The American Indian Parfleche

A TRADITION OF ABSTRACT PAINTING

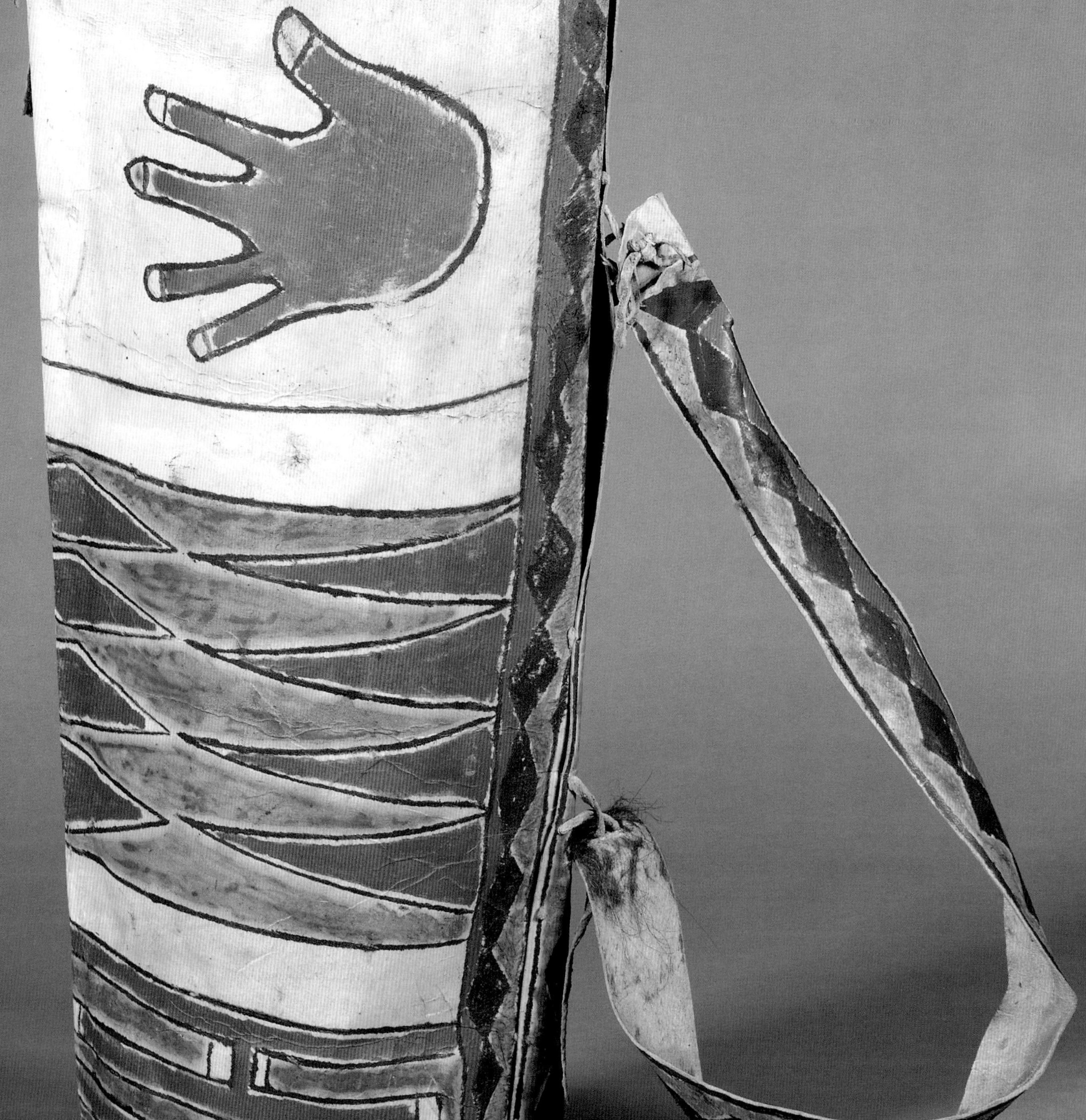

The American Indian Parfleche

A TRADITION OF ABSTRACT PAINTING

Gaylord Torrence

University of Washington Press in association with the **Des Moines Art Center**

98 97 96 95 94 5 4 3 2 1

Printed in Hong Kong
Design by Audrey Meyer
Composition by G&S Typesetters, Inc.

University of Washington Press
P.O. Box 50096
Seattle, WA 98145-5096

Library of Congress Cataloguing-in-Publication Data

Torrence, Gaylord.
The American Indian Parfleche : a tradition of abstract painting / Gaylord Torrence.
p. cm.
Catalog of an exhibition held at the Des Moines Art Center.
Includes bibliographical references and index.
ISBN 0-295-97332-3 (alk. paper) — ISBN 0-295-97333-1 (pbk. : alk. paper)
1. Parfleches—Exhibitions. 2. Indians of North America—Leather work—Exhibitions. 3. Indians of North America—Painting—Exhibitions.
I. Des Moines Art Center. II. Title.
E99.L4T67 1994
745.53′1′097—dc20 93-39709
CIP

The paper used in this publication meets the minimum requirements of American National Standard for Information Sciences—Permanence of Paper for Printed Library Materials, ANSI Z39.48-1984.

Frontispiece: Oto cylindrical case (pl.4), ca 1820 *(see also page 88).*
Photograph by Dietrich Graf.

Contents

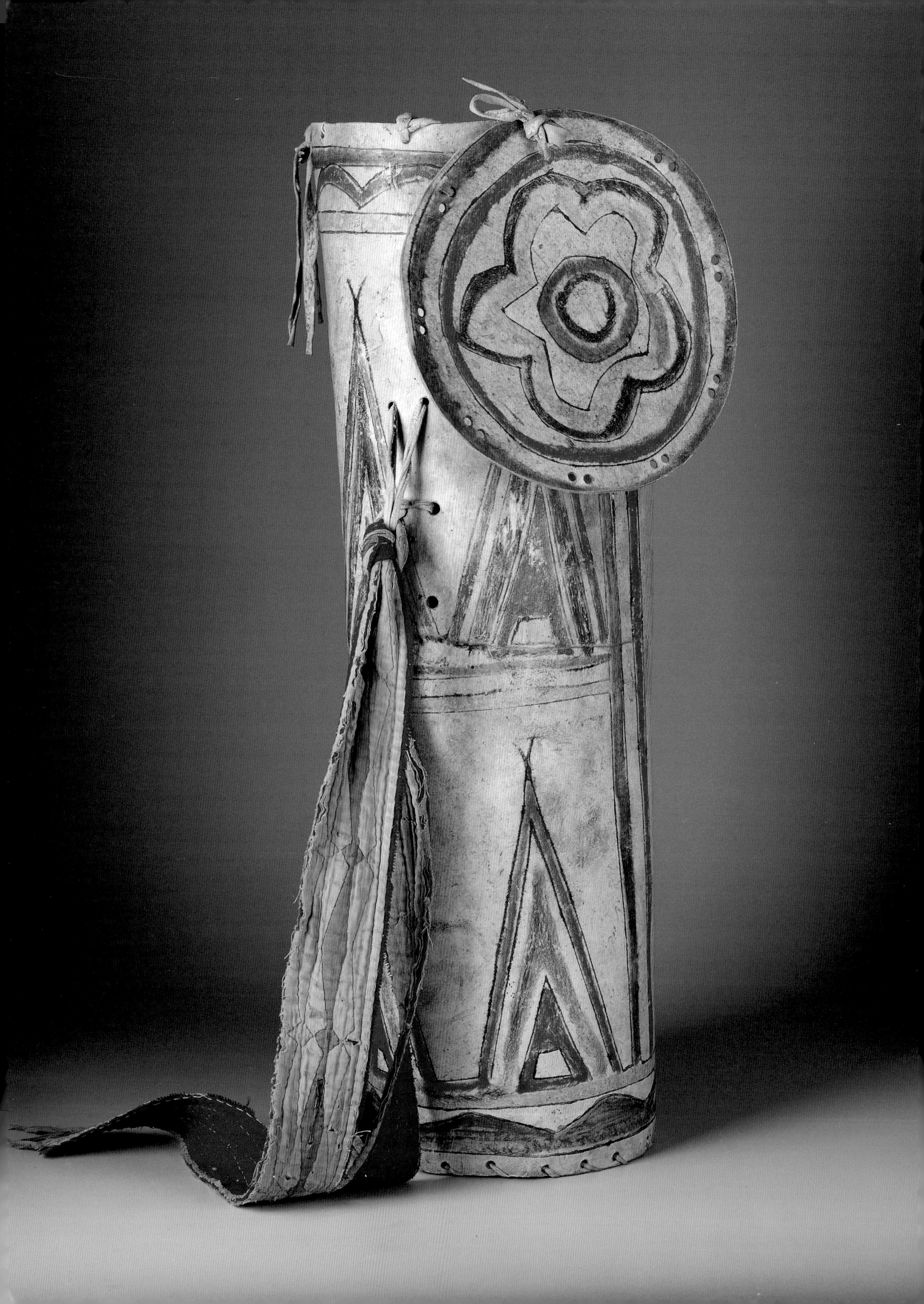

Foreword

The Des Moines Art Center is honored to present this important exhibition and accompanying publication. No doubt, these will be the definitive efforts in the field for decades to come. To say this is to pay tribute to Gaylord Torrence, who has dedicated a significant part of his life to exhaustive research on this art. But that research is only the raw material. As this catalogue and the selection of works exhibited indicate, Mr. Torrence has brought to bear on the material his remarkable intelligence and sensitivity. The result is an exhibition and publication of rare beauty and educational richness.

It is my pleasure to thank the many sponsors who have made possible this important undertaking. The exhibition "The American Indian Parfleche: A Tradition of Abstract Painting," its related public programs, and the national tour were made possible by a major grant from the Lila Wallace-Reader's Digest Fund. The Meredith Corporation, the Edwin T. Meredith Foundation, the Meredith family, and the Mid Meredith Zuendel Endowment Fund have underwritten this extraordinary publication. Additional crucial support for the exhibition has been provided by Kirke-Van Orsdel, Inc., the Rockefeller Foundation, and the National Endowment for the Arts, a federal agency. Further funding has been provided by Alicia M. and William A. Miller and the Continental Corporation Foundation. The exhibition poster has been underwritten by Harriette Lubetkin.

This exhibition has been in production at the Art Center for five years. I am grateful to Associate Director M. Jessica Rowe, who has coordinated many aspects of this complex project during that entire period. I also wish to thank the many staff members who have worked on the project.

I. Michael Danoff

Director

42 / **Kiowa cylinder, ca. 1850**

H 23 1/2 in., D 8 in. Buffalo rawhide, pigment, wool and cotton cloth

Collected by James Mooney. National Museum of Natural History, Department of Anthropology, Smithsonian Institution, 152966

This book and the national exhibition that accompanies it constitute an important achievement in the scholarship of American Indian art. They represent the definitive study of this subject and the first major presentation to the public that focuses on parfleches as significant works of art. The challenge for a museum is to utilize objects of the past to actualize experience, to assist a society in rediscovering and developing its ability to respond to its heritage. In providing a brilliant chronicle of this aspect of Native American painting, the Art Center establishes a union between the past and present, between traditional Native American cultures and contemporary American society by personally involving individuals with an artistic vision of the past.

This project has been at once familiar and unusual to the Art Center, which is primarily committed to presenting the art of our time. It is familiar because the Art Center simultaneously advances its mission, as reflected in various programs, by focusing on tribal art. It is unusual because here the unexpected vigor of the parfleche is experienced as a powerful tradition of abstract painting. Our goal for this project is to present tribal culture authentically, clearly, and respectfully. This aspect of the project has been aided by a Native American advisory committee for educational programs. The committee has supported the museum's efforts to provide greater audience exposure and innovative learning opportunities.

The Art Center approached Gaylord Torrence in 1989 to be curator and author of this project. His extensive work spanning more than ten years has been a search for knowledge of the art form and has taken him to collections throughout North America and Europe. His quest was painstakingly thorough, requiring a discerning eye, critical understanding, and perseverance.

The exhibition and this book augment the visual power of the parfleches themselves. They allow us to reflect upon their diversity and beauty, and help us to capture the essence of these richly handsome, meaning-laden parfleches and the historical conditions under which they were created.

M. Jessica Rowe
Associate Director

Acknowledgments

In many respects this project had its beginning in an exhibition I curated for the Kansas City Art Institute in 1984. It provided my first opportunity to explore parfleche painting in depth, and established the foundation for continuing research that has extended over the past ten years. During that time I have surveyed more than one hundred public and private collections throughout the United States, Canada, and Europe in an effort to expand and clarify my understanding of this great tradition. I have been aided in this endeavor and in the attempt to present this publication and exhibition by many people in many ways, and I am profoundly grateful for the help they have provided.

I began this project as Guest Curator for the Des Moines Art Center in 1989, and it has been my privilege to work with three exceptional directors during its course. I wish to express my sincere thanks to former Director Julia Brown Turrell for her interest in this Native American art form and for her commitment of the Art Center as the organizing institution. M. Jessica Rowe, in the roles of Interim Director and, currently, Associate Director, has provided the essential continuity in guiding the complexities of this project from its beginning. She has been a source of constant encouragement, valuable advice, and unfailing support throughout our collaboration, and it is with a deep sense of gratitude that I acknowledge her contribution. Director I. Michael Danoff has enthusiastically endorsed the project from the time of his arrival and has generously devoted considerable effort to its success.

The extraordinary efforts and contributions of the staff of the Des Moines Art Center in the planning, organization, and realization of this project are deserving of our greatest thanks. Suzanne Wood played an essential role in preparing the manuscript, organizing the loans and the logistics of the traveling exhibition, and handling correspondence and countless details associated with the production of the publication. She accomplished these tasks in the most dedicated and efficient manner. Wayne Masterson created an effective installation design with his usual care and skill; Connie Tartt Granberg and Peggy Leonardo organized the educational components and outreach programs associated with the exhibition; and Susan Burgess and Sheryl West contributed their professional assistance in a variety of ways.

I would also like to express my appreciation to the Board of Trustees of the museum for their interest and endorsement of the project, and especially to Jacqueline Blank and Melva Bucksbaum for their steadfast support and encouragement.

The visual power of the great majority of objects presented in this book has been conveyed through the superb photography of Mark Tade. His commitment as an artist, his sensitivity and perceptive understanding of the objects, guided every aspect of his work, and his remarkable technical skill enabled him consistently to achieve the highest quality even when working under difficult studio conditions as we traveled to different locations. His contribution to this project is one of immeasurable importance, and it has been my great pleasure to work with him. I also wish to acknowledge the special efforts of those photographers listed elsewhere who closely followed our specifications in providing images of objects in their respective collections.

This project has been generously funded by a number of institutions, corporations and individuals, and I am deeply grateful for their support. Grants from the Drake University Center for the Humanities and the Friends of Drake Arts provided me with funding that aided in research and the first stages of manuscript preparation. Production of the book was made possible by support from the Meredith Corporation, Edwin T. Meredith Foundation, Mid Meredith Zuendel Endowment Fund, and the Meredith family. Support for the exhibition, "The American Indian Parfleche: A Tradition of Abstract Painting," its related public programs, and the national tour were made possible by a major grant from the Lila Wallace–Reader's Digest Fund. Additional support was received from the National Endowment for the Arts, the Rockefeller Foundation, Continental Corporation Foundation, Kirke-Van Orsdel, Inc., and Alicia M. and William A. Miller. A contribution to underwrite a poster for the exhibition was received from Harriette Lubetkin.

We are greatly indebted to the institutions and private collectors that have lent objects to the exhibition or allowed their inclusion in the publication, for it is their willingness to share such remarkable objects that makes this endeavor possible.

Colleagues from a number of museums have enthusiastically provided access to their collections and records, and in every case, extended the resources of their institutions in the most generous manner. Many offered their personal encouragement and support as well. I wish especially to thank Stanley Freed, Belinda Kaye, and Anibal Rodriguez, American Museum of Natural History, New York; Judy Hall, Canadian Museum of Civilization, Hull, Quebec; Marsha Bol and Deborah Harding, Carnegie Museum of Natural History, Pittsburgh; Richard Conn, Denver Art Museum; Joyce Herold, Denver Museum of Natural History; David Penney, Detroit Institute of Arts; William Grewe-Mullins, Christine Gross, Jonathan Haas, and Janice Klein, Field Museum of Natural History, Chicago; Staffan Brunius, Folkens Museum–Ethnografiska, Stockholm, Sweden; Dan McPike and Chris Moore, Thomas Gilcrease Institute of American History and Art, Tulsa, Oklahoma; Daryl Betenia and Gerald T. Conaty, Glenbow Museum, Calgary, Alberta; Marsha Gallagher, Joslyn Art Museum, Omaha; Axel Schulze-Thulin, Linden-Museum Stuttgart, Staatliches Museum für Völkerkunde, Germany; Jane Ketchan, Logan Museum of Anthropology, Beloit College, Wisconsin;

Marian Rodee, Maxwell Museum of Anthropology, University of New Mexico, Albuquerque; Carter Lupton and Nancy Oestreich Lurie, Milwaukee Public Museum; Marcia Anderson, Sherri Fuller, and Linda McShannock, Minnesota Historical Society, St. Paul; Marie Fauvet, Musée de l'Homme, Paris; J. C. H. King, Museum of Mankind, The British Museum, London; Susan Crawford and Candace Green, National Museum of Natural History, Smithsonian Institution, Washington, D.C.; Lee A. Callander, Sharon E. Dean, Gary Galante, Cecile Gauteame, Molly Herron, and W. Richard West, Jr., National Museum of the American Indian, Smithsonian Institution, New York; Julie Droke, Oklahoma Museum of Natural History, Norman; Viva Fisher, Barbara Isaac, Martha Labell, and Kathy Skelly, Peabody Museum of Archaeology and Ethnology, Harvard University; Susan Bean and Lucy Butler, Peabody and Essex Museum, Salem, Massachusetts; Emma I. Hansen, Plains Indian Museum, Buffalo Bill Historical Center, Cody, Wyoming; Peter Bolz and Richard Hass, Staatliche Museen, Museum für Völkerkunde, Berlin; Jodi Evans and Jerome Thompson, State Historical Society of Iowa; Cathy L. Wright, Tayor Museum, Colorado Springs Fine Arts Center; Jeff Martin and Christopher D. Roy, the University of Iowa Museum of Art, Iowa City; and Lucy Fowler Williams, University Museum, University of Pennsylvania. In addition to these museum professionals, I wish to thank Douglas Drake, Elisabeth Kirsch, and Steven J. Smith representing Continental Corporation, and Ellen Napiura Taubman and Richard Pohrt, Jr., of Masco Corporation.

I am indebted to many dedicated scholars who have generously shared findings of their own research with me. In particular, Craig Bates, Winfield Coleman, Benson Lanford, and Gary Galante have been especially generous. I also thank Jonathan Batkin, Ron Bork, Steven Honnen, Evan Maurer, Richard Pohrt, Sr., Steven Shawley, Bruce Shackelford, and David Wooley.

A number of individuals have made their collections available to me or have directed me to important pieces, thus providing a significant body of works for study in addition to those preserved in museum collections. For this I would especially like to thank Kenneth and Barbara Canfield, and in addition, Nicholas and Jerrie Campagna, Jr., Ralph T. Coe, Jerry Cooke, Richard Edwards, Jr., Roger Foltz, Jerry Fowler, Larry Frank, Ed Garratt, H. Malcolm Grimmer, Toby Herbst, Imre Nagy, Gerald Lamb, Dennis Lessard, Harriette and Robert Lubetkin, T. N. and Marilyn Luther, Mark Miller, Ramona Morris, John W. Painter, Ralph Velich, and Hermann Vonbank. Bill and Kathy Brewer, David Christensen and Mark Miller generously provided information regarding traditional hideworking techniques gained through years of experience.

I also wish to express my great appreciation to those Native Americans who have provided guidance and help in our efforts to respectfully and properly present this aspect of their cultural heritage, and in our endeavor to develop the most effective outreach programs. My thanks to Gene Fracek, Abraham Conklin, Mary Goose, Lawrence H. Hart, Leo Keahna, Everett Kapayou, Joe Medicine Crow, Larson Medicine Horse, John Pretty On Top, Mable Pretty On Top, Amy Whiteman, Tom Yellowtail, Robin Young Bear, and other individuals who wish to remain anonymous. I am grateful to Gerald Conaty, Gary Galante and Gary Johnson for their roles in facilitating communication with some of these cultural leaders.

It has been a pleasure to work with the professionals at the University of Washington Press on the production of this book; I wish especially to thank Donald Ellegood, Director, for his interest and support, Marilyn Trueblood for her sensitive and discerning editing of the manuscript, and Audrey Meyer for her outstanding and thoughtful design. In Des Moines, Connie Wilson contributed to the production by developing the map, Sean O'Connor provided illustrations of parfleche patterns, and Nicole Anderson contributed her efforts as a research assistant.

Finally, to my dear friends who have sustained me through all with affection and faith, my deepest thanks.

62 / **Pueblo cylinder, ca. 1890**

H 15 1/2 in., D 4 1/4 in.; fringe 12 1/2 in. Rawhide, pigment, native leather

Collected at Cochiti Pueblo, New Mexico. Collection of William A. Miller

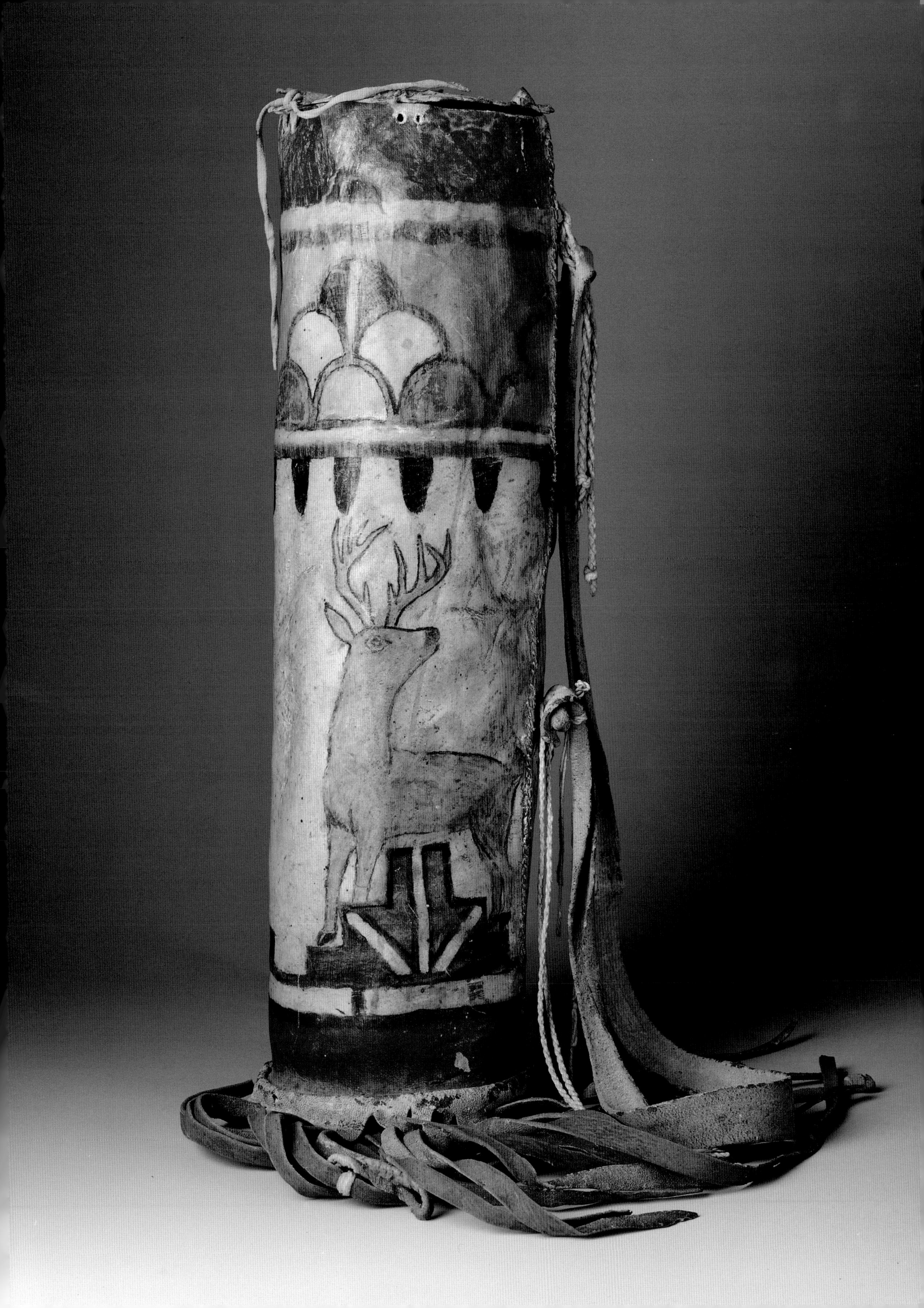

This book has been made possible by a gift from the Meredith Family, Meredith Corporation, the Mid Meredith Zuendel Endowment Fund, and the E. T. Meredith Foundation in memory of Mid Meredith Zuendel, 1954–1988. Mid was a member of the Des Moines Art Center Board of Trustees and had an abiding interest in and love for American Indian art and history.

As the women who made these parfleches live on in their art, Mid continues to enrich our lives through her three beautiful children and our treasured memories. We celebrate Mid's special gift for living. It is our hope that this book will touch a place in other people who carry special gifts.

The Meredith Family

The exhibition "The American Indian Parfleche: A Tradition of Abstract Painting," its related public programs, and the national tour were made possible by a major grant from:

Lila Wallace–Reader's Digest Fund, Inc.

This publication was made possible by:

Meredith Corporation
Edwin T. Meredith Foundation
Mid Meredith Zuendel Endowment Fund
Meredith Family

We are grateful for additional funding from:

Rockefeller Foundation
Kirke-Van Orsdel, Inc.
National Endowment for the Arts, a Federal Agency
Continental Corporation Foundation
Harriette Lubetkin
Alicia M. and William A. Miller

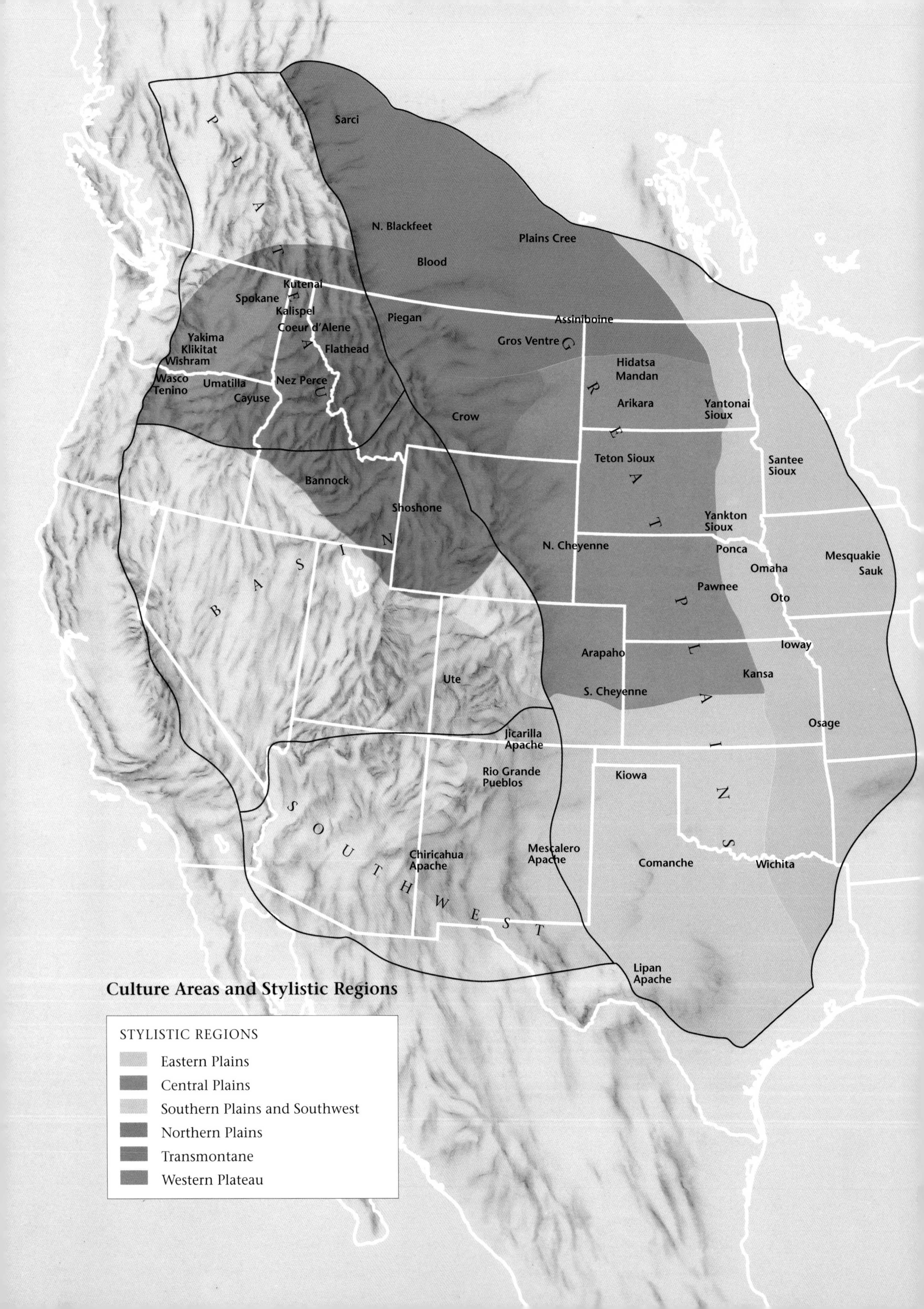

Culture Areas and Stylistic Regions

The American Indian Parfleche

A TRADITION OF ABSTRACT PAINTING

Introduction

At the close of the nineteenth century and during the first decades of the twentieth, a great wealth in material objects was collected from Native American peoples, including those tribes of the Great Plains, Intermontane, and Plateau regions whose former nomadic ways of life had vanished with forced settlement onto reservations. It was during this period that the great public ethnographic collections were formed, as thousands of objects were secured by museum-sponsored research and collecting expeditions sent into the field. At the same time, a number of important collections and studies originated through the efforts of academic institutions, individuals, and traders. This great endeavor to acquire both factual data and the material culture of traditional Native American societies had complex and far-reaching ramifications for Indians and non-Indians alike. It resulted in the preservation of a vast body of works that is still emerging to ever larger audiences and has formed the basis for various interpretations of Native American artistic expression. Found within this context is a class of objects known as parfleches—containers of folded or sewn rawhide elaborated with painted images on their exposed surfaces.

This publication and the exhibition produced in conjunction with it present a comprehensive overview of the American Indian parfleche, a powerful tradition of abstract painting created by the women of more than forty tribal groups throughout the western half of North America during the eighteenth, nineteenth, and early twentieth centuries. Parfleches were integral to the nomadic ways of life of the Plains, Intermontane, and Plateau tribes in that they provided for the transportation of each family's food and material possessions. At the same time, they served an intellectual, emotional, and spiritual purpose. The painted images that covered their surfaces were rich in associative and symbolic meanings, and provided the women who painted them with a powerful means for personal artistic expression and a way to affirm their cultural identity.

It is my purpose in this book to reveal the great diversity and exceptional quality of this art form, and to establish its significance by analyzing its formal characteristics and by exploring the aesthetic, symbolic, and utilitarian function of parfleches within American Indian cultures. In doing this, I will identify those features that define distinct tribal and regional painting styles, and differentiate each of these groups within their shared tradition. I will also describe the techniques of rawhide production, painting, and parfleche construction. The beliefs and meanings invested in the imagery and in the forms themselves will be discussed, along with the various types of parfleches and their associated uses. Finally, I will provide an explanation of the origin, evolution, and chronology of this art form, and reveal the manner in which Native American artists responded to cultural change by documenting the transition of parfleches from utilitarian objects to purely aesthetic symbols of a passing way of life.

Words alone, however, cannot fully depict the complex visual relationships embodied in these forms. A complete understanding of the concepts and descriptions presented in the text requires that they be considered in relation to the illustrations of the actual objects. The photographs are therefore an invaluable element of the book. This may seem self-evident but, in fact, relatively few parfleches have been photographically illustrated in the literature. Most previous studies have utilized schematic drawings of the designs, which fail to show the subtle qualities of line, color, and surface—the essential features that define these objects as paintings and expressive works of art.

Essentially, it has been my intention to present the finest extant examples of this art form. They have been chosen on the basis of aesthetic quality and condition and, within these criteria, they include the widest possible representation of tribes. Many are inspired examples of well-known types, painted by women working within the closely defined parameters of established tribal styles; others are highly unusual and are distinguished by the singular artistic inventiveness of their makers. There has also been an effort to include examples of all the variations of basic parfleche forms that were constructed by different tribes.

Many of the parfleches included are unpublished and unknown to all but a small number of scholars, museum professionals, and collectors. These objects have been preserved either in museum storage from the time of their acquisition or in the hands of private collectors. The fact that such masterworks of Native American art remain to be discovered and presented to the public is exciting, but it also serves as a reminder that this nation's knowledge and recognition of indigenous artistic traditions is still emerging. In the last two decades, a large number of important museum exhibits and publications have been devoted to the arts of Native Americans. Splendid objects have been presented for the first time, and many items originally collected and displayed as souvenirs, mementos of war, or ethnological specimens have been reinterpreted in the light of an increased sensitivity to and respect for the creative achievements of Indian artists. Of equal importance, there has been a steadily increasing involvement of Native Americans in the study, interpretation, and preservation of their cultural heritage. This project is intended to contribute to this movement and firmly establish parfleche painting as a cohesive tradition within the larger context of Native American arts.

Parfleche is a French Canadian word originated by voyageurs at the time of their earliest contacts with Prairie and Eastern Plains tribes in the late sixteenth and early seventeenth centuries. It is derived from *parer* (to parry or turn aside) and *fleche* (arrow), apparently referring to war shields that were made of heavy rawhide. The term was used to describe the untanned skin itself and, by extension, any object constructed from that material. Eventually it became the common name for the large, folded, envelopelike containers of rawhide, as distinct from other types of rawhide cases. Within the last few decades, the term parfleche has come to designate all of the various forms of painted rawhide. It should be noted, however, that the French Canadian word was never adopted by the individual tribes, whose languages included specific words for rawhide and the objects produced from it.

Each object illustrated in this publication is described according to its regional and tribal origin, date of manufacture, size, materials of construction, and collection history. The tribal attributions and dates are those of the author and are based on a comparative study of more than fifteen hundred parfleches in nearly a hundred public and private collections in the United States, Canada, and Europe. In many instances, these designations correspond to and confirm museum attributions based on the collection history of the objects or on the findings of previous scholars; in others, different conclusions are presented. Nearly half of the parfleches included here, however, have no recorded history and were without attribution. Their identification is based on an analysis of those features that define their distinctive painting styles and details of construction, in relation to the body of documented works that provides a basic framework of known types. These characteristics of style and form are discussed at length within the text, as is the specific nature and relevance of documentation.

It should be understood that even the attribution of documented parfleches requires judgment based on stylistic features because the documentation invariably concerns the collection of the objects rather than their origin. No parfleche has been found for which the name of the maker and the place and date that it was produced have been recorded. Instead, the most complete information we have for any piece consists of the name of the collector, the date of acquisition, and the tribe from which the item was obtained. To accept an identification on the basis of such collection history alone, without other supportive evidence obtained from comparing significant numbers of similar pieces, is problematic.

The same holds true with regard to determining the age of a parfleche. Most were collected some years after they were made. For this reason, the date assigned to these parfleches is also a matter of the author's judgment, based on several factors discussed in the text. In most cases it is reasonable to assume that the designated date might extend ten years earlier or later, thereby placing the time of production within a twenty-year period. In a few cases this might have to be expanded, particularly for some of the pieces made around and before 1850. For example, a parfleche dated about 1850 that is made of buffalo hide and painted with native pigments in the earliest style might very well date before 1840. Only the greater probability of its survival suggests the later rather than the earlier date. Age must be determined on the basis of style and materials rather than on appearance. The effects of wear, or patina, on a parfleche may make it appear to be much older than it actually is; conversely, some of the earliest examples were nearly new when collected and now appear to be more recently made.

As parfleches are somewhat irregular in shape, especially after they have been used, some explanation of their recorded dimensions may be helpful. First, all of the works have been measured as they are photographed. Suspensions of various kinds such as trade cloth tabs or thongs used in tying are not included, nor are the flaps of flat cases. With envelopes, the greatest length is indicated, as is the width along the folded end of the case, even when side flaps might extend beyond this dimension. Because envelopes might be viewed either vertically or horizontally as they were used, it seems appropriate to record their greatest dimension as length rather than height; because they were painted according to their vertical axis, length is indicated first. All other objects are measured conventionally by height, width, diameter, and depth. Fringe is measured separately, or may sometimes be included as it forms the overall height of the object when suspended.

Although the materials used in the creation of parfleches and the chronology associated with them are discussed extensively in the text, minimal information regarding these elements is given in the illustration captions. Without laboratory analysis, it is difficult and often impossible to determine accurately the kind of hide used to make a particular parfleche or the types of pigments used to paint it. Such testing is beyond the scope of this project and is, at any rate, of limited value. With the exception of buffalo, all types of hides and pigments might have been available to most of the tribes discussed in this publication at the time when most of the surviving parfleches were made. Although we may correctly assume that most of these objects made prior to the 1850s were created with native materials and that most produced after 1890 were painted with trade pigments on domestic cow hide, the great body of existing parfleches were created within the forty-year period between these dates, when any combination of materials was possible. Therefore, even if exact pigment types and hides were known, it would be of little help in determining either tribal origin or more precise dates of production. This conclusion is further reinforced by the fact that there are no detailed records that indicate when each tribe adopted materials introduced by Euro-Americans; there seems to be every indication that the transition occurred somewhat sporadically in different regions throughout the last half of the nineteenth century. Also, there are no discernible differences in techniques between the uses of wild and domestic hides or between native and trade pigments. Most significantly, aesthetic quality and power of content are never determined by materials alone.

Of all the types of hides used for parfleches, only buffalo may be easily recognized; therefore, it is designated in the captions. Its use is helpful in dating because few parfleches were made of this material after 1880. Buffalo hide is distinguished by its dark brown epidermal layer, which may range from a deep chocolate to a pale caramel color. This layer is the unpainted, inner surface of most parfleches, but is readily visible as the outer surface of incised cases (for example, pl. 88). Another distinctive feature of buffalo rawhide is its texture as it begins to break down with use; the surface becomes richly patterned with creases and wrinkles (see pl. 101) to a much greater extent than other hides. Even those buffalo hide parfleches that have had their epidermal layer removed by scraping may often be identified by the appearance of their outer surface texture.

Other hides are not so easily categorized. Once made into a parfleche, the skins of elk, horse, moose, and domestic cattle are usually impossible to differentiate on the basis of physical appearance alone. There are simply too many variables in the production and in the inherent qualities of the hides themselves. Color, thickness, and texture can vary greatly depending on the age and sex of the animal as well as the season in which the skin is taken. These differences are then further compounded by the number of technical variations possible in the processing and sizing of the rawhide, each producing distinct effects. Together, these factors make visual identification a matter of conjecture. The hides of different animals may sometimes appear very similar or, just as often, hides of the same type may vary considerably. Probably the most readily identifiable hides other than buffalo are those of domestic cattle, but even they are sometimes in question.

The identification of pigments according to native and trade varieties presents a similar problem. Many subtle variations in color existed in both classes of pigments, and although some hues appear to fall into one group or the other, a great many are seen that might be of either type. It is important to consider that the final color of the paint as it appears on a parfleche could be significantly affected by several factors. These include the manner in which pigments were prepared and applied, specifically, their density and opacity; the type of sizing used, its thickness and the way it was combined with the paint; the various colors and textures of the different types of rawhide that provided the ground for the painting; and, finally, the effects of wear—abrasion, exposure to the elements, smoke, and handling, all combining to create a surface patina that usually darkened and softened the colors. Thus, the colors we see on a parfleche today may have been different in appearance when it was newly painted, and even colors freshly applied may not look the same as pure pigment. So the identification of paint types based on what we see is, as with hides, often a matter of conjecture. However, in surveying large numbers of parfleches, one repeatedly observes certain colors associated with each of the three time periods previously mentioned. This frequency provides the most reliable key to identification when combined with our knowledge of the hues deriving from native pigment sources and those of later, somewhat standardized commercial types. With the exception of red—the most common trade color—the earliest parfleches are far more likely to have been created with native paint and the latest pieces commonly done with trade colors. Thus, a recognizable pattern emerges separating the early and late periods. Those produced during the decades between 1850 and 1890 are far more varied through an expanded palette of native colors and the use of early, less standardized trade pigments. These parfleches may have been painted with either type of pigment and, undoubtedly, many combined both within the same painting.

Some typical examples may be helpful in visualizing these groups. The parfleches illustrated in plates 1, 17, 22, 25, 45, 69, and 122 are representative of those executed in what appear to be native pigments. Those pictured in plates 15, 20, 92, 102, 109, and 119 reveal the trade colors seen extensively on many pieces after 1890. The cases in plates 12, 27, 41, 54, and 70 are typical of those in which the types of pigments remain in question.

None of the illustrated works is identified according to the artists' names because they are unknown. Our sense of the individual maker must therefore begin with a general understanding of the artist's role in Native American societies. Traditionally, there was a clear division of labor and responsibility between men and women based on the skills necessary for the survival of the household unit. These roles included the manufacture of items needed to sustain daily life and manifest religious belief, and they extended to artistic traditions as well. Working within established parameters of tribal style, each gender produced a variety of culturally defined forms; they were guided by traditions that directed the kinds of objects they made and the manner in which they worked. In painting, for example, Plains women created abstract geometric images on the surfaces of parfleches and robes; because rawhide containers were essential to nomadic life and great numbers must have been required, they were undoubtedly one of the most commonly produced aesthetic forms.

Words for "art" and "artist" do not exist in the languages of parfleche-making peoples because the creation of aesthetic objects was an integral part of life. In viewing their creative traditions, however, it is obvious that these societies possessed a highly developed aesthetic sensibility and recognized standards of technical excellence, content, and beauty in their artistic forms. Nearly everyone was more or less capable of producing the objects needed for daily existence, but exceptionally talented individuals were recognized and honored for the superior quality of their work. In tribal groups, where everyone's creative efforts were well known and compared, the people formed a critical audience that valued exceptional ability. Industry, virtuosity, and innovation were highly esteemed. Although there were no professional artists as that term is defined by Western standards, individuals recognized as masters of a particular art form tended to specialize in the production of that form to a much greater degree than has generally been acknowledged, and often created a body of objects that were stylistically distinctive.

Considering that each woman's work was so well known within the context of her own community, it is sad that we do not know the name of a single artist whose work is represented in this book. This seems all the more unfortunate and especially poignant when a number of parfleches, obviously made by the same person, are discovered in widely separated collections (pls. 71, 72); at such times, the living presence of the artist is most deeply felt, and we realize how very far these works have been removed from the impetus of their creation. This lack of information is the result of limited documentation, but this itself results from many early researchers treating Native American cultures as generic and by the failure of collectors to learn and record the names of those who made and used the objects they acquired. It is encouraging that increasing numbers of scholars in recent years have sought to recognize individual artists in publications and exhibitions, and undoubtedly this effort will continue. Research thus far, however, has failed to establish the identities of the women who produced this tradition of parfleche painting, and these extraordinary objects remain an anonymous contribution to the artistic heritage of North America. The works illustrated here, then, must stand for the achievement of all Native American women who, in the creation of this form, have shared the richness, integrity, and intensity of their expressive vision.

Origin and History

The development and production of parfleches are most closely associated with the nomadic tribes of the Great Plains. Parfleches probably originated in this area and, as an object essential to the way of life practiced by these groups, were made in the greatest numbers during the height of Plains culture from 1750 to 1880. The formal potential inherent in this type of painting was also explored most fully in this region, resulting in the greatest diversity of techniques and styles. The superb utility of these objects, their compelling beauty as works of art, and their inseparable association with the horse, all contributed to their importance as a Plains form. These same qualities also resulted in their adoption by many tribes of the Southwest, Rocky Mountain, and Plateau regions. These groups appropriated attributes of Plains culture along with the horse and created their own distinct styles of parfleche painting. Ultimately, painted rawhide containers had a wide distribution throughout western North America. Although they were developed by the Plains people, by the end of the nineteenth century at least fifty tribes are known to have made or used parfleches of some type (Douglas 1936: 107).

The Plains region is a vast area extending from the Mississippi basin in the east to the Rocky Mountains in the west, and from the Rio Grande in southern Texas to the upper Saskatchewan River in central Alberta. It has been characterized as a land of sky and earth, as a limitless expanse of grass, wind, and light. It is a high country, one of subtle beauty, dramatic climatic changes and, in some areas, richly varied geographic features. Prior to the settlement of Euro-Americans, it was exceptionally rich in wildlife, particularly in the great herds of buffalo and pronghorn antelope that provided the primary food source for most of the tribes inhabiting the region.

For thousand of years, this land had supported various Native American peoples. In precontact times, small pedestrian bands followed the herds and subsisted by hunting large game and gathering wild fruits and vegetables. From at least A.D. 1200, semisedentary and sedentary tribes who had migrated into the eastern region were settled in permanent villages of earth or grass lodges in the major river valleys. These groups supplemented their agricultural subsistence by hunting buffalo and trading with the nomadic hunters. Other tribes lived in the woodlands and prairies along the eastern edge of the region or in the Rocky Mountains to the west, and ventured onto the plains for seasonal buffalo hunts.

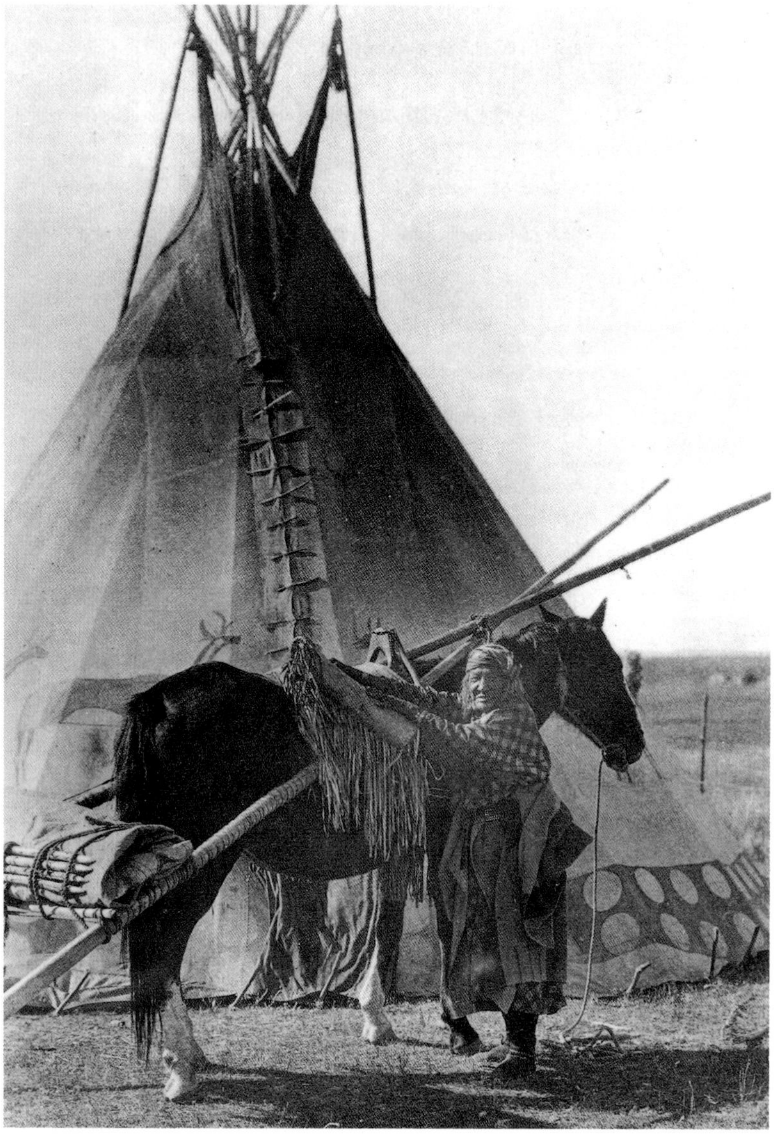

"Transporting the Ceremonial Bag and Tipi Cover." A Blackfeet woman packing her horse in preparation for travel, hanging a large, fringed cylinder containing sacred objects from the saddle. The tipi cover is carefully folded and wrapped around parfleche envelopes on the travois. Photograph by Edward S. Curtis. Courtesy Edward E. Ayer Collection, Newberry Library

This was the pattern of life found in the region by the first Europeans.

The emergence of historic Plains culture resulted from two concurrent forces: the introduction of the horse by the Spanish in the 1600s and its diffusion northward, and the westward movement of displaced Great Lakes tribes in response to the pressures of Euro-American expansion. Whether they were ancient occupants or newly arrived, there by choice or by necessity, all of the mounted Plains groups could cover the great distances necessary to effectively hunt the migrating herds of buffalo, to move their villages at will with relative ease, and to wage war more efficiently on neighboring tribes. As a result the protohistoric nomadic bands grew in wealth and power, expanding upon the basic features of their previous existence; many of the river tribes abandoned their permanent villages forever, adopting a fully nomadic way of life; and many of the groups inhabiting peripheral regions moved onto the Plains as permanent residents. This great transition occurred during the

1700s and, with it, the development of the parfleche. Nomadic tribes living in portable tipis needed to transport and store all their possessions and food supplies, and containers that were lightweight, durable, weatherproof, and manufactured from readily available materials were a necessity in maintaining their way of life. Also, the greatly expanded ability of these societies to hunt and wage war resulted in a substantial increase in possessions and material wealth. Both factors significantly increased the need for parfleches.

It is not known when and under what circumstances the first parfleches were made. We do not know if they originated in a single area or had their beginnings in several places simultaneously, later becoming essentially uniform in design as a result of tribal interaction. Undoubtedly, objects and containers of rawhide were made in prehistoric times; the nature of the material itself and the fact that rawhide is a primary resource of any hunting culture make its use a logical development. The fact that the French voyageurs created a word for rawhide—and presumably the containers made from it—suggests the existence of parfleches at the time of earliest contacts in the late 1600s and early 1700s. However, the absence of any detailed descriptions in eighteenth-century accounts indicates that, in pre-horse times, parfleches were either uncommon or else unpainted and so lacking in artistic distinction

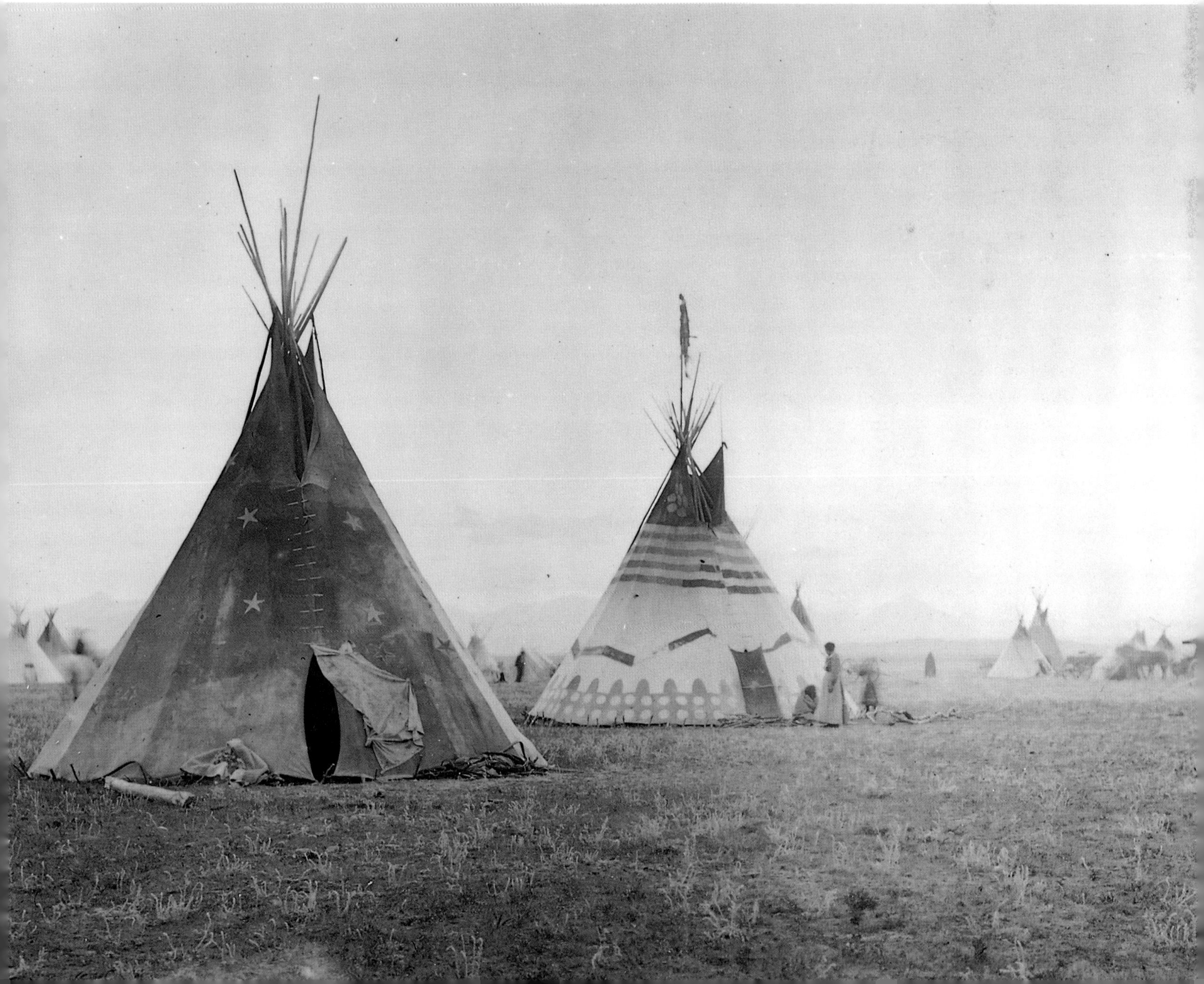

A Blackfeet camp, ca. 1900. Photograph by Walter McClintock. Courtesy Beinecke Rare Book and Manuscript Library, Yale University

as to be unworthy of special attention. It was only after the full emergence of Plains culture during the mid to late 1700s that painted parfleches were widely produced. By the time they were specifically mentioned in the literature and collected, their development as an artistic tradition was well established throughout much of North America.[1]

Teit (1930: 50) describes flat, undecorated rawhide bags in use among Plateau tribes before they acquired horses. Similar rudimentary bags in the form of large flat cases that are undoubtedly an archaic type were collected from seminomadic groups inhabiting the Eastern Plains (pl. 8). A very few envelopelike cases made of undecorated sheets of rawhide and that probably date from the mid-1700s have also been preserved. These were fashioned by cutting the corners away from a rectangular piece of hide and folding the resulting ends inward toward the center where each pair was secured by ties, forming a case which was nearly square.[2] Containers of this type are probably typical of those produced by all hunting cultures living in dry climates during prehistoric times and are the forerunners of historic parfleches. However, two additional factors were instrumental in their development: more effective and varied patterns of folding and the dramatic transformation of the object through elaborately painted surfaces.

It has been suggested by several writers that parfleches were conceptually patterned after bark containers made in the Eastern Woodlands and the Northwest. Bark was cut, folded and sewn with root splints into various forms and used for the same purposes as parfleches. This relationship between bark containers and parfleches seems plausible, not only because the physical properties of the two materials and the techniques of construction are similar, but also because many of the Woodland peoples who originally fashioned containers from bark later made parfleches after adopting Plains culture. Another affinity often cited is that both types of containers were decorated with incised and scraped designs.

Whatever its origins as a folded container, the parfleche is part of a long tradition of hide painting practiced by the Woodland tribes of the Northeast and Western Great Lakes regions. This was an extensive tradition and a variety of elaborately painted objects were produced. The materials, techniques, and aesthetic sensibility were well defined long before Woodland peoples migrated onto the Plains and turned their knowledge and skill to creating parfleches and other forms of Plains painting. The earliest surviving examples—specifically the extraordinary robes collected by Marquette in 1673[3] (see illustration, opposite) and a number of other ornately painted robes, coats and bags collected during the eighteenth century[4]—reveal the pictorial elements from which parfleche designs evolved. This fundamental vocabulary of visual forms consisted of geometric motifs, both straightedged and curved, organized into complex compositions within some type of rectangular frame. The images were based on highly elongated triangles, hourglass shapes, diamonds, rectangles, lines, and circular forms. It is interesting

1. Ewers (1955: 114) cites Edwin James's mention of the use of parfleches by the Omaha in 1819 as the earliest known reference (James 1823, vol. 1, p. 212), and none has been found during the present study that predates this.

2. Three envelopes of this type, identified as Salish (Thompson River) are preserved in the collections of the Musée de l'Homme, Paris; the date of their acquisition could not be determined. Also, Benson Lanford has described to me an unpainted envelope of similar construction found in a cave site in Utah, believed to date from the protohistoric period (ca. 1700). It is part of a group of hide items discovered in several related caches in the area, that includes three painted robes, two painted burden straps and a small, painted parfleche flat case.

3. Two additional examples from this group are illustrated in Maurer (1977: 125) and Feest (1980: 81).

4. See the painted coat illustrated in Ewing (1982: 182) and the bag illustrated in Phillips (1987: 60) as excellent examples of these object types; others may be found throughout the literature. In addition to the Marquette robes, a number of beautifully painted and quill-decorated tobacco bags from the Great Lakes region, of the type shown in Phillips, are located in the collections of the Musée de l'Homme and constitute what is probably the greatest concentration of these works. Dating from the eighteenth century, all are painted with complex black and red designs on their upper sections and ornamented below with panels of netted quillwork. One of these is illustrated in Feest (1980: 59).

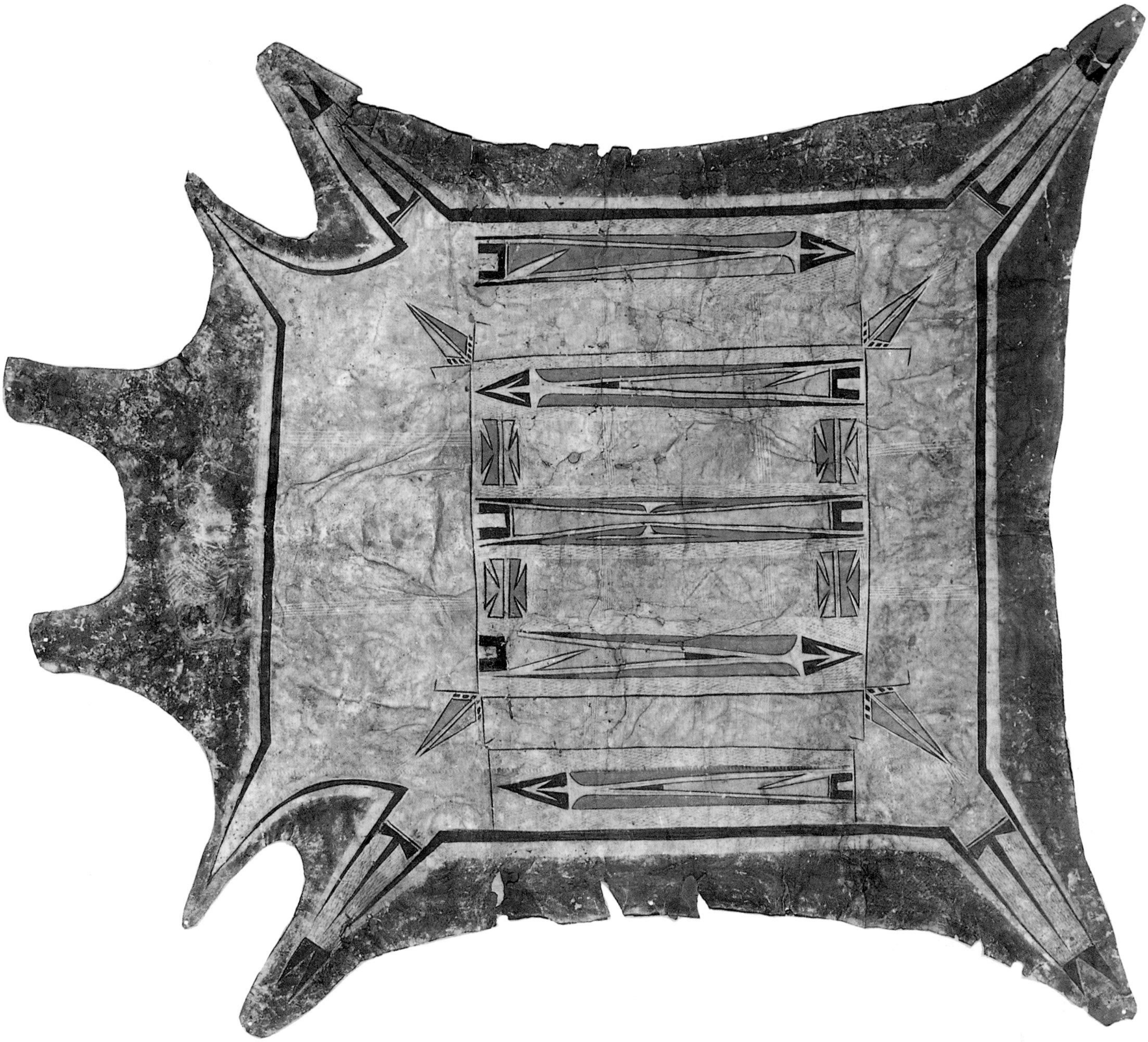

Painted robe, Western Great Lakes, ca. 1670. Collected from the Illinois by Pere Jacques Marquette in 1673. Collection Musée de l'Homme, Paris, 78.32.131

to note that these same motifs also formed the designs observed in tattooing during the earliest contact period.[5] Colors were usually limited to red and black, with white lines created through sizing. Other colors, primarily yellows, were used in limited amounts. This same palette was maintained throughout much of the Woodlands area, prevailing in quillwork, textiles, and other art forms as well as in painting, and extended to the earliest painted garments and robes produced by the Plains tribes.

It must have been common for nonequestrian Woodland people to wrap their possessions in soft-tanned robes, both for storage and during their limited, seasonal camp movements. This would have occurred as a practical necessity, in addition to their use of woven bags, soft leather bags, and bark containers. Some of these hides were undoubtedly painted—their striking designs transforming common packs into beautifully patterned objects—and it may be that the concept of painted

5. One of the best existing depictions of early tattooing is the portrait of Sa Ga Yeath Qua Pieth Tow, a Mohawk chief, included in a 1710 painting by John Verelist; illustrated in Phillips (1987: 82).

rawhide cases was first formed through this common visual experience. This is further implied by the fact that some of the earliest surviving parfleches replicate painted robes in their basic format. Their tightly structured rectangular compositions were arranged in the center of the hide, which was then folded into a flat envelope with little regard for the relationship formed between the painted design and the folded surfaces. This is in contrast to the later careful alignment of painted image to volumetric form, which constitutes one of the primary features of all Plains parfleches.

Only two parfleches of this early type are known to exist, suggesting that production stopped early in the nineteenth century. Both examples were collected by Duke Paul in the Eastern Plains region during the 1820s and are among the oldest rawhide containers of any type to be preserved. In fact, the earliest of the two was probably made during the closing years of the eighteenth century (pl. 1). La Flesche collected a third parfleche of this type from the Omaha (pl. 2) at a much later date, suggesting either that the form persisted among this tribe, which is unlikely, or that this parfleche was made specifically for him as an example of the type commonly used in earlier times. It was not unusual for researchers working in the late nineteenth century to commission objects that were no longer made or could not be purchased. A fragment of a fourth example was illustrated by Franz Boas, who assumed he was diagramming the painted panel of a Mesquakie trunk (Boas 1927: 28). The painting is not Mesquakie, however, but Siouan in style, and was clearly cut down from a larger, flat envelope acquired by the Mesquakies from one of the neighboring tribes to the west.

These four envelopes with robelike format are the only remaining evidence of a transitional, or developmental, stage of parfleches which feature elaborate painting, and it is likely that they always remained a regional type associated with Eastern Plains tribes. All other surviving examples, even the earliest that date from the first decades of the 1800s, are typical of the classic forms produced throughout the history of the tradition. Significantly, this would seem to indicate that the basic parfleche types—standard folded envelope, cylinder and flat case—came into being with the development of historic parfleches during the eighteenth century.

It is interesting to note that even after the traditional formats of parfleches and painted robes were separately defined in nineteenth-century Plains culture, a definite affinity remained between certain parfleche designs and those appearing on particular types of women's robes. Specifically, the elongated, rectangular "box" that forms the central element of "box-and-border" designs contains many of the same motifs and compositional conventions found on parfleches; on some robes, the box element even assumes the same general proportion as a parfleche envelope.[6] This relationship is most evident in the paintings created by Central Plains women, particularly among the Sioux and Arapaho.

Beyond what has already been discussed, our knowledge of the earli-

6. For this comparison, see particularly the robes illustrated in Dunn (1968: 150), Schulze-Thulin (1976: 78), Ewers (1982: 44), Feder (1967: cat no. 11) and Barbeau (1960: 61).

Painted buffalo robe with box and border design, Arapaho, ca. 1860. Courtesy Metropolitan Museum of Art, Michael C. Rockefeller Memorial Collection of Primitive Art, 1978.412.128

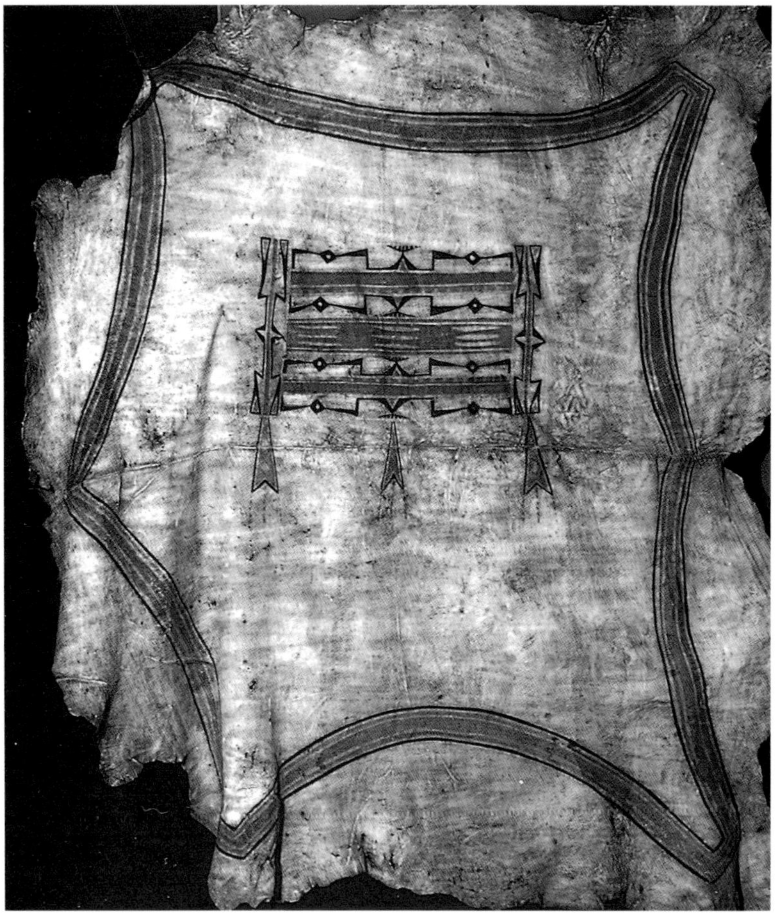

est parfleche traditions is limited because of the small number of surviving pieces from that period. The great majority of parfleches in collections today were both made and acquired after 1880. Those dating from the preceding three decades are far fewer in number, and those created prior to 1850 are extremely rare. Even the majority of those made before 1880, however, were collected during the final years of the nineteenth century and early decades of the twentieth when confinement of tribes on reservations allowed greater access to their material culture by outsiders. At this time, the great natural history museums and independent agents collected intensively, seeking to acquire and preserve artifacts of native peoples rapidly losing their traditional ways of life. Prior to that time, a much smaller body of Plains and Plateau objects, including parfleches, had been obtained by military personnel or explorers. In fact, many of the earliest documented pieces were acquired by Europeans during their travels to the western regions of North America between 1820 and 1850.

That there were few early pieces left to be found by the time major collecting expeditions were undertaken is the result of several factors. Parfleches are made of perishable material and did not survive once abandoned. All of those buried with the deceased and those cached for future use and never recovered have long since returned to the elements. In addition, traditional parfleches were functional objects, made with the intention of being used. The length of their utility varied depending on their type and contents. For example, envelopes received harder use than containers for ritual objects, so many of the oldest pieces in collections today are sacred medicine cases. Beautifully painted envelopes used to store elaborate clothing undoubtedly lasted longer than those used for the storage of food because finely painted cases were highly regarded and were surely handled more carefully than more common ones. Unless they were collected by non-Indians, however, all were destined to be consumed through use over time.

When parfleches were worn to the point that they were no longer serviceable, they were usually cut up and recycled into the construction of other objects requiring rawhide parts. Moccasin soles bearing fragmentary painted images may be commonly seen. Pieces of old parfleches also appear as the rawhide elements of baby carrier hoods, various types of horse equipment, knife cases, dance bustles, headdresses, small bags, belts, arm bands, drums, and dance shields. Occasionally, large parfleches were cut up and reconstructed into smaller cases. It was not until the tribes were settled on reservations that older parfleches were put away and preserved as mementos of the old way of life.

In one instance, however, recycling helped to preserve pieces that would otherwise have been used up. During their confinement on a reservation in eastern Kansas during the years 1846 to 1857, and perhaps even before, Mesquakies acquired envelopes from Western Plains tribes through trade. They refolded these according to the pattern of their traditional trunks, often in such a way as to utilize the original painted panels as decorative elements (pl. 6). Once constructed, these trunks were used as storage containers, particularly for sacred materials, and were kept in permanent lodges. They were neither exposed to the elements nor subjected to hard wear, and were thus preserved until many were collected during the first years of the twentieth century. At least eight Plains parfleches dating prior to 1850 have survived in this manner, most of which appear to be of Cheyenne, Arapaho, or Southern Plains origin. Included in this group are trunks collected from the Potawatomi and Kickapoo; although these peoples may also have fashioned trunks from Plains envelopes, it seems more likely that the majority of trunks obtained from them were of Mesquakie manufacture and acquired through trade. Of the few surviving parfleches that date before 1850, even fewer are accompanied by any information regarding their origin. At best, this consists of when, where, and by whom the object was collected; tribal identification is usually in question and the date of manufacture and name of the maker is always left unknown. Limited as the information may be, the few pieces described below comprise our earliest historic framework.

Although Ewers (1955: 115) cites a painted rawhide case described by Frederic Douglas as collected prior to 1789,[7] the earliest parfleche for which we have reasonably precise documentation is the extraordinary

7. This parfleche, reportedly in the collection of the Musée de l'Homme, could not be located during the present study.

envelope collected by Prince Maximilian and illustrated by Karl Bodmer (pl. 22). Maximilian acquired this piece during his famous expedition up the Missouri River in the years 1833–34 probably in the vicinity of Fort Pierre. Judging from its condition, it was new or nearly so at the time of its collection. Maximilian recorded the parfleche as being typical of those produced by the Dakota (Bodmer 1984:339), but its design indicates that it was painted by a Cheyenne woman. While elements within the composition may also be found in later parfleches of the Sioux, Arapaho, and Gros Ventre, the painting reflects all the tenets of classic Cheyenne style.

Three parfleches collected by Duke Paul are believed to predate the Maximilian envelope, but the exact years of their acquisition is unknown. The Duke made four separate journeys to North America during the years 1822–24, 1829–31, 1849–56 and 1857 (Lottinville 1973: xxiv). Most of the Native American objects in his collection were obtained during the first and second trips, and it is reasonable to assume that the parfleches all date from before 1830. The magnificent envelope previously mentioned, probably obtained from the Eastern Sioux, appears to be one of the very oldest parfleches of any type to have survived (pl. 1). Another envelope of the same construction, apparently new when collected, is adorned with images similar in many respects to those of the Maximilian envelope and may represent its antecedent.[8] The third is a beautiful cylinder with a striking design incorporating human hands (pl. 4). It was apparently collected from the Oto and contained an elaborate ornament known as a raven belt. Belts of this type were worn by distinguished warriors of several Prairie tribes and embodied an interrelated set of religious and military concepts. The association of the belt with the parfleche attests to the fact that, even at this early date, cylinders were used to store sacred objects.

A fragment of a parfleche, probably painted during the late eighteenth century, was collected by Costantino Beltrami in 1823 on the upper Mississippi River and is now preserved in Bergamo, Italy.[9] Although tentatively catalogued as part of a tipi door, its proportion and what appears to be a fold bordering the painting suggests that it was the painted panel of an envelope. Its design is remarkably similar to an envelope collected in the Western Plateau region, which was probably made during the same period (pl. 111). It is impossible to know if this affinity is the result of a general uniformity in some of the earliest painting styles or if, indeed, a Plateau piece found its way back to the Midwest through trade.

An incised knife case collected before 1828 (pl. 3), possibly by Lewis and Clark during their expedition of 1804–6, is ornamented with a design featuring rows of elongated triangles. Its pattern is essentially identical to the configurations found on the Oto cylinder just mentioned and on many of the earliest painted hide bags collected in the Great Lakes area. This case may date from the late eighteenth century, suggesting that incised rawhide, even if derived from bark incising, was quickly adapted to the imagery of painting.

8. This parfleche is illustrated in Torrence and Hobbs (1989: 25).

9. This object is in the collection of the Civico Museo E. Caffi, Bergamo, Italy.

A member of the Wilkes expedition to the Northwest in 1841 obtained an exceptionally beautiful flat case at Fort Vancouver on the Columbia River (pl. 122). Although there is no record of its tribal origin, it was undoubtedly produced in that region. It conforms in all its basic features to a large number of cases of the same type collected from Western Plateau groups during later years.

Two other important parfleches were collected by Count d'Otrante, a native of France and a naturalized Swede, during his travels in the upper Missouri region during the years 1842–44 (Brunius 1990: 31). Although the Count provided no tribal attributions, one envelope is undoubtedly Cheyenne (pl. 23) and the other is probably Blackfeet (pl. 68). Both of these, like the Wilkes case, appear to have been recently made when acquired; all three are quite distinct in their style of painting, suggesting that by 1840 at least some tribal and regional styles were clearly defined.

At the same time, stylistic similarities may sometimes be observed in the early parfleches produced in widely separated regions. For example, the flat, fringed cases created by the women of the Southern Plains feature painted designs that are nearly indistinguishable from those produced among the Western Plateau peoples. This general similarity may be seen in comparing two early cases collected from the Comanche with those from the Plateau. The first Comanche case was acquired by Jean Louis Berlandier in Texas between 1828 and 1851.[10] Its basic composition conforms with at least three other documented Comanche pieces, which helps confirm its origin—but still it might easily be mistaken for a Plateau case. The other case, probably collected by George Catlin during his meeting with the Comanche in 1834, also has many design elements similar to those found on Plateau cases. Yet, one significant difference consistently distinguishes these cases and others from the Southern Plains from their Plateau counterparts. Those collected from the Plateau groups are always horizontally rectangular (pls. 121, 122, 123), while those produced by the Apache (pls. 51, 52, 53), Comanche (pls. 45, 46), and Arapaho (pl. 38) are square or somewhat vertical in format.

This small group of parfleches constitutes the main body of works for which we have documentation indicating that they were collected before 1850. One feature is consistent among them all: the exclusive use of red, green, and black in their coloration. This feature, more than any other, identifies them as belonging to the earliest period. The three discernible periods in parfleche production based on color preference and paint type (see Introduction) seem to extend to all tribes and transcend the distinctive features of tribal design. This transition in color is therefore one of the best indicators of time period, particularly when considered in relation to the use of buffalo hide which was seldom available after 1880.

As the Woodlands painting style with its limited palette was adapted to parfleches, an interesting transformation occurred. Green became

10. See Berlandier (1969) for an illuminating account of the Indian tribes of Texas and illustrations of the objects he collected, including some of the earliest documented Comanche material.

an important color within the compositions, essentially replacing black as the predominant color counterbalancing red. Black, in turn, became the color used for the fine outlines delineating major motifs and for small units within the designs. In a sense, this intricate use of black replicated the linear activity originally created by white, sized lines, which never appeared as an element in parfleche painting due to the uniform coat of sizing that covered the entire object. This basic color scheme of red and green outlined in black distinguishes nearly all parfleches produced in every region before 1850.

The number of documented parfleches collected between 1850 and 1880 is somewhat greater, but still relatively small. The major difference distinguishing this group from those of the preceding period is an extended range of colors, primarily blues and yellows. Usually these colors are of native origin or may be a combination of native and trade pigments, which differentiates the parfleches of this period from most of those produced after 1880.

Beginning about 1870, the transition to the exclusive use of trade paints accelerated, until by 1890 most parfleches were painted in commercial pigments using a more standardized set of colors.

Other changes in the evolution of individual tribal styles correspond to the transition in color. These include the types of motifs, the structure of compositions, the character of the drawing, the details of construction, and the quality of craftsmanship. Again, because of the small number of documented works to provide a chronological framework and the fact that the materials used in construction defy precise dating, these changes in style are difficult, sometimes impossible, to discern consistently. In most cases they can be traced only in the most general and fragmentary way.

The evolution of distinct tribal styles is best understood when considering those tribes from which large numbers of parfleches have been collected. In such instances, the chances of a greater number of documented examples are combined with the opportunity to examine several pieces and determine those characteristics by which a tribal style is defined. In some cases, it is even possible to reconstruct the different phases in their evolution.

The tribal groups are represented in collections to differing degrees and this both directs and limits our vision. The Cheyenne tradition, for example, is represented by parfleches dating from 1830 to the late nineteenth century, spanning all phases of stylistic development. Even though most of these were produced from 1850 through 1880, we have a relatively complete picture of Cheyenne painting, including what preceded and followed this middle period.

The collections from most tribes, however, are usually insufficient to form such a complete picture of their stylistic development. A great number of Crow parfleches have been preserved also, but most date after 1880; those predating the reservation period are rare, and very few are known that apparently date prior to 1860. Consequently, our understanding of the Crow tradition is confined to the last half of the nineteenth century in general, and the reservation period in particular.

In contrast to the Cheyenne and Crow, very few Kiowa parfleches of any type have survived. Fewer than twenty-five are known to the author, and it is doubtful that many more exist. All appear to date from 1850 to 1880. Our knowledge of Kiowa parfleche painting, therefore, is extremely limited. We really have no idea how early Kiowa parfleches differed from those of the other Southern Plains tribes, and we do not know if or how long Kiowa parfleche painting continued into the reservation period.

The production of parfleches began to diminish as soon as tribes accepted or were forced onto reservations throughout the nineteenth century. The stressful effects of confinement and economic hardship, combined with the impact of forced cultural change brought about by intolerant government officials and policies and by missionaries, resulted in dramatic upheaval in every aspect of life. This included artistic production as well. Certain art forms, particularly those with a continuing function or economic potential, continued to be made, and these were often instrumental in helping the people maintain and preserve their valued traditions.

Other forms, including parfleches, were ultimately abandoned and this apparently occurred rather quickly among many Plains tribes, who ceased most, if not all, production by the end of the nineteenth century. These tribes include those originally inhabiting the Eastern Plains who were removed to Oklahoma, the peoples of the Southern Plains and intermontane Southwest, the Gros Ventre and Assiniboine in the Northern Plains, and probably the Missouri River tribes placed on Fort Berthold Reservation in North Dakota. Other tribes, however, continued to create various types of rawhide containers after the turn of the century. The Northern Arapaho in Wyoming, and possibly their relatives in Oklahoma, continued to produce at least until World War I. Western, or Teton Sioux, women produced a significant number of parfleches throughout the same period and continued rawhide painting to a limited extent until the 1930s. Their works were often acquired by other tribes as gifts or through trade and may have met the limited need these groups had for such objects, thus contributing to their own abandonment of the form. The Blackfeet tribes also created parfleches during this time—many undoubtedly intended for tourists—and continued to do so at least until the 1920s.[11] Many Western Plateau tribes were active into the twentieth century as well. It was the peoples of the Transmontane region, however—particularly the Crow, Shoshone, and Nez Perce—who probably produced the greatest numbers during the twentieth century. These objects were made as parade items and for sale and trade, as well as to be used in the traditional Plateau wedding ceremonies.[12] This production ended during the 1940s, and with it, the old tradition of parfleche painting.[13]

11. For a thorough and insightful discussion of the effects of the tourist trade on Blackfeet artistic traditions, see Walton et al. (1985).

12. The traditional exchange of parfleches and corn husk bags associated with weddings has long been a custom in the Plateau region (Morrow 1975: 95, 105), but became highly formalized about 1910 and continued until the end of World War II. This resulted in a resurgence of parfleche production during this period of the twentieth century and, even though it diminished somewhat after 1920, encouraged the continuation of excellent work long after production by most other tribes had ceased (Steven Shawley, pers. com., 1992).

13. Shawley, pers. com., 1992. This fact is also confirmed by other specialists who have spoken with Indian informants regarding Plateau artistic traditions after 1930.

Materials

In our highly industrial, consumer-based society where nearly everything we use in our daily lives has been prepared for us, it is easy to underestimate the difficulties, and the achievement, of producing what we may be inclined to consider a simple object. The parfleche is just such an object—deceptively simple in its design and use of natural materials and so perfectly suited to its function as to appear a most obvious solution. In fact, the creation of a fine parfleche involved several steps, each requiring technical knowledge, experience and considerable skill. And prior to the entire process of construction, the specialized tools needed to accomplish the work had to be made and pigments had to be gathered and expertly prepared.

Hide

The primary material used in the construction of a parfleche is rawhide, an untanned skin which has been treated to insure its preservation. In its finished state, it is 1/16 to 3/16 inches in thickness, tough, durable, waterproof, and unbreakable. It has a smooth, hard surface and, although quite stiff when new, it can be folded without cracking and becomes more pliable with use.

The preparation of rawhide was physically demanding, heavy work, but the subtle beauty of the painted image was ultimately dependent upon the quality of the finished hide. Expertly prepared rawhide possesses a beautiful, uniform color ranging from soft tan to off-white; it has a remarkable depth of tone and subtle luminosity. Its surface never appears flat or dead, but is imbued with a luster which animates the rich, glowing color of the painting and sustains the presence of the total form. The hide functioned not only as the physical ground for the painting but as an integral part of the completed image because unpainted areas were always contained within the design. The painting techniques unified the surface, integrating colored areas with the hide itself. It is a common assertion that the production of rawhide is the simplest means of preserving hides. While this may be true in comparison with the degree of skill and labor required to prepare finely tanned skins, not everyone could prepare rawhide equally well. In surveying a large number of parfleches it is apparent that considerable differences

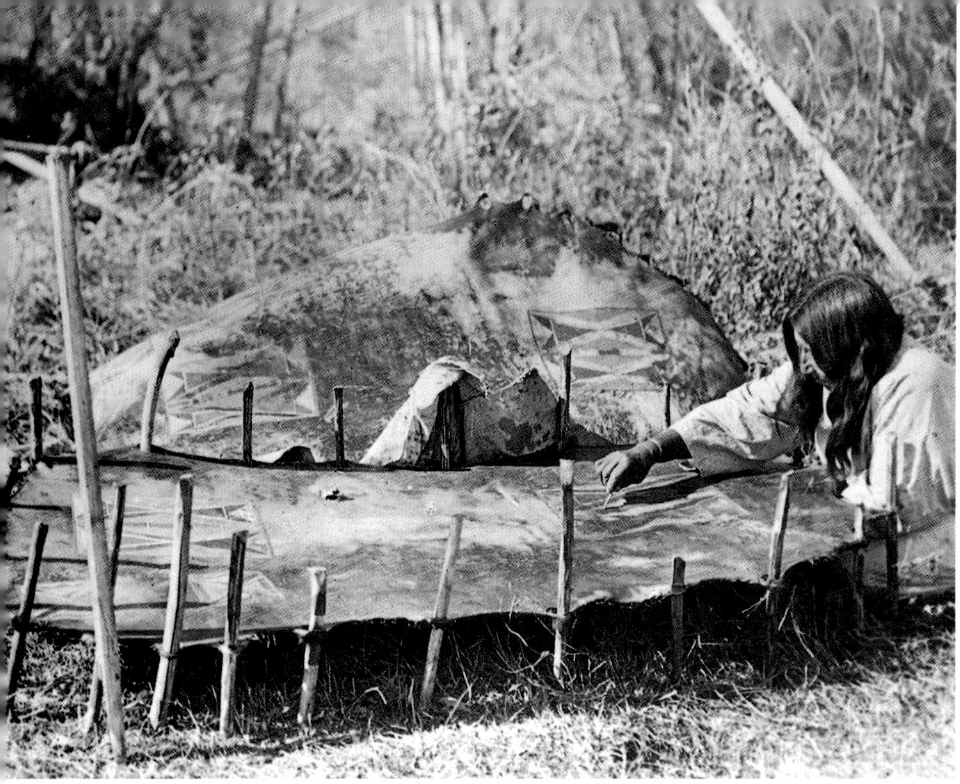

Takes Five, a Crow woman, painting a parfleche at Lodge Grass, Crow Reservation, Montana, ca. 1900. Visible on the hide in the background is the finished painting for another parfleche. Photographer unknown. Courtesy National Museum of the American Indian, Smithsonian Institution

existed in the skill of the makers and the quality of the objects produced.

Parfleches could be made from the skins of any large, readily available animals, but whenever possible the choice was determined by the preference of the maker for particular properties of the different types of hides. Each kind of animal skin has distinctive structural characteristics, which, together with the age and sex of the animal and the season in which the hide is obtained, make it more or less desirable as a material for rawhide.[1] Indian women were experts at hide preparation, and were undoubtedly very sensitive to these factors in determining which type of skin yielded the best results.

Buffalo was clearly the most favored hide until the destruction of the great herds in the 1870s, and the majority of surviving parfleches that predate 1880 are made of this material. It is ideal in every way for the construction of these objects and was one of the most abundant resources available to the Plains tribes. Having a relatively coarse and loose-fibered structure, the hide is comparatively easy to work, is extremely tough and durable, bends easily when folded, and becomes more pliable with use. Its weight and texture possess a tactile richness that makes it a pleasure to touch and handle, and the color and surface, when finely processed, are visually beautiful and provide a perfect ground for painting. Some of the earliest surviving parfleches, however, are made from other hides, indicating that elk, horse, moose, and possibly even deer were always utilized to some extent for this purpose, either being valued for their own qualities or used out of necessity.

As soon as they became available, the hides of domestic cattle were used as well. The skins of these animals are hard and tightly fibered; they are more difficult to work and usually result in rawhide that is somewhat inferior to that made from wild animals. Increasingly toward the

1. Much of my information regarding hides has been provided by contemporary craftspeople who are experts in working with all types of animal skins using traditional Native American techniques. I am grateful to Bill and Kathy Brewer, David Christensen, and Mark Miller for generously sharing their extensive knowledge of this field with me.

end of the nineteenth century, however, they must have been the only hides obtainable for many groups. By the mid-1880s, cow hide had become the most commonly used material by the Plains tribes who were confined to reservations where the native animals had nearly or entirely disappeared. At the same time, the federal government's program of beef rationing made cattle hides readily available, especially when the Indians themselves were allowed to kill and butcher the animals issued to them. After this practice was discontinued and reservation slaughterhouses provided the people with their beef allotment, hides must have become more difficult to acquire, and this factor undoubtedly contributed to the decline of parfleche production as an art form among some tribes.

Throughout the Plateau region there was probably less reliance on domestic cattle for hides following the disappearance of the buffalo, as elk and horse hides could be obtained in great numbers. This readily available, traditional material may account in part for the continued production of fine parfleches in this area well into the twentieth century. As long as they could be obtained, however, buffalo hides were probably most preferred here just as they were on the Plains. This is suggested by the fact that nearly all of the earliest surviving examples from the Plateau are constructed of buffalo, and many of these were collected from the Western Plateau tribes who resided along the Columbia River near The Dalles, far from the Plains buffalo ranges. Although there were great concentrations of herds in the Eastern Plateau country at an earlier time, by the nineteenth century most buffalo hides had to be acquired by the Plateau people through a trade network with the Plains tribes to the east, or by their own seasonal hunting excursions onto the plains of present-day Alberta, Montana, and Wyoming. As the numbers of buffalo declined, the Plateau groups began to rely heavily on elk and horses for their hide production, in addition to an increasing use of domestic cattle. Elk were always an important resource in this region, and remained abundant in the mountainous areas even as the adjacent country became more settled. Rawhide made from elk is flexible and whitens easily, and it seems to have been favored by many painters; undoubtedly some Plateau parfleches were constructed of this material even before 1880, and it was used extensively after that time. Many of the Plateau tribes were also extremely wealthy in horses, and large, individually owned herds provided a ready and convenient supply of hides. This resource may have become increasingly important as the tribes became more acculturated and devoted less time to hunting. Some twentieth-century informants, among the last Plateau parfleche-makers, indicated that they preferred horse hide to all other types, stating that it possessed an exceptional whiteness which was highly esteemed (Shawley, pers. com., 1992).

In conclusion, it is clear that buffalo hide was most commonly used before 1880 and that the use of domestic hides increased greatly during the last half of the nineteenth century. However, the often expressed idea that all early parfleches were made of buffalo hide is inaccurate. A survey of existing pieces reveals that throughout the history of parfleche production, a variety of hides were utilized, and the type of skin alone is not a decisive factor in determining age.

Paint

Painting on leather has been practiced in varied forms by Native American artists since prehistoric times, and it is this tradition that determined the materials and techniques of parfleche painting, as well as the aesthetic sensibility that formed the basis of its imagery.

The Indians' knowledge of paint sources grew out of their intimate familiarity with the natural world in which they lived and their expert utilization of its resources in providing for their physical and spiritual well being. The material culture and technology of most American Indian tribes, into which artistic expression is so thoroughly integrated, reflects intelligence, sensitivity, and inventiveness in the creation of objects needed to facilitate their chosen way of life. These characteristics extended to their use of trade materials as well, as Native Americans appropriated Euro-American materials into their evolving artistic traditions during the eighteenth and nineteenth centuries.

Native paint was obtained from a variety of sources.[2] Most pigments are of mineral origin, but a significant number of vegetable and animal substances were utilized as well. Some pigments were common enough to be available in most areas, while others were far more difficult to obtain, often requiring paint gatherers to travel long distances. We know that specific paint sources were well known to many tribes over a wide region, suggesting the great value and importance placed upon them. Some pigments were collected in a relatively pure and refined state, but other types required some degree of processing, usually demanding skill and experience on the part of the maker. This is clearly evident in the description provided by Frances Densmore (1918: 116) of what was involved in the preparation of a fine red pigment:

> On the Standing Rock Reservation is found a yellow ocherous substance which, after being reduced to a fine powder, is used by the Indians in making yellow paint. This substance, when treated by means of heat, yields the vermilion used on all ceremonial articles as well as in painting the bodies of the Indians. The baking of this ocherous substance—a process which requires skill—is done by the women. First, the substance mixed with water is formed into a ball. A hole is dug in the ground in which a fire of oak bark is made. When the ground is baked, the coals are removed, the ball is placed in the hole, and a fire is built above it. This fire is maintained at a gentle, even heat for about an hour, which is sufficient for the amount of the substance usually prepared at a time. The action of the heat

2. The listing of various pigment sources has been compiled principally from Ewers (1939: 3), Dunn (1968: 161), and Morrow (1975: 33); others are noted separately.

changes the color of the substance to red. When the ball is cold, it is pounded to powder.

It was necessary to know how hot to make the fire, how to make a fire without smoke, and exactly how long to keep the paint in the heat (Morrow 1975: 34). When taken from the fire, the transformed pigment might vary from a beautiful, bright red if processed perfectly to a dark, brownish hue, according to the ability of the maker in regulating the temperature and timing. Other desirable pigments must have required comparable effort and knowledge, so it is not surprising that the finer varieties were very highly valued and an important item of local as well as intertribal trade.

It is also important to recognize that among many tribes paint was regarded as a sacred substance. Its color functioned as a potent symbol in a variety of contexts and the pigment itself was believed to embody sacred powers. Ceremonies often attended its collection, and it was used in nearly all religious activities.

The most specific description of the variety of colors used by a Plains tribe at an early date was provided by Alexander Henry, a fur trader during the first years of the eighteenth century. Writing about the Piegan division of the Blackfeet tribe, he noted ten different colors. These were "a dark red, nearly a Spanish brown; a red, inclining to pale vermillion; a deep yellow; a light yellow; a dark blue; a light or sky-colored blue; a shining and glossy lead color; a green; a white; and charcoal" (Henry and Thompson 1897: 731). Although we may assume that most, if not all, of these paints were of native origin, it is possible that even at this early date some of them may have been procured from traders. A variety of natural brownish blacks, reds, and yellows was readily available throughout the Plains, Intermontane, and Plateau regions, but most tribal groups managed to manufacture or trade for a wider range of colors.

Black was obtained from several sources, nearly all of which rendered pigments that inclined toward brown—ranging from a warm, sepia-colored hue to a deep, rich, rusty black in its greatest density. Paint often referred to in the literature as "earth" black was the most common type, and was derived from various clays and mineral deposits usually containing high concentrations of iron oxide. A rich brownish black of similar appearance was also obtained from lignite, a soft coal with high carbon content. Charcoal derived from burning certain types of wood and grass was commonly used, and George Bird Grinnell (1923, vol. 2: 19) described a Cheyenne method of producing a dark brown-black by mixing the ashes of burned rye grass with fresh buffalo blood. Graphite may have been used to some extent, and was probably the source for the paint Alexander Henry described as having "a shining and glossy lead color." It is found in far fewer locations than other mineral blacks, but is present in the country occupied by the Piegan. Other blacks were available from vegetable sources, such as the boiled roots of the black walnut tree, walnut hulls, and from the helianthus or sun flower.

Morrow's informants indicated that they considered brown and black to be the same (1975: 34), both in their thinking and in their use of it to achieve desired effects in their paintings. It was used almost exclusively for outlining and for very small elements placed throughout the image, the only known exceptions to this being a very few parfleches from the Plateau region in which black is used to cover larger forms. This restrained use of black only intensifies its subtle character and inherent richness. It may be significant that native black was rarely if ever replaced by commmercial trade pigments as were all other colors in parfleche painting, perhaps indicating that certain religious concepts were associated with it.

Red—the color often associated by Native Americans with life-force and sacred power—was the most extensively used color in hide-painting of all types. A wide variety of relatively pure pigments ranging from pale vermillion to a dark brownish violet were obtained from concentrated mineral deposits rich in iron oxides and, as previously mentioned, the Sioux, Blackfeet, and probably many others produced a bright, beautiful vermillion by subjecting yellow ochre pigment to heat. Although other reds were extracted from such vegetable sources as buffalo berries, pussy willow buds, savoyenne root, and ripe cactus fruit, most parfleche painting was executed with mineral pigments. Another paint commonly appearing on even the earliest surviving parfleches is a mercury vermillion from China. It was introduced to North America during the eighteenth century and was the first commercially prepared pigment obtained by the western tribes. A common but highly valued trade item, it was also presented as a gift by early travelers and delegations (Ewers 1939: 4), and was widely utilized as soon as it became available.

A full range of natural ochre yellows was easily obtained from iron oxide earth, the most common source for this hue, but variants could also be produced from buffalo gallstones and Wolf's moss, a variety of lichen.

Beautiful native greens were created from both mineral and vegetable sources. At the beginning of the nineteenth century, Lewis and Clark (1904, vol. 6: 161) reported that a green earth paint was in use among the Indians living near the Rocky Mountains; this was probably derived from copper carbonate, which renders a delicate bluish-green. Other greens were produced from dried water plants, particularly the green algae slime found along river beds or collected as lake scum (McClintock 1910: 215). This soft, native green was particularly favored by many of the Plateau groups, who continued to use it in combination with trade colors up until the end of the nineteenth century.

A dark blue mud or blue earth found in crevices between layers of rock along some rivers furnished paint of this color for many tribes. Some of Father Powell's Northern Cheyenne informants recalled that a blue clay used by women to paint parfleches was obtained near their Sacred

Mountain, Bear Butte, in South Dakota (Powell 1977: 36). He also noted that blue clay was found along certain streams flowing into the Yellowstone River and in the colored paint pots in Yellowstone National Park. Morrow states that the Sioux procured this substance near the present-day sites of Blue Earth and Mankato, Minnesota. In appearance, most natural blues are dark and similar to what would be referred to as "Prussian blue" in a commercial pigment; some tend toward a dark blue-green. Another pale blue, or turquoise, which is distinct from the one just described but which also appears to be of natural origin, is sometimes found on early Arapaho and Cheyenne parfleches. Ewers (1945: 14) mentioned that the Blackfeet produced a blue pigment from dried duck excrement, and other dark blues may have been obtained from berries or crushed flowers.

White paint was readily available in the form of various clays and chalk, but was never used on parfleches. The lightest values in these paintings were established by the areas of unpainted hide that were always incorporated into the image.

Pigments were first prepared in dry, powdered form by grinding in a shallow stone mortar. Each color was then stored in its own small buckskin bag or combined with sizing to form a disk of paint which was wrapped in a piece of buckskin and preserved in that manner for future use. The paint bags themselves were sometimes elaborately decorated with beadwork, but were most often plain or even made of canvas.

Commercial pigments introduced by European and American traders as early as the eighteenth century became increasingly popular once they were available. They virtually replaced most native paints by the last quarter of the nineteenth century. Trade paints came in the form of dry pigments packed in small wooden boxes or paper packets and because they were perfectly suited to traditional painting techniques, they were easily adopted. Trade colors commonly employed included vermillion, red lead, chrome yellow, Prussian blue, an ultramarine blue, and chrome green (Mallery 1886: 52); whites and blacks were also available but were never adopted for parfleche painting.

Variants of these or perhaps other unspecified colors must have had occasional use as well, considering that a wide range of pigments was traded to Indians by Spanish, French, English, and American traders. The varying character and quality of these pigments contributes to the difficulty in identifying some colors as commercial paint and visually differentiating them from natural pigments. By the last quarter of the nineteenth century, however, trade colors had become more standardized because they came from fewer sources and consequently are more easily recognized.

The transition from the use of native pigments to the use of trade paint must have occurred over an extended period of time and was determined by several factors: the distribution and availability of trade goods, the attitudes of different tribal groups toward new materials, and the taste and preference of the individual artist. Although using trade paints was more convenient than collecting and processing natural pigments, paint obtained from the earth and other natural sources was regarded as sacred among many tribes and was therefore considered more desirable or even essential for certain uses. This may have resulted in greater restraint by some groups in accepting the new materials for parfleche painting, in the same way that the Cheyennes initially resisted using commercial glass beads in place of natural dyed porcupine quills in the decoration of sacred garments (Powell 1977: 40). Ultimately the adaptation took place, but probably later than for many neighboring tribes.

Beliefs associated with particular pigments may account for the continued use of certain native colors in combination with trade paints long after trade colors of the same hue were readily available. A distinctive native green of the type found on the oldest parfleches and corn husk bags was used well into the twentieth century by several Plateau tribes, and it persisted as a border color even when a commercial green was included within the painting (pl. 113). Similarly, Eastern Apache and Ute parfleche painters utilized an oxide red for both the outermost borders and side flap painting (pl. 50).

The acceptance of trade colors must also have varied from artist to artist even within the same small group, and this points to one of the difficulties in attempting to date parfleches precisely on the basis of paint type alone. Consider that in the same Sioux village in the year 1879, one might find a young, progressive woman enthusiastically incorporating the new commercial colors into her work, while an older, highly conservative woman continued to utilize the same natural colors that she had used and preferred since she began painting in the 1850s. One parfleche would thus appear quite similar to the great majority of those painted during the late nineteenth century, while the other would have the appearance of parfleches painted almost a half century earlier. Consider also that in 1879, some bands of Teton Sioux had been settled on reservations for a decade or more and had easy access to trade colors; at the same time, Sitting Bull's Hunkpapa people were still living the final years of their old nomadic way of life. This dramatic difference manifested itself not just in the availability of trade materials, but undoubtedly extended to the attitudes of the people as well.

In keeping with the three distinct phases of color usage (see page 22), generally parfleches from all regions painted before the 1850s exhibit a restrained use of color, primarily red, green and black; occasionally limited amounts of yellow, dark blue, or dark green were incorporated. This color range is consistent with other types of painting on hide of this period and corresponds with the limited range of color seen in porcupine quill embroidery and beadwork from the same era. Parfleches from about 1850 to the early 1880s reveal an expanded palette and in this respect mirror the same transformations that occurred in bead embroidery as tribes began to replace pony beads with seed beads. A wider variety of reds, yellows, blues, greens, and browns appear in combination with black at this time, and it is probable that many of the parfleches painted then combine both native and trade colors within the same compositions.

After 1890 there is again a greater consistency in color as trade pigments came to be universally adopted by all those who continued to produce parfleches. Although distinctive preferences of color combina tions, dominancy, and sequence were maintained by different groups, the same blues, reds, yellows, and greens were apparently available throughout the country and appear on parfleches of tribes widely separated geographically and stylistically.

Colored crayons were also used to a very limited extent during the late nineteenth and early twentieth centuries in the ornamentation of parfleches. Although occasionally they were used to brighten worn parfleches, a few examples are known on which crayon was incorporated with paint in the original design to establish one or two areas of new color. It appears that the crayon was added after the parfleche was painted, sized, and completely dry, perhaps in response to areas of color that may have been judged too weak after the painting was completed.

Tools

The implements used for applying paint in parfleche painting were fashioned from bone, wood, horn (Ewers 1939: 4), and stone. Like the parfleche itself, they were deceptively simple in design and taken from readily available natural materials, but were well suited and highly effective for their purpose. A common type of bone brush, which was more precisely a stylus, was cut from the porous parts of large bones or joints. Buffalo bones were preferred because of their fine grain, and the edge of a shoulder blade or the end of a hip bone was especially favored. These were carved into flat, oblong shapes, ranging from 2 1/2 to 4 inches long, rounded at the corners and tapered to a sharp edge. Although buffalo bones were the best material for these implements, bones from domestic cattle and other large mammals were used as well. The porous bone soaked up and held the paint, and allowed it to flow smoothly when the tool was applied to the surface of the hide. Held in one direction, it produced a sharp, thin line; turned to the side, the broad edge could be used to spread the paint over a wide area. The hard surface of the bone also made them an ideal tool for working the paint into the surface of the hide when necessary. One brush of this type was used for each color.

Sticks of willow or cottonwood were also used for applying color. They were carved to a point and then chewed to produce a loose, stiff fibrous brush. Although these brushes were used extensively, they do not appear in painting kits preserved in collections because they

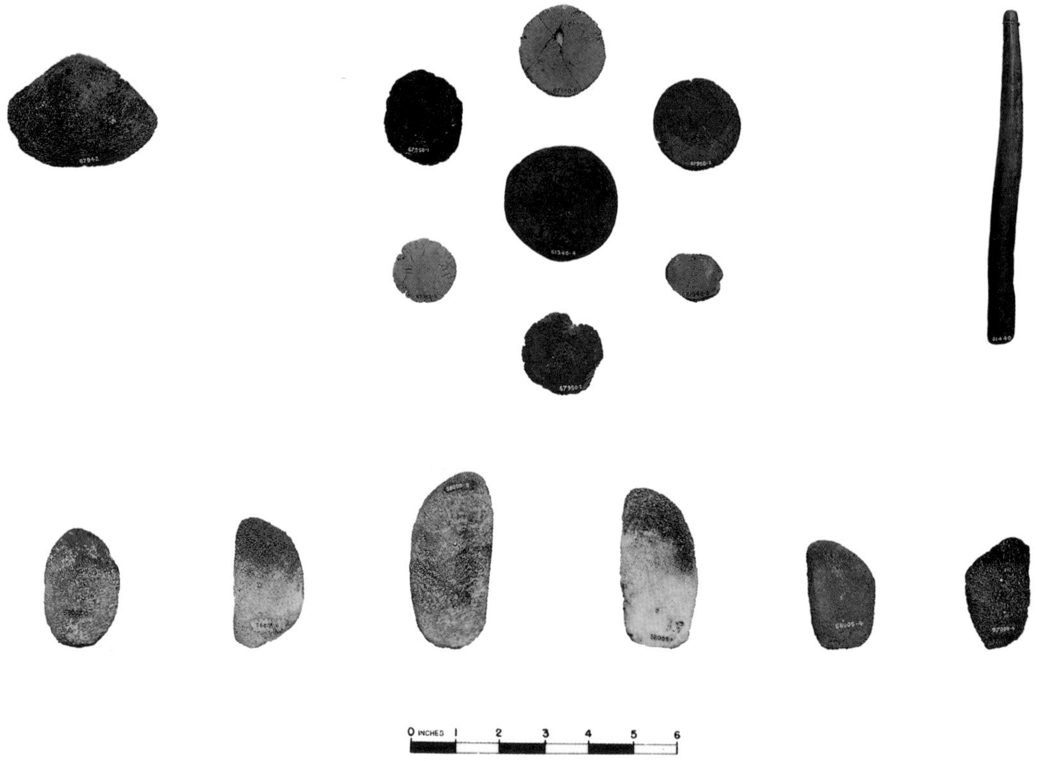

were made from green wood and were discarded after use. Other sticks were sometimes carved to a flattened end with a sharp edge that could render linear elements, and the rounded ends of sticks were used to create dots. Mountain sheep horn was also carved into a long, narrow spatulate form with a sharp edge to create an outlining tool. This implement could not hold much paint but was capable of producing a very fine line and could also be used for scouring the surface of the hide before applying color. Similarly, a stone tool was reportedly used for outlining by Northern Blackfeet women (Morrow 1975: 73), and this practice undoubtedly extended to other tribes as well.

Many painters also kept in their kits a bundle of peeled willow sticks that were used to lay out designs and, by some artists, as a straight-edge, or rule, in painting. These sticks, in addition to brushes, containers for holding liquid paint, sacks of pigments, and cakes of paint, comprised the artist's painting kit.

Artists' tools, including porous bone brushes, or styli (bottom row and upper left), for applying liquid paint; disks of pigment (top center) for applying color directly to wet rawhide; and a stylus of mountain sheep horn (upper right) for outlining. Arapaho, nineteenth century. Courtesy Field Museum of Natural History.

Techniques of Painting and Construction

Although many descriptions of the preparation of rawhide and parfleche painting exist in the literature, none is so detailed and thorough as that of Mabel Morrow (1975: 28–33, 35–39). She was the only researcher with a specific interest in parfleche working at a time when the many variations in their production could still be observed. She systematically sought out and interviewed traditional parfleche workers, some of whom were active even during the prereservation years of the nineteenth century. That the Native American women she met responded to her enthusiasm and respect for their artistic accomplishment is apparent in their willingness to discuss their craft in such detail. It is this body of information which is perhaps Morrow's greatest contribution to our knowledge of parfleches, and much of the basic technical information in the following description is taken from her account.

In considering any description that outlines the creation of a parfleche, however, it is very important to recognize that the process and technique varied among tribal groups and even among individual workers within a band. Morrow points out that the characteristics of the hide, the weather, the location and conditions under which the work was accomplished, plus those factors that determined the timing of the process, all had an impact on the quality and appearance of the finished parfleche, as well as on the manner in which it was produced. The impact of these variables on the finished work is confirmed by contemporary craftspeople who make rawhide and replicate Indian parfleches today, even though they usually work under more controlled conditions.

The process began with a freshly killed animal, usually skinned by a man, who then turned the hide over to a woman whose responsibility it was to transform it into rawhide or a tanned robe to be used in many ways. After the animal was skinned, it was first necessary for her to remove the fragments of muscular and connective tissue, congealed blood, and fat from the inner side of the hide. This process, called fleshing, was accomplished with hacking and raking strokes using a chisel-like tool of bone or metal that has a serrated blade. If the hide began to dry out before the fleshing was finished, water was applied to keep it soft and workable. Although Wissler describes this work as "an unpleasant and laborious process requiring more brute strength than skill" (1910: 64), it nonetheless required great care. The flesh side of the skin ultimately became the exterior surface of the finished parfleche, so cuts or deep gouges at this stage could ruin the skin as a surface for painting.

The fleshed hide was then staked horizontally six to ten inches above the ground, hair-side down, with heavy wooden stakes intermittently spaced around the edge of the hide. These stakes were similar to those used to hold down edges of tipis. This process stretched the hide so that it would have a smooth and even surface when it shrunk and dried. As with fleshing, the procedure demanded skill and experience: it was critical that the maker establish precisely the proper tension in staking and stretching in order to achieve the desired results.

After the hide was staked, but while it was still wet, it was thoroughly washed. This was done by throwing water upon it and scraping it off with a dull knife or piece of bone; occasionally the rough side of a buffalo's tongue, soaked in water, might be used for the same purpose. This process was repeated until the hide was completely clean, thereby insuring that it would be white when finished.

At this point, a woman could proceed in one of two ways. If the skin was being prepared as an unpainted rawhide, it was allowed to dry and bleach in the air and sun at this time. This process was carefully controlled because it was important for the hide to dry evenly. As the stretched skin dried, it became hard and stiff. The stakes were then removed and the hide was placed on the ground where the worker scraped it to an even thickness. She accomplished this by standing on the hide and, leaning over it, chipping away the inner surface until it was smooth and even using the adzlike tool made from elk antler with an attached blade of flint or metal. She might then turn the hide over and remove the hair using one of methods described on page 53, thus completing the finished rawhide. It could be utilized for a number of purposes at this point, or it could be stored and made into parfleches at a later time. If that was the case, the dried rawhide would need to be again thoroughly soaked in water to prepare its surface for sizing and painting. This was usually accomplished by submerging it in a stream of running water where it would become thoroughly softened and washed. It would then be staked out and allowed to dry to the point that it was ready to be painted.

Most women, however, preferred to make parfleches from fresh hides. When this was done, the skin was worked to an even thickness through fleshing and scraping, and then staked and washed in the manner described, but it was not allowed to dry completely. When the hide had dried to precisely the proper stage, it was ready for sizing and painting, and the artist could begin her creative work.

The sizing consisted of a thin glutinous wash applied to the flesh side of the skin which ultimately became the painted, external surface of the parfleche; when dry, it formed a hard, lustrous coating. Sizing served the primary purpose of making the rawhide water resistant, thereby sealing and protecting the contents of the parfleche from the elements. It also sealed and protected the painting from fading, soiling, and abrasion. As an element of the painting itself, it brightened the colors and established a smooth, uniform surface, helping to unify the painted and unpainted areas of the design into a cohesive whole. Many parfleche makers sized the hide prior to painting, and then applied a second coating over the painted image when it was completed. Others preferred to paint directly on the unsized rawhide and then cover the entire surface with a coat of sizing when finished. In both approaches, the hide as well as the painting were thoroughly covered by this protective glaze.

Sizing could be made from several materials, but the two most preferred and utilized were the juice from prickly pear cactus and scrapings from the hide itself. In addition, Morrow lists juice from other types of cactus, antler or horn glue, fish roe, the lymph from a fish, a gland froman elk or buffalo, wax from the tail of a beaver, buffalo gallstones, or liquid from animal eyes. She also notes that a kind of varnish, which differed somewhat in appearance from the usual sizing, might be made from resin or gum from wild cherry, pinon, tamarack, and other trees. The Pueblo groups are reported to have produced a sizing from peach juice.

The first step in creating the painting consisted of defining the outside dimensions of the image and establishing the primary compositional structure. This was often accomplished with the aid of straight, peeled willow sticks which most women included in their painting kits. These sticks, about the diameter of a common lead pencil, served as both rulers and straightedges; their lengths generally corresponded to the length and width of the design area, and they were used as guides in painting. The painter first determined the borders and basic compositions by arranging sticks on the surface of the hide; when the desired image was visualized, it was impressed onto the wet hide as a guideline for the painting. Once the drawing began and color was applied, however, variations in this initial configuration must have taken place along with the spontaneous incorporation of additional small-scale elements.

Indeed, the character of many parfleche paintings suggests that the artist relied more upon her experienced eye than in guidelines or templates. This is clearly apparent in those which are quite freely painted, but is also evident on close observation in those which have the appearance of being precisely measured. The finest parfleche painting always transcends the static, mechanical quality that would be imparted by too great a reliance on measuring devices. These paintings are animated by an active tension arising from the subtle interplay of the highly formal, symmetrical structure of their forms and spatial divisions combined with the dynamic and improvisational quality of drawing.

This essential *character* is lost in the schematic drawings so often used to illustrate parfleche painting in earlier publications, and it is for that reason that these representations fail completely in depicting the artistic achievement in this form. For it is not simply the designs that define these paintings as inspired works of art—indeed, the designs alone may be easily misconstrued as mechanical and purely decorative—rather, it is those expressive qualities of line, color density, spatial organization, and surface texture that are inseparable from their creation as paintings.

It seems likely that many artists used guidelines to define the borders of the painting and to determine the central vertical and horizontal axes of the field and perhaps the major motifs. Once these parameters were set, the painting was completed by visual measurement alone.

Two basic methods were employed in painting. In the first, dry powdered pigments were mixed with hot water or sizing to form liquid paints which were applied to the hide with the implements previously described. Each color had its own container, which was commonly the shell of a box turtle or mussel shell, and its own brush or stylus. In the second technique, the painter applied color directly to the wet hide using a dry disk of paint, formed of pigment and sizing. These were usually 3 to 4 inches in diameter when new, and were basically handled like a bone stylus; the edge was used to draw relatively narrow lines and the broad sides could be used to cover large areas with color.

Kneeling on the ground next to the hide, the painter aligned herself with the longitudinal, or vertical, axis of the painting. This position was dictated by the act of drawing the image in that the long lines, both straight and curved, were most effectively executed and controlled by a downward stroke, with the painter drawing her arm toward her body. In this manner she first established the vertical lines and edges of the forms within the borders of the painting and then moved around the hide as the painting progressed. In order to draw most effectively, the artist maintained a tension and muscular control in her entire upper body, and the drawing resulted from the integrated action of her eye, hand, arm, and back.

The painting was executed while the hide was at a certain stage of wetness. The pigment penetrated the hide to some degree and established a continuity of surface between painted and unpainted areas of the

A Brulé Sioux woman painting a parfleche, Rosebud Agency, South Dakota, ca. 1900. She is completing the second of a matched pair. A single hide was generally large enough to produce two envelopes, and it was customary to paint them with identical designs. Photography by John Anderson. Courtesy Nebraska State Historical Society

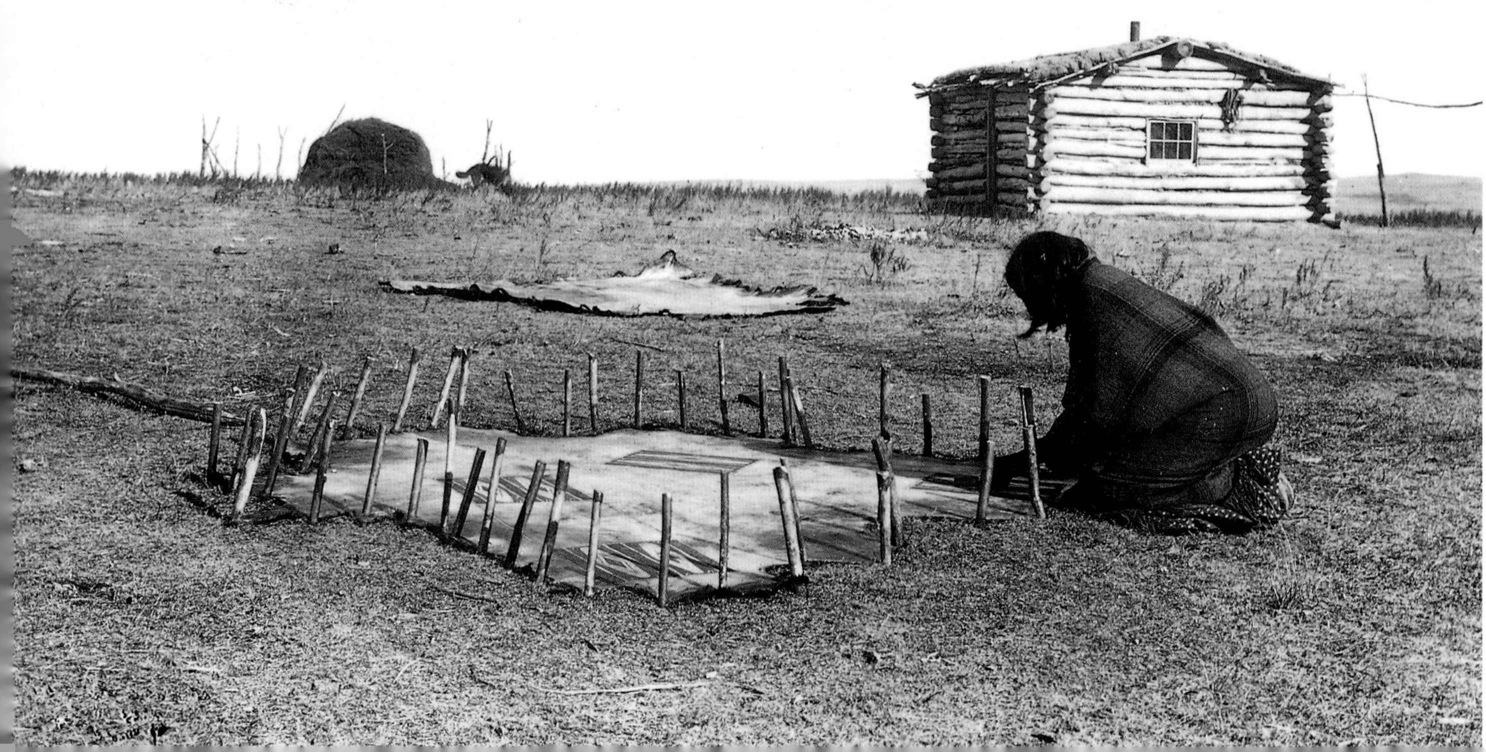

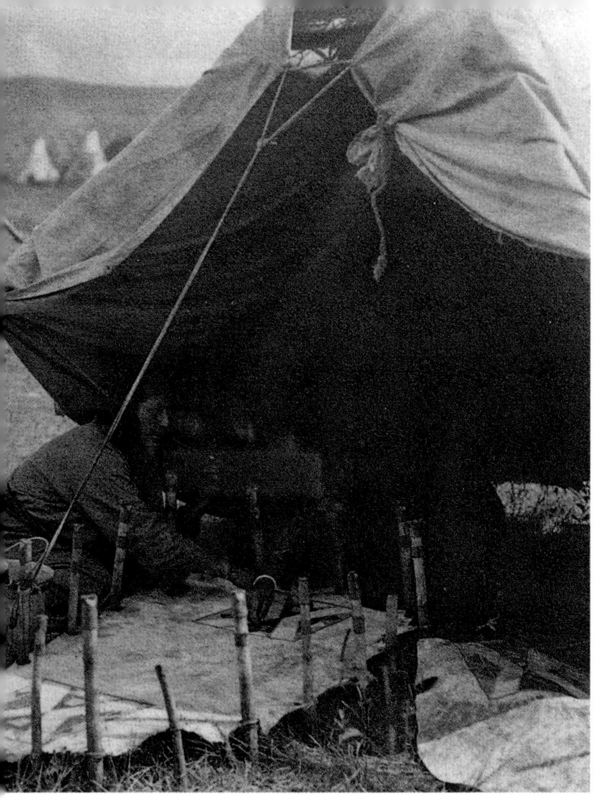

Crow women painting a parfleche. They are working under a temporary shelter erected to protect the damp, staked hide from drying too quickly in the sun. Photograph by Throssel, 1911. Courtesy Barbara A. Hail

design; because of this, the painted images never appear to be applied on top of the surface, but rather seem to be thoroughly integrated with and inseparable from the hide itself. In this respect, parfleche painting is similar to fresco and related watercolor techniques.

Like a calligrapher, a skilled painter worked with a speed and sureness gained through experience and the knowledge that the painting must be completed before the hide became too dry. That the painting had to be finished in a limited time is reflected most clearly in the decisive character of the drawing; this time constraint is evident in the bold angularity of some styles, but it also manifests itself quite beautifully in the delicate, complex designs that possess a remarkable fluidity of contour and line. Some painters worked under sun shades to slow the drying and in order to quicken the work utilized assistants to fill in areas of color once the design was established.

Finally, in considering the aesthetic and technical achievement of the finest parfleche painting, it is important to remember that no revision was possible once the painting had begun. It was necessary for the artist to conceptualize her design in its entirety before beginning—to visualize fully the complex relationships of line, shape, and color and, then, holding this vision in her mind, proceed to give it tangible form.

After the painting was completed and a coat of sizing had been applied, the hide was allowed to dry. As noted earlier, this was an important step because it was during this stage that the necessary structural change occurred which transformed the untreated hide into rawhide and produced the desired whiteness in its color. It was preferable to dry the hide as slowly and evenly as possible, and experience was required to control the process under various atmospheric conditions. Temporary shelters were often erected to shade the hide from the sun to help extend the drying process which, ideally, lasted at least two weeks.

Once the hide was thoroughly dry, the hair was removed by one of two methods. The oldest technique, which was the most difficult but produced the most beautiful rawhide, was pounding the hide with a heavy, smooth, flattened stone. Stoning could also be accomplished by using the back of an ax as Buffalo Bird Woman, a Hidatsa, demonstrated for Gilbert Wilson in 1913 (Gilman and Schneider 1987: 43). The hide was removed from the stakes, turned over with the hair side up, and placed on a pad of dried grass or native tanned leather to protect the painting. Beginning in the center and working toward the edges, the maker began to pound off the hair with hard, glancing, overlapping blows that followed the lay of the hair. This process not only removed the hair, but also intensified the whiteness of the hide and helped create the creamy, opaque surface that distinguishes the finest rawhide. In addition to making the rawhide more pliable without reducing its natural thickness, stoning also left the epidermal layer of the hide intact, which provided a smooth unbroken surface for the interior of the finished parfleche. A stoned surface more effectively repelled moisture and could be easily cleaned.

The hair could also be scraped off with an elk antler scraper after the hide was dry, either before or after it was painted. Standing on the hide and holding the scraper in both hands, the person preparing the hide removed both the hair and epidermal layer of skin by a series of short, hoeing strokes. This method was less desirable for the reasons previously cited and, according to Morrow, was not generally practiced until after 1880. However, parfleches finished in this way which appear to predate this time do exist, so the method was probably utilized to some extent throughout the period of production. In fact, scraping may have been combined with stoning because some pieces that show the marks of a scraping tool also possess a very beautiful color and surface. Laubin, in writing for hobbyists, suggested that the hide be pounded with the rounded back of an axe after it was scraped in order to produce the desired whiteness and pliability (Laubin and Laubin 1971: 71), and it seems quite likely that this was practiced by Indians as well.

At this point the parfleches were cut from the finished hide and folded into their intended shape. Although Morrow mentions that the cutting could be done with a piece of flint, clam shell, or beaver tooth, using such tools for this process would be very difficult. It is more likely that metal knives were commonly used; one of Ewers's Blackfeet informants even cites the lack of knives in pre-horse times when such trade items were not available as proof that parfleches were not made during that period (Ewers 1955: 116). Folding the stiff hide of a new parfleche for the first time was difficult, and was accomplished by pounding the corners and edges and weighting the piece until its shape was maintained.

Once the folding was completed, holes were burned for the ties and, on flat cases and cylinders, the lacing. The number and location of holes used for tying parfleche envelopes varied among the different tribes but was fairly consistent within each group, which makes this a helpful feature in determining tribal identification. Burning the holes with a hot metal rod or piece of bone created a hard edge which resisted tearing and was far more durable than holes made by cutting. Sometimes stake holes were used for the ties to secure the inner flaps of envelopes,

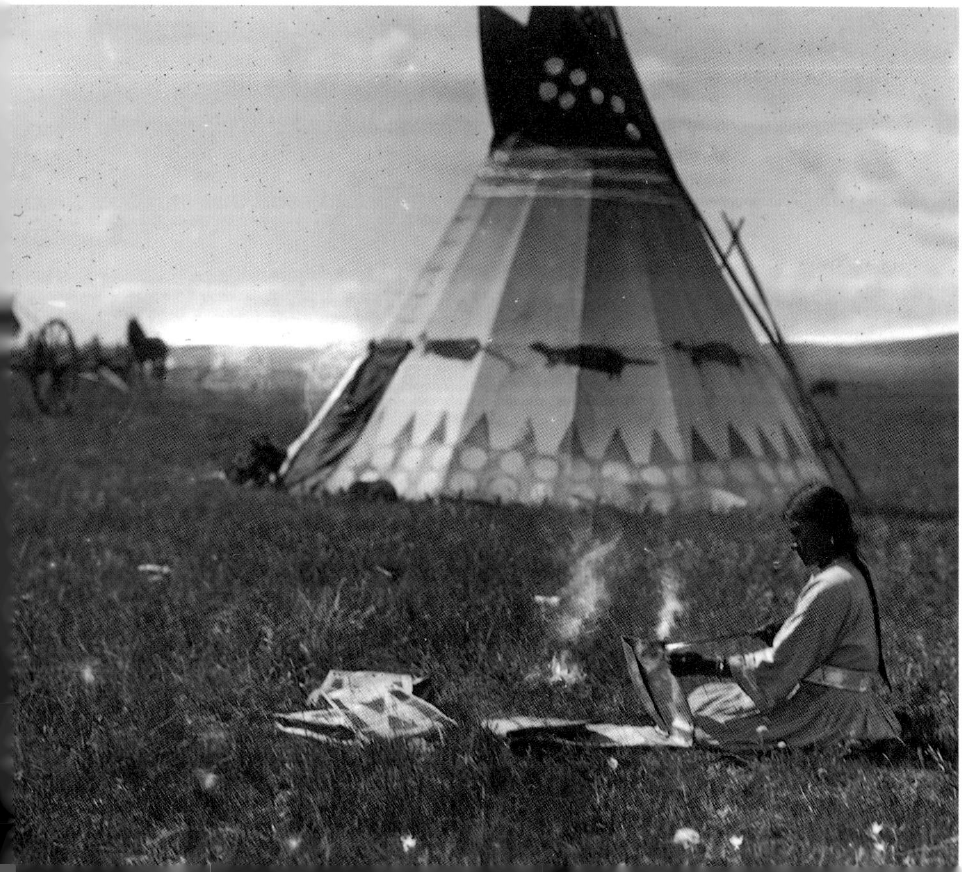

Blackfeet woman burning tie holes in a finished parfleche, ca. 1900. Photograph by Walter McClintock. Courtesy Beinecke Rare Book and Manuscript Library, Yale University

although a few large envelopes from the Ute, Jicarilla Apache, Kutenai, and Western Plateau region are made so that stake holes are also used to close the outer flaps (pl. 84). With the addition of native-tanned leather ties, the basic envelope was completed. Other forms, which required lacing or sewing or the addition of other structural elements such as fringe, were completed at this time as their construction demanded.

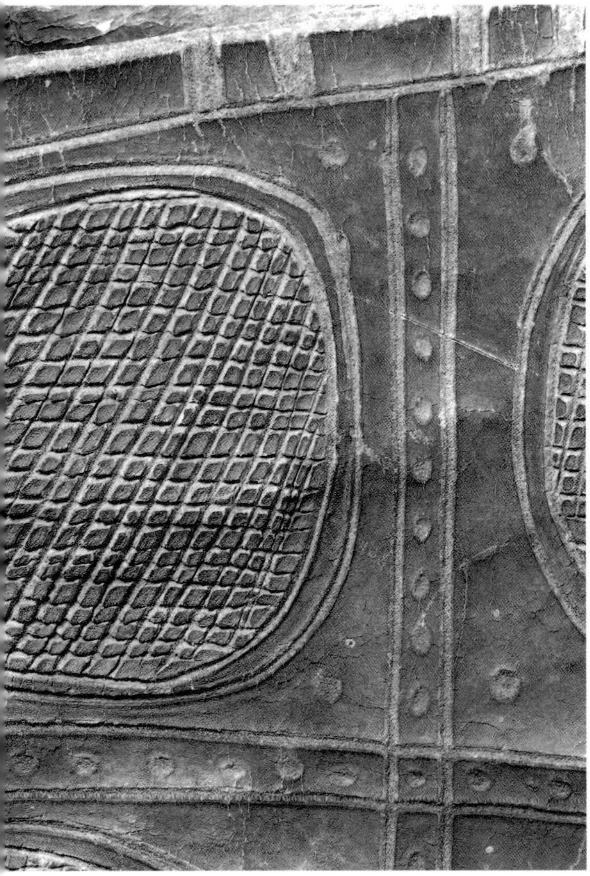

Detail of an incised parfleche envelope, Western Plateau, ca. 1850. Collected from the Umatilla. Benson Lanford Collection

Incising

Several tribes created incised parfleches in addition to those ornamented with painting. These were made of heavy buffalo hide and constructed so that the darkly pigmented, epidermal layer of the hide formed the outer surface of the parfleche, rather than being folded to the inside as on painted pieces. The technique consisted of cutting and scraping away areas of this dark brown upper layer to reveal a lighter colored layer beneath, thus creating a contrasting design in light and dark brown (pl. 88). The images were comprised of fine lines, cut into the damp surface, that widened slightly as the hide dried; often these lines formed large areas of crosshatching. In addition, the compositions usually contained some shapes or broader lines in which all of the epidermis was completely scraped or peeled away leaving larger, light-colored areas.

Incising is an old technique. Surviving examples of fully incised parfleches are extremely rare—fewer than twenty are known to exist—and their historic relationship to painted parfleches is fragmentary and not fully understood. It is often asserted that incised containers predate painted ones, suggesting that they were a preliminary step in the development of the painted form, but there is no concrete evidence to support this. Actually the reverse was perhaps more feasible. The earliest documented parfleches as well as those which appear to be even older are painted, not incised, and reveal that the tradition of painted rawhide was well established less than half a century after the introduction of the horse and the full development of Plains material culture. It seems doubtful that an extensive tradition of incising was developed and then given up in favor of painting within that short span. Both methods of ornamenting rawhide were surely practiced in precontact times, and it is more likely that the two techniques were developed and produced concurrently, with incised pieces always being somewhat rare. The process was undoubtedly favored by some tribes—probably those from which the greatest numbers have been obtained—and never developed by others.

Wissler recorded the Sioux tradition that incised parfleches were made before painted ones (1904: 256), yet it should be noted that the Sioux were producing painted rawhide containers long before his informants were born and the accuracy of their statements may be open to question. This tradition does, however, indicate that incising was widespread from the Eastern Plains to the Western Plateau region at a very early date, before the technique began to disappear in the 1860s. Although some of Morrow's twentieth-century informants were familiar with the technique and even spoke of using elkhide darkened with blood as a substitute, it is doubtful that any fully incised parfleches were made after 1880 when buffalo hides were no longer readily available. All of the known examples in collections today appear to be of great age, dating from the mid-nineteenth century or earlier, suggesting that even before 1870 the production of incised parfleche was diminishing. These dates seem to be confirmed by an examination of Crow lance cases and sword scabbards (see Galante 1980). The shafts of these objects dating before 1880 are constructed of buffalo hide with incised designs. After 1880 and until 1930, this element was made from cowhide and ornamented with painted designs; the pattern does not change, only the materials and techniques of production.

Nearly all of the known fully incised parfleches have been collected from the Plateau tribes and the Crow who were so closely associated with them through trade. The design elements and compositional structure of the images adorning these pieces directly correspond to those that were painted, confirming that they were produced by these peoples and not acquired through distant trade. Some of the most beautifully executed envelopes were obtained from the Crow, who also produced incised cruppers and lance cases, and depict classic Crow designs composed of angular forms derived from combinations of isosceles triangles and tapering lines. Many of those acquired from Plateau tribes have compositions based on freely drawn, curvilinear elements, closely replicating the painting style developed by the Western Plateau groups. Others have angular designs which seem more typical of the Nez Perce and other Eastern Plateau tribes. A number of these Plateau pieces have trapezoid-shaped outer flaps, indicating that this was an early construction feature in the region and suggesting a strong relationship with Blackfeet style. Only one incised envelope is known, however, which appears to be unquestionably of Blackfeet origin; the proportion of this case, its construction, and its surface designs duplicate the Blackfeet type of painted parfleche in every detail. An incised and beaded knife case attributed to the upper Missouri region also affirms that this technique was practiced by tribes in that area. Finally, a very few pieces, including a flat case (pl. 5) and knife sheath (pl. 3), have been collected from the Eastern Plains. The case was reportedly collected from the Ponca but is without precise documentation, and its design motifs and composition strongly suggest that it may have been made by a Sioux artist.

In a related technique, incising and painting were combined within a single work, in which elements of the painted design were articulated by a finely incised outline. This was practiced most elaborately by the

Mescalero Apaches in the creation of both envelopes and flat cases that are distinguished by the clarity and precision of their intricate designs (pl. 54). It was also used by the Pawnees and other Eastern Plains tribes in the ornamentation of their burden straps (pl. 9), but the combination has not been found on other types of parfleches from this region. Limited amounts of this type of incising have been observed on a very few envelopes from the Plateau region, but it was apparently not a convention in this area.

The origin of incising techniques stems from two possible sources and it is likely that both contributed to its development. First, it has been noted that parfleches were conceptually patterned after birchbark containers made in the Eastern Woodlands and Northwest. These objects were often decorated with incised and scraped designs in the same manner as parfleches, and several writers have suggested that they undoubtedly served as the precedent. It should be noted, however, that since prehistoric times Woodland peoples have decorated a great variety of objects made from wood, horn, shell, bone, and clay with incised designs. Although rawhide and birchbark have similar physical characteristics, the basic pictorial concepts embodied within the general tradition probably established a basis for the development of incised rawhide as much as any single object type. For example, the incised geometric designs on a few wooden feather box lids bear a close visual affinity to some parfleche designs, as do the patterns on certain types of pipe stems, cradle boards, and awl handles.

The second antecedent and certainly the most direct influence in the creation of Apache incised parfleches is the decorated leather work produced by Spanish and Mexican colonists in the Southwest. A variety of objects, particularly horse gear, was ornamented by incising, piercing, and tooling. Saddles, especially the covering over the top, known as the mochilla, were decorated with incised cutwork done with a knife. Mexican pommel bags were incised and painted; the designs were cut into the leather, then rubbed with red paint so that the color filled the incised lines while the excess was wiped away. A variety of flat bags, trunks, and leg-wraps, or botas, were also decorated in various ways using these techniques (Bruce Shackelford, pers. com., 1992). Many of these items were also decorated with serrated or scalloped edges, an element often seen on the fringes of Apache parfleches and saddlebags but also represented in painted designs along the edges of major motifs and borders on Southern Plains, Apache, and Western Plateau parfleches.

By 1750 these Spanish items were all in common use throughout the southwestern ranching industry, which was centered in New Mexico. There is strong evidence that the southern tribes were influenced by this aspect of Hispanic culture, and it is also reasonable to assume that this influence spread northward to the Plains and Plateau regions with the rapid diffusion of Spanish horses and their associated trappings during the last half of the eighteenth century.

Although incising was undoubtedly a difficult procedure, many parfleches of this type are notable for their linear delicacy and intricate compositions. An interesting transformation in their appearance also occurred as they were subjected to wear. When new, the effectiveness of the design was dependent on the precise edges and sharply contrasting values produced by incising, but as they became worn through use, the incised areas that lacked the smooth, hard epidermal surface became fibrous with a slightly raised nap. These areas also became soiled and darkened, so they more closely resembled the surrounding areas in color and value. The result provided the viewer with a far more subtle visual experience in that the incised image was transformed into a dark, richly textured relief pattern covering the surface of the weathered hide.

Diagrams of parfleche types prior to folding, showing location of painted panels. Dotted lines indicate folds.

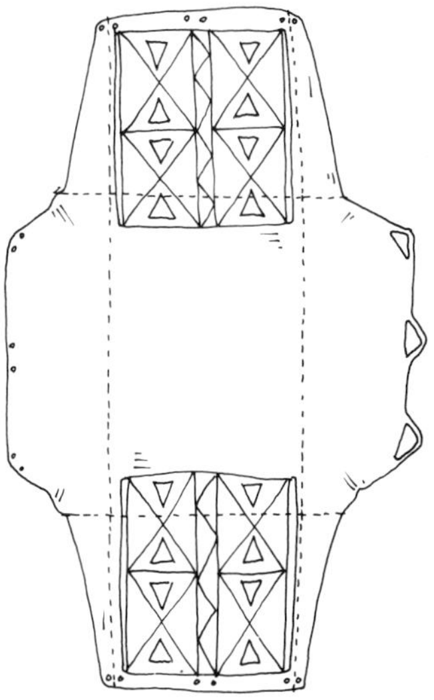

envelope

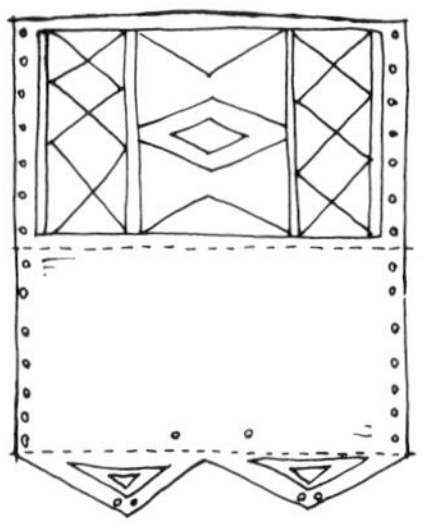

flat case

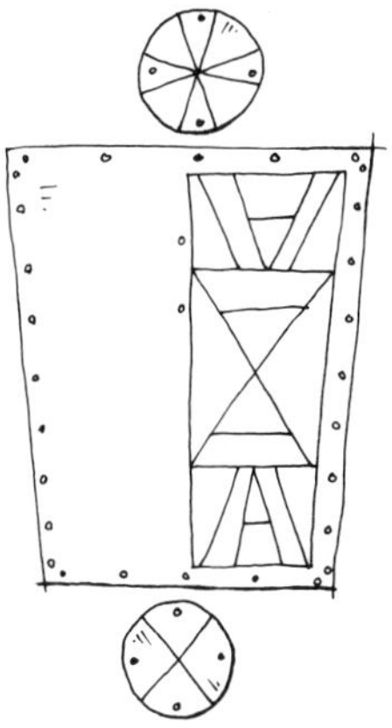

cylinder

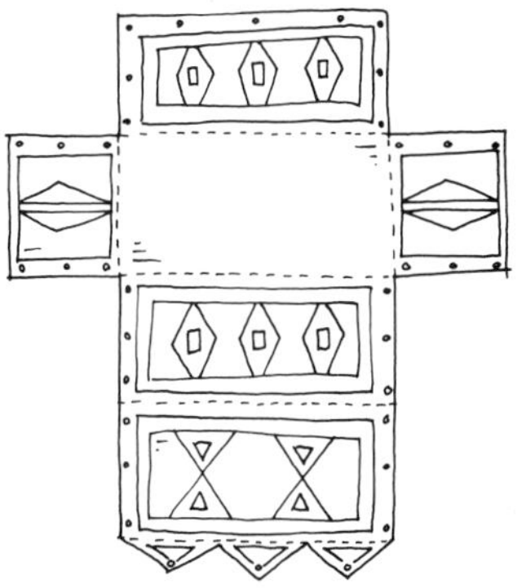

box

Forms and Functions

Parfleches were constructed according to four primary forms: folded envelopes, flat cases, cylinders, and boxes. Many variations of these basic types differing in proportion, size, and construction details were produced by the different tribes, but all were fundamentally the same in concept as their archetype. Each was made to fulfill a different function or was traditionally associated with specific contents in that certain items were usually kept in parfleches of a particular type. Sometimes special cases were made for individual items such as knives or rolled feather bonnets, and these containers closely echoed the shape of the objects to be stored, but most often the shape of the parfleche was not indicative of the contents.

While it is sometimes useful, and often convenient, to generalize about the distribution and specific use of the different types, numerous exceptions existed in the practices of individual tribes. Not all of the four forms were made by every group producing parfleches, and some types may have been made only during certain periods. In addition, the same types of containers, or variants, sometimes had differing functions among different tribes or during different eras.

This is clearly illustrated in a partial survey of tribal customs regarding flat cases. Unfringed cases of this type (pl. 37) are universally described in the literature as women's utility cases or work bags, used to gather foods or store such items as sewing materials. In contrast, flat cases with long, heavy side fringes (pl. 46) are referred to as ceremonial bags or medicine cases, which were used to store sacred objects. These designations probably derive from Wissler's study of the Blackfeet and have become somewhat standardized by subsequent writers in discussing the material culture and art of all Plains and Plateau tribes. While this pattern of use is well documented among the Blackfeet people, it does not extend to all other tribes.

For example, there is undisputable evidence that the Cheyenne used unfringed cases for their personal medicine bundles (pl. 30); several examples acquired with their contents intact may be found in museum collections. In fact, no side-fringed Cheyenne cases are known to exist and, considering the numbers of other parfleche types collected from this tribe, it seems highly unlikely that they were ever produced. Although we have fewer examples upon which to base a judgment, the same use-pattern is apparently true of the Kiowa. The Arapaho, however, who were very closely associated with the Cheyenne and Kiowa, produced both heavily fringed and unfringed cases for their sacred objects (pls. 38, 39). In addition, all three tribes also made various types of flat cases intended for secular, utilitarian purposes.

Similarly, the exclusive use of side-fringed cases as medicine containers may not be assumed without question after considering the traditions of all the tribes who produced them. It is known that this practice was well established among the Blackfeet and Crow (pl. 94) since a great many bundles complete with contents have been collected from these people or discussed in studies describing their religion, arts, and material culture. However, comparable information regarding their use by other tribes is largely unavailable. For instance, none of the extraordinary fringed cases collected from the Apache (pl. 52) has been acquired with contents, nor has their use been discussed by early observers. In fact, Apache parfleches of any type are barely mentioned, which is perplexing in itself considering that the women of this tribe created a highly distinctive and exceptionally beautiful style of rawhide painting. In contrast, several fringed medicine bags of softly tanned leather, painted with religious imagery and containing amulets, have been collected, suggesting that bags of this type may have been the exclusive containers for the sacred items of Apache warriors and shamans.

Apart from those of the Blackfeet and Crow, the greatest number of side-fringed cases have been collected from the tribes of the Plateau region, particularly those western groups living along the Columbia River (pls. 121, 122). While it seems probable that some were used for religious or medicinal items when considered within the context of other material culture traits adopted from the Plains tribes along with the horse, this is an assumption; none has been located in museum collections with its contents intact. Plateau religious practices varied within the region and were different from those of the Plains peoples, and we cannot be certain that these tribes followed the same customs or that the contents of their fringed cases were always sacred. It is, in fact, doubtful. In his discussion of the Coeur D'Alene, Teit notes that flat bags with long fringes were used "as canteens or saddlebags by women when traveling and hung up in the lodges as receptacles for odds and ends, women's tools, etc." (1930: 50). This notion is further reinforced by the fact that comparatively few unfringed cases have been acquired from Plateau tribes, suggesting that they were an uncommon form and that fringed cases must have been regularly used for both religious and secular purposes.

There is also clear evidence that the sacred function of side-fringed cases changed in accordance with the secularization of religious objects that occurred among many tribes during the reservation period of the late nineteenth and early twentieth centuries. Within this context and because of their dramatic appearance, they, along with parfleche cylinders, were adopted as decorative horse trappings (pl. 75) to be displayed during the mounted parades that were a standard feature of tribal gatherings, powwows, and Wild West Indian shows. Significantly, this change took place primarily among the Northern Plains and Plateau tribes, including those groups which had historically made exclusive use of these cases as containers for ceremonial items. During the first years of this transition, Northern Plains and Plateau peoples probably used the empty cases to symbolize the ownership and spiritual prerogatives associated with sacred bundles. Southern Plains tribes, however, did not follow this practice and generally ceased to produce parfleche medicine containers of any type during the early reservation period.

Clearly, the specific uses of the various types of parfleches were not as rigidly standardized as has often been described. The function of a parfleche was generally prescribed by its form according to tribal customs, which varied from tribe to tribe and, to some extent, with the preferences of individuals. Our knowledge of the details of tribal life is often fragmentary and incomplete and what we know of one tribe may not always be applicable to another. This sometimes leads to perplexing questions. For example, parfleche cylinders are quite often cited as containers for rolled feather headdresses, and Kiowa informants told Ewers that they used cylinders exclusively for this purpose (1955: 119). Their statement seems verified by the fact that nearly all of the known Kiowa cylinders are quite large and would accommodate elaborate objects of this type. Yet the Sioux, with whom spectacular eagle feather war bonnets are synonymous, apparently produced few parfleche cylinders, and most of those found in collections today are relatively small and were probably intended for other types of ceremonial objects. Perhaps only a fraction of the larger cases survived, but considering the great numbers of other types that were collected, this seems doubtful; it is more likely that many Sioux men stored their headdresses in envelopes rather than cylinders.

Envelopes

The most common form of parfleche was a flat, rectangular, folded envelope capable of considerable expansion when filled. This was the most widespread type throughout North America and was undoubtedly produced in the greatest numbers; most parfleches preserved in collections today are of this kind. This form is often designated in the literature as the true "parfleche" as distinct from other kinds of painted rawhide cases. These envelopes are usually described as containers for dried foods such as meat, berries, pemmican, and tallow, but they were also used to store and transport a great variety of other materials. As the general, all-purpose packing case, they held elaborately decorated clothing and ceremonial items, blankets, household goods, and personal possessions. A prosperous family would have required several envelopes to meet their needs,[1] undoubtedly reserving some for special

1. None of the early studies reveals the total number of parfleches that an average Plains family might possess. Perhaps the most specific indication was obtained by Weltfish (1965: 195), who recorded that a Pawnee family of six required for its 1867 summer buffalo hunt at least six to eight large envelopes packed with food and a few small items in addition to a few soft-skin sacks. This number is surely small in relation to the numbers needed by fully nomadic Plains peoples, in that the Pawnee left many of their possessions in their permanent villages during a buffalo hunt, and relied on daily hunting to supplement their food supply. Also, by this date, the Pawnee had far fewer horses than most Plains tribes, which would have restricted the amount of baggage they could carry.

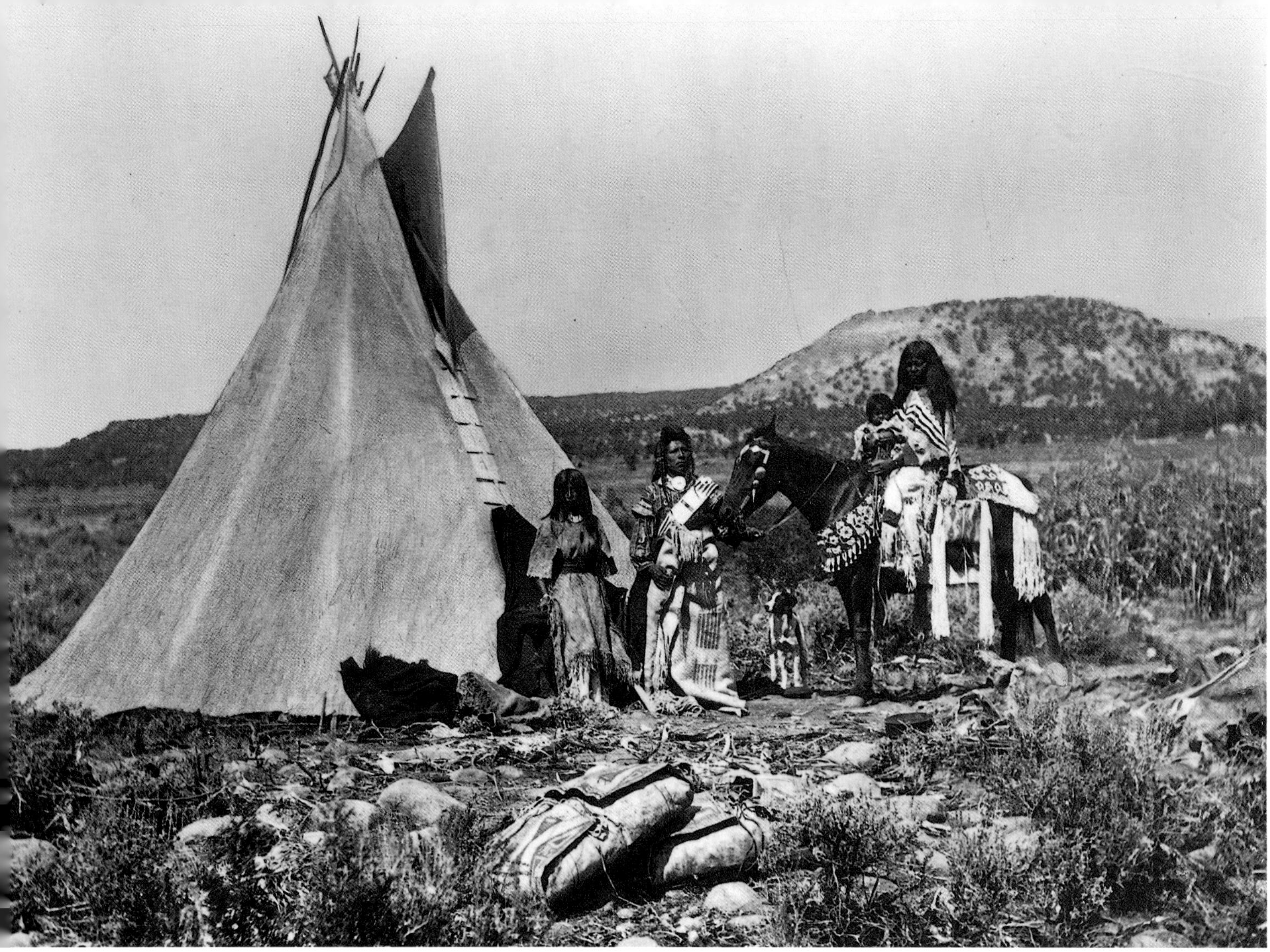

items that were always stored in the same case while appropriating others as needed during the activities of daily life.

The sense of order connected with the use of these containers is reflected in the statement of Buffalo Bird Woman, a Hidatsa: "Our clothes we put away in parfleche bags which were used only for this purpose. We never used these bags or cases to pack meat or foods in, as we wanted to keep our clothes clean. . . . there was just one bag for the man's suit and that of his wife. The warbonnet and trail were kept in the bag, along with the clothes" (Gilman and Schneider 1987: 42). Grinnell observed that "parfleches carried sacks of dried berries and dried roots, gathered during the proper seasons and kept for use during the winter and spring; and in others were ornaments, wooden bowls and dishes, small horn spoons, and any odds-and-ends. In fact, the contents of a parfleche were a perpetual surprise, for it might contain anything from an elk's tooth to a twenty-dollar gold piece." He went on, "When a woman was looking for something that was not easy to find, she might drag out from between or under the beds half a dozen parfleches, one after the other, to be unlaced and its contents picked over in the search for the missing article" (1923, vol. 1: 244–45). We are reminded by these statements of the universal need to organize one's

Sai-ar and family at their camp. Uintah Agency, Utah, 1871. The material wealth of this Ute family is prominently displayed in this portrait. Visible are their richly beaded and painted articles of clothing, elaborate horse trappings, including a fringed parfleche case, and packed parfleches stacked in the foreground. Photograph by E. O. Beaman. Courtesy Smithsonian Institution

possessions, and it is interesting to know that this problem extended even to the Plains peoples, where efficiency and organization were essential to their way of life.

Envelopes were made from large rectangular pieces of hide with straight-cut ends and somewhat irregular sides which widened toward the center. These long side-edges were first folded inward until the center sections met or overlapped forming a longer, narrower rectangle; then the top and bottom ends were folded toward the center where they met forming the closure flaps. Both the side flaps and outer flaps were secured by ties at the edges. When the envelope was packed, the contents were placed in the center of the open case; the side flaps were then folded over covering the contents and tied in place, followed by the outer flaps covering the seam formed by the inner flaps. Each full-size envelope required the use of nearly half a hide, so they were usually made in matched pairs with identically painted images (pls. 25, 65). While making two at once was the logical outcome of production techniques, the practice of creating matched paintings was probably derived from the custom of packing a parfleche on each side of the horse suspended from the packsaddle, thus establishing in the symmetrical pairing of the paintings an arrangement that echoed the practical distribution of weight and symmetry of form.

Curley, a Crow warrior who gained considerable fame as one of Custer's scouts in the Battle of the Little Big Horn, stands beside a horse that is packed for travel with parfleches and storage bags. A painted crupper is also visible. Photography by F. A. Rinehart, ca. 1900. Courtesy David Wooley

The size of envelopes varies, but most are from 12 to 16 inches wide and from 22 to 29 inches long. An exception to this is the unusually large envelopes produced by Ute and Jicarilla Apache women (pls. 57,

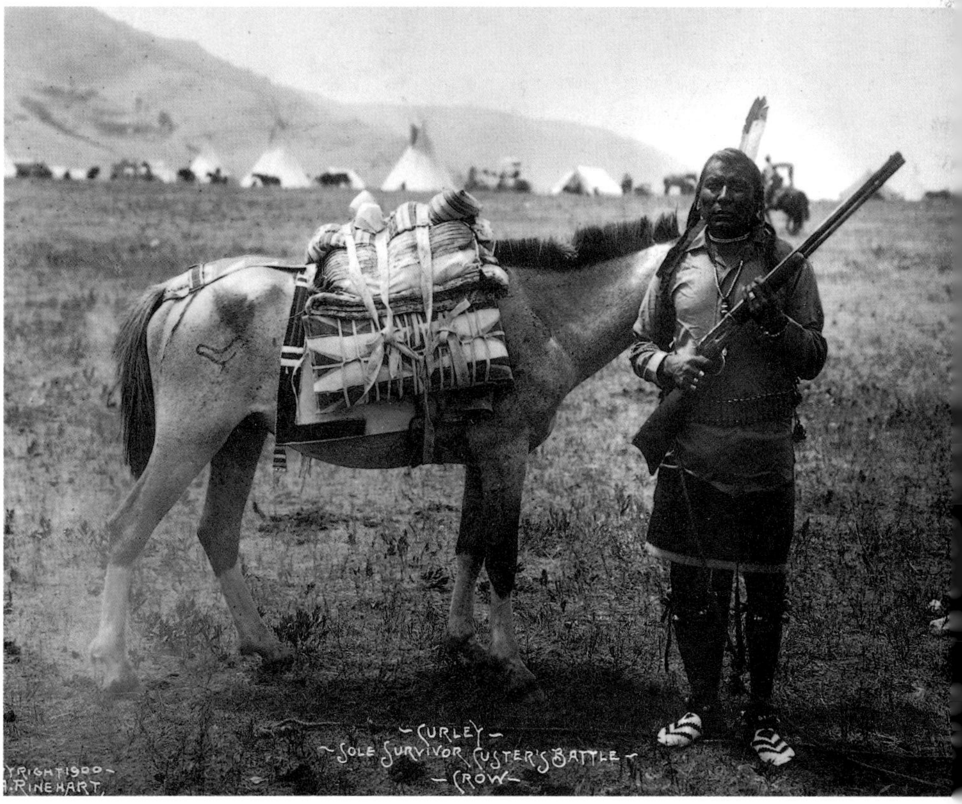

59). Some of these are 36 inches long and must have taken an entire hide. These groups may not have produced pairs for this reason, and the fact that none are known to have ever been collected further supports this probability. Envelopes that were smaller than the standard sizes were also made. Some may have been produced to store special items, but most were probably created for children (pl. 108). Some of these small envelopes were functional in that the possessions made for Indian children often replicated in miniature those of adult life, while others that were too small to serve a practical use were undoubtedly intended as toys.

Envelopes were painted on the surfaces of the two outer flaps forming a single image across the upper side of the entire case, with the painted panels usually extending somewhat over the ends to the back of the parfleche. Some groups painted the inner flaps as well (pl. 50, interior), which became more visible when the case was filled and expanded, but—except for those made by the Kutenai—this was always executed in a somewhat more restrained or rudimentary fashion. The back of the envelope was relatively undecorated. According to the traditions of some tribes, the backs were often left unpainted, while other groups joined the outer edges of the front panels with lines of color to form a border along the edges of the back of the folded container. Some Plateau tribes also framed the back panel completely with a single colored line. While the first format tended to focus the viewer on the delineated plane of the parfleche's uppermost surface, the two latter treatments created a sense of extended containment, by integrating the painted image with the various contours and planes of the folded form.

A variation of the standard envelope, and quite possibly its predecessor, originated among the tribes of the Eastern Plains at a very early date (pls. 1, 2). This form is undoubtedly archaic and only a few are known to have survived into the twentieth century. Examples differ conceptually from the conventional envelope in the relationship of the painted image to the folded form. While the designs adorning common envelopes are carefully adjusted to cover the surfaces of the outer flaps, these early ones are designed according to a different set of artistic principles. In their creation, a single, rectangular image, tightly composed and complex, was first painted in the center of a large rawhide, then folded into a flat envelope with little regard for the relationship between the painted design and the folded surfaces. The pictorial organization of these paintings was closely related in many respects to that of the earliest painted robes from the Western Great Lakes region. As previously mentioned, this suggests that they were probably derived from this source, and were a transitional form between the tradition of painted hides and the final development of the parfleche envelope produced by most tribes throughout the nineteenth century.

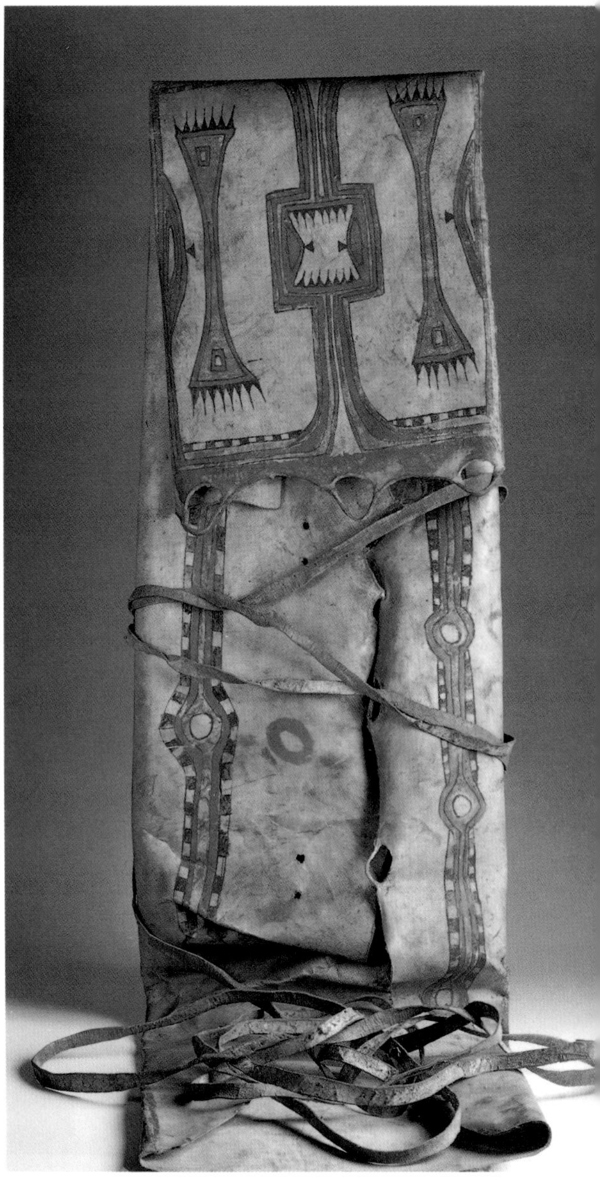

Apache envelope (pl. 50) partially opened to reveal painting on inner flaps.

Flat cases

A great many flat cases of varying patterns were produced to serve different functions, and probably all parfleche-making tribes produced some version of this type. In their most basic design, they were constructed by folding a single piece of rawhide at what would constitute the bottom edge of the case and sewing or lacing it along the sides, leaving a rounded or tapered projecting end which was folded downward to form the closure flap. These cases might be nearly square, or rectangular with either a horizontal or vertical format. The flaps of many horizontal cases, particularly those made by the Sioux and Arapaho, were cut to form two, three, or four triangular shapes running the length of the case. Some tribes also made distinctive boat-shaped containers without a closure flap to hold sacred objects (pl. 95).

Flat cases ranged considerably in size, the longest dimension usually being 10 to 14 inches, but smaller and larger cases were constructed as well. The edges were sometimes sewn with sinew, heavy thread, or cord, but were most frequently laced with leather thongs through holes punched or burned along the side. The lacing was sometimes executed as an overstitch extending around and over the edge of the case (pl. 37), while the other common method required that single or double thongs be laced in and out of the holes so as to lie parallel with the edge (pl. 39). Strips of red, dark blue, or green wool cloth were often incorporated under the lacing, either wrapped over the edges or, on fringed cases, attached at the front of the case along the seam; usually these strips extended below the case as short pendants. The edges of flaps were sometimes ornamented in a similar fashion.

Occasionally cases were further elaborated with various beaded or quill-wrapped suspensions, feathers, bells, metal cones, or simply pairs of buckskin thongs at the corners. There was usually some means of suspension extending from sets of holes burned in the back. This might be a single thong on smaller bags, but was usually a wide strap designed for heavy use on the larger containers. Crow and Nez Perce cases were sometimes elaborated with a wide rawhide strap ornamented with serrated edges and painted designs. Older cases of this type were generally strongly constructed and could withstand hard wear, while later examples perhaps intended as gifts or made for sale are more delicate.

Flat cases fall into two major groups: those just described and those that were further embellished with long, heavy fringes extending from the sides. Those without fringe are generally regarded as women's bags and, as such, were often used for collecting berries or other foods, or made to hold specific items or sets of objects such as sewing, hide-dressing, or painting materials. Numbers of these containers were essential for a nomadic family needing to organize a multitude of possessions during a life of constant movement. At the same time, they were undoubtedly used for diverse general purposes as immediate needs might dictate. An interesting statement first defining the traditional use of a parfleche type and then noting its exception was recorded in Gilbert Wilson's work (Gilman and Schneider 1987: 48). Wolf Chief, one of his Hidatsa informants, specifically referred to this type as a woman's bag, yet he used one himself to carry food or other items during an eagle hunt. As noted, however, unfringed cases were employed by some tribes to contain sacred objects and medicines used in healing.

The heavily fringed cases are more generally associated with ceremonial materials. Their function as containers for medicine bundles is well documented among the Blackfeet and Crow, and may also be true for many other tribes because parfleches of this type had a wide distribution throughout the Plains, Intermontane and Plateau regions. Notable exceptions were the Sioux and Cheyenne who never produced cases of this type; also, no such case is known to have been collected from the Kiowa even though fringed cases were utilized by their close allies, the Arapaho and Comanche, and were very common among neighboring Apache groups.

The long fringes were cut from a single piece of tanned leather or heavily pounded rawhide in such a manner that one continuous edge remained intact. This end was then inserted between the edges of the case and secured in place as they were laced together. Some groups preferred the attachment of a short fringe to the flap as well. The length of side fringes averaged about 30 inches, but might range from 15 inches to as long as 45 inches. Generally, the cases of the Blackfeet, Arapaho and Comanche tend to be constructed with proportionally shorter fringe than those of the Crow and Apache, while Plateau cases varied greatly in this aspect of their design.

The addition of the fringes significantly transformed the visual emphasis of the case from the painted image to a balance between surface ornamentation and sculptural form. In addition to changing the contour of the object to a shape extending beyond the painted field, fringes animated the form through their contrasting texture and potential for movement. Cases of this type were usually suspended from the pommel or cantle of the woman's saddle as they were transported; the long, trailing fringes responded to each movement of the horse and the ever-present motion of the wind. The visual effect was graceful and dramatic. In combination with other elaborate trappings, they transformed the horse into a remarkable assemblage of colors, shapes, and textures. In Plains camps, they were hung from tripods erected next to the owners' lodges along with cylindrical cases, shields, and other ceremonial objects, the physical embodiment of spiritual guardians and sacred power.

Flat cases were painted primarily on the front side, and related images were usually extended to the flap. The presence, amount, and type of painting on the reverse side varied according to tribal tradition. The back side of Crow cases are unpainted, as are many from the Plateau

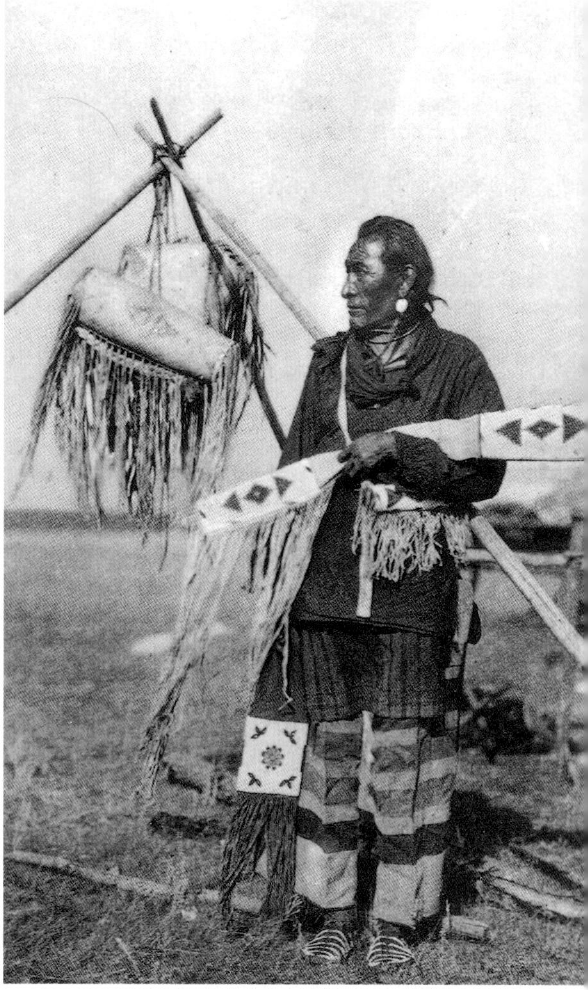

"In a Blackfoot Camp." This portrait of a Blackfeet man includes his sacred bundles in their parfleche cases, hung from a tripod erected behind his lodge. The cylinder in front appears to have a braid of sweetgrass attached to the fringe. Photograph by Edward S. Curtis. Courtesy Edward E. Ayer Collection, Newberry Library

tribes, particularly those eastern groups associated with the Transmontane style. On other Plateau pieces, like most of those from the Blackfeet divisions, the backs are framed with one or two lines of color. Sioux cases were sometimes elaborately painted on the reverse side with designs as complicated as those adorning the front (pl. 16), although the majority were painted with simple linear patterns or other motifs that were clearly secondary to the primary image. The reverse side of most Cheyenne cases for sacred objects feature identical designs consisting of crossed lines running from corner to corner within a single framing border forming an X, with a simple cross suspended within each quadrant. Although the meaning of this symbolic design has not been recorded, the Arapaho share this tradition on some of their medicine cases to the extent of dividing the field with crossed lines, creating a design intended to represent the *baaxoti,* or sacred hoop, one of the sacred tribal objects (Kroeber 1907: 116). When crosses are included, they are associated with the morning star. The Arapaho also adorned many of their later cases in a fashion similar to the Sioux style. The most distinctive are those with elaborate designs consisting of parallel lines, or lines combined with rows of dots (pl. 37 L). Many Apache cases, like those of the Comanche and Kiowa, feature a single colored line framing the reverse panel, but others are painted with linear designs or isolated, paired motifs that appear to be symbolic representations.

As containers for sacred materials, flat cases were made singly to house specific objects or bundles, but as parade items they were often made in matched pairs (pl. 75). The Crow produced a unique form for sacred objects that combined two flat cases (pl. 94). These featured a small, boat-shaped case suspended above a conventional side-fringed case; they were conceived as a single integrated form and were visually unified through the details of their construction and the relationships of their painted designs.

Another kind of flat case (pl. 8), one which is now extremely rare, should be considered separately from the examples previously described and those commonly illustrated in the literature. The few surviving examples were collected from the Wichita and represent an archaic type once widespread among the Eastern Plains tribes. These cases are horizontal in format and quite large, being about 30 inches in width; they are made of buffalo hide and are unpainted. Like other flat cases, they are folded at the bottom and laced along the sides, but these are also laced around the rounded corners and along the outer edges of the top, leaving an opening that could be laced shut by running a long thong through several closely spaced sets of holes. This manner of closing and the contour formed by the slightly rounded corners and subtle curvature of the sides are reminiscent of the woven fiber bags created by the Prairie and Great Lakes tribes since prehistoric times. The Wichita and the other semisedentary tribes living along the rivers of the Eastern Plains produced these twined bags, and it may be that the rawhide cases were conceptually patterned after their woven counterparts.

Other large, flat hide containers that are closely related to the Wichita cases but constructed with closure flaps have been collected from the Ponca and Osage. Both of these types were probably common forms throughout the region, perhaps favored for certain purposes over folded envelopes that were about the same size. On the Western Plains, only the Comanche, neighbors of the Wichita and Osage, adopted this large flat form as a painted case (pl. 47), and this may account for the fact that no Comanche envelopes are known to have been produced.

Elliptical cases (pls. 18, 19) are another distinctive type of flat container that was produced almost exclusively by the Sioux. They were constructed by folding a piece of rawhide in half and sewing it along the side, creating a flat, vertical form measuring about twenty inches by twelve inches. An elliptical piece of soft-tanned hide or canvas was sewn to the bottom and a short sleeve of the same material with a drawstring closure was added to the top, which allowed for greater expansion when the container was filled. The drawstring provided the means for the suspension of the case from the saddle. All of the seams were finely sewn rather than laced and were usually ornamented with a short fringe. The front and back of the case were established by the degree of elaboration of the painting on each panel. One side was ornamented with a complex image while the painting on the reverse was far more restrained, usually consisting of a simple linear design, either a cross within a frame or banded lines.

These cases were always intended for secular use and probably served a variety of functions. They have been described as containers for collecting berries, for the storage of foods such as coffee or sugar, or for clothing and headdresses. They have even been classified as lunch bags, probably because the drawstring opening would have allowed easy access to the contents while traveling on horseback. The form was apparently favored by Sioux women and must have been produced in significant numbers, considering that many are found in collections today. Although it may be a later development, the oldest examples, which date from the 1860s, indicate that their production was well established by the mid-nineteenth century, and they continued to be made until after 1900. It is surprising that such a well-designed form did not have a wider distribution, but except for a few made by the Arapaho and a variant produced by that tribe and the Kiowa in which an elliptical bottom was attached to a vertical case with a flap closure, none was made by other tribes.

An unusual Sioux case (pl. 17), dating from the mid-nineteenth century and shaped like a cylinder but having an elliptical rawhide bottom and flap closure, may represent the prototype for later elliptical forms. A similar case attributed to the Blackfeet (pl. 69) further supports the possibility of this being an older form that was generally abandoned at an early date.

Cylinders

Parfleche cylinders are the other type of container always associated with sacred objects, including many types of medicine bundles, ceremonial clothing, feathers, and rolled feather headdresses. All of the documented contents of these cases indicate that this was their exclusive function until they were adapted by some tribes as one of the common elements of parade regalia during the reservation period. Cylinders had a wide distribution, although some tribes favored them much more than others. They were far more prevalent throughout the Southern and Northern Plains and Plateau than among the peoples of the Central region who sometimes maintained different practices in the storage of medicine bundles. The Sioux, for example, often packed their sacred objects with an outer wrapper of soft tanned hide or, in later years, canvas. This custom was also practiced by the Cheyenne to some extent, by the Missouri River tribes, and probably by the peoples of the Eastern Plains, and may account for the relatively small numbers of cylinders collected from these groups.

Cylinders varied greatly in size, details of construction, arrangement and attachment of fringe, and in the relationship of the painted field to the form itself—all useful diagnostic features in determining the tribal or regional origin. They were basically constructed from a single piece of rawhide which was rolled to form a tube that usually tapered slightly toward the bottom. The single vertical seam overlapped and was secured either by lacing single or double thongs through a series of holes or by tying thongs or running long fringes through several pairs of holes spaced at regular intervals along the full length. The ends were covered by disks of rawhide which were also affixed by lacing or knotted thongs. An exception to this manner of construction are those cylinders made by the Pueblo tribes, who preferred to close the seam by sinew sewing and usually covered the top opening with a fitted cap of rawhide (pl. 61). The size of cylinders varied even within tribal styles, depending on the contents but as a type they range from 10 to 30 inches in length and 3 to 10 inches in diameter. Two holes from which the hanging cord was attached were burned into the case opposite the seam allowing the case to hang at a diagonal.

The most spectacular cylinders were the large elaborately fringed cases produced by the Crow and other Transmontane tribes (pls. 103, 110). These were embellished with finely cut fringes up to 36 inches long and attached along the full length of the side seam and around the bottom end, creating a dynamic sculptural form comparable to the side-fringed flat cases with which they were often combined in ornamenting horses during travel and parades. This tradition extended to the Western Plateau and to the Blackfeet as well, although Blackfeet cylinders tend to be more compact proportionally with fringes that are somewhat shorter (pl. 82). Using the same construction technique as for flat cases, fringes were sometimes cut from a single piece of tanned leather or pounded rawhide. The uncut edge was inserted into the seam and secured with lacing. Other cylinders were fringed by running exceptionally long separate or double thongs through closely spaced pairs of holes, creating the same visual effect. On some cases of this type, the length of the fringe is carefully graduated with longest fringes at the top, so that when the case is suspended at an angle, the flowing ends are approximately horizontal (pl. 110). These tribes also produced considerable numbers of cylinders lacking heavy fringes. The ends of the tied thongs which held them together extended to form a short, scattered fringe. Most Sioux cylinders are also constructed in this fashion, although on some the side seam is secured with a running overstitch, leaving a short fringe only at the top and bottom.

The Southern Plains tribes, specifically the Arapaho, Cheyenne, Kiowa, Comanche, Ute, and Apache, constructed their cylinders with a single or double thong lacing, producing a case with no side fringe and a relatively smooth, uninterrupted contour (pls. 40, 42). Those of the Comanche, Apache, and Ute, as well as those of the Pueblo groups, were further distinguished by the addition of a heavy fringe suspended from around the bottom edge of the case (pls. 48, 56, 60). The character of this fringe, which might range from short and wide-cut to long, finely twisted, two-ply strands, varied considerably, as did the method of attachment.

The placement of the painting in relation to the cylindrical form varied according to tribal and regional styles. The Crow and other Transmontane tribes and Western Plateau groups generally painted the front half of the cylinder, leaving the reverse side unadorned. Blackfeet women commonly established a major design on the front side and balanced this with a secondary, less elaborate image on the back, unifying both with a common border. The Sioux and other Central Plains groups shared the painting tradition of the Southern tribes; it was their practice to cover the entire rawhide panel with painted images, so that the designs completely encircled the form of the finished cylinder. Of these groups, the Kiowa utilized the cylindrical form to create their most elaborate parfleche paintings. They usually divided the field vertically into two parts, so that each side of the finished object was defined by a strongly contrasting image which precisely balanced its counterpart (pl. 42 and page 6).

Among most parfleche-making tribes, the disk that covered the top of a cylinder was almost always painted, usually in some type of four-part design (pl. 79). Painted in this manner, the simple piece of rawhide was transformed into a cosmological diagram; it defined the circle as a universal symbol of the unity and continuity of all life and evoked the four sacred directions and the supernatural powers with which they were identified.

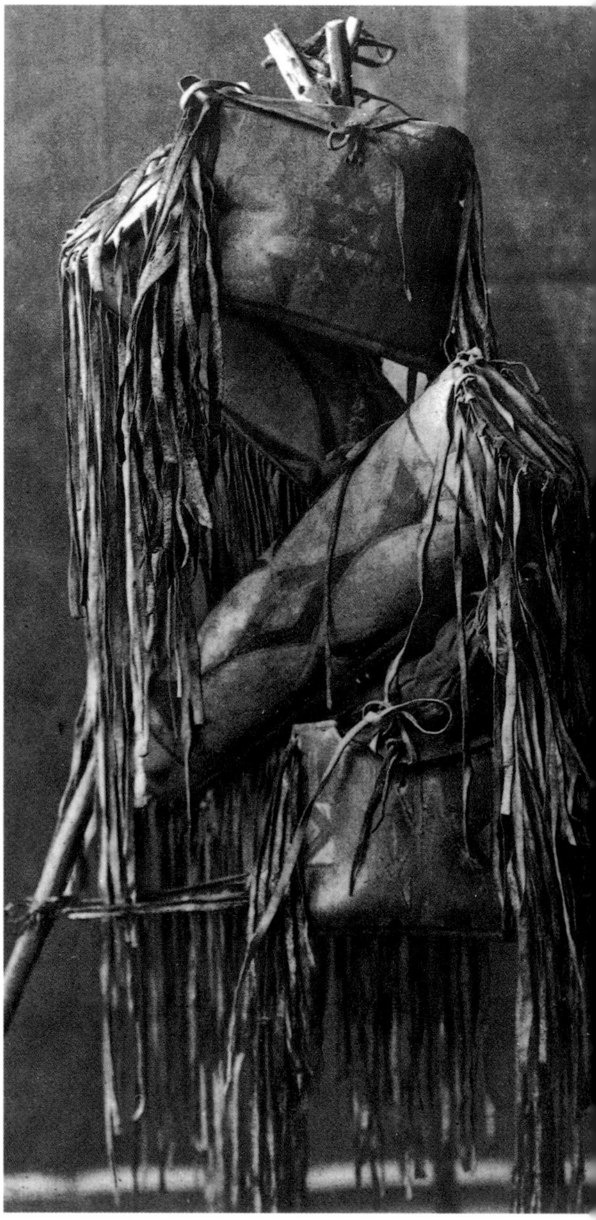

"Medicine Bags—Piegan." Fringed and painted parfleches containing sacred bundles, suspended from a tripod outside a lodge. Photograph by Edward S. Curtis. Courtesy Edward E. Ayer Collection, Newberry Library

Boxes and Trunks

The study of any specific type of American Indian art usually reveals an evolution of form, content, or function deriving from artists' responses to outside influences, changing cultural conditions, and the emergence of new concepts. The most recent creation in the development of parfleches was the painted rawhide box, a form produced by the Western Sioux and possibly by some of the neighboring Eastern Plains tribes during the reservation period. The earliest parfleches of this type date from the 1880s, but most were probably made during the first years of the twentieth century. They became popular after the tribes were relatively settled on reservation lands and had begun to use horse-drawn wagons as a common means of transportation. Not a traditional Plains form, boxes undoubtedly imitated commercial Euro-American containers that were readily available at the time. They were made in considerable numbers by Sioux women. Many were intended for sale to non-Indians, and they were a popular gift to be presented at giveaways, both among the Sioux people themselves and at the intertribal gatherings. The latter seems confirmed by the great number of Sioux boxes found in the possession of other tribes.

The distribution of the boxes also raises the question of which tribes in addition to the Sioux actually produced this form. Several authorities have suggested that they were also made by all of the Eastern Plains, Siouan-speaking groups, including the Ioway, Oto, Omaha, Ponca, Osage and Kansa.[2] This seems unlikely for several reasons. First, all of the boxes attributed to these groups are stylistically indistinguishable from the many, well-documented boxes produced by the Sioux; they are basically the same in their proportion, general size and construction, and in the pictorial elements that comprise the painting and its compositional structure. It is highly improbable that the respective painting styles of all these Eastern tribes would so closely replicate that of the Sioux. Second, it seems unlikely that these tribes would have maintained or revived an isolated tradition of parfleche boxes toward the end of the nineteenth century without producing other forms concurrently and without sustaining at least some continuous production from an earlier period. No evidence of either fact is visible in museum collections of their material culture. In fact, very few parfleches of any type with convincing documentation have been collected from Eastern Plains tribes and these few date before 1860, suggesting that these groups discontinued the manufacture of parfleches at an early date as they adapted to reservation life. The boxes in question all date from the late nineteenth or early twentieth centuries, a period when the Sioux were still producing considerable numbers of parfleches for trade, sale, and gifts, while the Eastern Plains and Prairie tribes had long since undergone dramatic changes in their cultures and in the production of their arts, resulting in the disappearance of most traditional forms. Finally,

2. See Morrow (1975: 224) for an example of Sioux boxes attributed to the Ioway on the basis of collection history alone. The acquisition of these boxes from the Ioway is recorded by Skinner (1926: 281–85), but he does not specify where they were made.

it would seem that the attribution of the boxes in question is based on their acquisition history alone, which is unreliable without some supportive evidence—which in this case is lacking. While it is possible that some of these tribes produced some type of box or trunk at an earlier time, it seems quite likely that most, if not all, of the later examples collected from them are of Sioux origin, obtained as gifts or through trade during the reservation period. We know, for instance, that large numbers of Sioux people were welcomed guests at the Ponca Sun Dances at the turn of the century. Such events would have provided the Sioux with the opportunity to present many gifts, including parfleches, to their hosts, and this probably accounts for the considerable numbers of Sioux parfleches residing in Ponca collections in museums today.[3]

A variety of box shapes were created. The most common was a horizontal box (pl. 21), but square and vertical forms (pl. 20) were produced as well. Most were constructed from a single piece of rawhide cut according to a pattern in which the sides extended from the bottom and the top was formed by a longer extension of one side. This piece of hide was folded into shape and sewn or tied along each of the four vertical edges. The lid was folded at the back to cover the top, where it was tied in place along the front and side edges. Often the leading edge of the lid was cut to form two or three triangular projections which were folded downward to overlap the front side. On many boxes, this basic form was elaborated by the addition of short fringes or cloth strips along the vertical seams; more rarely glass "seed beads" were incorporated in the sewing to form a band of beadwork at these edges, or quill-wrapped suspensions with pairs of metal cones were attached at intervals along the edges or at the corners. A cloth binding was often used to finish the edge of the lid on those which had strips of cloth at the seams.

Boxes vary in size as well as shape, the longest dimension usually averaging about 12 to 14 inches. They seldom exceed 20 inches in length and rarely measure less than 6 inches. They were always painted on the four sides and the top, leaving the bottom undecorated, and each plane was treated as a separate field. The designs that were applied to these five surfaces were sometimes identical, although adjusted to the scale and proportion of the differing panels. On other boxes, the same basic motifs were utilized throughout but were organized differently on the sides, ends, and top, creating a more complex set of pictorial relationships. Other painters treated these units as distinct elements, creating three separate designs, pairing the ends and sides in opposition to the top which stood as a singular composition. Regardless of the manner in which the painting was organized, the five planes comprising the painted form were always conceived as a unified, cohesive image. This was accomplished on many boxes by the use of a singular border throughout, by the continuity of color relationships, and by the sensitively balanced arrangement of pictorial elements over the entire surface.

A related, boxlike form having flat sides but a rounded base and entirely covered with painted designs was also made by the Sioux.[4]

3. During the late nineteenth and early twentieth centuries, the Ponca Reservation adjoined that of the Rosebud Sioux, allowing for considerable intertribal exchange at other times as well.

4. See Conn (1982: 72) for an example of this type of case.

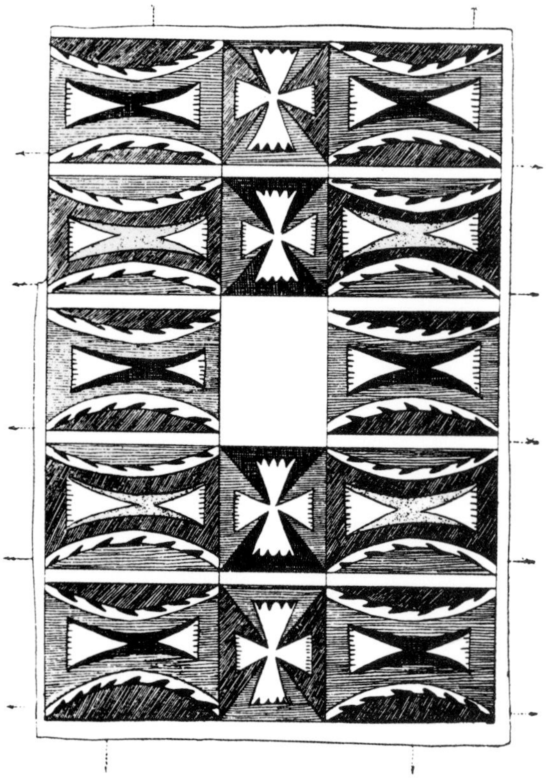

Diagram of the painting on the Mesquakie trunk, illustrated in plate 7, as it appeared before folding. After Boas, Primitive Art *(1927)*

Usually described as a utility case for tools, these boxes were probably fashioned after military cases of similar shape. A few rounded containers similar in size and shape to hat boxes were also produced.

Because they were a nontraditional form, it is doubtful that boxes were ever intended for a specific function, and no particular pattern evolved regarding their use. They generally held personal possessions or clothing in the same manner as Euro-American boxes, but a few have been collected that contain healing bundles and other sacred items. Perhaps their most important function derived from their extensive use as gifts and the many binding associations connected with this social interaction. And they were certainly important as a commercial product during the early, destitute years of reservation confinement.

Parfleche boxes may also have derived from an earlier tradition of elaborately painted, folded rawhide trunks (pl. 7) that were made in the Western Great Lakes and Prairie regions. Like the later Sioux boxes, they were used to store clothing and personal belongings; but to a much greater extent, especially in later years, they were the principal container for sacred medicine bundles. Trunks of this sort may have been produced by other Great Lakes tribes, but nearly all those in museum collections were obtained from the Mesquakie in Iowa, who probably originated this extraordinary form in the early nineteenth century.

Among the most interesting and beautiful of all types of painted parfleches, Mesquakie trunks were dramatically different in form and concept from the boxes of the Sioux. The artist first executed a complex painting on a large, rectangular piece of rawhide, covering the entire surface except for areas of unpainted hide integrated into the design. This painting was then folded into the form of a lidded rectangular trunk about 20 inches long and held in place by sewing the overlapping folds together at the side, thereby creating a somewhat random relationship between the structural organization of the painting and the planes of the finished trunk. It first appears that the effectiveness of the painting has been destroyed by the folding, but a sustained viewing reveals that another order, just as harmonious, has been created. Although the planes of the trunk and the design elements of the two-dimensional image do not precisely conform to one another, they are sufficiently aligned to create a dynamic visual tension between the pictorial structure of the painting and the form of the trunk, each holding the other in powerful counterbalance. The density of color, the soft luminosity of the surface, and the graphic energy of the drawing are still active elements, and the total effect is one of an immense richness. Apparently the painting's intrinsic power and symbolic or associative meanings were considered completely intact regardless of what shape the painting was given.

Miscellaneous Forms

In addition to parfleche containers, there were other objects made of rawhide and decorated using the same painting techniques. Burden straps, knife sheaths, quivers, horse cruppers and saddle ornaments, and sun visors were produced by various tribes. Not all of these items were made by every tribe or even within every region, and in some cases production was apparently quite limited. Some of these objects were more commonly decorated by other means, such as beadwork or quill embroidering, and some were often constructed without embellishment of any kind.

Rawhide knife cases (pl. 3) were numerous in all areas because both men and women customarily carried knives as tools and weapons. Most decorated sheaths were elaborated with beads, tacks, or quillwork, but a number of painted examples have been collected from the Crow, Sioux, Arapaho, and Eastern Plateau tribes. At least two incised cases without precise documentation have been collected as well. All were constructed from a single piece of rawhide which was folded and sewn along the trailing edge. On larger cases, particularly those made by the Crow, the upper portion of the back side was often extended to form a closure flap. Most sheaths were painted extensively on the front side, while the reverse was either unpainted or framed with simple lines. Only the Sioux varied from this practice, painting both sides of their later sheaths with equally elaborate images. The composition of their painted sheaths often replicated those ornamented with other techniques, suggesting the handle and blade of the knife in the arrangement of motifs.

A small number of beautifully painted and incised burden straps have been collected from the Pawnee[5] (pl. 9), Oto, Omaha, and Kansa.[6] These straps are made from a single piece of buffalo rawhide ranging in size from 1 1/2 to 4 inches wide and from 15 to 22 inches long, with long hide thongs attached at each end to secure the material being carried. The entire surface of one side is covered with intricate designs which were first cut into the leather and then painted, so that each color was separated by an incised line. The few surviving examples date from the mid-nineteenth century or earlier and are attributed only to the tribes just mentioned; most of these were obtained from the Pawnee. The Pawnee were especially noted for their use of cosmic symbolism on a variety of forms and this extended to the designs used on painted rawhide as well. It is interesting to compare the motifs on their burden straps with those used to adorn the carved and painted panels of their cradleboards (see Feder 1978). While burden straps must have been a common device among other tribes, the fact that none survives makes it impossible to know if other groups also decorated theirs with painted designs.

The quivers and bow cases produced by parfleche-making tribes were generally constructed of tanned leather rather than rawhide. Only two exceptions may be found. The first are the painted rawhide quivers

5. See the example attributed to the Oto or Pawnee illustrated in Myers (1984: 50) as well as those pictured in Morrow (1975: 189–90).

6. Only one burden strap attributed to the Kansa has been located; it is in the collection of the National Museum of the American Indian, Smithsonian Institution. A single Omaha strap collected by Francis LaFleche and originally in the collection of the Peabody Museum, Harvard University, is now preserved at the Nebraska State Museum, Lincoln.

made by the Western and Chiricahua Apache (pl. 58). These are also ornamented with cutout designs backed with red cloth, scalloped edges and pendant tabs, and metal cones. The second type consists of a few examples obtained from the Western Great Lakes region; only one of these has been found with elaborately painted designs,[7] so it is impossible to know the extent of this tradition. The single piece is embellished with designs which are quite similar to those found on Mesquakie trunks. Both the Apache and Great Lakes types are rather flat in shape, as distinct from parfleche cylinders that were never used for storing arrows.

Several tribes produced elaborate horse trappings. This tradition extended throughout the Transmontane and Western Plateau regions, and included the Plains Cree, Assiniboine, Gros Ventre, and Blackfeet groups of the Northern Plains and, to a more limited extent, the Central and Southern Plains tribes. Martingales, cruppers, saddles, saddle blankets, bridles, and stirrups were ornamented in a variety of ways with beadwork, trade cloth, paint, and other materials. The Crow people are especially renowned for their production, and most objects of that type which utilized painted rawhide as a central feature were created by the women of this tribe. The most common painted form was the crupper (pl. 99), used for both riding-horses and pack animals. It served a practical function in stabilizing the saddle or load in rough country, but was also adopted for purely decorative purposes during parades and other formal occasions. Painted cruppers were usually constructed of two broad, tapering rawhide strips that extended from a padded loop fitted under the horse's tail to the saddle, to which the ends were attached. The two strips were painted with matching designs, usually based on a sequence of motifs which established a rhythmic progression running the full length. It is interesting to note that at least a few Crow cruppers were decorated with incised rather than painted designs.[8]

7. This quiver is in the collection of the American Museum of Natural History and is attributed to the Mesquakie.

8. See the example illustrated in Lessard (1980: 63).

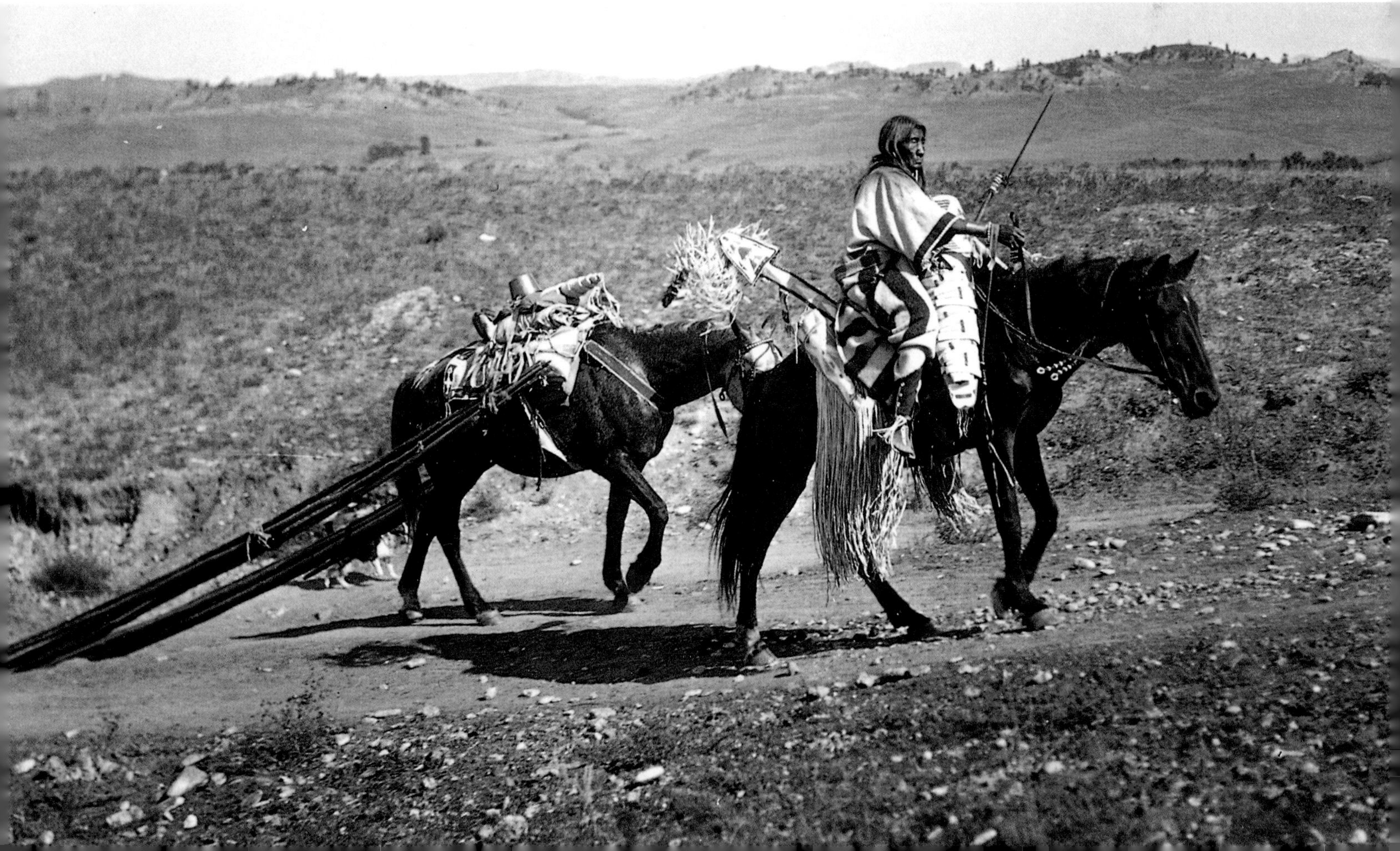

A Crow woman traveling, ca. 1880. She is impressively outfitted with fringed parfleche cylinders, beaded cradleboard, and lance case. Her pack horse is laden with lodge poles, parfleches, and other possessions. Courtesy W. H. Over State Museum

The Crow and possibly their Nez Perce allies also produced a distinctive saddle ornament of painted rawhide (pl. 100). It consisted of two pieces of hide, one for each side, which extended below the bottom edge of the saddle. Each piece was cut in the form of two large disks, joined horizontally by a narrow strip and a flaring projection extending from the upper edges, by which it was attached. The disks were painted identically with circular and triangular shapes, transected by a narrow band running horizontally across both.

These ornaments are an unusual form without any counterpart in Plains or Plateau horse gear, which raises interesting questions regarding their origin and meaning. One of the few known examples is widely separated by time and locale, which is also perplexing in view of their remarkable uniformity. At least four sets that date from the late nineteenth century and are so close in style as possibly to be the work of one woman, were collected from the Crow.[9] Another set, still attached to the saddle, was collected by the Reverend Henry Spalding from the Nez Perce in 1841.[10] It also is probably of Crow origin, considering the extensive trade between the two tribes and the preponderance of Crow material goods in the exchanges. All of these ornaments are nearly identical in form and iconography. The images appear to represent a cosmological or celestial structure, and their strict continuity over such a broad span of time strongly suggests that a precise concept was embodied in the design. Moreover, the fact that the Spalding example is almost certainly not a prototype reveals an even longer tradition. That none has been found dating midway between this early set and the later group only indicates that none survived, not that this form was not produced, for such a continuity of form would not have been sustained by oral tradition alone. This serves as a powerful reminder that our knowledge is based on what has been collected and our conclusions are often tenuous—without the Spalding example, we might very well assume that this object-type was a late and perhaps aberrant development rather than a traditional form with a very substantial history.

Another form of painted rawhide, a type of hat commonly referred to as a sunshade or visor (pl. 87), was collected from many of the Northern Plains and Transmontane groups.[11] These were made from a single piece of hide rectangular in shape, usually from 12 to 15 inches long, with a long brim and no real crown. The opening for the head was created by a series of bisecting cuts which formed a circle; the resulting long, triangular sections projected upward when the hat was worn, forming an open, serrated top. The edges of the entire object were often pinked, and feathers, ribbons, or strips of fur were sometimes added to transform it into a more elaborate headdress. Most visors were painted only on the upper side, but on a few the designs extended to both sides of the crown projection or to the underside of the visor. While the majority of these were specifically painted as hats, others were simply cut from the painted panels of old parfleche envelopes.

9. These sets are located in the National Museum of the American Indian, the Carnegie Museum of Natural History, the Denver Art Museum, and a private collection in the United States.

10. This object is preserved in the collection of Ohio State Museum, Columbus.

11. Several of these sunshades were collected from the Arapaho and Shoshone. It is noteworthy that the artist C. M. Russell frequently depicted his Indian subjects wearing them, which suggests that they were commonly seen during his early years in the West.

Formal Characteristics

In addition to the basic forms and the materials from which they are made, parfleches from all regions of North America share a number of formal characteristics in their painted imagery which unify them as a distinct body of works. The paintings are essentially abstract and geometric, with no apparent reference to representational imagery (the only exceptions are those relatively few sacred cases that are adorned with figurative designs of visionary origin). They are composed principally of lines, triangles, diamonds, and rectangles, although circular and curvilinear forms are common in the work of some tribes. These basic elements are combined in various ways to form larger, more complex configurations and these in turn form the overall composition. The resulting patterns might range from a rather simple arrangement to one quite intricate and refined. For this reason it is difficult to analyze a design by describing isolated elements because they visually combine or subdivide according to the changing perception of the viewer. Studies defining tribal styles based solely on this kind of analysis are often more confusing than informative. For example, an hourglass might also be described as two triangles joined at their points (pl. 91); or, the common configuration of a triangle joined to the point of a central diamond with a second triangle extending from the opposite point could also be seen as four stacked triangles or two stacked hourglasses (pl. 103).

The compositional organization of parfleche painting must really be considered according to two aspects: (1) as singular painted panels—those that cover each flap of an envelope (pl. 64), the face of a flat case, the surface of a cylinder, or the plane of a box; (2) as the total pictorial structure formed by these panels in relation to each other and to the finished shape of the case itself.

With rare exception, identical images were painted on each flap of an envelope, and these join visually to establish a single unified composition across the entire surface of both flaps. Two subtle variations of this format exist. Some tribes, especially those of the Central and Southern Plains and, to some extent, those of the Northern Plains, repeat a highly centralized design on each flap, establishing a dual repetition of elements over the entire field (pls. 15, 28). Other tribes, most notably the Crow and those peoples of the Basin, and Plateau regions, often structured the designs on each panel so that a single composite image uniting both flaps is perceived (pls. 88, 102, 105). Many parfleches may be seen in both ways (pls. 24, 107), so to a degree, this distinction is a matter of the viewers perception, of emphasis within the composition, and of the strength with which the border of each panel functions in isolating it from its counterpart. Still, it was possible for artists to achieve two very different effects utilizing the same basic format.

Each panel was defined by its own painted border, which contained the image and established its relationship with the physical planes and volumes of the parfleche. Panels have their own intrinsic order and may be analyzed separately, but many of the characteristics that distinguish them are equally descriptive of the kind of composite images just described. Nearly all compositions are bilaterally symmetrical on a longitudinal axis and most are latitudinally symmetrical as well. They are generally bold in appearance as they were intended to project visually and be seen effectively at a distance. This was often achieved through the use of strong color and invariably through the interplay of strongly contrasting light and dark elements. Painters always included some amount of the light-colored, natural hide background as an integral element of their composition; and this, in conjunction with painted areas, established a visually active figure-ground, spatial relationship. In the most effective and carefully balanced designs, the visual reversal of figure and background constantly changes according to the shifting perception of the viewer.

The use of color varied according to tribal style, paint type, and time period, from bold primary color systems to those formed of subtle and delicately modulated hues. Usually five or six colors including the natural hide ground composed the painting, and these most often included red, yellow, blue, and green; other colors appear less frequently. Many tribes also incorporated brown-black as an outline and for small elements within the painting. Considering the tradition of parfleche painting as a whole, it is remarkable that such diverse effects were achieved by artists of all the different tribes using essentially the same limited palette and the same basic vocabulary of painted forms. In itself, this constitutes a fascinating study in artistic invention. That such distinct tribal styles were created—as well as unique and intensely personal expressions—is yet another example of the extraordinary range that Native Americans artists achieved within a closely defined set of stylistic parameters and formal conventions. On parfleches, artists accomplished this by manipulating the amounts, combinations, density, and sequences of colors in relation to the forms they occupied.

The painted surface on different parfleches might range from opaque to nearly transparent. Color was always conceived and applied as a flat plane, yet varying degrees of translucency, surface modulation, and diffusion of edges tend to activate the color areas and provide them with a sense of life and energy. Still, the designs never convey an illusion of volume or physical weight; the flat planes of color are never shaded and planes do not overlap. Instead, forms are made to advance and recede visually, adhere or separate, through the adjacent relationships of shape, color, and value and the function of line. In the strongest paintings these elements are held in perfect suspension, so that the geometric symmetry and solidity of compositional structure are unexpectedly countered by the powerful sense of movement, rhythm, and inner tension arising from their interplay. Basically, the finest paintings are superbly balanced in their organization of line, shape, color, and tone in accord with the universal principles of design and composition.

On all parfleches with multiple painted panels, the singular images were always conceived in relation to the final form so that the different painted surfaces functioned as a unified pictorial field. At the same time, the painted images emphasized the form of the object itself. It is this relationship between two-dimensional imagery and three-dimensional form that distinguishes parfleches from all other types of hide painting. Just as the organization and scale of the painted image were adjusted to the picture plane of its two-dimensional field, these surface designs were adjusted to the volumetric form of the container. Image and object were thus beautifully integrated, again reinforcing the inherent sense of balance, tension, and order.

There are two basic ways in which parfleche paintings were conceived and executed, and the difference between the two is one of the most important features to consider in determining tribal and regional origin. These two approaches resulted in significant differences in the appearance of the finished work and in the sensibility of their pictorial structure. In one approach colored shapes were painted prior to outlining, while in the other, the image was first defined by line and then filled in with colors.

In the first method, artists applied colors to form the various shapes comprising the basic composition; they then further defined this image by applying a thin, brown-black outline that followed the contour of the primary forms and often separated color areas (pls. 13, 28). This outlining served a structural purpose in that it clarified the separation between painted and unpainted areas and visually sharpened the design and intensified the color. It strengthened and solidified the shapes and established a sense of unity and order. It also functioned as one of the most expressive elements in parfleche painting. The process of outlining was really an act of drawing and introduced a dynamic graphic energy into the work. The result establishes a subtle play of lyrical rhythms and directional movements that echo the painted forms, but is also possessed of its own dramatic intent. The resulting contrast between the linear configurations and the more static color masses creates a powerful tension that greatly compounds the strength of the painting.

Outlining has the appearance of being drawn with pen and ink although, as previously mentioned, the paint was applied with a stylus of horn, stone, or bone. The color of the lignite paint might vary from a pale brown to a full, rich, rusty black. The line also varies in width and color density with the manner of application. For this reason the line possesses an inherent richness, and even the most tightly controlled drawings never assume a mechanical quality.

In addition to the outlining, artists often incorporated small elements of black into the painting during this stage, thereby extending the scale of elements comprising the image and establishing concentrated focal points within the design in contrast to the larger areas of color (pls. 25, 26). These tiny units consisted of solidly painted geometric shapes—triangles, diamonds, hourglasses, squares, circles, rectangles, short lines, and scallops. They were commonly placed singly or in pairs throughout the design, often within small, delineated negative (unpainted) areas. They were also combined in repetition to establish rhythmic sequences of pattern and visual movement, either floating within negative areas in the design (pl. 23), or along the edges of major shapes thereby changing their contours from smooth to serrated or scalloped edges (pls. 86, 114). When used with skill and sensitivity, these elements add a sense of intricacy and refinement to the painting.

This tradition of painting utilizing black outlining was practiced by the tribes of the Central Plains, by most of the Southern Plains and Southwestern groups including both the plains- and mountain-dwelling Apache and the Ute, and by most tribes of the Northern Plains. It was also an early tradition among the Western Plateau tribes and southern divisions of the Blackfeet Confederacy—sustained to some extent by the Plateau peoples but generally abandoned by the Piegan and Blood during the last half of the nineteenth century. Some artists from the Central Plains, notably Sioux and Arapaho, and the Gros Ventre of the Northern Plains, also omitted outlining during their final period of production following the turn of the century. In some cases this was the result of deteriorating standards of quality brought about by changing values on the part of the makers, who by that time were producing large numbers of pieces for what they may have considered a less discriminating audience. Others may have taken this step in response to outside influences resulting from the new exchanges of ideas and material goods which intensified during the reservation period.

A second method of painting was practiced by the Crow people of the Northern Plains and other Transmontane tribes of the Basin and Eastern Plateau, throughout much of the Western Plateau region, and by the Piegan and, to some extent, the Blood tribes of the Blackfeet Confederacy. In this approach the artist first defined the image through drawing; a linear structure formed of colored lines was established, and the shapes created by this subdivision of the pictorial field were then filled in with additional colors (pl. 92). It is often possible to discern the strokes of the artist in the surface texture of the paint, clearly revealing how the colors were applied and contained within these predefined areas. A number of variants of this approach were produced by different tribal groups, but all generally adhered to this basic concept. The structural lines that formed the linear framework were usually dark blue. This choice of color never varied among the Crow and Wind River Shoshone, who produced great numbers of parfleches for trade and sale as well as their own use during the late nineteenth and early twentieth centuries. The same is generally true of the Nez Perce and other Eastern Plateau groups as well, although dark green was occasionally substituted for this element by these tribes and throughout the Plateau region (pl. 120). It was also common for the women of the Blackfeet and some Plateau tribes to combine two or even three colors of structural line within a single painting to create especially complex color relationships among the solidly colored shapes and their contrasting outlines (pl. 108). Occasionally, rather heavy black outlines were introduced within the designs of Yakima and other Western Plateau parfleches, delineating isolated motifs and unpainted areas (pl. 119). Some Plateau parfleches also feature the addition of secondary outlines in different colors bordering the primary lines in order to emphasize isolated motifs (pl. 113).

The lines that form the design are usually about 1/8 inch in width, although they might range from 1/16 to just over 1/4 inch. On highly controlled paintings the width of the lines was sometimes intentionally varied according to the different design motifs, so that the primary image was drawn in lines of one width while smaller units within the painting were composed of finer lines. It was also common for artists working in this style to taper the width of the outlines of principal design elements so that they converged from a wide base to a sharp point along the length of the line (pls. 93, 109). Lines of this kind were always paired to form the two sides of a triangle, or two pairs might be combined to form the sides of a diamond. This device was one of the most characteristic features of this style of painting and, when used effectively, was responsible for the dramatic sense of tension and spatial activity contained in the strongest images.

The paintings created in this fashion are distinguished by their bold, flat angularity and the subdivision of major elements. Those from the Crow and Transmontane groups of the Eastern Plateau and Basin are composed of straightedged and precisely drawn motifs, with structural lines nearly always separating the colors. Their compositions are highly formal and tend towards a strict geometry. The sequential subdivision of the pictorial field and major motifs into successively smaller configurations is easily discernible if one attempts visually to reconstruct the process. In doing so, the viewer may become attuned to the linear complexity and movements within the design. It is interesting to note that the elements comprising this style of painting are closely related to the designs of beadwork and later twined basketry bags created in this region, and quite probably form the basis of their development (see Lanford 1980, 1984).

The later parfleches of the Western Plateau and Southern Blackfeet groups are generally the same in technique to those painted in the Crow-Transmontane style, but tend to be more freely drawn and often have sweeping curves incorporated into their compositions (pls. 115, 118). Also, colors within the major motifs are not always separated by structural lines. These traits perhaps reflect the earlier painting tradition of this region in which designs were first painted and then outlined in black in the manner of most Plains tribes.

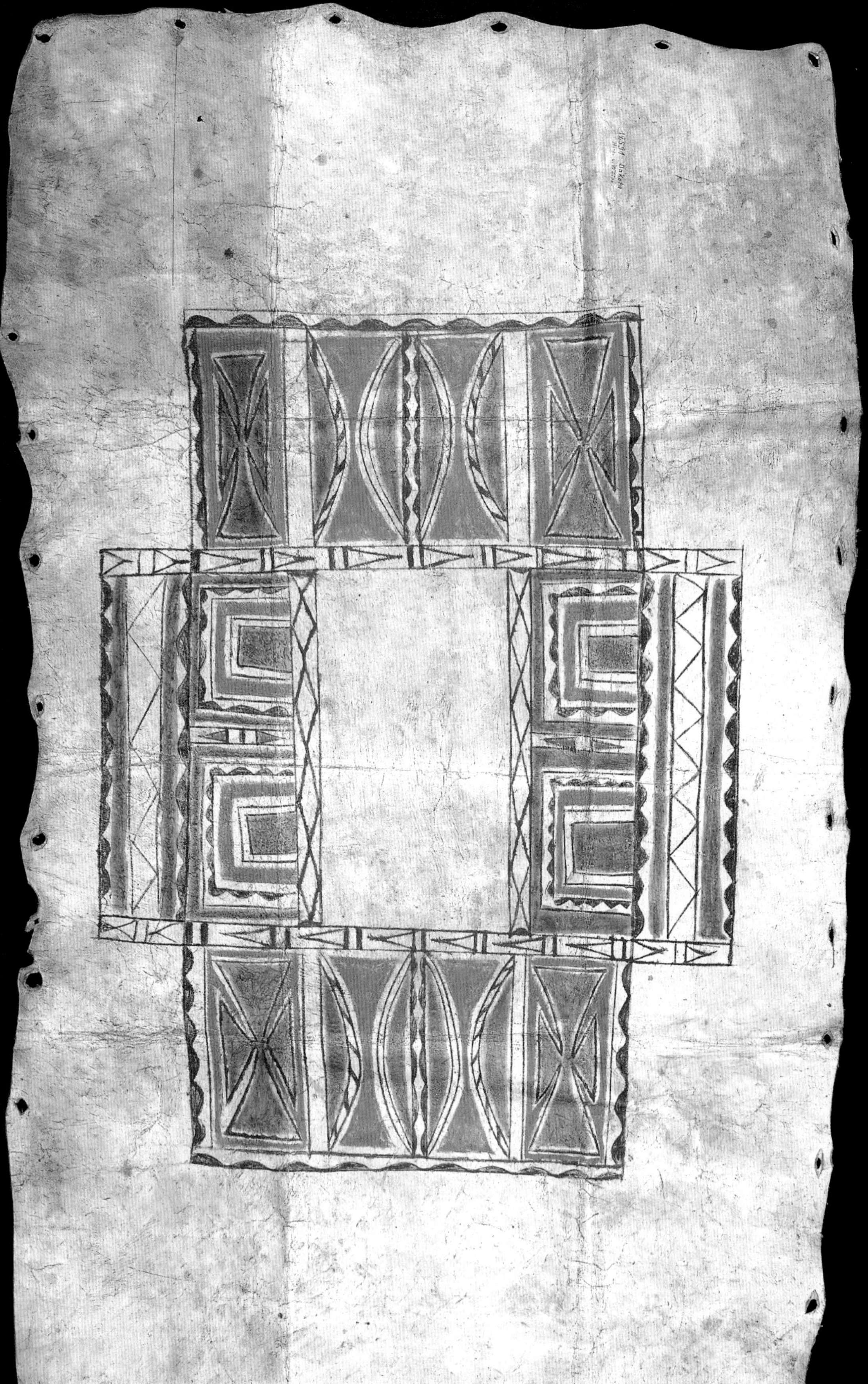
12591 Dakota

Regional and Tribal Styles

The tradition of parfleche painting included the development of both tribal and regional styles. These are defined by the conventions established and generally maintained by each group regarding construction, painting techniques, color, design elements, and composition. These formal characteristics also function as diagnostic features in identification. Envelopes generally contain the greatest number of elements for analysis and usually provide a key for the identification of other forms within a tribal tradition. The elements include the basic compositional formats, the types of borders, the size and proportion of flap shape, the number and placement of tie holes, the presence of side-flap decoration, the use of lines joining the painted panels on the reverse side, and the presence or absence of black outlining and the manner in which it is incorporated. These characteristics must be interpreted in relation to other important but less explicit features such as the character of the drawing and application of paint, the surface quality of the painting, and the choice of colors and their sequence within the individual motifs and the overall design. However, it should be understood in attempting to identify tribal and regional styles on the basis of these characteristics that significant exceptions can always be found in the work of any group, and that each tribe's style usually changed over time.

The parfleches in this book are organized according to six geographic regions that generally correspond to artistic styles: the Eastern Plains, Central Plains, Southern Plains and Southwest, Northern Plains, Transmontane, and Western Plateau. Each of these regions was inhabited by a number of tribes that produced parfleches characterized by similar traits. In this context, each tribe developed and maintained its own distinct style, which was more or less consistent with those of other groups within its region. The degree of stylistic uniformity, however, could vary considerably. In the same manner, the tribes in some regions were culturally similar, while in others they were quite distinct. Likewise, the geographic features in each region might be similar or diverse. Basically, the relationship between artistic styles, cultural similarities, and geographic proximity assumes varying degrees of cohesion within each region, yet some combination of these elements differentiates the six areas and unifies the tribes within them.

The peoples of the Eastern Plains, or Prairie region, for example, inhabited a geographically homogeneous area and shared many cultural

1 / **Eastern Plains envelope, ca. 1800**

L 64 in., W 37 in. (unfolded). Buffalo rawhide, pigment

Collected by Friedrich Paul Wilheim, Duke of Wuerttemberg, probably during the first of his four journeys to North America, 1822–24. Linden-Museum Stuttgart, Staatliches Museum für Völkerkunde, 12591

attributes, but it is highly doubtful that they all produced parfleches that were stylistically consistent at any time in their history. Rather, it appears that several distantly related styles prevailed. Similarly, the Sioux and Cheyenne of the Central Plains, although neighboring tribes closely related through political alliance and basic ways of life, created parfleches that were stylistically quite distinct, while the Arapaho—the third major tribe of this region—developed their own style encompassing features of both.

In other regions, one basic style predominated throughout. For example, the women of the Kiowa, Comanche, and Eastern Apache tribes of the Southern Plains and Southwest produced parfleches that, while differing in a number of significant details, shared many of the same features and collectively constituted a more uniform Southern Plains style. This style extended to the Rio Grande Pueblos to some extent and northward to the mountain-dwelling Utes. It also influenced or was perhaps partly derived from the work of the Southern divisions of the Arapaho and Cheyenne. A single style also dominated the Northern Plains, unifying the three divisions of the Blackfeet Confederacy as well as the Sarsi and Kutenai. Again, though many differences might be noted that separate the individual painting styles of these groups, all shared many of the same motifs and basic compositional structures and all constructed their envelopes with trapezoidally shaped outer flaps. Only the Gros Ventre and possibly the Assiniboine of this region must be considered apart: their parfleches reflect multiple influences from both Northern and Central Plains tribes.

The Transmontane style completely transcended geographic boundaries and included the Crow of the Northern Plains, the Shoshone of the northeastern Great Basin, and the Nez Perce and other tribes of the Eastern Plateau. While these tribes differed in many aspects of their cultures and inhabited diverse geographic regions, they produced parfleches that are so closely unified in style as to be nearly indistinguishable.

Finally, in the Western Plateau, the prevailing painting styles and the geographic region are synonymous. In fact, no individual tribal style may be consistently identified with assurance. Although distinct features undoubtedly developed in the work of different tribal groups during various periods, their origins are no longer discernible. Also, stylistic changes that surely took place over time cannot be traced except in the most general way because of the tremendous cultural exchange that occurred among the tribes of this region throughout their history. The tribes were joined through extensive trade, intermarriage, and shifting political alliances; aesthetic concepts were freely borrowed throughout the area and this merging of ideas was compounded by the continuous exchange of actual objects, with the result that individual tribal styles ceased to exist and were blended together into an indivisible regional type.

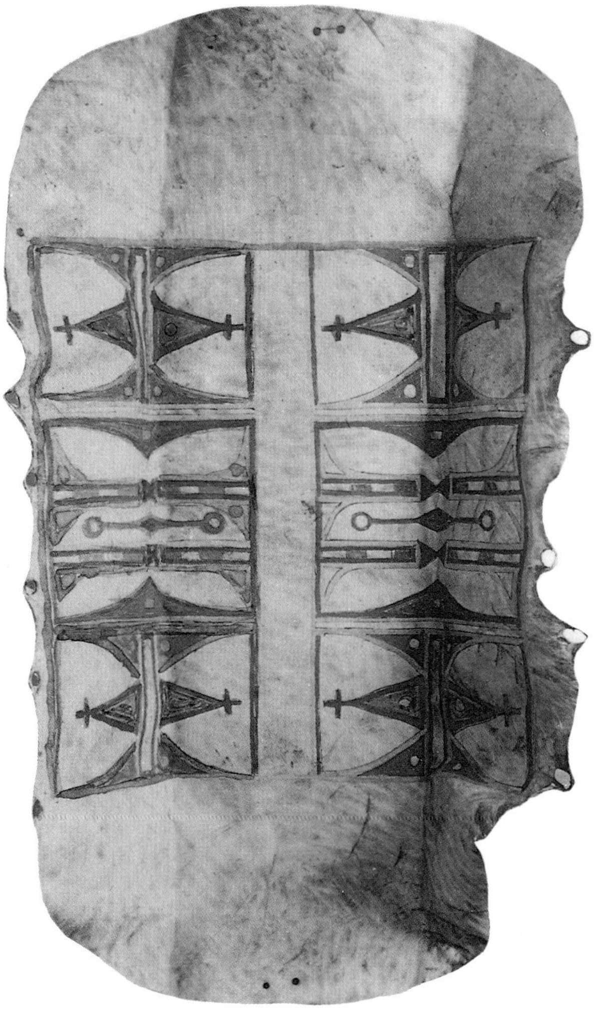

2 / **Omaha envelope, ca. 1870 (?)**
Size unknown (unfolded). Rawhide, pigment

Collected by Francis LaFlesche; present location unknown. Photograph from the original manuscript, An Illustrated and Descriptive Catalogue of Articles used by the Omaha Tribe of American Indians collected by Francis LaFlesche (Member of the Tribe), 1898 *(photo no. 35), in the collection of the Staatliche Museen, Museum für Völkerkunde, Berlin, IV B 2240*

Eastern Plains

A number of tribes resided in this region during the historic period, including the Eastern Sioux groups, Mesquakie, Sauk, Omaha, Ioway, Ponca, Oto-Missouri, Kansa, Osage, Wichita, and Pawnee. They were all semisedentary peoples living in villages along river valleys where they subsisted by maintaining a yearly cycle of farming and seasonal buffalo hunts. While retaining various aspects of the Woodland societies from which most had descended, they also adopted many elements of Plains culture, particularly after acquiring significant numbers of horses. Our vision and understanding of the parfleche traditions of these tribes are limited because of the exceedingly small numbers of surviving pieces. In fact, collections comprised of all types of traditional material objects from this area are fragmentary at best and, for some tribes, nearly nonexistent; very little remains from the time that these cultures were intact and flourishing, especially when compared to the collections obtained from Western tribes.

The primary reason for this dearth of material is that the tribes of the Eastern Plains and Prairie suffered the effects of Euro-American expansion during the first half of the nineteenth century, long before any systematic efforts were made to collect and preserve Indian objects. Indian populations were greatly diminished by epidemics of smallpox and cholera, and the patterns of their traditional lives were forever disrupted by forced relocations into reservations and by intolerant government policies of assimilation. It was a tragic cultural transformation, which for many tribes became a struggle for survival amidst disease, hunger, and economic hardship, and it resulted in the loss of many art forms that were inseparably tied to the activities and beliefs of traditional life.

If parfleche production among most of these tribes did not cease altogether during the middle decades of the nineteenth century, it was greatly diminished. This fact, together with the availability of commercial containers from traders and the practice of recycling older, worn parfleches into moccasin soles and other items requiring rawhide, left these tribes with few rawhide containers of their own manufacture after 1880. At the same time, as the Western Plains tribes became settled on reservations during this period, there was greater opportunity for the Eastern tribes to acquire parfleches from them, through trade or as gifts during intertribal visits. In addition to these contacts, intermarriage surely occurred as well, quite possibly resulting in a few Sioux women living among Eastern tribes and continuing to produce parfleches for both commercial purposes and local use.

The result was that a variety of late, intrusive rawhide containers were in the possession of Eastern groups by the time museum collectors were most active—during the late nineteenth and early twentieth centuries. The parfleches that were acquired were accessioned according to the tribes from which they were obtained, and this misidentification has persisted in some cases to the present day. Many parfleches in museum collections or illustrated in the literature that are designated as Ponca, Ioway, Omaha, Pawnee, Oto, or Eastern Sioux were, in fact, produced by women of the Teton Sioux, Cheyenne, Arapaho, or other Western Plains tribes. This is also true of the Plains envelopes that were remade into folded trunks by the Mesquakie, Kickapoo, Potawatomi, and Winnebago, and into flat cases by Eastern Plains tribes living to the west. It has usually been assumed that the envelopes from which these containers were made were produced by the same tribes, but this is extremely doubtful. Instead, they all appear to be constructed from parfleche envelopes originally painted by, and obtained from, the Cheyenne, Arapaho, or Southern Plains tribes.[1] Taken collectively, the body of parfleches obtained from Eastern Plains tribes consists of a few, very early, prereservation examples that in all probability were made among the tribes from which they were collected, and a larger number of pieces originally made by Western Plains groups.

Much of what can be said regarding the parfleches of the Eastern Plains region has been previously discussed, in that most of what we know concerning the early history of this art form is based on the few remaining works from this area. In summary, it is apparent that the tradition was well established by the late 1700s; that it was closely related to other types of painting, porcupine quill embroidery, and incised ornamentation originating in the Woodland area; and that the vocabulary of motifs provided the basis for the development of later designs produced by the Western Plains tribes. We can see that incised designs were produced concurrently with painted ones, and that both shared the same elements and compositional structure. We know that a variety of forms were constructed and that certain types were associated with specific functions. It is also clear that parfleche painting sometimes embodied religious concepts and symbolically communicated a variety of meanings.

At the same time, it is impossible to reconstruct a knowledge of individual tribal styles, for these have been lost along with the great body of objects themselves. Still, two observations might be made. First, it is apparent that no single style dominated the area, judging from the diversity of surviving pieces. Second, certain regional affinities are nonetheless clearly visible if one notes the similarity of designs between the early envelope illustrated in plate 1 and those of a Mesquakie trunk painted much later (pl. 7), or compares the designs of the Omaha envelope (pl. 2) and Ponca (?) case (pl. 5) with those of later Teton Sioux parfleches, or relates the triangular motifs comprising the design of the incised knife sheath (pl. 3) with those of the painted Oto cylinder (pl. 4).

1. A notable exception is the large Osage flat case made from an envelope illustrated in Morrow (1975: 125). The features of the painting suggest an Eastern Plains origin, which greatly increases the probability of the Osage collection data being accurate.

3 / **Eastern Plains knife case, ca. 1800**

L 10 11/16 in., W 3 in. (not including suspensions). Incised buffalo rawhide, native leather, porcupine quills, metal cones

Possibly collected by the Lewis and Clark expedition, 1804–6; accessioned by the Peale Museum, 1828; identified as Ojibwa. Peabody Museum of Archaeology and Ethnology, Harvard University, 99-12-10/53027

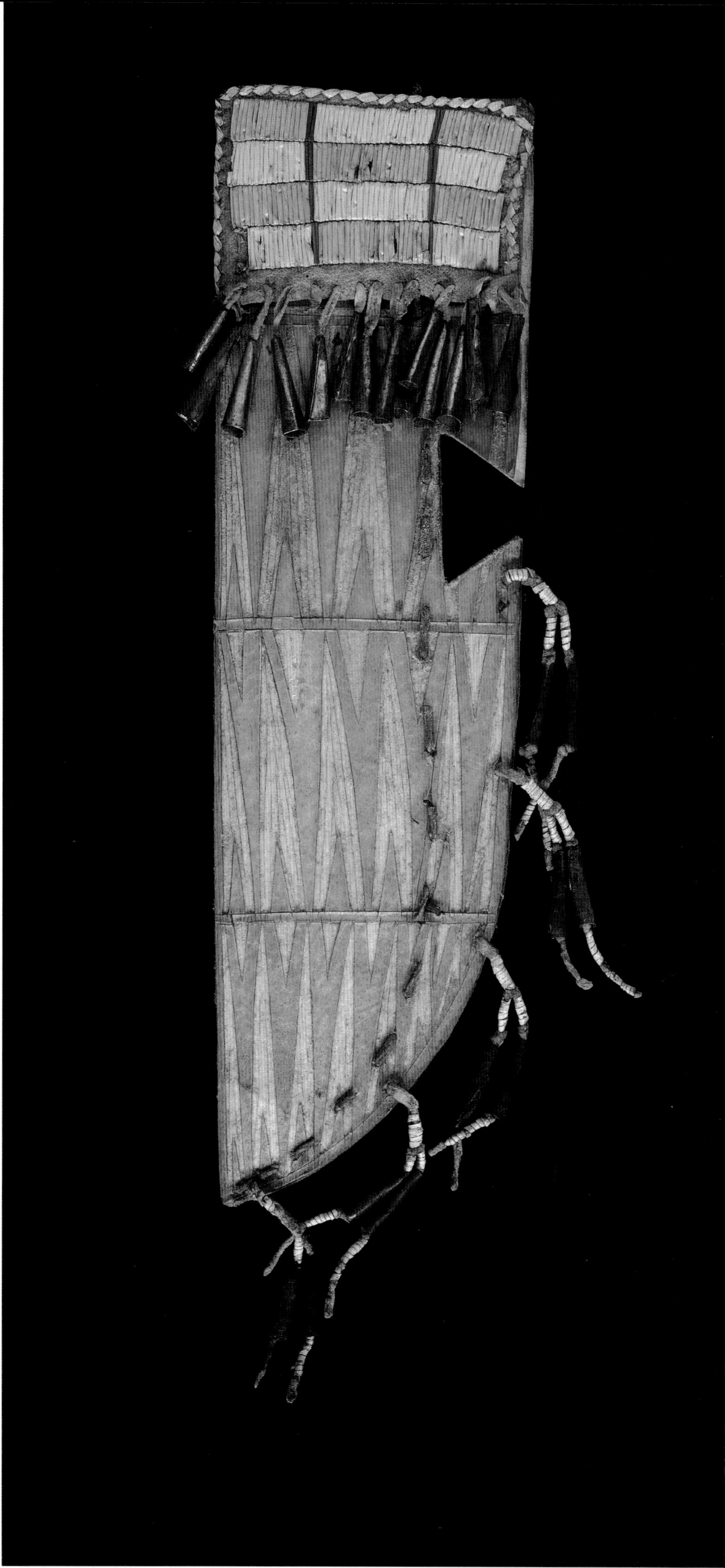

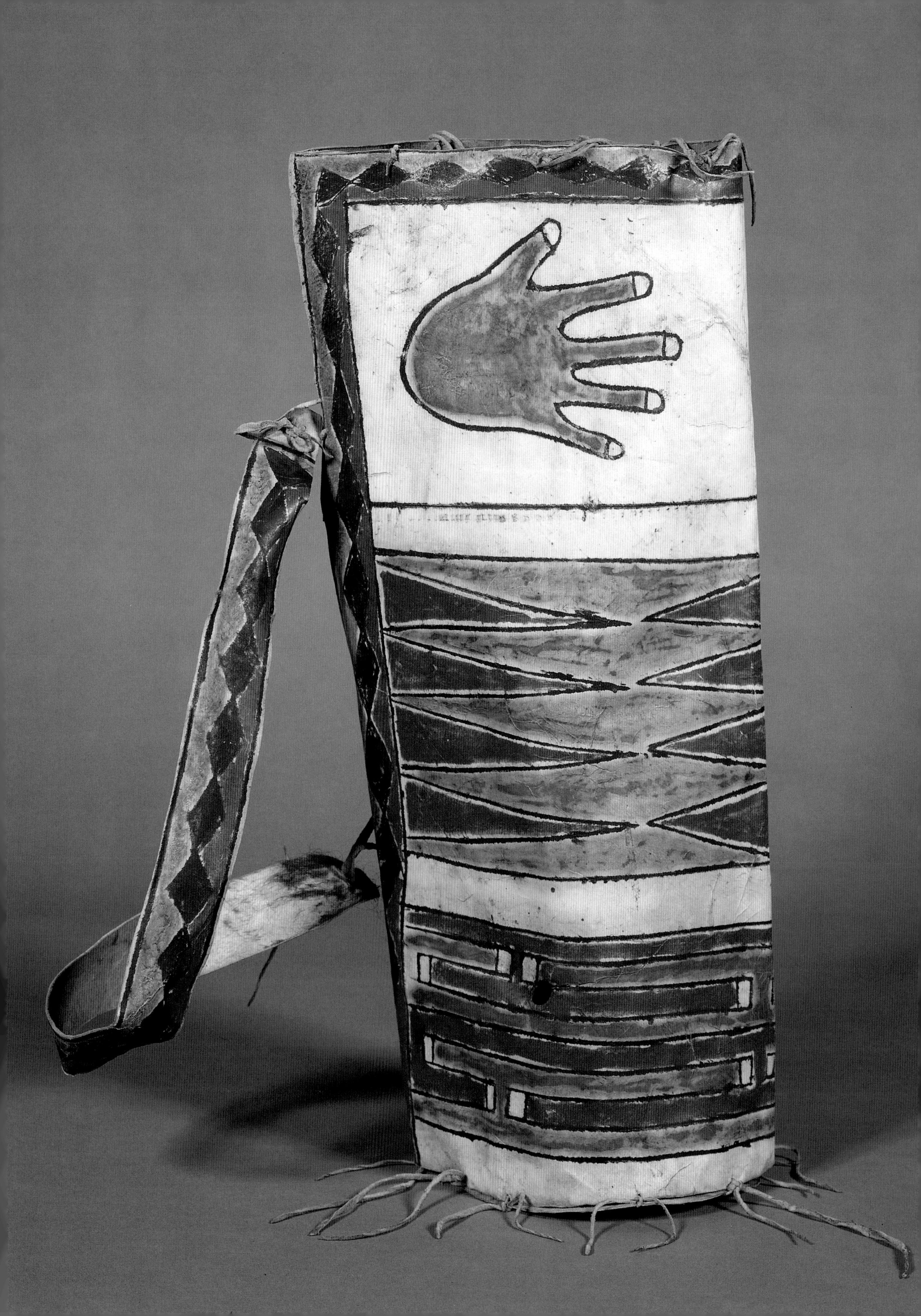

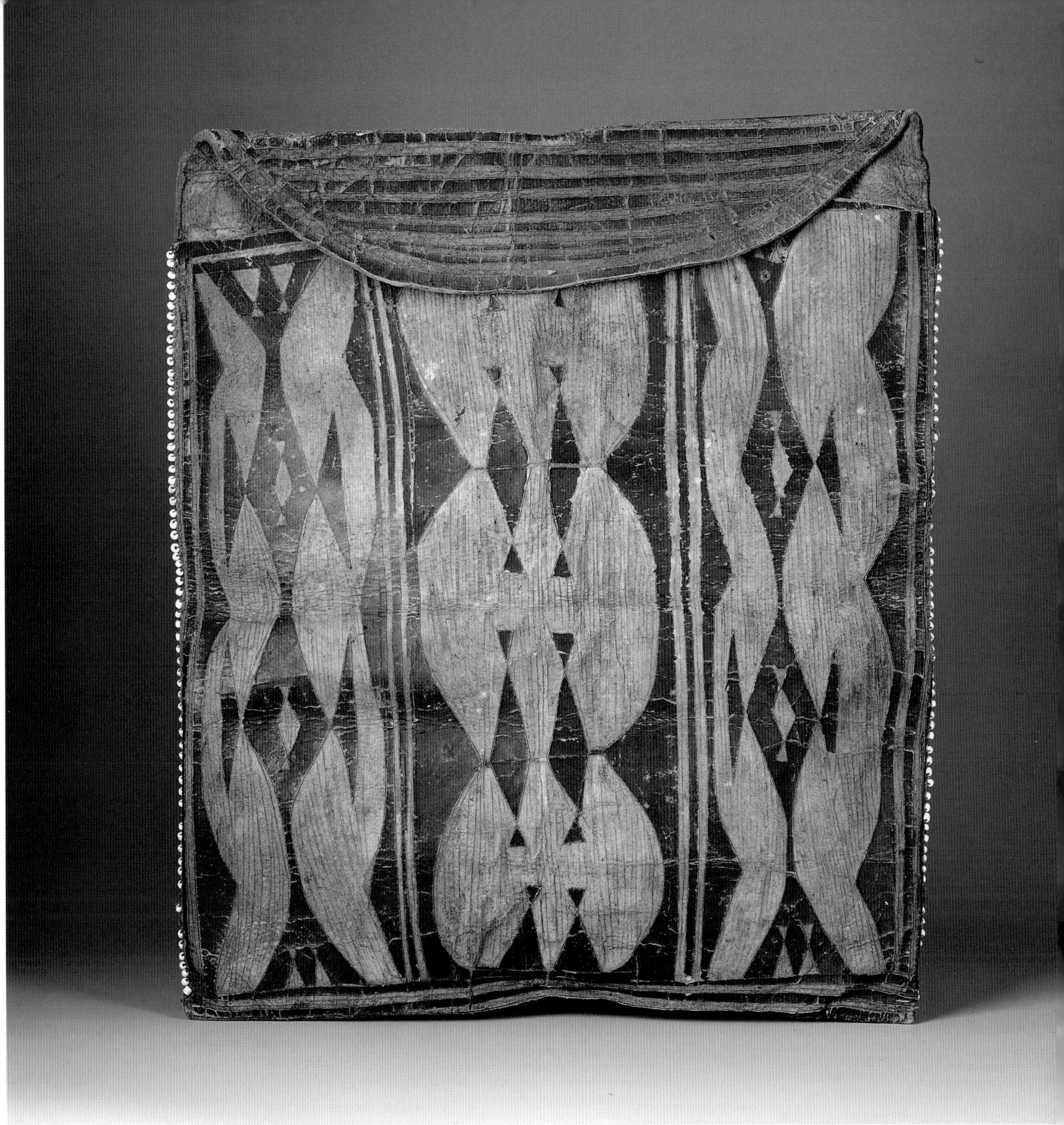

4 / **Oto cylindrical case, ca. 1820**

H 25 in., W 11 in. Buffalo rawhide, pigment

Collected by Friedrich Paul Wilheim, Duke of Wuerttemburg, probably during the first of his four journeys to North America, 1822–24. Staatliche Museen, Museum für Völkerkunde, Berlin, IV B 296

See other side of this case on page 2

5 / **Eastern Plains (Ponca?) flat case, ca. 1830**

H 15 1/2 in. (not including flap), W 15 1/2 in. Incised buffalo rawhide, glass beads

Collected by T. R. Roddy, possibly from the Ponca in Oklahoma. National Museum of the American Indian, Smithsonian Institution, 6/4077

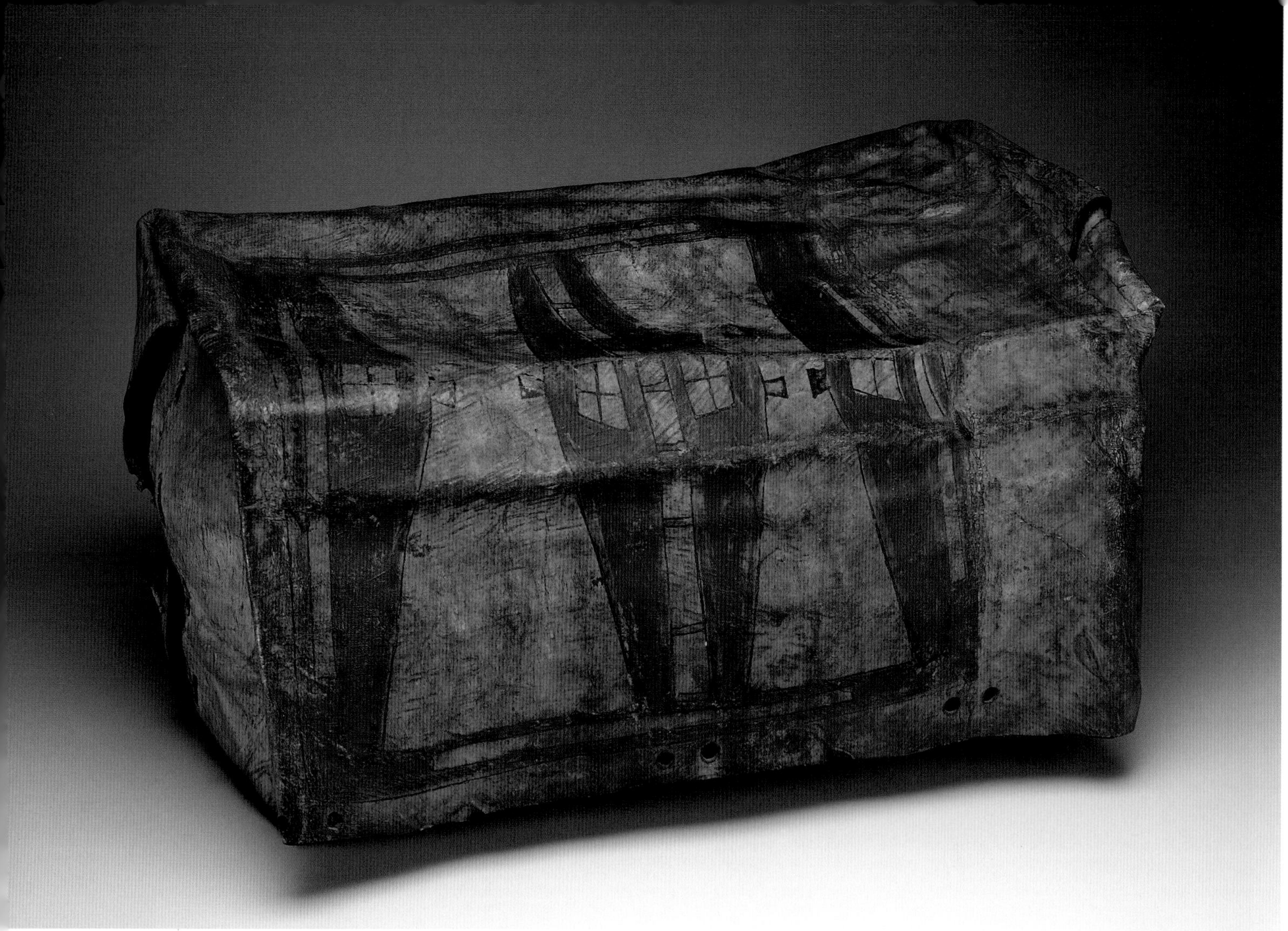

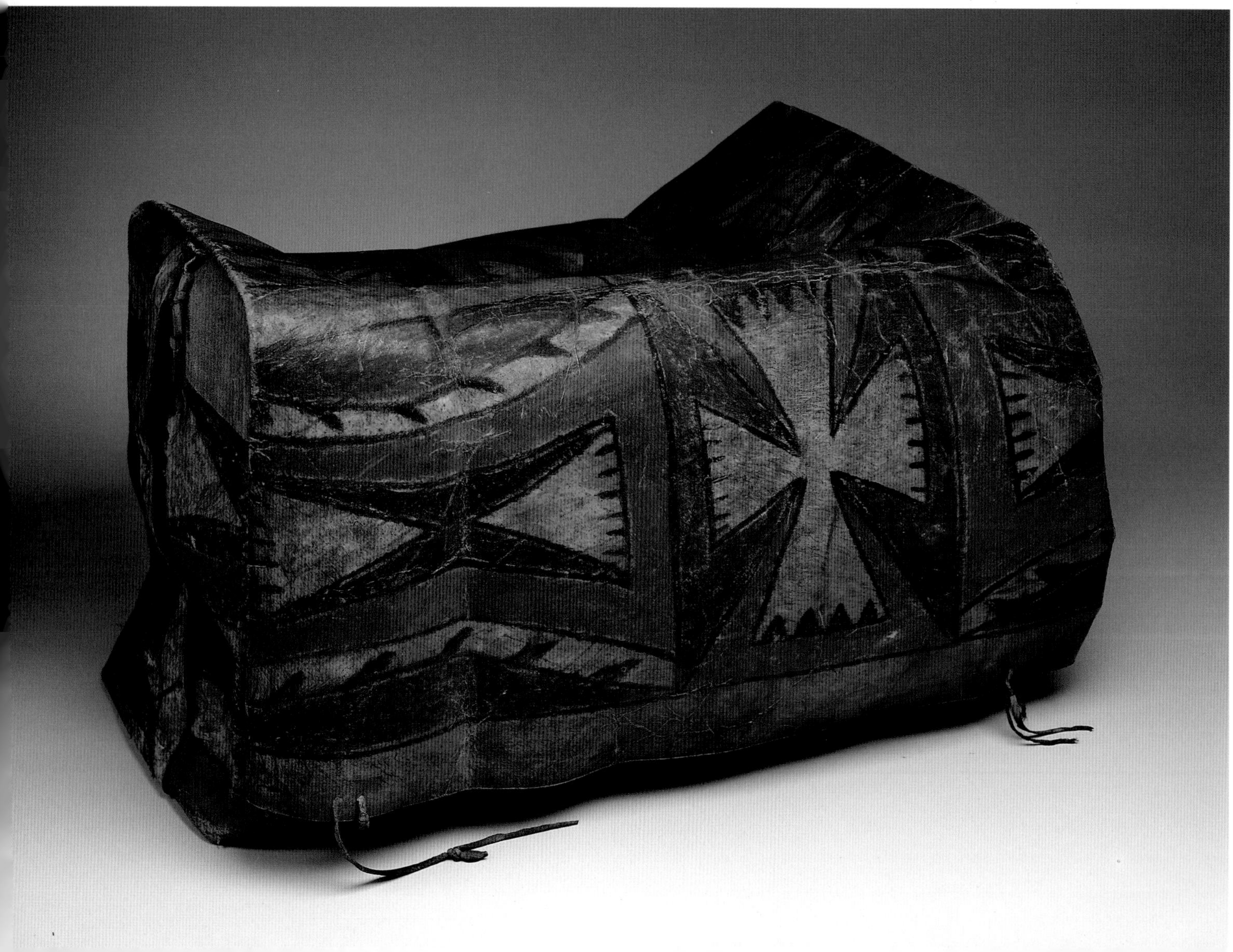

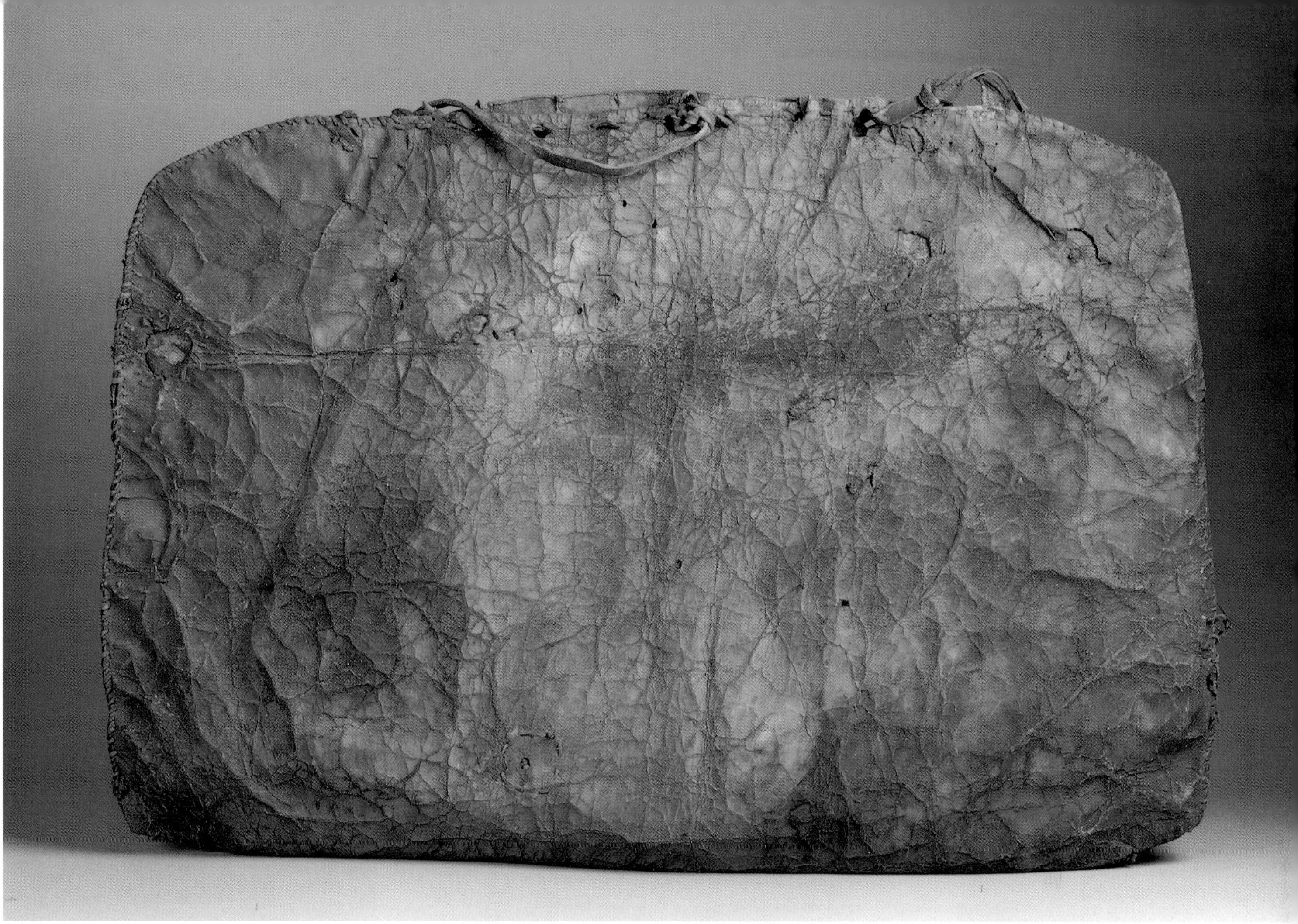

6 / **Mesquakie trunk, ca. 1850**
H 10 in., L 19 in., W 10 in. Buffalo rawhide, pigment

Constructed from a Southern Plains envelope, ca. 1830. State Historical Society of Iowa, 2424

7 / **Mesquakie trunk, ca. 1860**
H 12 1/2 in., L 21 3/4 in., W 10 in. Buffalo rawhide, pigment

Collected by William Jones at Mesquakie Settlement, Iowa, 1902. American Museum of Natural History, 50/3594

8 / **Wichita flat case, ca. 1850**
H 20 1/2 in., W 29 1/2 in. Buffalo rawhide

Collected by George Dorsey in Oklahoma, 1903. Field Museum of Natural History, Chicago, 71922

9 / **Pawnee burden strap, ca. 1850**
L 20 3/4 in. (not including ties), W 2 5/8 in. Incised buffalo rawhide, pigment, native leather

Collected by George Dorsey in Pawnee County, Oklahoma, 1901. Field Museum of Natural History, Chicago, 59503

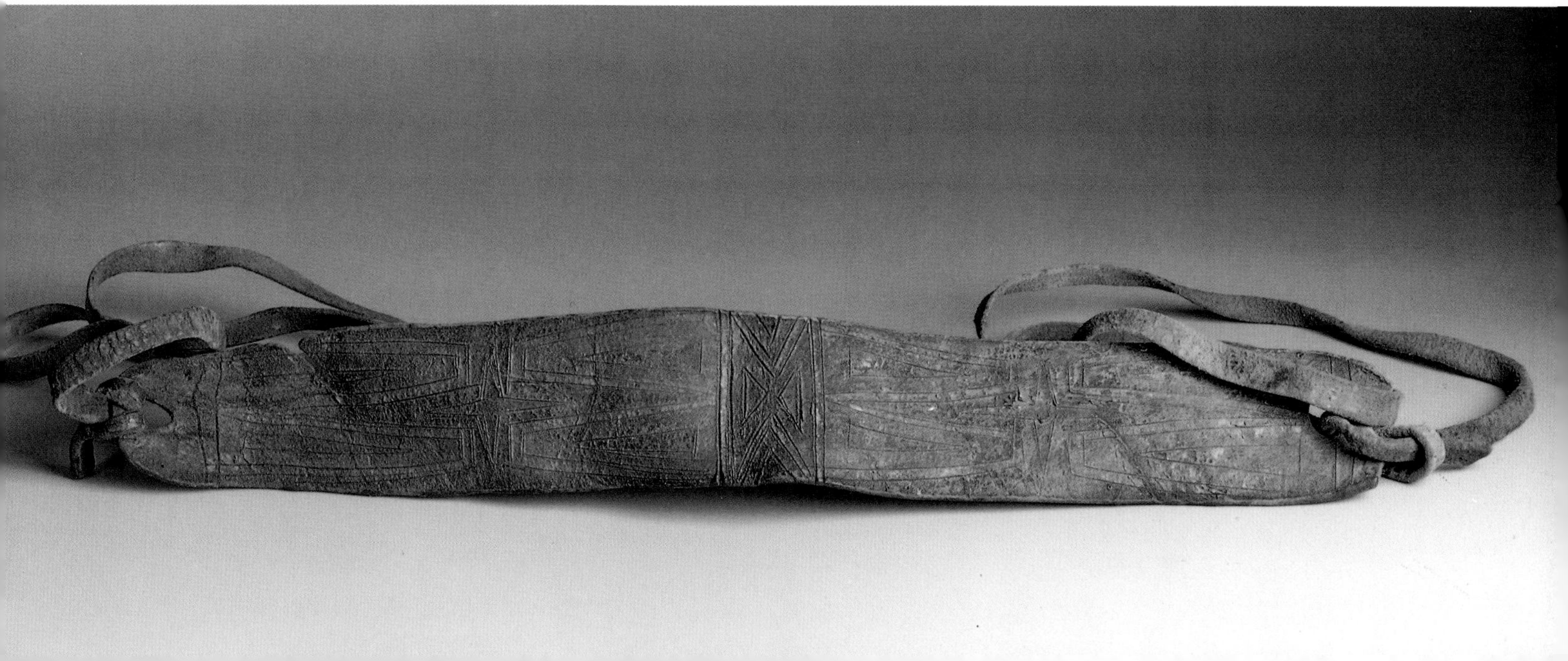

Central Plains

SIOUX

The Lakota, also known as the Teton or Western Sioux, comprise seven closely allied tribes: the Oglala, Brulé, Minniconjou, Sans Arcs, Two Kettles, Blackfeet, and Hunkpapa. Together they were the largest of the Plains groups and, with the Cheyenne and Arapaho, the dominant power inhabiting the central Plains during much of the nineteenth century. Their history as a people and the vitality and splendor of their artistic traditions are well known; both are well represented by the hundreds of objects preserved in museum collections. Each of the seven tribes must have developed distinctive features in the creation of their various art forms, but the prevailing lack of documentation prevents us from differentiating the style of each group. Consequently, Sioux parfleches must be viewed as a collective tradition.

Sioux parfleches are distinguished by their bold designs, strong saturate color, and heavy black outlining (pl. 13). The painted surfaces are rich and opaque. Brilliant reds, blues, and yellows in their primary forms are the predominant colors, usually combined in relatively equal amounts throughout the painting. Smaller areas of green are almost always included, and only rarely do other colors appear. Most of the surface of the designs is covered with paint, and unpainted areas are thoroughly integrated within the shapes as smaller, repeated elements. In the few surviving mid-nineteenth-century pieces, color is limited to dark blue and red, sometimes with small amounts of yellow, in contrast to the nearly universal use of red and green during that period by other tribes. The unpainted ground in these early designs also functions more clearly as a background space, a feature that is generally rare in Sioux painting until the final phase.

Black outlining is used extensively throughout the compositions, not only separating painted and unpainted areas, but also as a division between colors thereby framing each element. Sioux drawing tends to be forceful and heavy, effectively enhancing the vivid, primary colors; together, these elements impart a sense of directness, clarity, and expressive power. Small black units such as dots, bars, or triangles are sometimes included, but Sioux women relied on these devices less frequently than their Cheyenne and Arapaho allies, or other tribes who commonly employed them. More often in Sioux painting, these small figures were executed in color and outlined in black. Bars and triangles were common and several parfleches, including a number collected at Standing Rock Reservation, have small circles incorporated within their designs.

Crosshatching composed of colored lines, or areas filled with parallel lines of color, forms another distinctive feature of Sioux parfleches.

10 / **Sioux envelope, ca. 1850**

L 20 in., W 16 in. Buffalo rawhide, pigment

Collection of Michael and Sherry Maxwell

11 / **Sioux envelope, ca. 1865**

L 25 1/2 in., W 16 in. Buffalo rawhide, pigment

Collected by George H. Pepper from the Arapaho, 1901. National Museum of the American Indian, Smithsonian Institution, 21/7308

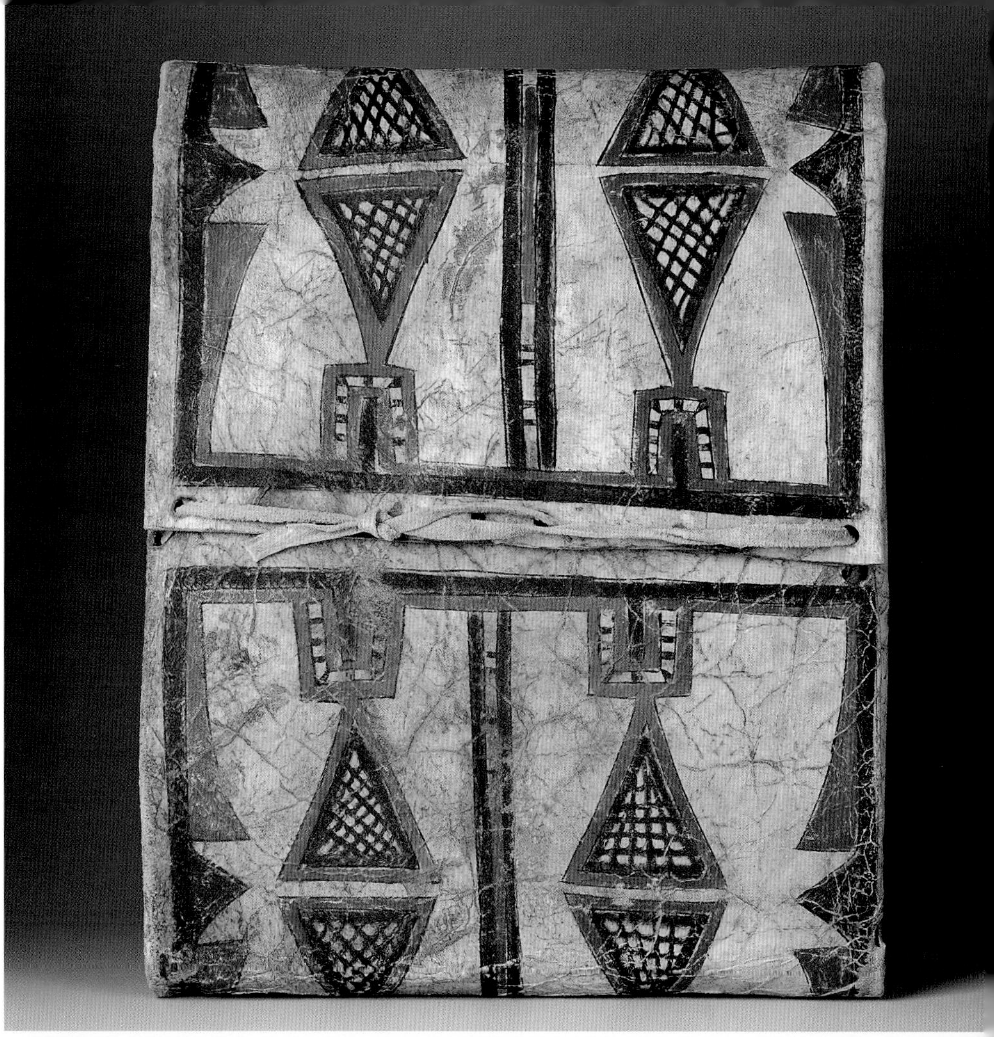

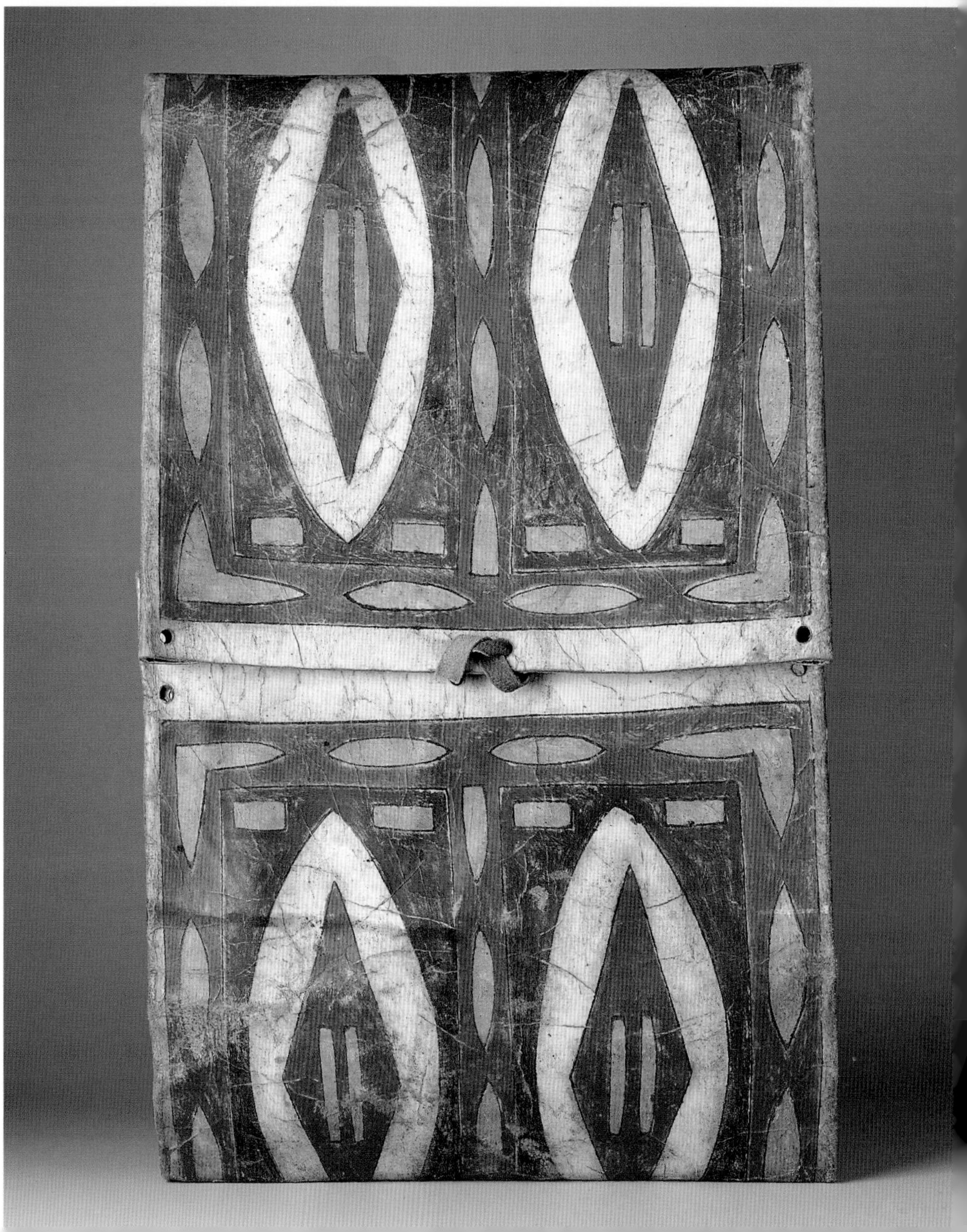

This practice is sometimes described as a late development and one held in low regard because it supposedly indicated a shortage of paint. In fact, its use occurs throughout the history of Sioux parfleche production and, in most cases, was clearly included as the result of an aesthetic decision by the artist in preference to solidly painted motifs. It was often used with great effect as the most inventive and dramatic component within the painting (pl. 20). The origin of this element was probably the crosshatching of sized lines often included in the designs of painted robes. Crosshatching is used almost exclusively by the Sioux, although Arapaho women occasionally included it as a result of Sioux influence.

Sioux designs almost always consist of both straightedged and curved elements. Compositions are most often based on either a central motif, usually a diamond or hourglass (pl. 15), or a two-part vertical division of the field with each area enclosing a diamond or hourglass configuration (pl. 11). In the first format, the primary element is often joined to the borders by triangles, either at the ends thereby emphasizing the verticality of the composition or on all four sides. A third format sometimes seen but not illustrated here is based on a triangle-diamond-triangle configuration running vertically through the panel either as the central motif or paired side by side between the borders and separated by a central band.

The basic composition of both flat and elliptical cases is often structured by a horizontal and vertical central division, separating the field into four rectangular areas filled with smaller motifs (pl. 18). It should be stressed, however, that the vocabulary of Sioux design elements is extensive and complex. While certain configurations were favored and often repeated, such as the classic design of the envelope illustrated in plate 13, a great variety of singular designs were achieved through combining traditional motifs in innovative ways. New motifs were also introduced in response to outside influences. A striking example of this is the inclusion of American flags within the design adorning a box (pl. 21). Images of the flag and other patriotic symbols were incorporated into a variety of artistic forms produced by many tribes during the reservation period but were especially favored by the Sioux. Objects created for the great Fourth of July celebrations, which for a time replaced the tribe's annual Sun Dance as the foremost tribal gathering of the year, were often embellished with such images because of their patriotic and military association. Other unusual designs, such as those covering the back of the remarkable flat case illustrated in plate 16, were possibly derived from woven or printed fabrics, oriental rugs, Navajo textiles, or American quilts, all of which had become a part of Sioux experience by the end of the nineteenth century.

The borders of Sioux parfleches, particularly envelopes, are generally wide and ornate, being formed of two narrow bands of the same color, enclosing a wide band of contrasting color that serves as a background for repeated, regularly spaced figures that are usually triangles. This border typically surrounds the field (pl. 15). When a central band is used

12 / **Sioux envelope, ca. 1865**

L 25 1/2 in., W 15 in. Buffalo rawhide, pigment

Private collection

13 / **Sioux envelope, ca. 1880**

L 26 in., W 14 1/2 in. Rawhide, pigment

Private collection

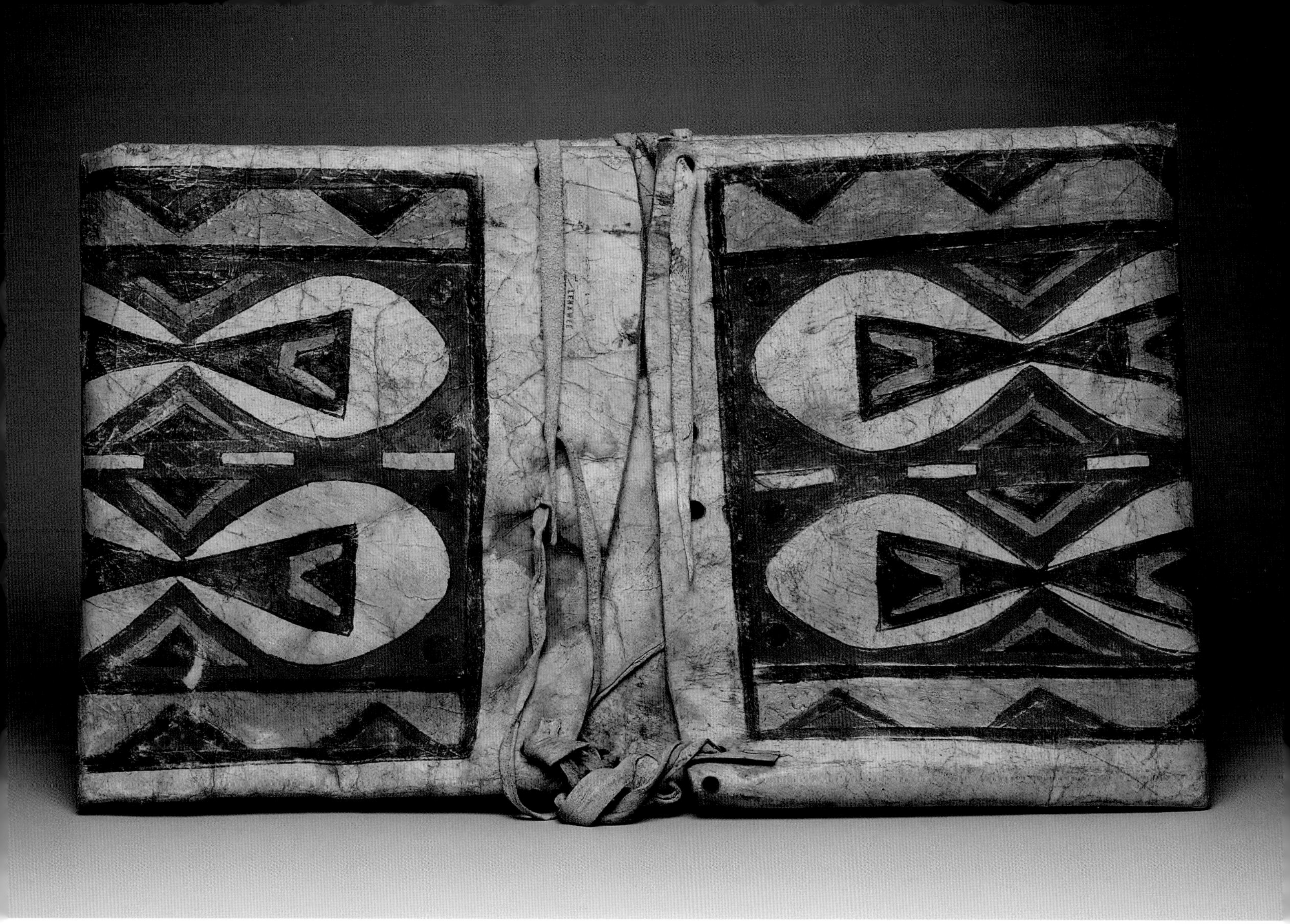

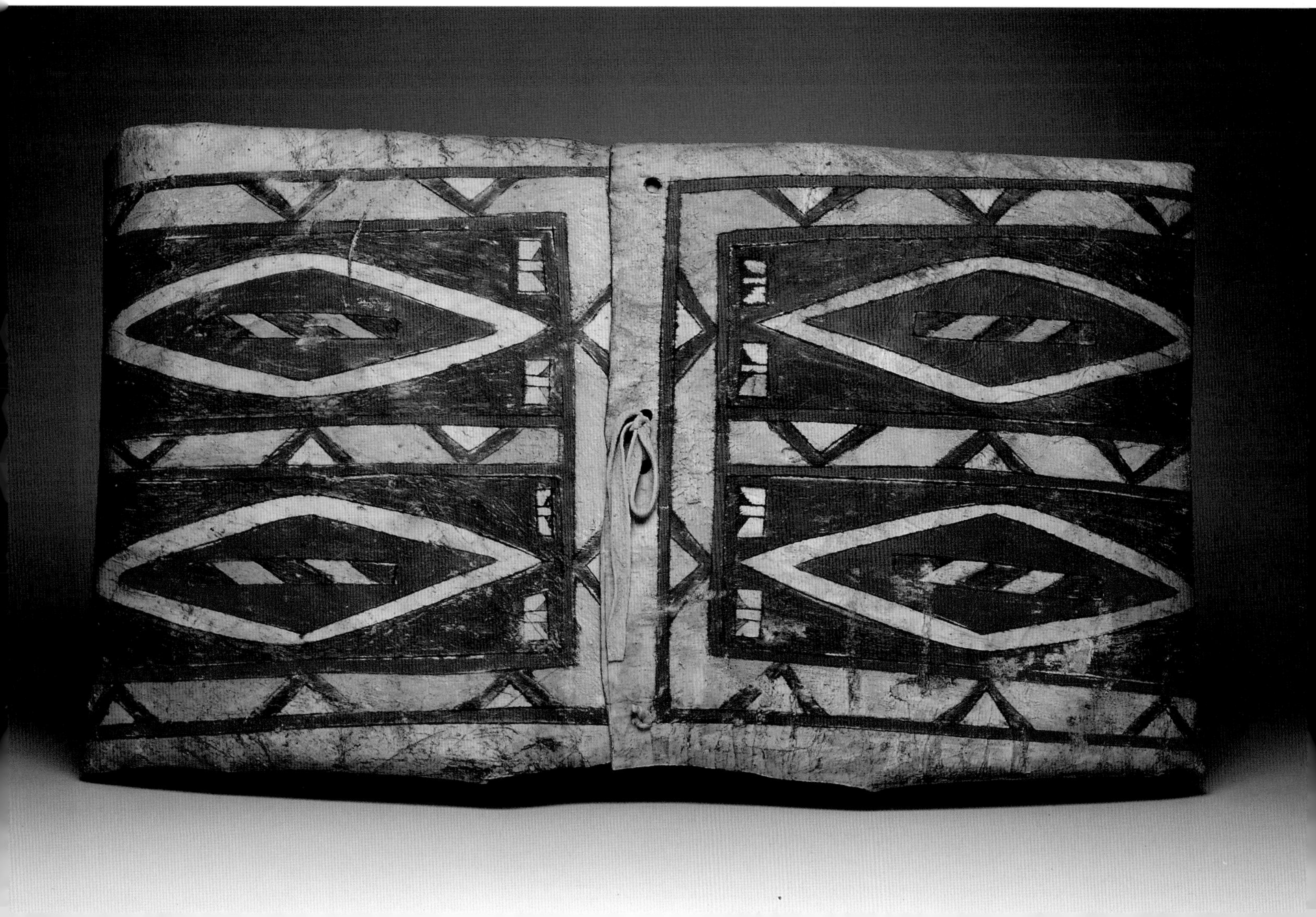

to divide the field vertically, it is most often painted in the same manner as the border. However, what we now consider to be the traditional Sioux border may have developed during the last half of the nineteenth century. Two of the earliest surviving Sioux envelopes dating from mid-century, one of which was collected from the Yankton, have borders that are quite similar to those found on early Cheyenne envelopes. The borders of these Sioux envelopes consist of joined bands of contrasting color, with the inner band forming triangular configurations at spaced intervals, thereby becoming an active component of the central design (pl. 10). This use of the single or double band border persists especially in the painting of elliptical and flat cases and boxes.

Sioux envelopes vary considerably in size and proportion, probably more so than with most other tribes. The earliest tend to be more nearly square, while later pieces are more elongated. The same is true of the painted panels that adorn them. The Yankton envelope previously mentioned, which was accessioned by the National Museum of Natural History in 1869 but made several years earlier, has panels that are square in proportion, quite similar to the envelope illustrated in plate 10. Regardless of time period, the panels of Sioux envelopes are joined by two lines, one extending along each edge of the reverse side. Side flaps were traditionally left unpainted, but later pieces were sometimes elaborated in this manner (pl. 14). Each closure flap has a pair of holes in the center and single holes at each side of the joining edge for ties.

The range of technical skill revealed by surviving Sioux parfleches varies greatly. Early pieces are finely crafted and beautifully painted. Although some excellent examples continued to be made into the twentieth century, a general deterioration, particularly in the quality of the rawhide itself, began during the reservation period and steadily continued until production ceased.

Relatively large numbers of Sioux parfleches may be found in collections today, owing partly to the great size of this tribe and the corresponding number of containers that were made, and in part to the continuation of production well into the twentieth century. In addition to envelopes, significant numbers of elliptical cases and flat cases have also been preserved. The latter tend to be rectangular in shape, usually with a horizontal format, and are never elaborately fringed. Cylinders were also produced, but few have survived. Large numbers of boxes may be found, however, due to the great popularity of the form after 1890. These are found not only in Sioux collections, but in those of numerous tribes who acquired them as gifts or through trade.

14 / **Sioux envelope, ca. 1900**

L 25 in., W 9 1/2 in. Rawhide, pigment

Private collection

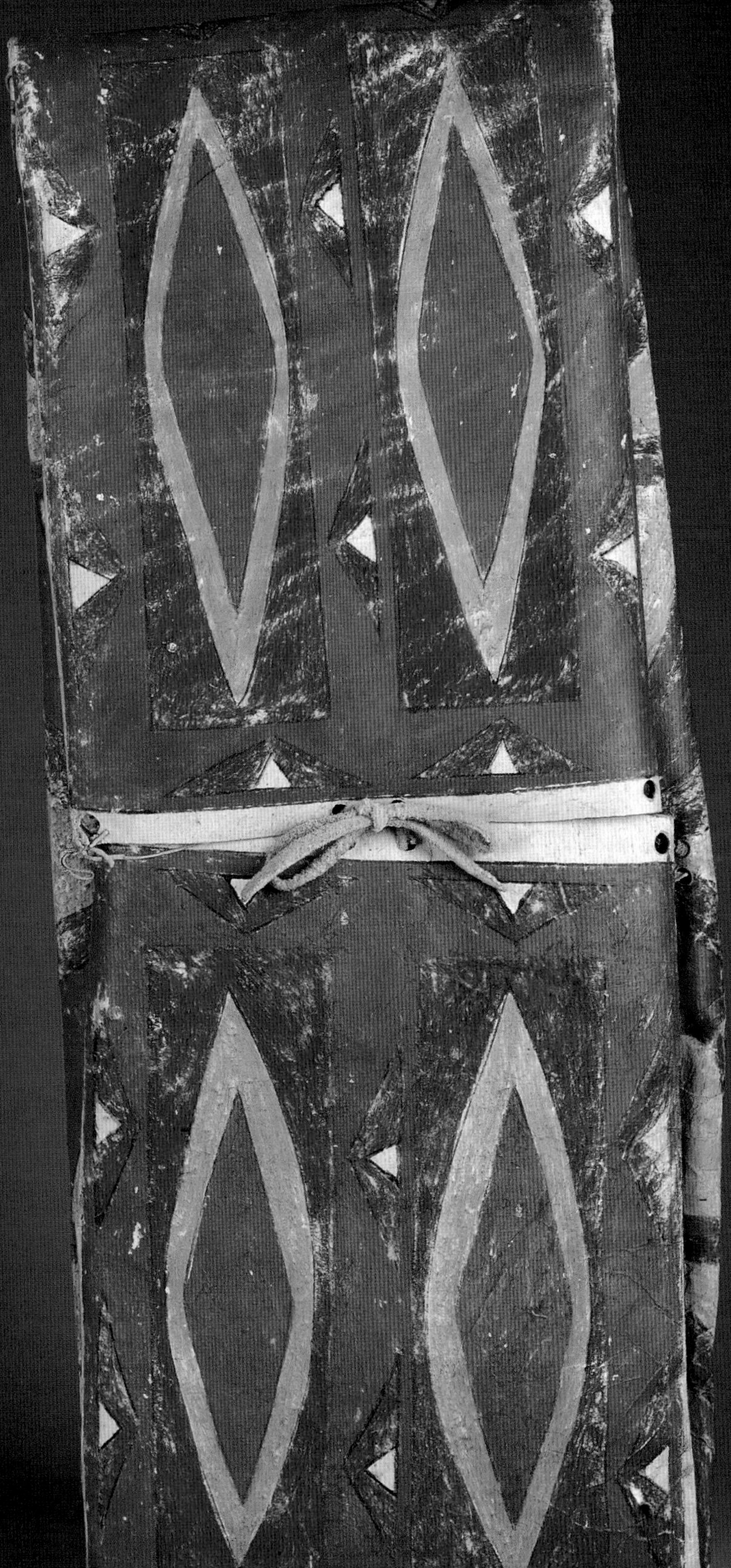

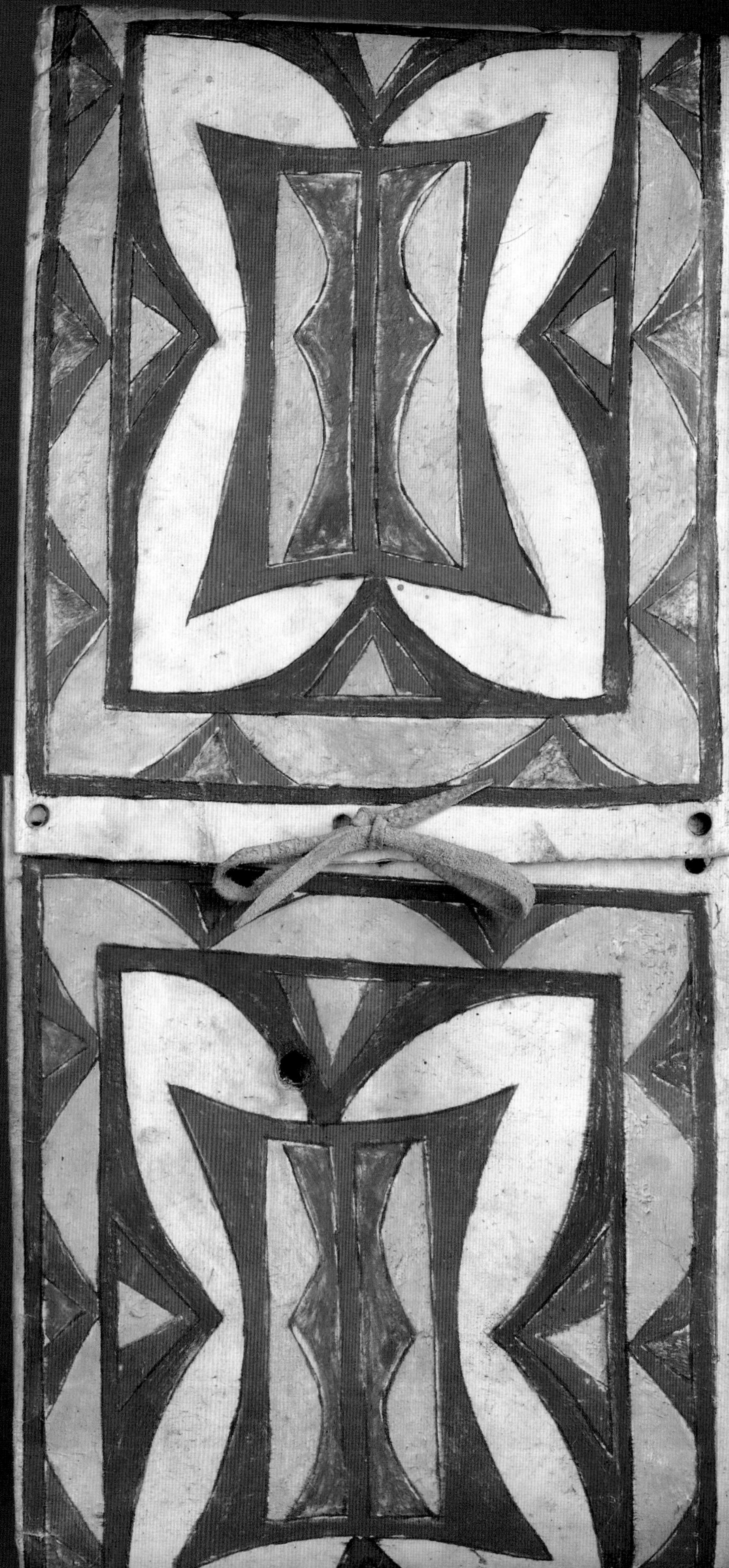

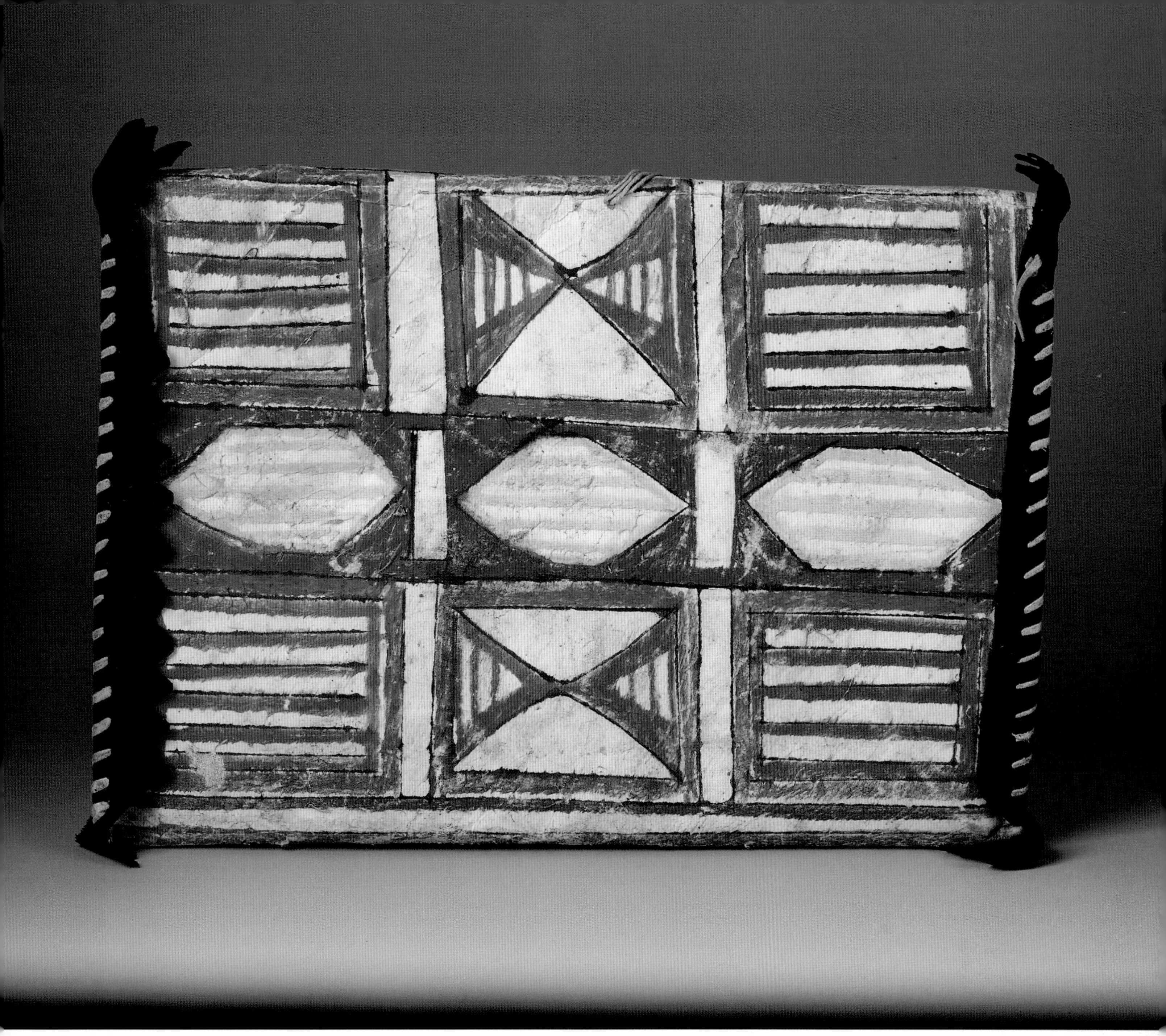

15 / **Sioux envelope, ca. 1900**

L 28 in., W 13 in. Rawhide, pigment

Collected by Gilbert Wilson from the Mandan or Hidatsa, Fort Berthold Reservation, North Dakota, 1909. American Museum of Natural History, 50.1/5425

16 / **Sioux flat case, ca. 1890**

H 10 in., W 14 1/2 in. Rawhide, pigment, wool cloth

Oklahoma Museum of Natural History, NAM 9-?-2; E/54-5/1/128

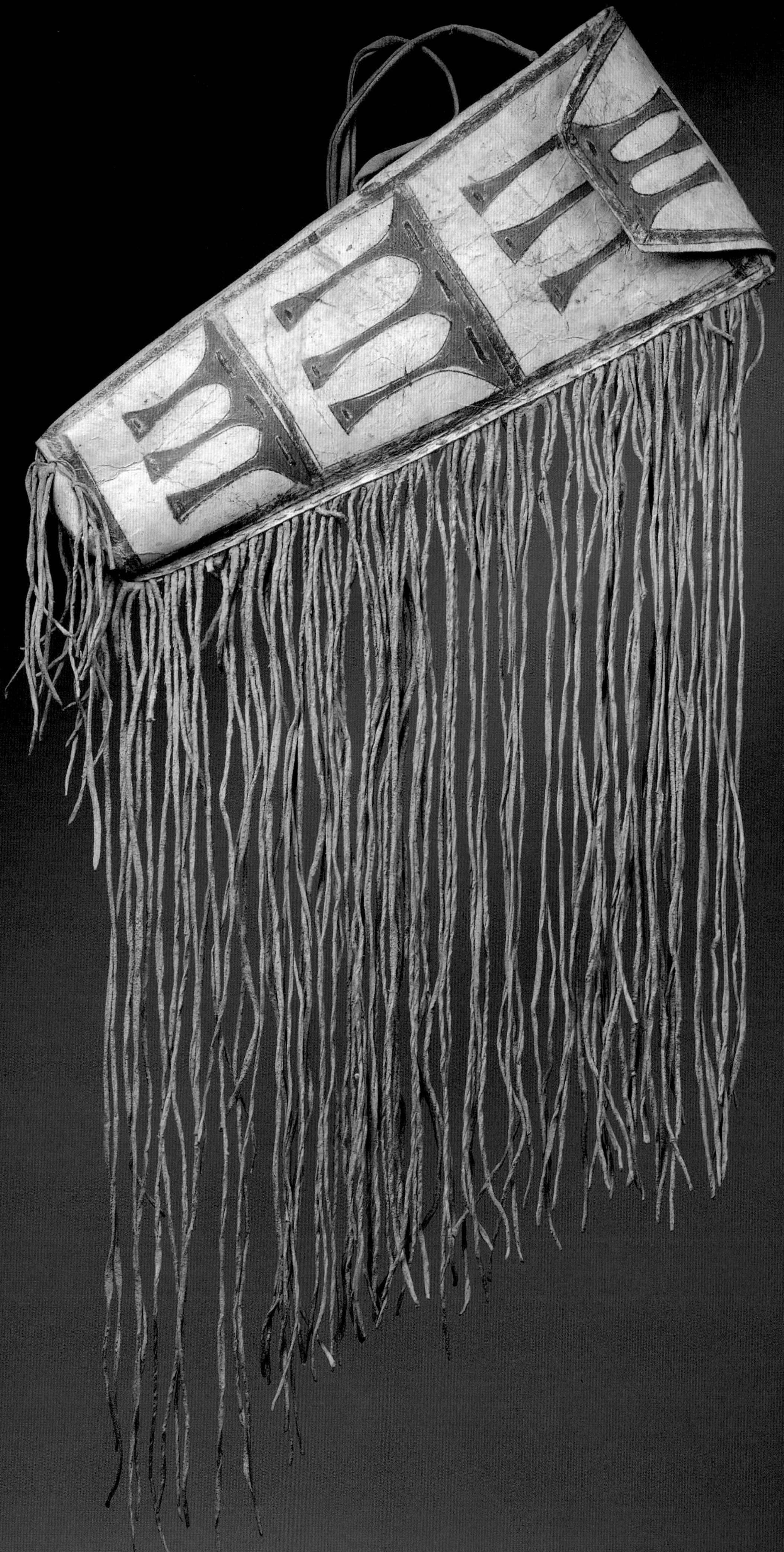

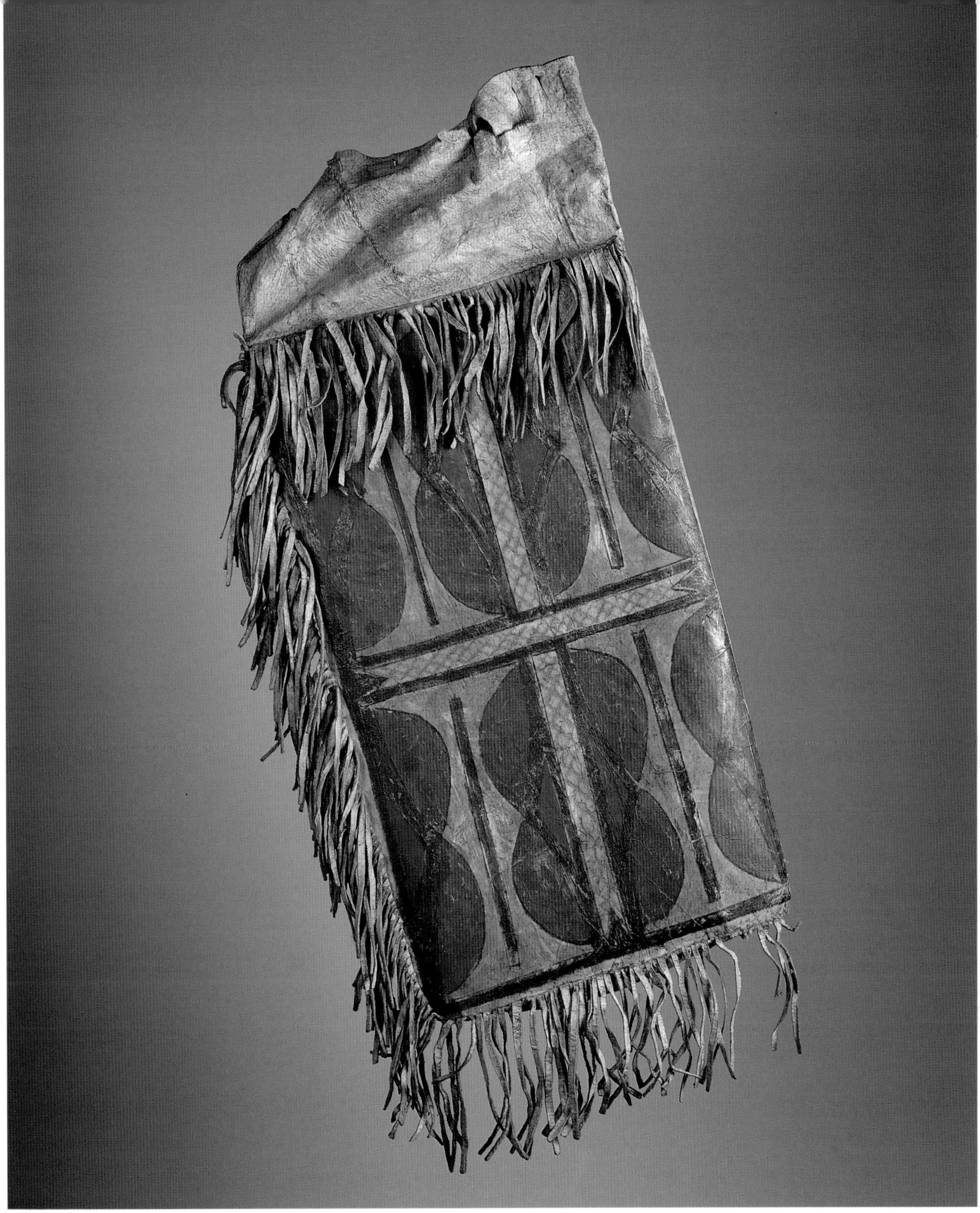

17 / **Sioux elliptical case, ca. 1850**

H 19 in., W 8 in.; fringe 23 in. Buffalo rawhide, pigment, native leather

Collected in North Dakota, 1863. National Museum of Natural History, Department of Anthropology, Smithsonian Institution, 76836

18 / **Sioux elliptical case, ca. 1865**

H 21 3/4 in., W 12 1/2 in. (not including fringe and leather top). Buffalo rawhide, pigment, native leather

Collected by H. Marsden Hazzard from the Santee Sioux, Devils Lake Reservation, North Dakota. National Museum of the American Indian, Smithsonian Institution, 18/1965

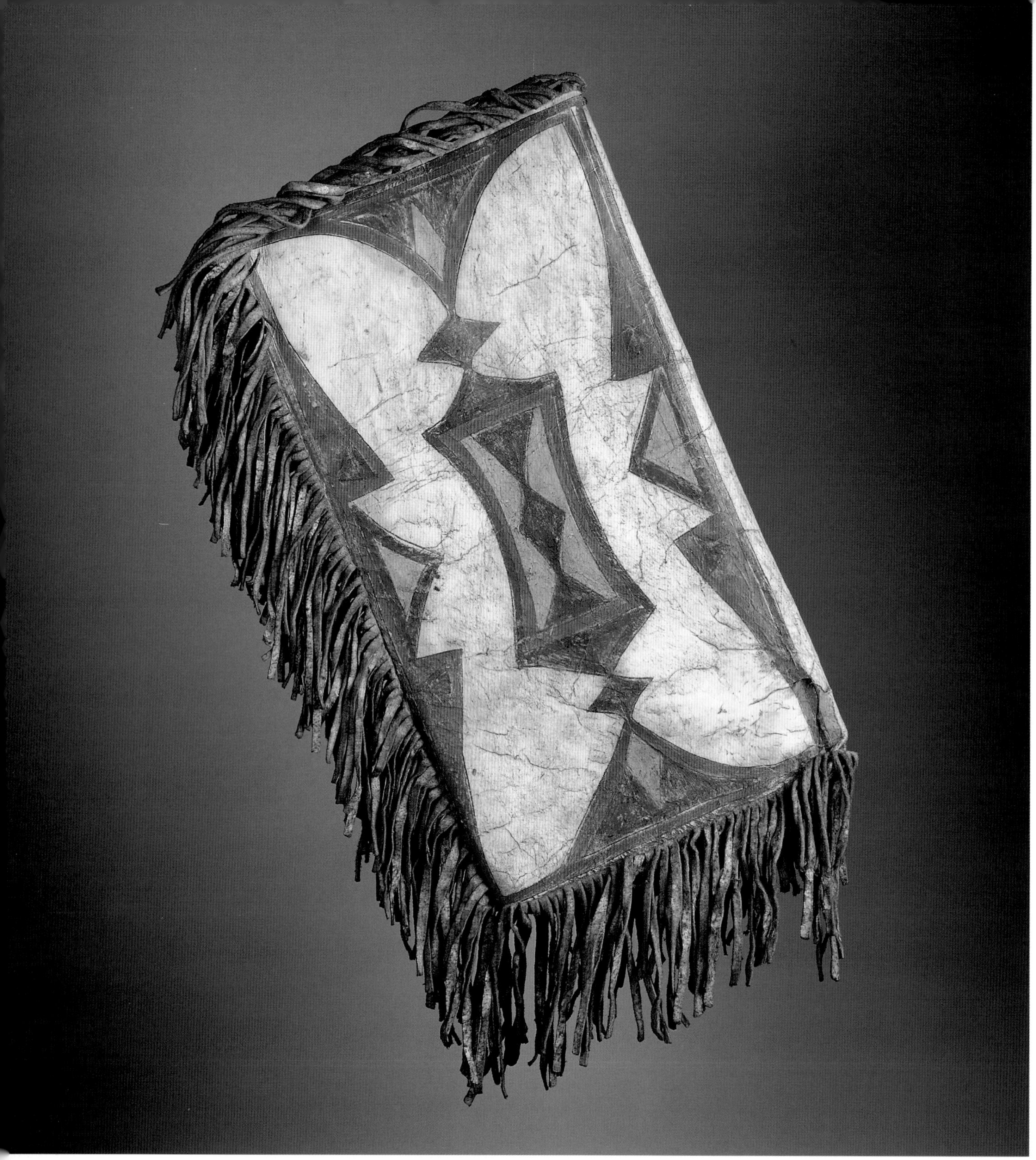

19 / **Sioux elliptical case, ca. 1865**

H 22 1/2 in., W 12 1/2 in. (not including fringe). Buffalo rawhide, pigment, native leather

Collected from the Blackfeet in Montana. National Museum of the American Indian, Smithsonian Institution, 14/3398

20 / **Sioux box, ca. 1889**

H 18 3/4 in., L 10 in., W 10 in. Rawhide, pigment, cotton cloth

According to an old label, this box was presented to a physician on the Standing Rock Reservation, North Dakota, 1889. Private collection

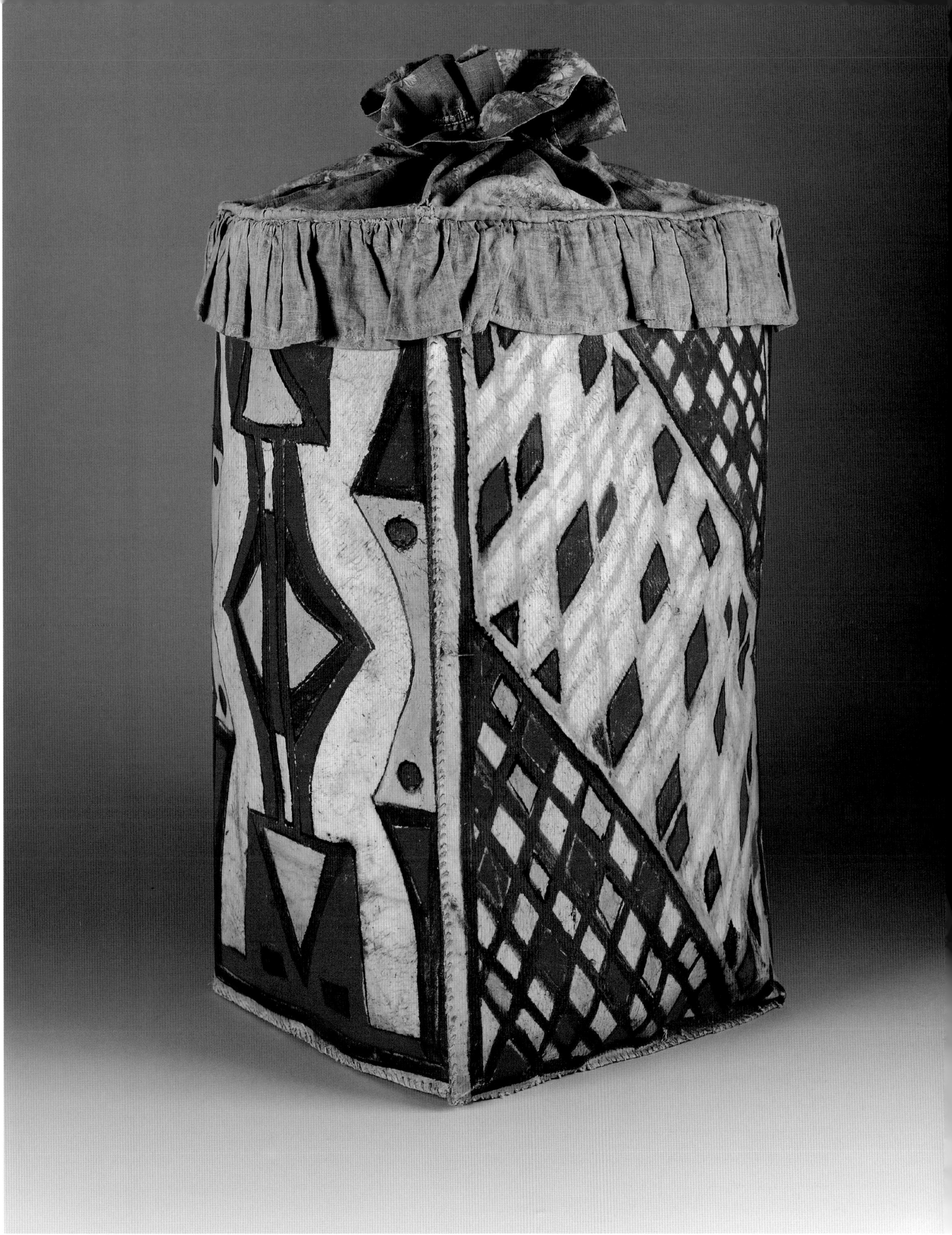

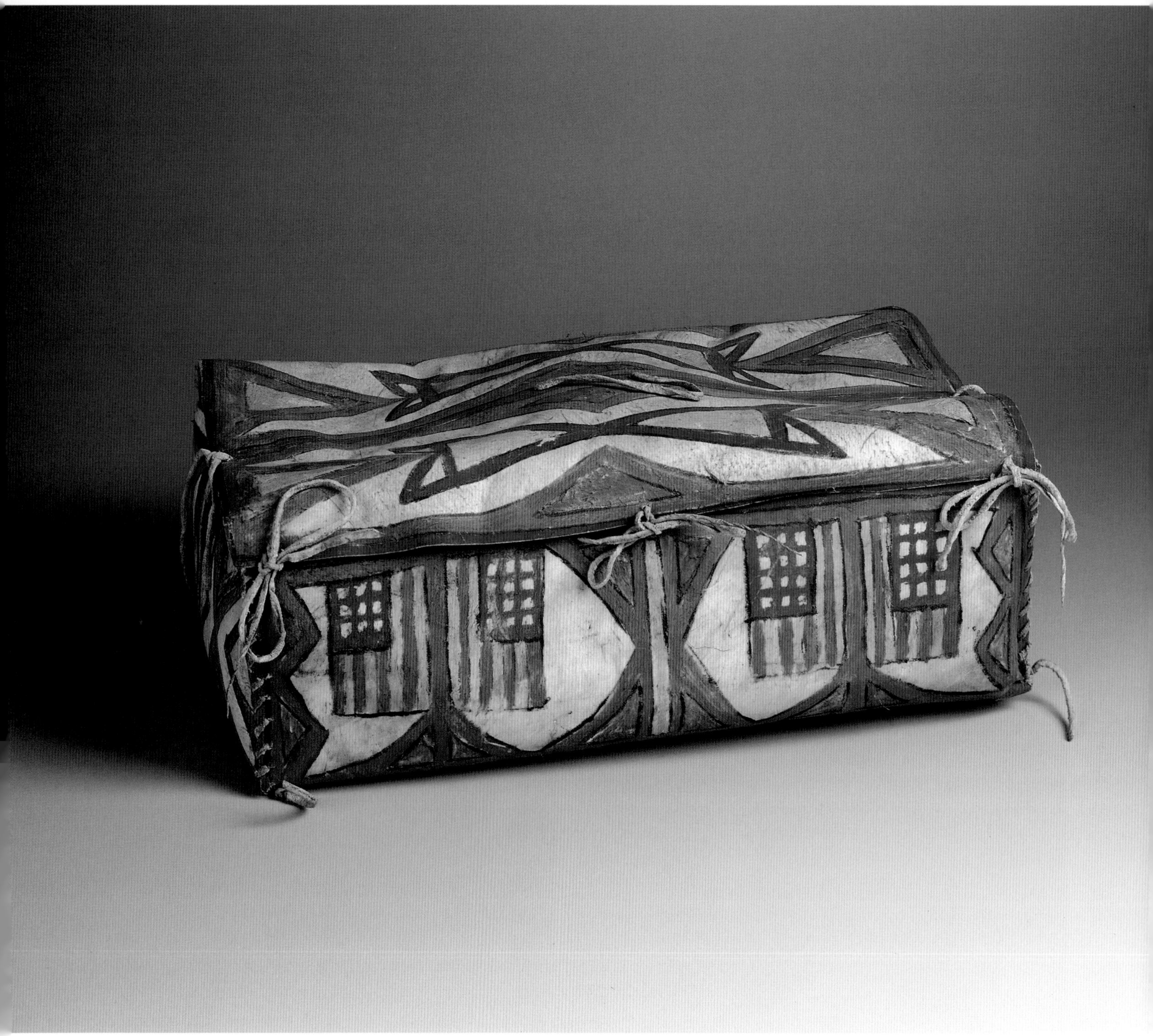

21 / **Sioux box, ca. 1900**

H 4 1/2 in., L 14 1/2 in., W 8 in. Rawhide, pigment

Denver Museum of Natural History, Crane American Indian Collection, 3383

CHEYENNE

The exceptional quality of Cheyenne artistic traditions is widely recognized and is clearly visible in the technical excellence and unsurpassed elegance of their parfleches. Among the Cheyenne, artistic expression was a manifestation of religious belief, and the creation of various art forms was directed and strictly maintained by guilds comprised of elected women recognized for their skill, character, and spiritual knowledge. For this reason alone, Cheyenne parfleche painting must be considered as a single tradition, even though the tribe divided into Northern and Southern bands toward the middle of the nineteenth century. While there were undoubtedly subtle differences in style that developed following their separation, these are impossible to discern at this time because of the relatively small number of surviving pieces for comparison and the lack of documentation regarding makers. One might assume that the close alliance of the Northern Cheyenne with the Sioux influenced their painting, as did the Southern band's association with the Kiowa and Comanche, but even this cannot be determined with certainty.

Two facts, however, suggest that most Cheyenne parfleches in collections today are of Southern origin. The first is simply that most were acquired in Oklahoma, from members of the Southern branch, and it is likely they were made there. The second fact is the tragic and nearly total loss of Northern Cheyenne material wealth during the destruction of Dull Knife's village in 1876 by General Mackenzie's forces. The Northern people never recovered from this blow in the creation of traditional art forms (Powell 1976: 7), and evidence suggests that few parfleches were produced after they were resettled in Montana following their return from Oklahoma in 1879.

The distinctive character of Cheyenne parfleches emerges from the power of the drawing. The images possess a sense of tension and a precise linear structure deriving from the artists' emphasis on fine, brown-black outlining, which is the primary activating element of the paintings. This effect of line is frequently enhanced by the placement of small black units throughout the design; these units—which might include triangles, hourglasses, diamonds, short lines, squares, circles, and distinctive, ball-tipped finials (pl. 24)—establish shifting focal points and rhythmic directional movements. They also dramatically extend the complexity and scale of elements comprising the image. These units are integrated within the order of larger colored forms through the linear framework established by the outlining, which also separates painted and unpainted areas and borders all colored shapes.

The refinement and delicacy created by drawing is echoed in other components as well. Compositions are controlled and precisely balanced, with nearly equal amounts of painted and unpainted surface area, creating a subtle, yet active, figure-ground reversal in most designs. The contours of primary forms are often gently curving and rhythmic, yet taut and seemingly possessed of an inner structure. The use of color is elegant and restrained; usually the paint was relatively transparent resulting in softly luminescent tones that appear imbued with light and space. In addition to various reds and yellows, a range of distinctively pale, beautiful blues and greens were used to create forms that illuminate the rawhide surface and contrast effectively with the black outlining. The deep ultramarine blue so favored by the Sioux and Crow, as well as many other tribes, was rarely used by Cheyenne artists. Only on parfleches produced by a few Southern Cheyenne women during the final decades of the nineteenth century does it appear.

There are three basic compositional formats used by Cheyenne women, although this number might be expanded depending on the interpretation of the variations that were created. These three are defined by the primary motifs that form the designs, all of which were produced concurrently throughout the nineteenth century. Cheyenne artists did not deviate from these traditional configurations, and this continuity, in addition to the great consistency of technical excellence, affirms the powerful influence of the women's craft guilds on the production of parfleches as well as on other arts.

The first format is based on an arrangement of rectangular motifs that extend from the borders at the ends of the panels toward the center, while triangular forms extend from the sides (pls. 23, 24). Quite often the center of the panel in these designs remains open. The second format might be considered a variation of the principal Arapaho design (pl. 32), in that the field is divided vertically into four sections with three triangular shapes arranged along each side of the central band and along the outer vertical borders (pls. 25, 28). The two remaining bands located midway between these are usually elaborated into wide lines composed of two colors that flair as they join the borders at their ends.

The third format is based on a vertical division of the field into two parts, each containing an unpainted hourglass shape in its center. The hourglass is formed by large triangles extending from the sides and the central band (pls. 26, 27). This configuration may also be perceived as an elongated diamond in the center of the field, with a triangle (or matching half-diamond) at each side. Usually the contours of these forms are subtly curved, enhancing the delicate character of the painting. The two unpainted hourglass shapes almost always contain some figure: either a flaring line extending from top to bottom or a floating, highly elongated hourglass (pl. 27) or simple bar of color terminating with flared lines (pl. 26). This design is applied almost exclusively on flat cases of the type used to contain sacred materials (pl. 30).

A significant observation may be made in comparing plates 26 and 27. There is a dramatic difference in effect derived from the varied emphases of line and color. Although both artists used the same compositional format, one relied greatly on the linear structure and radiant energy

22 / **Cheyenne envelope, ca. 1830**

L 33 3/4 in., W 16 in. Rawhide, pigment

Collected by Prince Maximilian zu Wied-Neuwied on the upper Missouri River, 1833; accessioned as Dakota. Staatliche Museen, Museum für Völkerkunde, Berlin, IV B 160

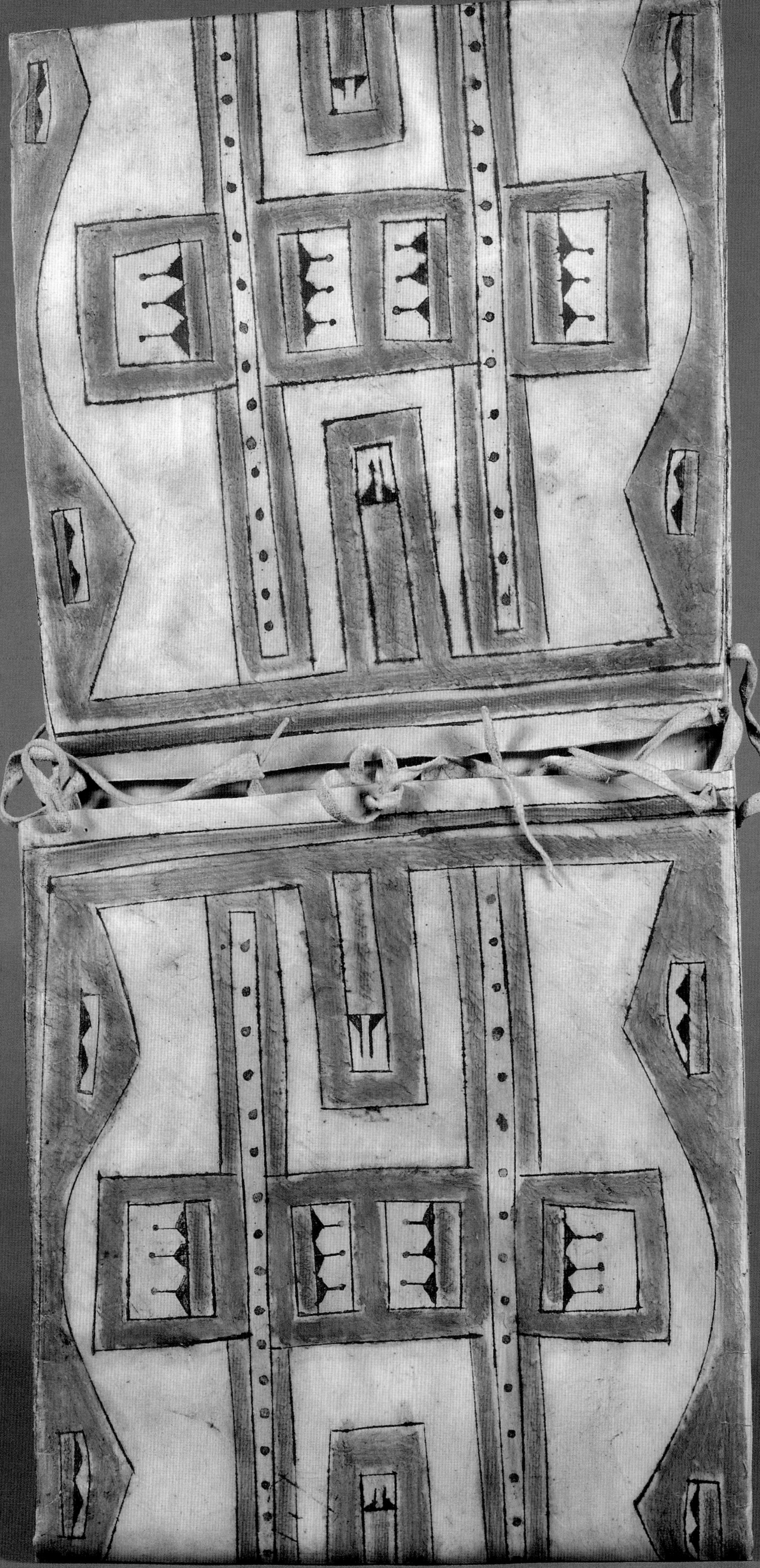

achieved through the strength and clarity of her drawing (pl. 27). The pale color of the forms only amplifies the definition and activity created through line. The other artist chose to utilize the power of color to create a dramatic image emphasizing solid, light-dark contrasts and carefully balanced shapes (pl. 26).

It is also worth noting that even this seemingly simple design may be perceived in two very different ways, either as two distinct panels—each containing an hourglass—or as a unified composition dominated by a central diamond. This points to the difficulty and confusion arising from attempts to classify parfleche designs according to a singular description of composition or the arrangement of motifs alone.

Cheyenne borders consist of two narrow bands of the same color enclosing short bars of contrasting color, usually at the corners and quite often at the centers of each side of the panel. On many designs the inner band extends into triangular shapes, assuming a configuration along the sides, thereby becoming a part of the central image.

The proportion of the painted panels of envelopes is rectangular, but often nearly square. These panels usually extend to the back of the folded envelope because of its compact proportion, and they are joined by bands of color on the reverse side in the same manner as those of the Sioux. Side flaps are never painted. The arrangement of holes on the outer flaps always consists of a pair in the center and a single at each side.

Cheyenne parfleches found in collections today are considerably more rare than those of the Sioux and Arapaho, and consist of a limited number of forms. Although envelopes are most common, a number of flat medicine cases may also be seen. These are rectangular and unfringed, with a vertical format (pl. 30). No elliptical cases were produced and only a very few cylinders have been collected; these are nearly indistinguishable from the type most commonly produced by the Arapaho (pl. 40 L). Although George Bird Grinnell (1923, vol. 1: 245) mentions the use of trunks, none has been found that bears Cheyenne characteristics, suggesting that those he saw were acquired from the Sioux.

The painter of the case illustrated in plate 31 was not bound by the traditional conventions of Cheyenne design, because the extraordinary images and the instruction to create them were received in a vision. This container for sacred objects has been transformed by its painting into a cosmological diagram, composed of many of the symbols of sacred power that appear on other forms of Cheyenne religious art. On the front is the Sun, greatest of the Above Powers; at the corners are the Four Sacred Persons who dwell at the Four Directions; descending through the center of the panel are the tracks of buffalo, also sacred to the Northern Cheyenne people; and along each side is a row of black circles of unknown significance but undoubtedly symbolizing some dimension of supernatural power. In the center of the reverse side is a crescent moon, and at each corner a horned lizard, possibly denoting the power of water creatures. Drawn near the border at each side is the "Man-

23 / **Cheyenne envelope, ca. 1840**

L 29 in., W 20 in. Rawhide, pigment

Collected by Count Armand Fouche d'Otrante during his travels in the Northern Plains region, 1842–44. Folkens Museum–Etnografiska, Stockholm, 1854.2.11

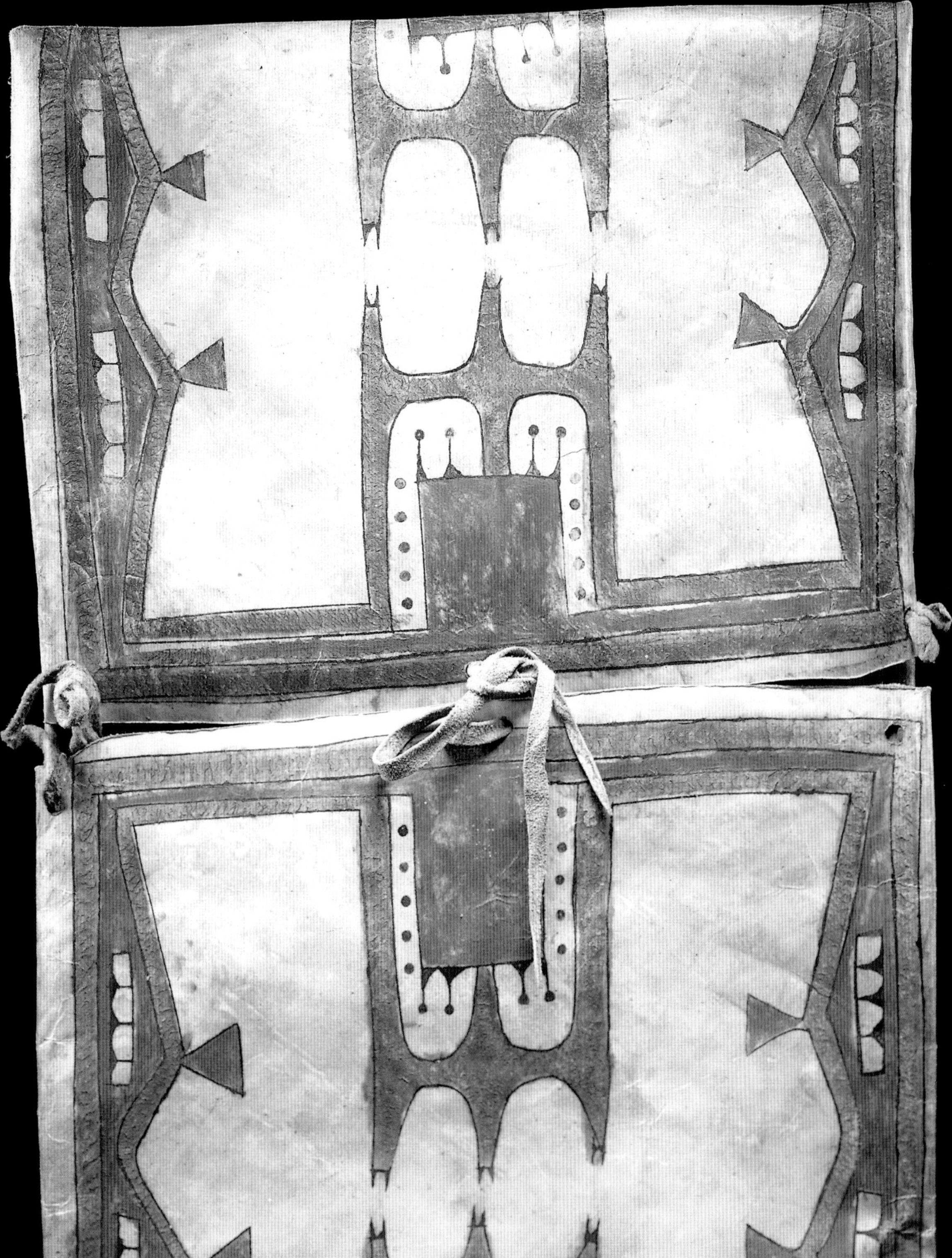

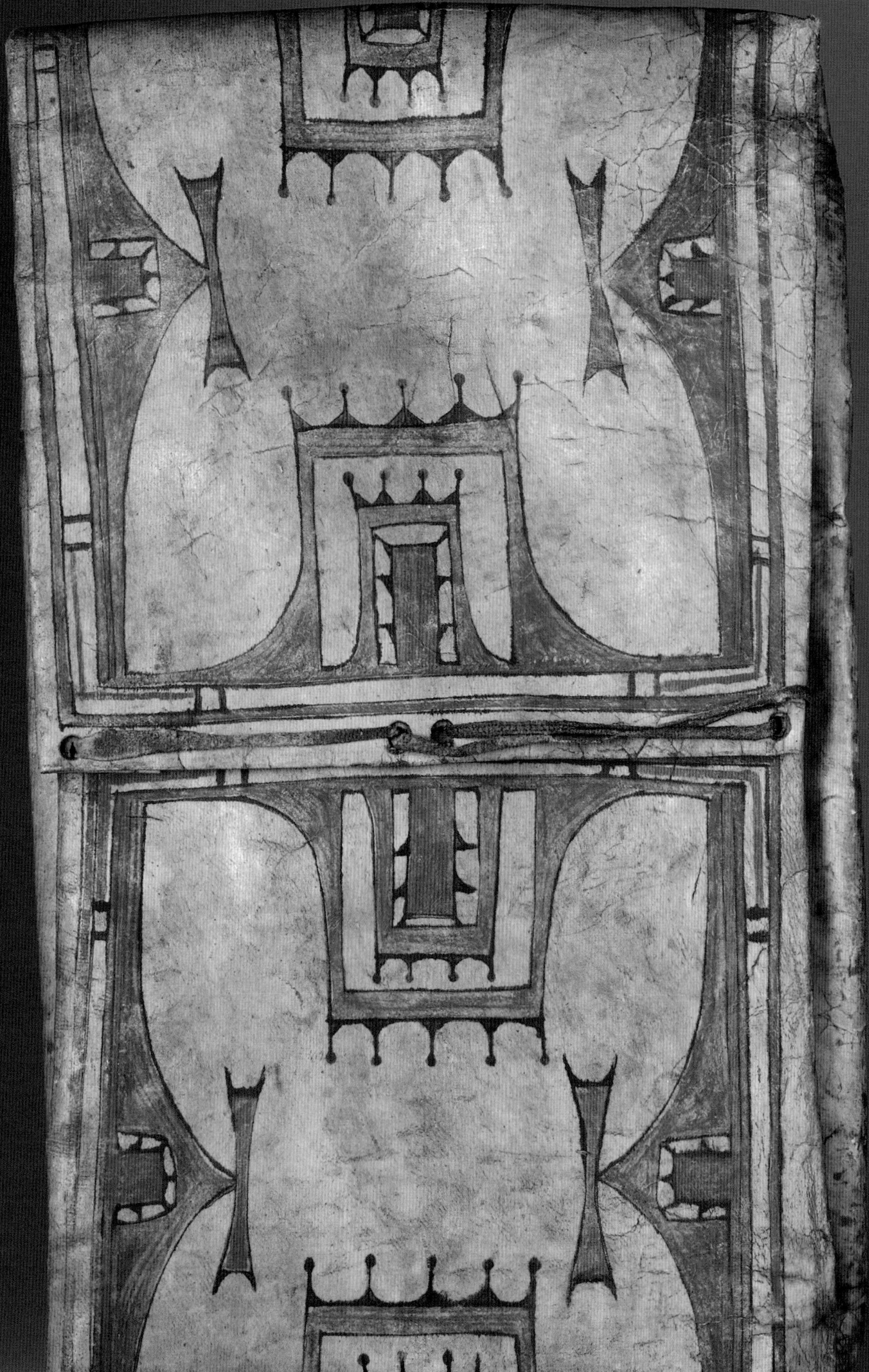

24 / **Cheyenne envelope, ca. 1850**

L 25 1/2 in., W 14 3/4 in. Buffalo rawhide, pigment

Collected by A. E. Jenks at the Cheyenne Settlement, Canadian River, El Reno, Oklahoma, 1899. Collection of Gary and Fran Spratt

25 / **Cheyenne pair of envelopes, ca. 1850**

L 24 in., W 14 in.; L 24 1/4 in., W 14 in. Rawhide, pigment

Private collection

power" symbol that appears engraved on the horns of the Sacred Buffalo Hat and other religious objects (Powell 1969, vol. 2: 437–38), and next to these is a progression of smaller black circles. Bordering the case and encompassing all of this spirit world is a rainbow. The buffalo tail and horsehair suspensions and the rawhide cutout of a horned dragonfly extend the symbolic content embodied in this object even beyond the painting.

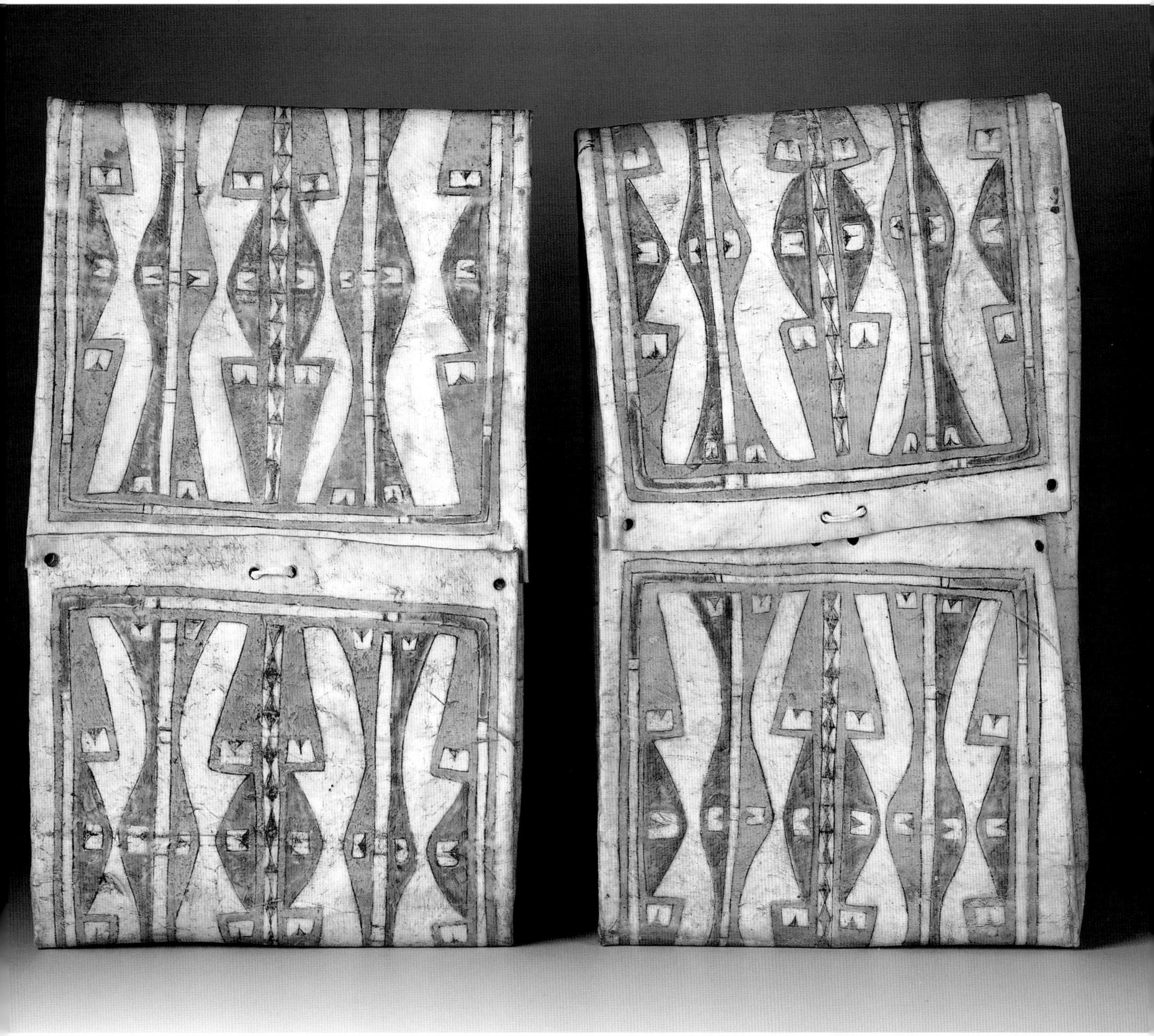

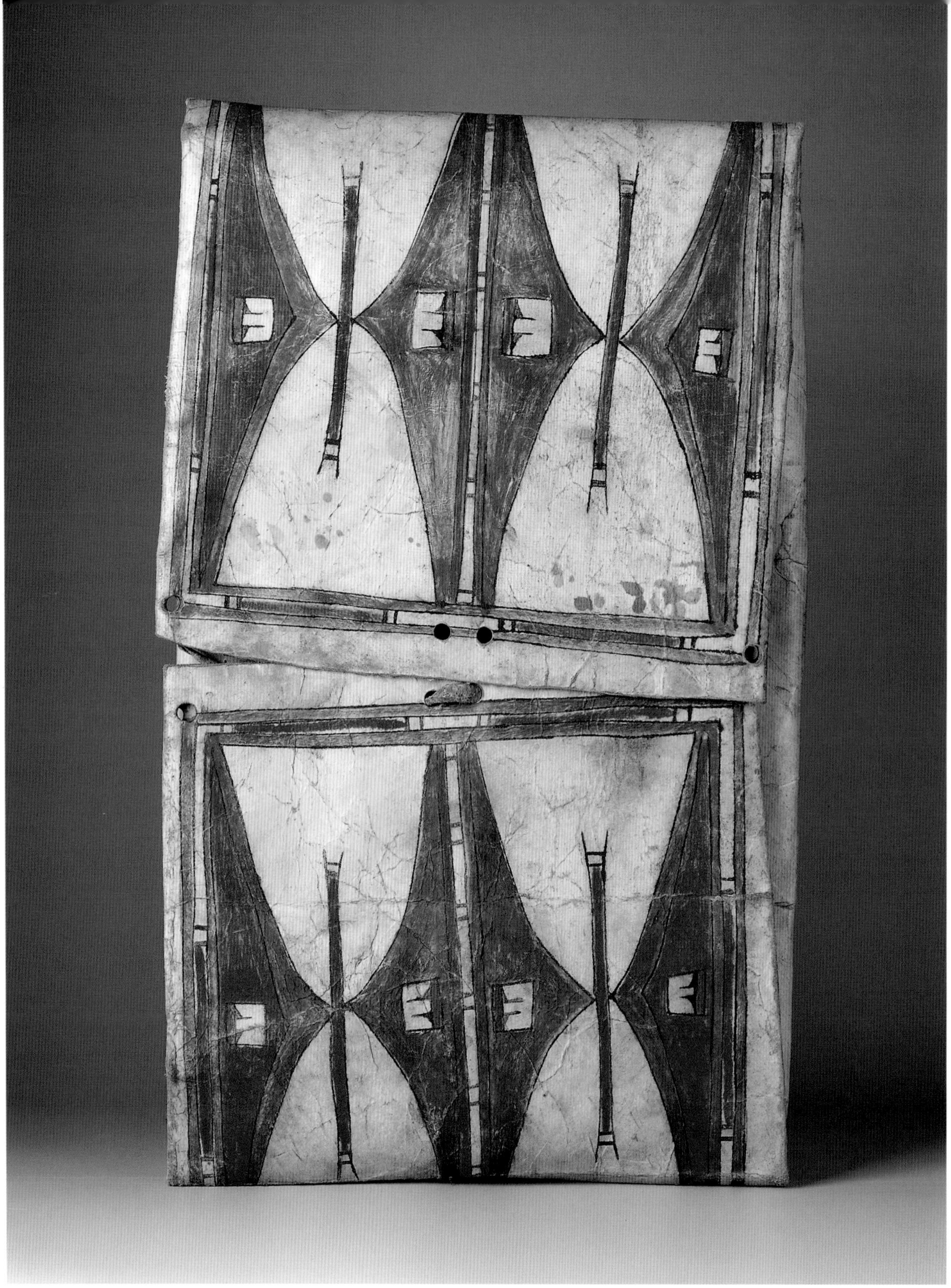

26 / **Cheyenne envelope, ca. 1860**

L 26 1/2 in., W 15 1/2 in. Buffalo rawhide, pigment

Catalogue entry states: "Captured from the Kiowa Indians; General George A. Custer, Lt. Col. of the U.S. Cavalry commanding expedition. Wichita Mountains. Indian Territory [Oklahoma]: Capt. C. S. deGraw, Asst. Surgeon, U.S. Army, Fort Dodge, Kansas"; probably acquired during the campaigns of 1868–69; one of a pair. National Museum of the American Indian, Smithsonian Institution, 15/8681

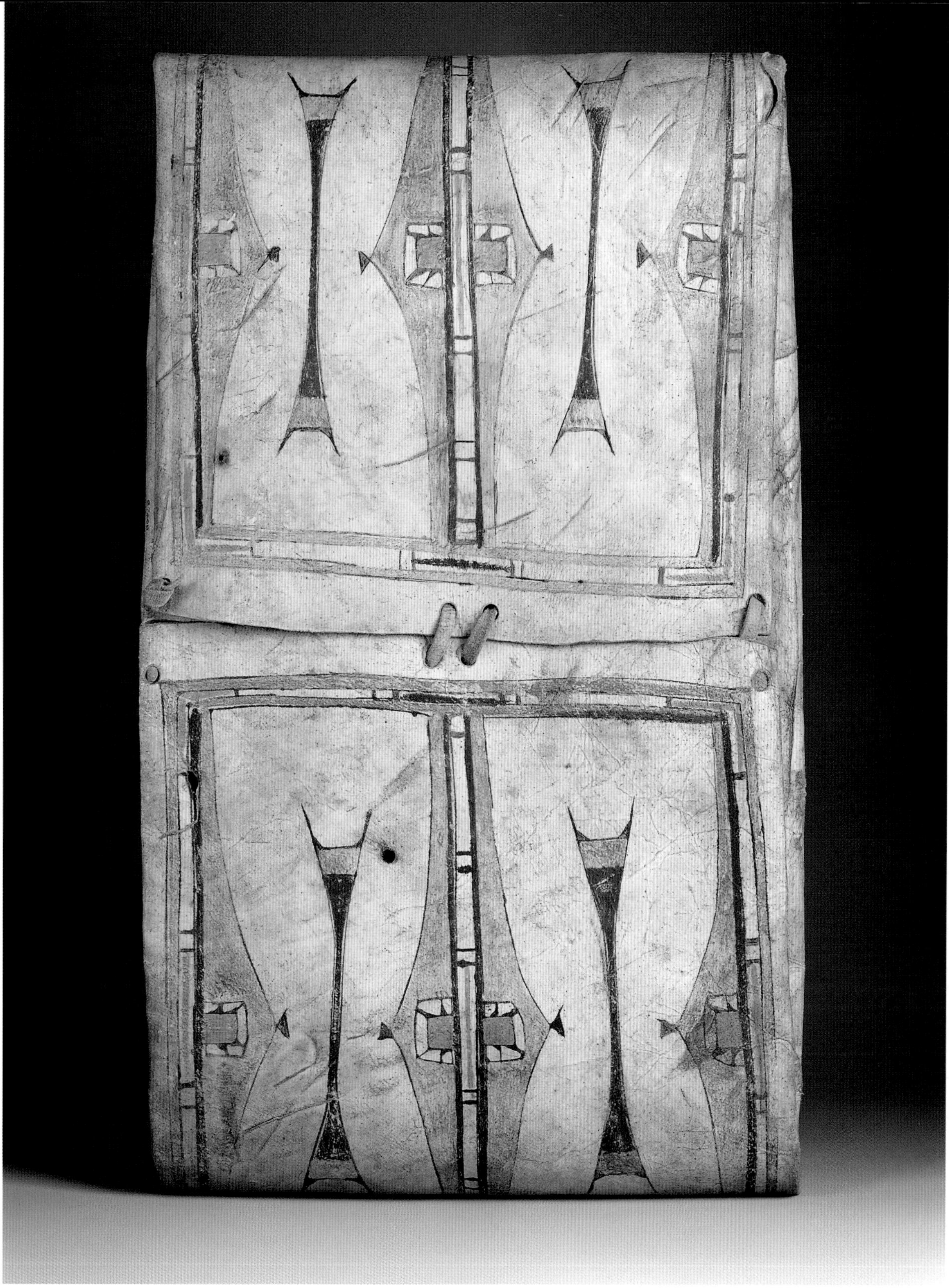

27 / **Cheyenne envelope, ca. 1865**

L 29 in., W 16 1/2 in. Rawhide, pigment

Collected by H. R. Voth when missionary to the Southern Cheyenne and Arapaho in Oklahoma during the 1880s; possibly acquired in 1889. Field Museum of Natural History, Chicago, 67468

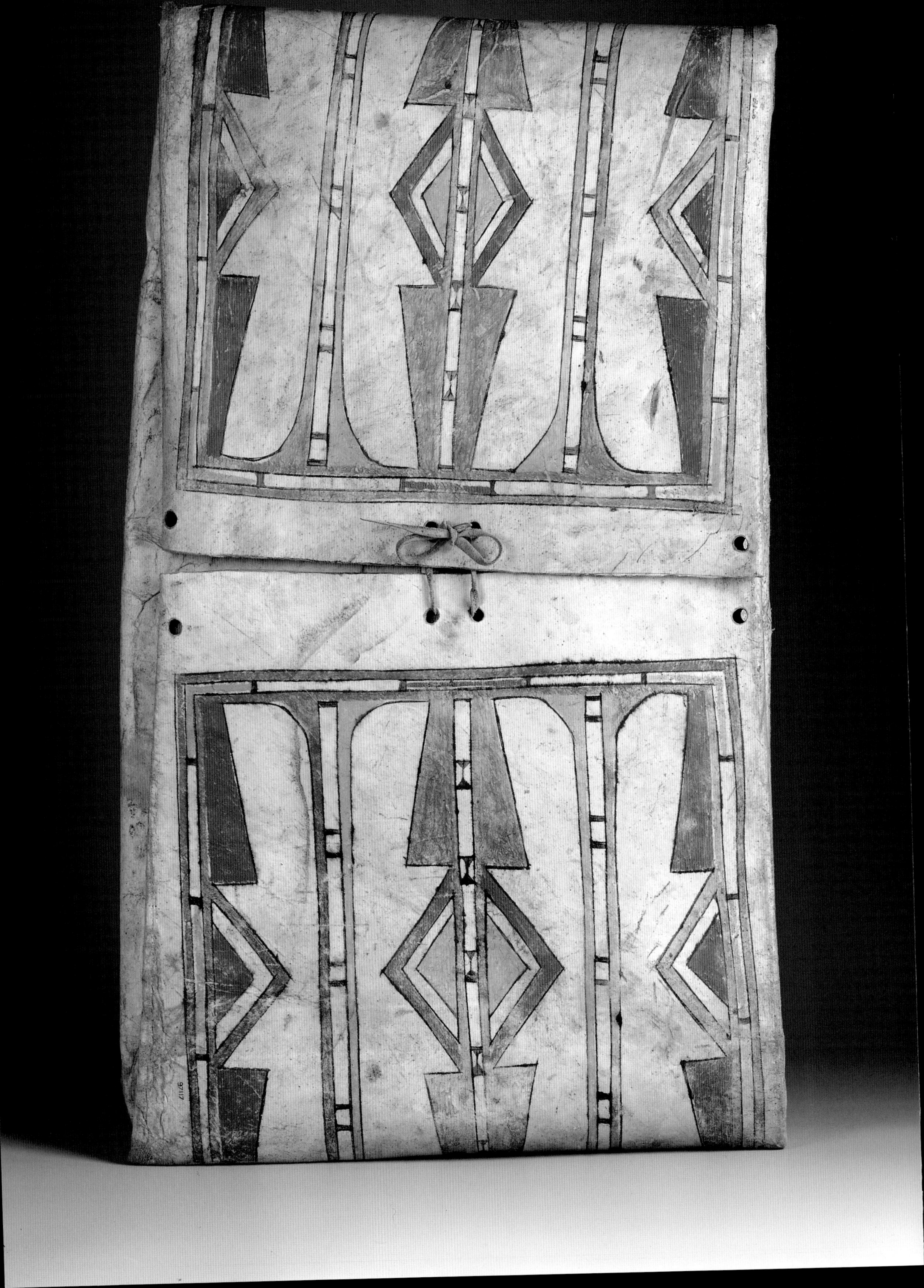

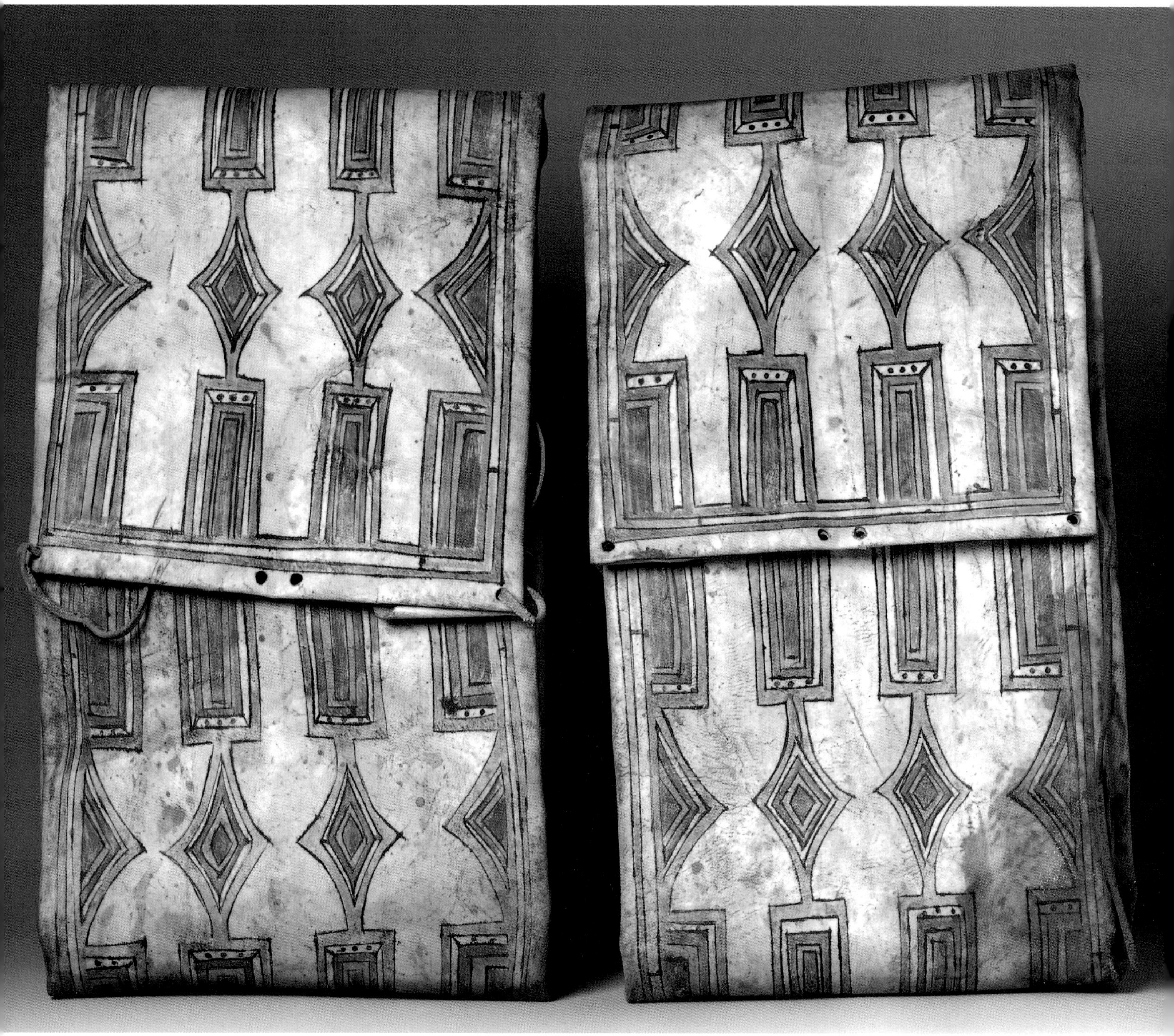

28 / **Cheyenne envelope, ca. 1875**

L 27 in., W 15 1/2 in. Rawhide, pigment

Collected by James Mooney at Darlington, Oklahoma, 1904; matching envelope in the collection of the Buffalo Bill Historical Center, Plains Indian Museum, Cody, Wyoming. Field Museum of Natural History, Chicago, 97117

29 / **Cheyenne pair of envelopes, ca. 1885**

Each L 25 in., W 14 in. Rawhide, pigment

Field Museum of Natural History, Chicago, 179795

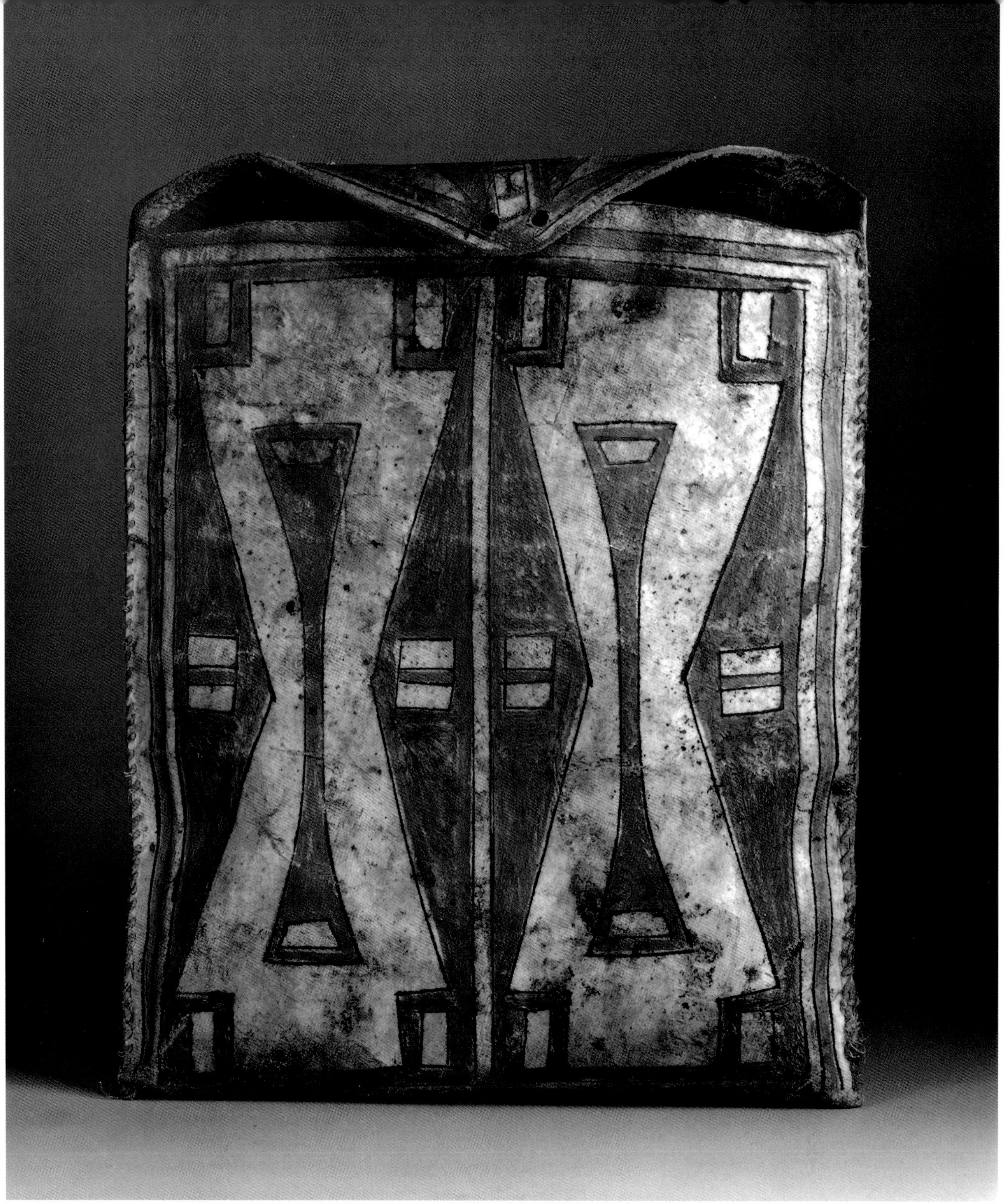

30 / **Cheyenne flat case, ca. 1860**

H 13 in. (not including flap), W 12 in. Buffalo rawhide, pigment

Collected at Fort Keogh, Montana, 1893; accessioned as Sioux. National Museum of Natural History, Department of Anthropology, Smithsonian Institution, 395583

31 / **Cheyenne flat case, ca. 1860**

H 15 in. (not including flap and suspensions), W 15 1/2 in. Buffalo rawhide, pigment, horse hair, buffalo tail

Collected by William Wildschut in Montana. National Museum of the American Indian, Smithsonian Institution, 13/5303

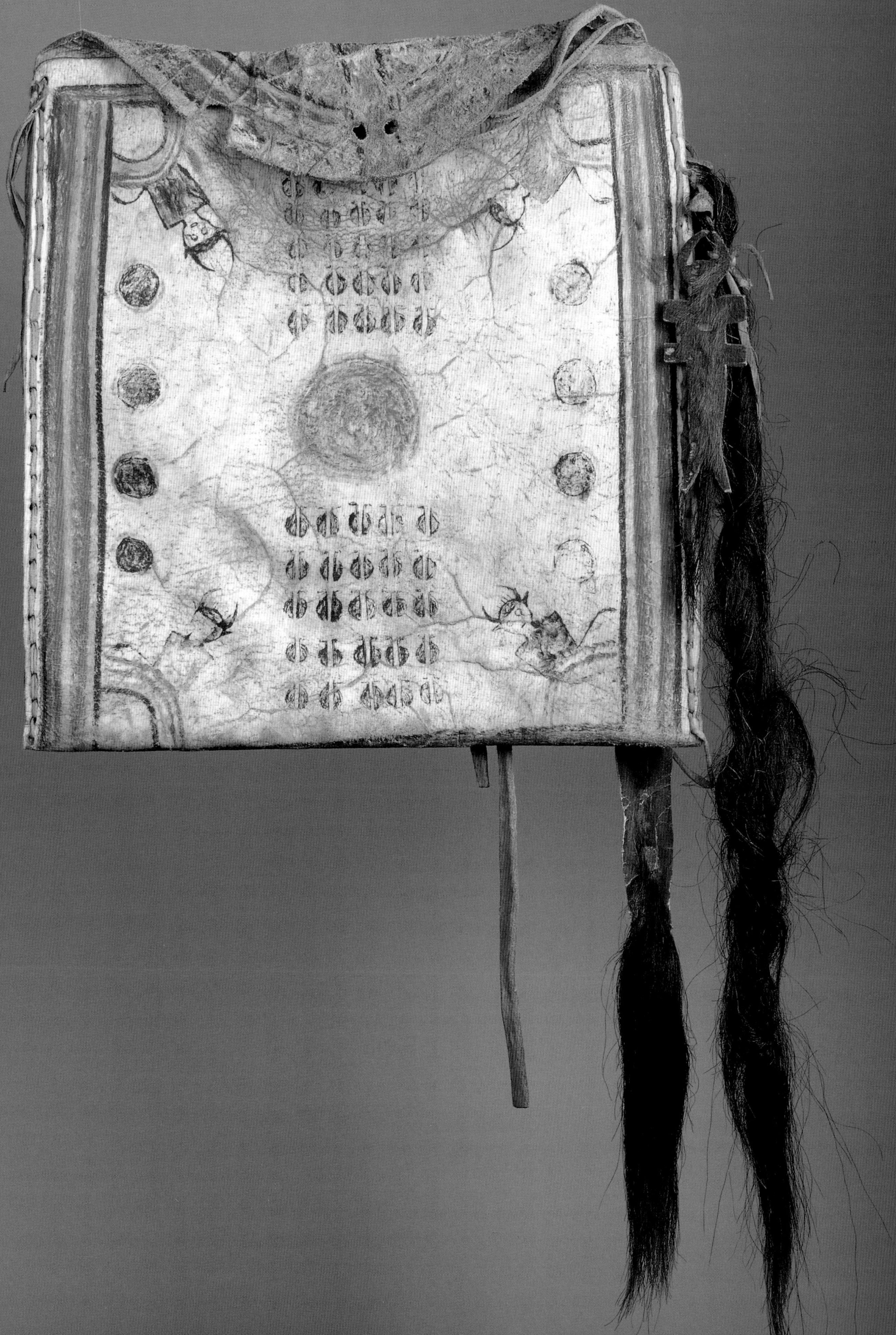

ARAPAHO

The Arapaho were closely allied with the Cheyenne and, like that tribe, separated into Northern and Southern bands by the mid-nineteenth century. They also maintained close ties with the Sioux, and the stylistic traits of their parfleches reflect both of these associations. Indeed, the most finely painted Arapaho parfleches are often misidentified as Cheyenne because of their close similarity in composition, delicate coloration, and precise outlining (pl. 33); others are clearly derived from Sioux designs, incorporating the strong color and heavy drawing preferred by that tribe (pl. 37 R). It should also be noted that the Arapaho people were once joined with the Gros Ventre, and this distant relationship is visible in the early parfleche patterns of the two tribes. Morrow notes that the Arapaho themselves acknowledged the influence of Apache painting on their designs, and one may discern a close affinity with Kiowa painting as well. It is not surprising, then, that the elements of Arapaho style are difficult to characterize and the parfleches sometimes hard to identify.

Large numbers of Arapaho parfleches are preserved in museum collections, largely due to the efforts of Alfred Kroeber and George Dorsey at the turn of the century. A survey of these pieces reveals not only a great range of stylistic features but of technical skill and care in the preparation of rawhide and application of sizing. This diversity extends to the character and quality of painting and drawing as well.

Although they share many of the same features of design and style, Arapaho parfleches do not often possess the sense of reserve that distinguishes most Cheyenne work. In general, Arapaho designs are more freely painted than those of the Cheyenne, and the definition of elements is less exact. The outlining is expressively drawn and rendered less precisely in the delineation of colored forms. Arapaho artists often integrated small black-brown elements within their paintings in the same manner as the Cheyenne, but had a greater tendency to divide primary shapes into radiating bands of different colors (pls. 33, 37 R).

Conversely, Arapaho parfleches that reflect the influence of Sioux designs, in comparison with parfleches actually produced by the Sioux, project a more delicate sensibility in their drawing and subtle coloration. Sioux influence is most apparent at the turn of the century, but parfleches closely associated with Cheyenne style continued to be made as well, and both types are equally present in collections obtained from the Southern and Northern divisions.

The relative importance of color and its particular character varies considerably, from soft, nearly transparent hues to dark, saturate tones. In some paintings, the strokes of the artist's tools in the application of color remain quite visible, imparting visual texture and color modulation (pl. 35). Arapaho women used an exceptionally wide range of colors, and these were often combined in unusual and unexpected ways. In addition to the relatively pure reds, yellows, blues, and greens, vari-

32 / **Arapaho envelope, ca. 1850**

L 29 in., W 16 3/4 in. Buffalo rawhide, pigment

Collected by Col. John Upham in the 1870s. Milwaukee Public Museum, 327

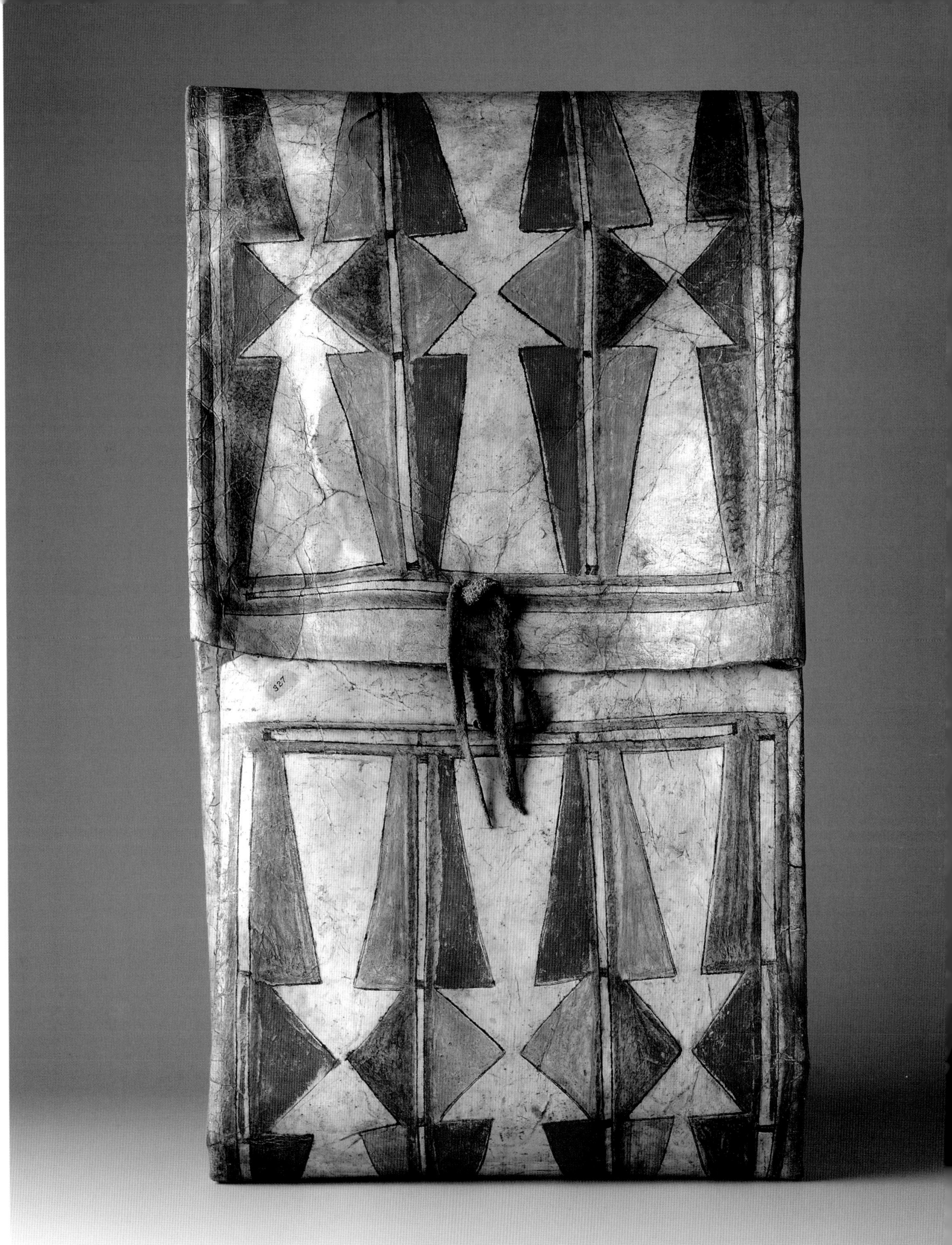

ous shades and tints of these hues were common, possibly achieved through a mixture of paints. A number of Arapaho parfleches may be seen which include a distinctive dark brown (pl. 35) as one of the principal colors. This unusual feature is seldom found in the work of the Cheyenne or Sioux. Pale rose, golden orange, and remarkable blue-greens are common as well. Many paintings are formed of medium-value colors, while others rely on strong contrasts for their effect.

Two compositions used on envelopes are recognized as the oldest and most traditional (Kroeber 1902: 109). The first is illustrated in plate 32 and is unique to the Arapaho, although the principal design unit from which it is composed appears in the composition of several tribes, particularly the Cheyenne (pl. 28), Kiowa (pl. 41), and Blackfeet (pl. 80). This unit is formed of an equilateral or isosceles triangle joined at each side by an elongated right triangle and the three triangles are aligned so that their bases form a continuous edge. In the Arapaho composition, the panel is divided into three rectangles; the triangular units are placed along all the vertical edges, creating a complex pattern that is horizontally and vertically symmetrical, leaving an unpainted, stepped hourglass in the center of each rectangle. The alignment of the central triangles establishes a horizontal band through the center of the image. The resulting composition, which is beautifully organized but somewhat static due to the repetition and symmetry of the elements, is dramatically offset by the unexpected transposition of color throughout the painting. This design (or variants of it) often appears on flat cases as well as envelopes.

The second design (pl. 33), said to be the older of the two, is called by the Arapaho *wasixta,* or "bear foot" (Kroeber 1907: 110). It is more commonly known as "five-box" or "five-spot," and its use was also widespread throughout the Plateau region (pl. 113). The image is basically composed of a square or rectangle in each corner of the panel with a larger rectangle located in the center. Usually the central figure is attached to the border by triangular forms at the top and bottom, and the corner boxes are frequently rendered as truncated triangles as in the design of the envelope illustrated in plate 33. Often, pointed elements were incorporated into the blocks to represent bear claws, but these might also be depicted as tiny black squares. Variants of the five-box design were created by the Gros Ventre (pl. 63) and, occasionally, by the Piegan Blackfeet. A closely related composition that probably evolved from this pattern was produced by several tribes. It was created by inserting triangles between the corner elements and substituting a diamond for the central box (pl. 74).

A third composition favored by Arapaho women, for both envelopes and flat cases, is based on an elongated central diamond (pls. 35, 36). This composition is essentially the same as one of the primary Cheyenne designs previously described (pl. 27); the main difference distinguishing the two lies in the definition of the larger forms: the contours of Cheyenne designs are generally curved, while those of the Arapaho

33 / **Arapaho envelope, ca. 1875**

L 28 3/4 in., W 15 in. Rawhide, pigment

Collected by George Dorsey for the Fred Harvey Company, 1903. Courtesy of The Carnegie Museum of Natural History, Pittsburgh, 31-79-309

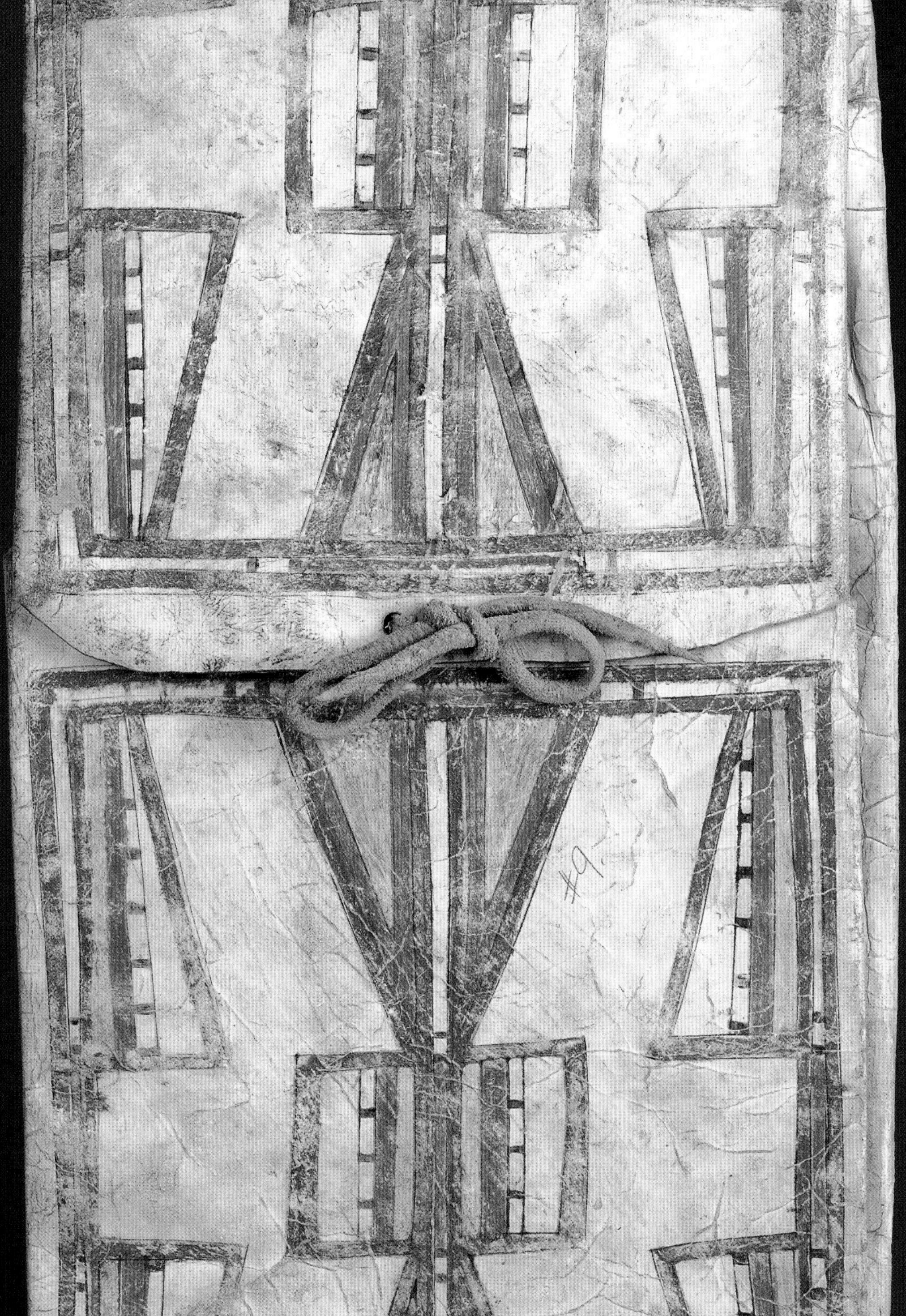
#9

are straightedged. Other Arapaho compositions are formed of triangle-diamond-triangle configurations either as the central figure or placed side by side between wide borders at the sides and a matching central band down the center, in imitation of Sioux patterns.

The borders of Arapaho parfleches are nearly identical to those of the Cheyenne, in that they are formed of two narrow lines of identical color with bars of contrasting color enclosed at regular intervals. The Arapaho, however, tended to place these elements only at the center of each side of the panel, leaving the corners open; Cheyenne artists placed them at the corners and often along the sides as well. Arapaho women did not paint the inner flaps of envelopes, nor did they join the panels with colored bands on the reverse side.

The most consistent feature differentiating Arapaho envelopes from those of the Cheyenne and Sioux is the number of holes used to secure the outer flaps. Arapaho women preferred one pair of holes located in the center of each flap, while the other two groups consistently used a single-pair-single pattern. The large numbers of well-documented Arapaho parfleches indicate that this structural feature never varied.

In addition to standard envelopes, the Arapaho produced a variety of flat cases. Some of them were elaborately fringed (pl. 38); others resemble Sioux cases in proportion, construction, and design (pl. 37). Still others closely resemble the unfringed cases of the Cheyenne. Elliptical cases were made that were similar in construction to those of the Sioux although some have flap closures like those of the Kiowa, but boxlike forms were never adopted. Several sun shades, knife sheaths, and at least one crupper have also been preserved.

A number of very beautiful, unfringed cylinders were collected, which were used for the storage of ceremonial objects (pl. 40). The compositions painted on these cases usually consist of horizontal bands, with inverted triangles arranged within the resulting panels; the design completely encircles the cylindrical form. Other images that are vision-inspired utilize the same banded format but incorporate symbolic figures. All of these cylinders are particularly distinguished by the lustrous, reddish brown color of their exterior surface. Kroeber (1907: 132) suggests that this color is possibly the result of their having been smoked. While this may account for part of their remarkable color, it appears to have been achieved mainly by the application of a thin, transparent coating of sacred red paint over the surface of the entire object. In some instances, the paint may have been mixed with sizing. Flat cases that served the same function were also embellished in this way (pl. 39). Whether cases and cylinders of this type were used for a singular class of sacred objects, or indicated the custom of a particular religious or warrior society, or reflected tribal practice during a specific time period, or differentiated the Northern from the Southern branch is unknown—but all were associated with ceremonial use. Other flat cases not finished in this manner were also used to hold ritual items, while others were intended for secular use.

34 / **Arapaho envelope, ca. 1885**

L 25 in., W 13 1/2 in. Rawhide, pigment

Collected by Alfred L. Kroeber, 1900, probably on the Wind River Reservation, Wyoming. American Museum of Natural History, 50/1045

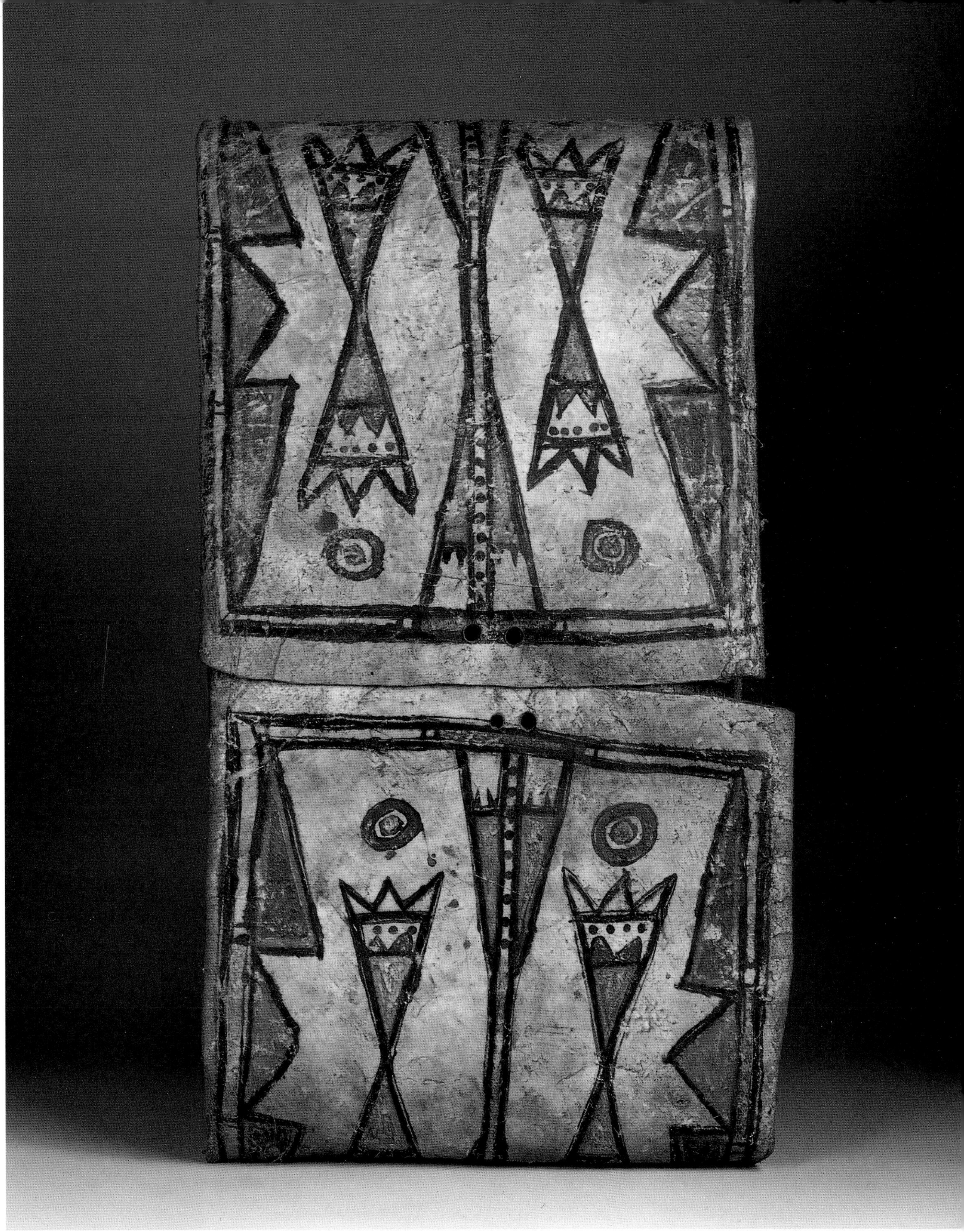

123 CENTRAL PLAINS

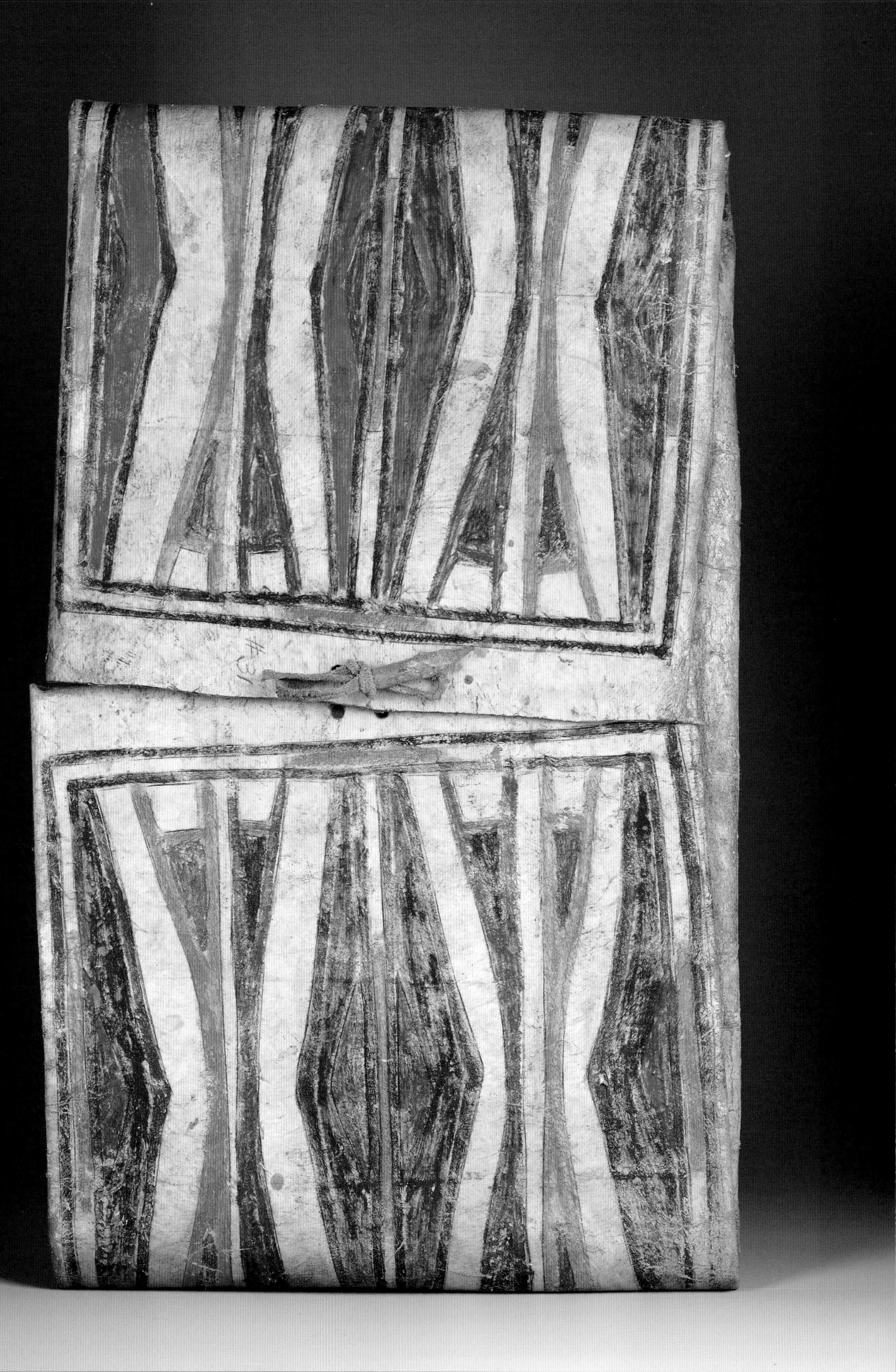
#31

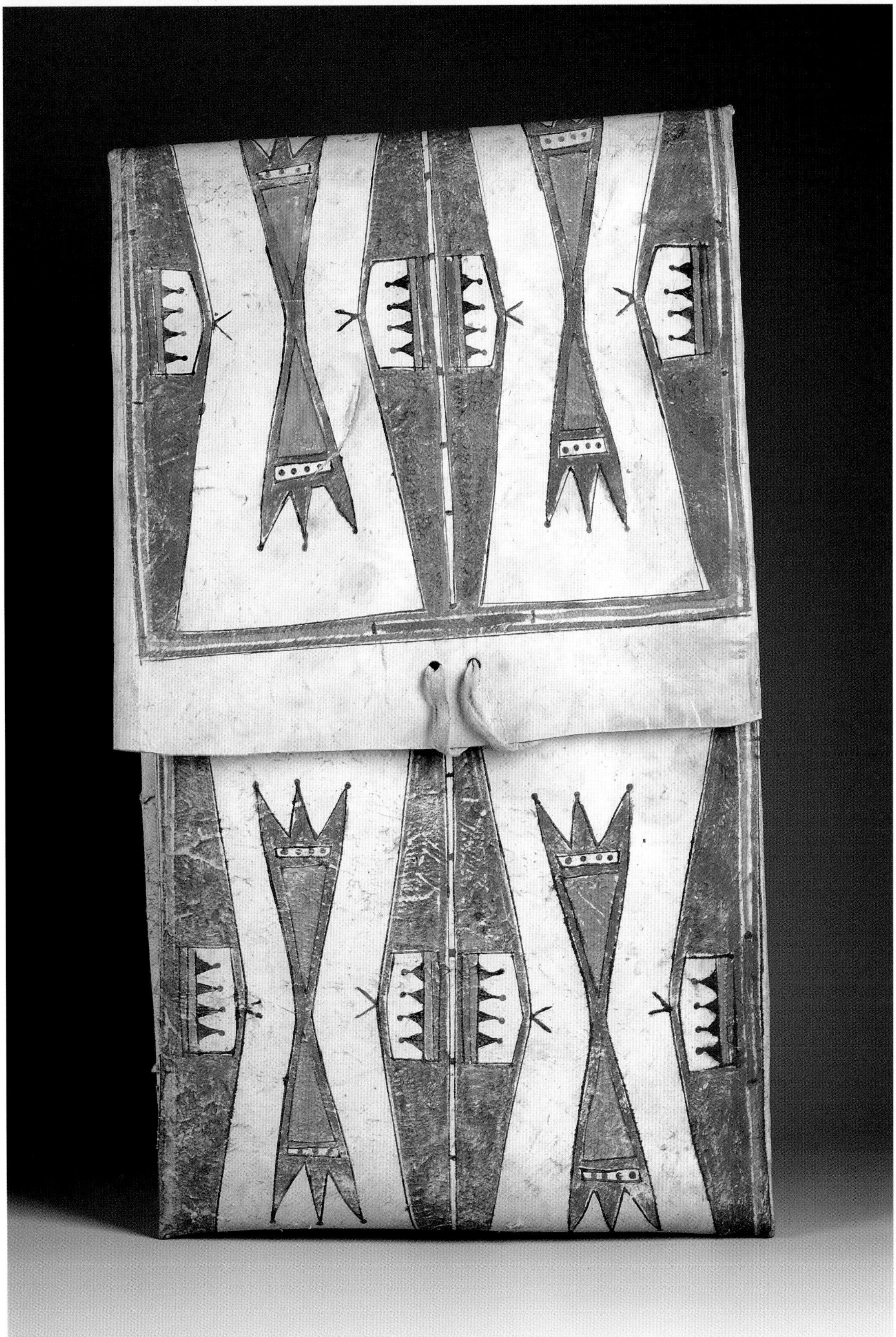

35 / **Arapaho envelope, ca. 1885**

L 27 in., W 15 1/2 in. Rawhide, pigment

Collected by George Dorsey in Oklahoma, 1903.

Field Museum of Natural History, Chicago, 71962

36 / **Arapaho envelope, ca. 1900**

L 26 in., W 15 1/2 in. Rawhide, pigment

Collected by George Dorsey in Oklahoma, 1903.

Field Museum of Natural History, Chicago, 71960

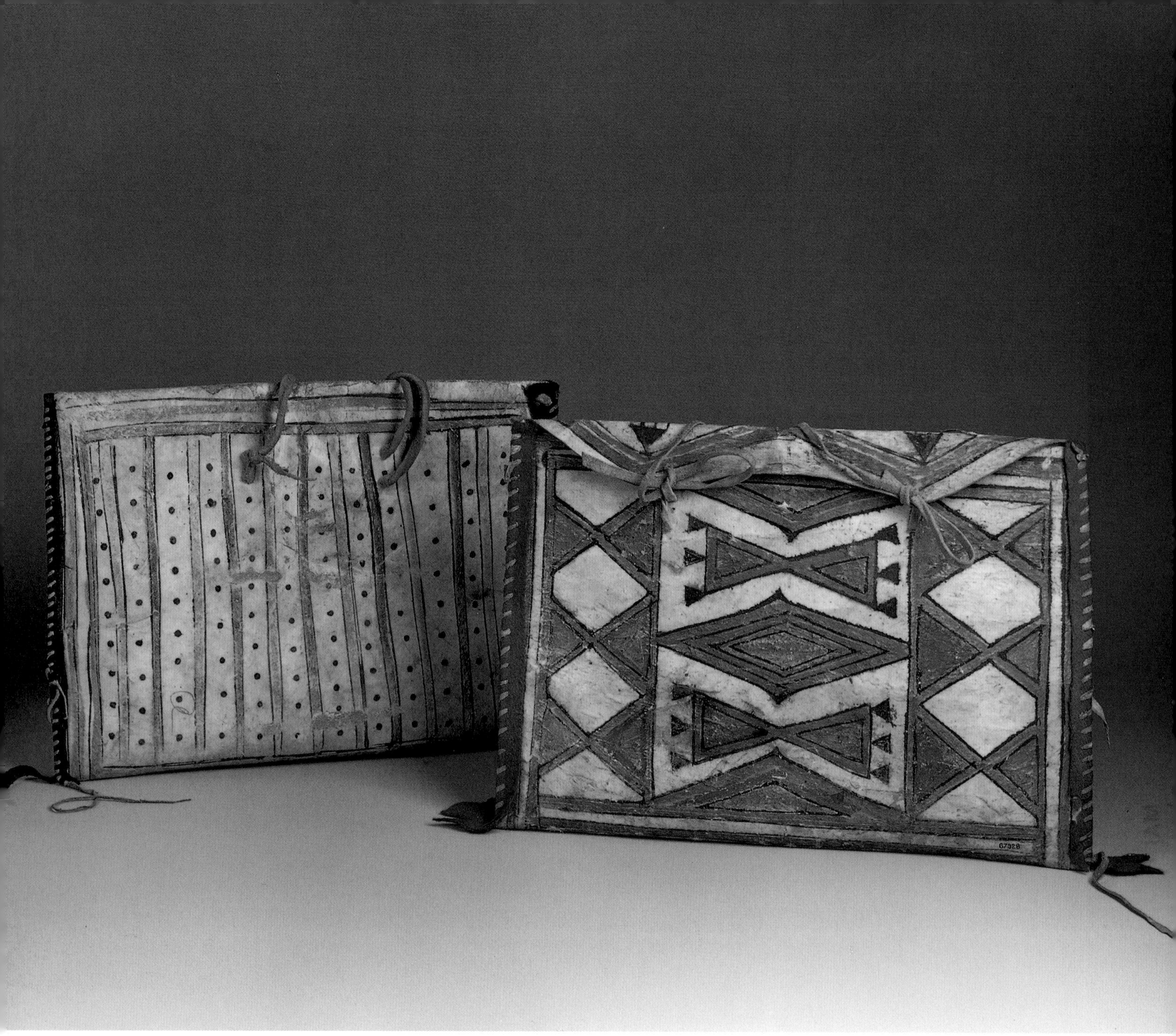

37 / **(right) Arapaho flat case, ca. 1900**
H 11 in., W 16 1/4 in. Rawhide, pigment, wool cloth

Collected by Fred Harvey in Oklahoma, 1905.
Field Museum of Natural History, Chicago, 67328

(left) Arapaho flat case, ca. 1900
H 10 3/4 in., W 15 in. Rawhide, pigment, wool cloth

Collected by George Dorsey in Oklahoma, 1903.
Field Museum of Natural History, Chicago, 71970

38 / **Arapaho flat case, ca. 1850**
H 9 1/2 in. (not including flap), W 9 3/4 in.; height with fringe 28 in. Buffalo rawhide, pigment, native leather, glass beads, porcupine quills

Masco Collection

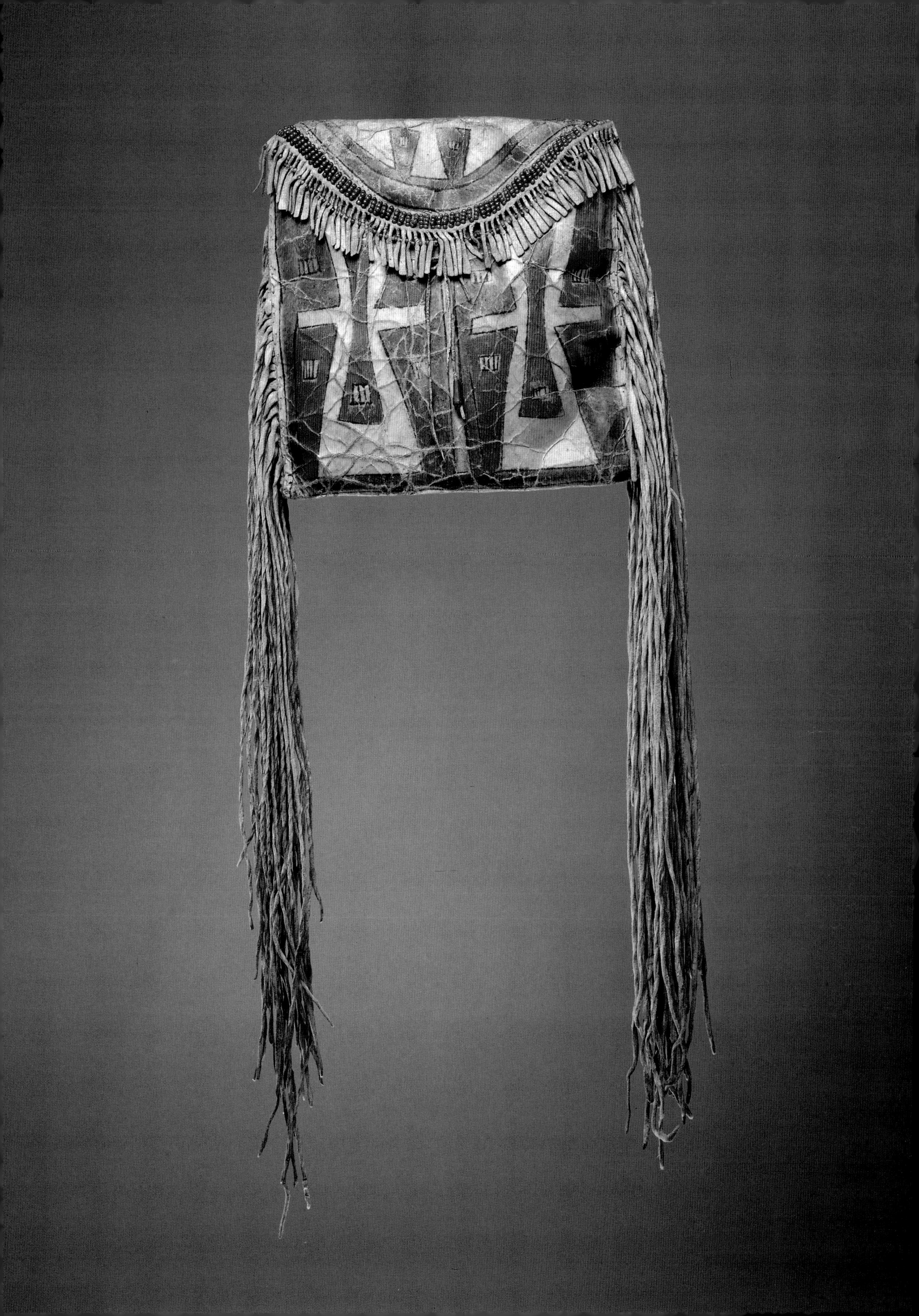

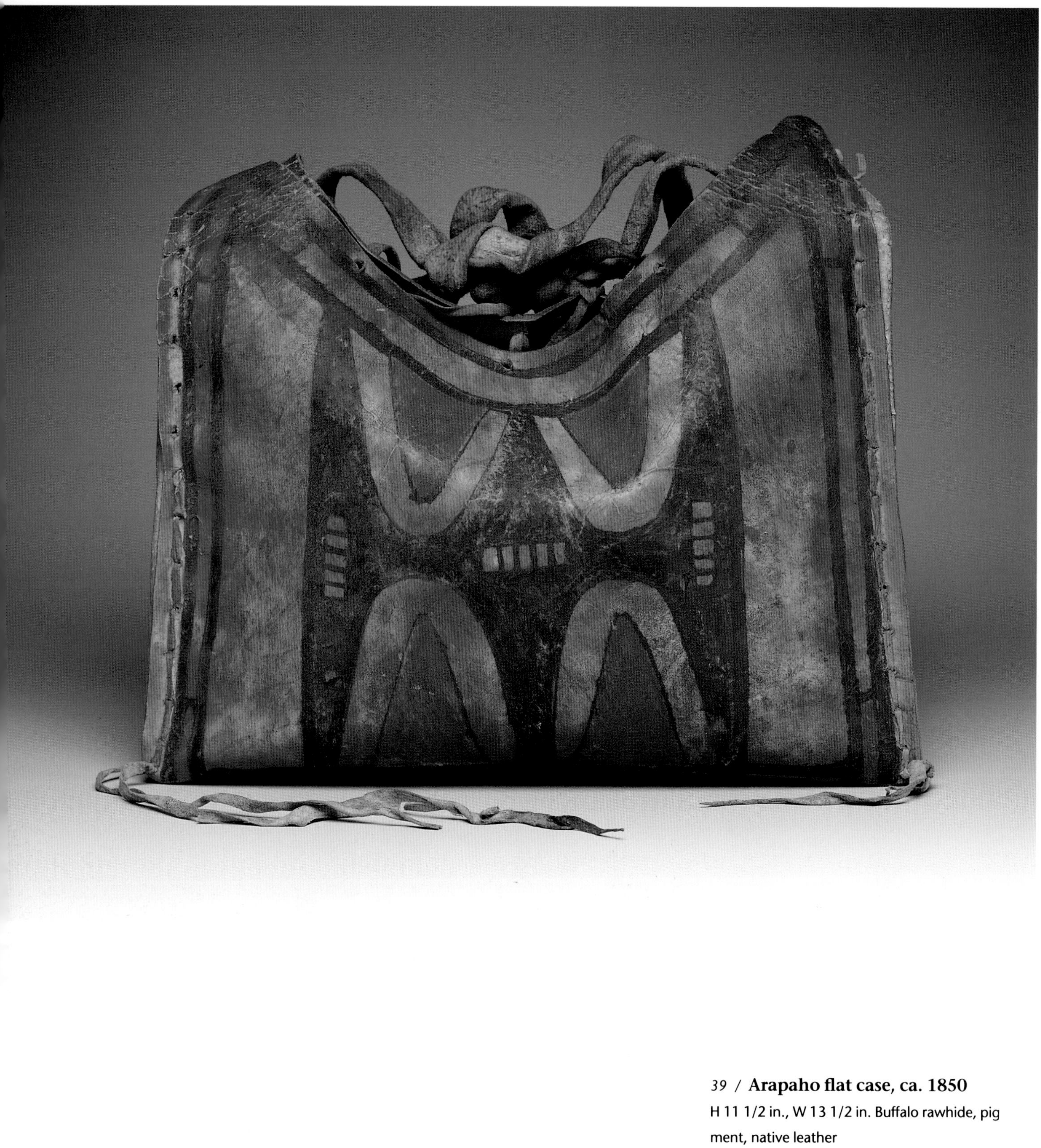

39 / **Arapaho flat case, ca. 1850**

H 11 1/2 in., W 13 1/2 in. Buffalo rawhide, pig ment, native leather

Collected in Oklahoma. Private collection

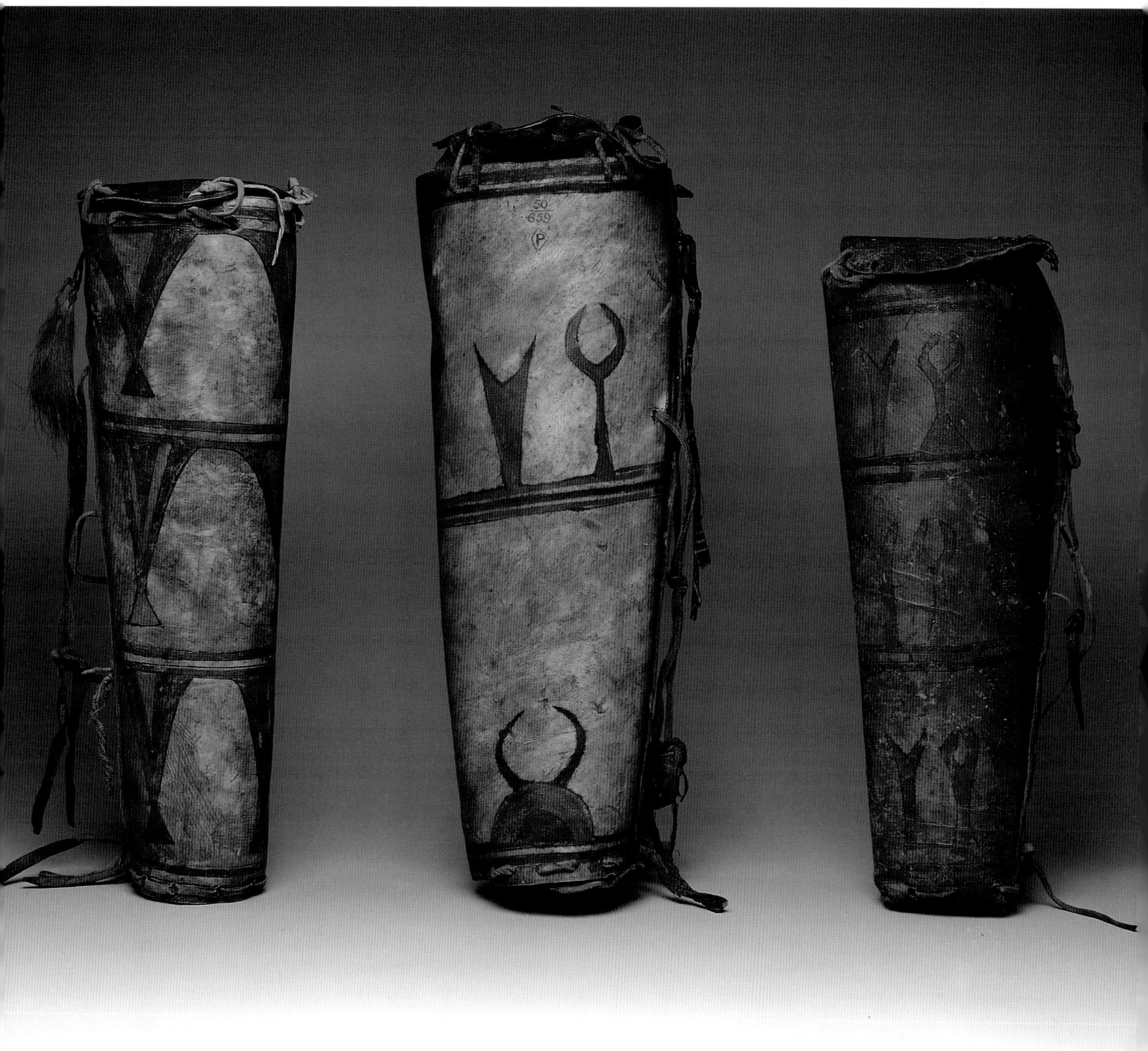

40 / **Arapaho cylinder, ca. 1860**
H 18 1/2 in., D 6 in. Buffalo rawhide, pigment

Collected by Alfred L. Kroeber, 1899. American Museum of Natural History, 50/688

Arapaho cylinder, ca. 1850
H 19 in., D 6 in. Buffalo rawhide, pigment

Collected by Alfred L. Kroeber, 1899. American Museum of Natural History, 50/659

Arapaho cylinder, ca. 1850
H 17 in., D 5 in. Buffalo rawhide, pigment

Collected by Alfred L. Kroeber, 1899. American Museum of Natural History, 50/401

MANDAN, HIDATSA, ARIKARA

The Mandan, Hidatsa, and Arikara inhabited permanent earth-lodge villages along the upper Missouri River, subsisting by agriculture and buffalo hunting. After their numbers were severely decimated by smallpox and cholera epidemics during the first half of the nineteenth century and, to some extent, as a result of warfare with surrounding tribes, they settled together on the Fort Berthold Reservation in North Dakota.

Little is known of the parfleches produced by these peoples. None that predates the reservation period is known to exist, and those few collected at Fort Berthold around the turn of the century are indistinguishable from Sioux work.[2] Some of these are even specifically recorded as having been acquired from the Sioux in trade; all the others are stylistically inseparable and are, in fact, probably of Sioux origin (pl. 15). This is not surprising, considering the active trade relations these tribes maintained with the Sioux, the close proximity of Standing Rock Reservation, and the extensive parfleche production maintained by Sioux women during this period. Indeed, the Missouri River villages were always important centers of intertribal trade,[3] and it may be that the majority of painted rawhide containers used by these peoples were always obtained through exchange. If not, Mandan, Hidatsa, and Arikara women had so thoroughly adopted the tenets of Sioux painting by the reservation period that any distinguishing features remaining from an earlier style had completely disappeared.

2. Several of these are pictured in Gilman and Schneider (1987), and provide an excellent indication of the types of parfleches collected from the Fort Berthold peoples during the early years of the twentieth century.

3. See Taylor (1984) for an informative discussion of selected aspects of the trade systems joining the tribes of the Central Plains and Plateau regions. Essays by Galante and Lessard in the same publications provide additional information on this subject, particularly as it affected artistic production.

Southern Plains and Southwest

The Southern Plains region was dominated by the Comanches from the early 1700s, after they migrated in from the northwest and displaced a number of Plains-dwelling Apache groups. At the beginning of the nineteenth century, they were joined in the area by the Kiowa, who became their close allies. About 1840 the two tribes then formed an alliance with the southern divisions of the Cheyenne and Arapaho, thus extending their power and influence into the Central Plains. The Eastern Apache bands—specifically the Lipan, Mescalero, and Jicarilla—established themselves in the intermontane regions of eastern New Mexico, surrounding the Rio Grand Pueblos on three sides. To the north of the Jicarilla, in Colorado, were the Ute.[4] All of these peoples produced parfleches with related characteristics, resulting in the formation of a generally unified regional style.

4. For excellent historical overviews of the Southwest, including multicultural and intertribal relations within the region, see Fehrenbach (1974) and John (1975).

KIOWA

Kiowa parfleches, particularly their envelopes, are similar in many respects to those of the Cheyenne and Arapaho, and the general features of their painting are consistent with other neighboring tribes in the region. Yet in details they remain a distinct body of works. Those found in collections today consist principally of envelopes, cylinders, and a distinctive type of flat, unfringed vertical case with an elliptical bottom and flap closure at the top.[5] The Kiowa apparently did not produce the elaborate, side-fringed flat cases seen throughout the Southern Plains region that were in common use by their Comanche and Arapaho allies and by their Apache enemies. One large flat case of the type favored by the Comanches (pl. 47) and possibly produced by a woman of that tribe was collected from the Kiowa, which probably indicates its use among both peoples. Most Kiowa cylinders are large and, like those of the Arapaho, unfringed. Only one exceptionally beautiful early case believed to be of Kiowa origin (pl. 43) has been found that is embellished with long twisted fringe in the manner of those produced by the Comanche, Apache, and Pueblo groups. Small flat cases were surely made in considerable numbers, but only one painted with conventional geometric designs is known to have been preserved. As with the other tribes of the Southern region, no boxes or trunks were ever produced.

5. See the examples illustrated in Morrow (1975) on pages 110 (center) and 111 (right). Although the case pictured on page 111 is identified there as Comanche, it was collected from the Kiowa and accessioned accordingly by the National Museum of Natural History, Smithsonian Institution. The painting style confirms its Kiowa origin.

The number of Kiowa parfleches known to have survived is very small—fewer than twenty-five have been located in this study. Nine of these are cylinders, seven are envelopes, and the remainder are flat cases of various types. All appear to date from the mid-nineteenth century to about 1880, which may account for the strong uniformity of style. It also suggests that parfleche production ceased soon after the Kiowa people were settled on their reservation, which would help explain the small numbers collected.

The majority of Kiowa parfleches are painted in red, yellow, green, and a dark Prussian blue, in addition to brown-black outlining. On some pieces, either blue or green is omitted from this limited palette, and a few are painted only in red and yellow.

The designs are outlined in dark brown or black; the quality of the drawing tends to be spirited and rather fluid, yet conveys a sense of refinement. This outlining is always used to separate the major painted configurations from unpainted areas, but adjacent colors within the larger forms are not always separated by line. Occasionally, distinct elements within larger figures are not outlined at all but used in conjunction with others that are. All of these features are clearly seen in the painting on a large early cylinder (pl. 42). Also visible in this work are two other distinguishable features of Kiowa painting. The first is the practice of leaving narrow, unpainted areas—actually bands—between bands of color comprising larger design configurations. The second is the inclusion of small, unpainted, outlined blocks within the design; these are often trapezoidal, but might also be square, rectangular, triangular, or somewhat irregular in form. Similar small, unpainted elements, often of circular form are commonly seen in Comanche and Apache designs as well (pl. 53). Kiowa women also included small black units within many of their designs, sometimes using them in repetition with great effect.

The painted designs of most Kiowa envelopes are organized in similar fashion (pl. 41). Nearly all feature a central band vertically dividing the panel into two parts; this band is elaborated with a configuration of elements that forms a central design running from top to bottom. It is notable that this band, which is always unpainted and filled with some arrangement of black elements either simple or complex, is generally wider than the same band in similar Cheyenne or Arapaho designs. The elements along the sides usually mirror those of the central figure, but this is not always the case. The motifs comprising the predominantly straightedged compositions often incorporate curvilinear forms, and the overall panels are usually square in proportion.

The borders of Kiowa envelopes provide the greatest aid in identification. They consist of two narrow bands of colors with an unpainted space between. Each of the bands is composed of one color at the sides and another color at the ends; these colors are then transposed in the inner and outer bands. The only other tribe to practice this reversal of border color was the Gros Ventre of Montana, and other than this single feature, the parfleches of the two groups are quite distinct. Kiowa women often painted a bar of contrasting color between the bands in each corner in the manner of the Cheyenne, and sometimes included a few lines or blocks of brown-black.

Side flaps were never painted nor were bands of color used to connect the panels on the reverse side. The holes used to secure the outer flaps

41 / **Kiowa envelope, ca. 1865**

L 29 1/4 in., W 16 in. Rawhide, pigment

Collected by Brig. General James D. Glennan; entered in his catalog as "Kiowa trunk, . . . Purchased 1892, belonged to Hawgone's brother's child." National Museum of Natural History, Department of Anthropology, Smithsonian Institution, 385871

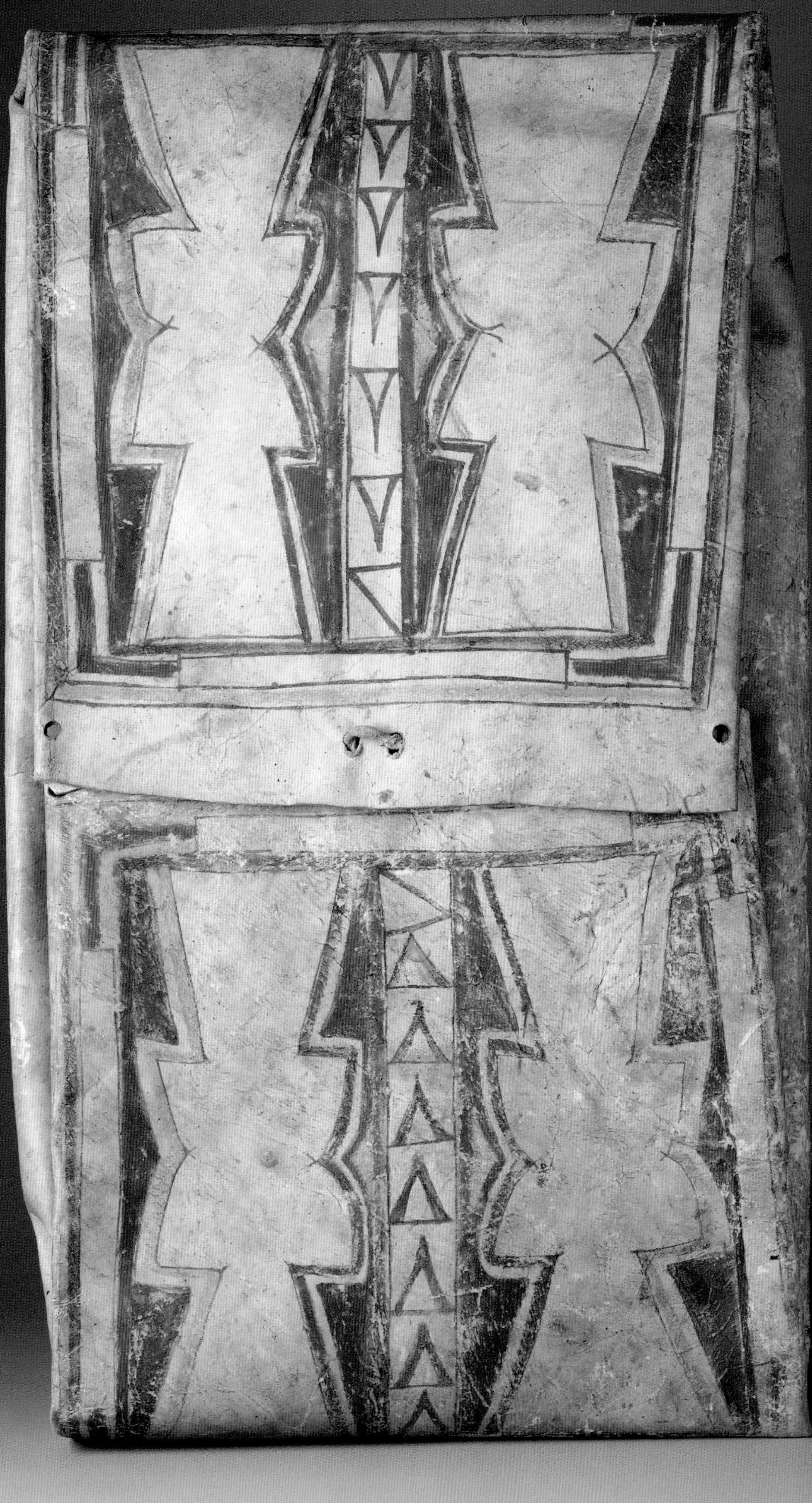

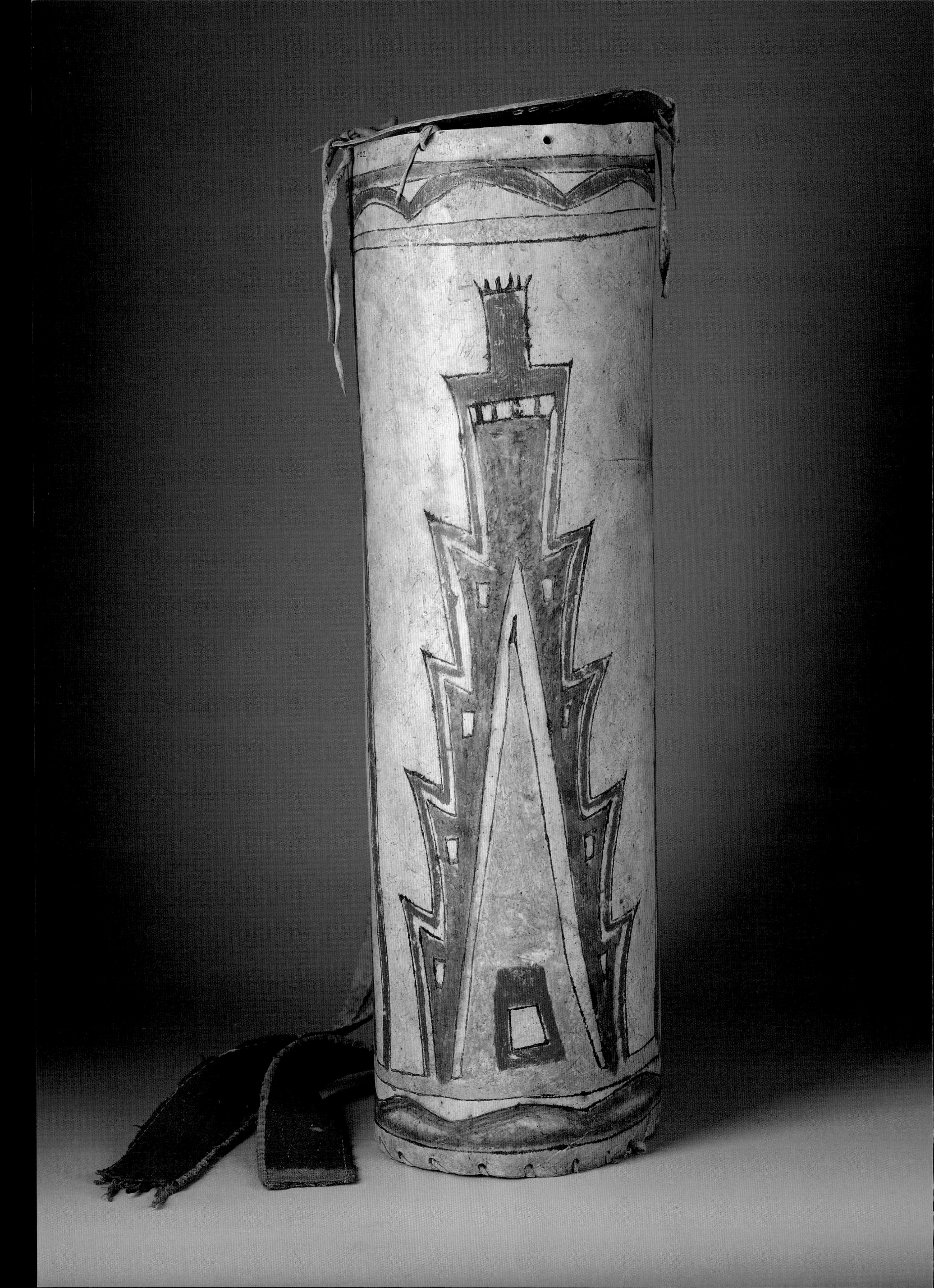

42 / **Kiowa cylinder, ca. 1850**

H 23 1/2 in., D 8 in. Buffalo rawhide, pigment, wool and cotton cloth

Collected by James Mooney. National Museum of Natural History, Department of Anthropology, Smithsonian Institution, 152966

See other side of this cylinder on page 6.

43 / **Kiowa cylinder, ca. 1850**

H 14 3/4 in., D 4 in.; fringe 21 in. Buffalo rawhide, pigment, native leather

Collection of Michael and Sherry Maxwell

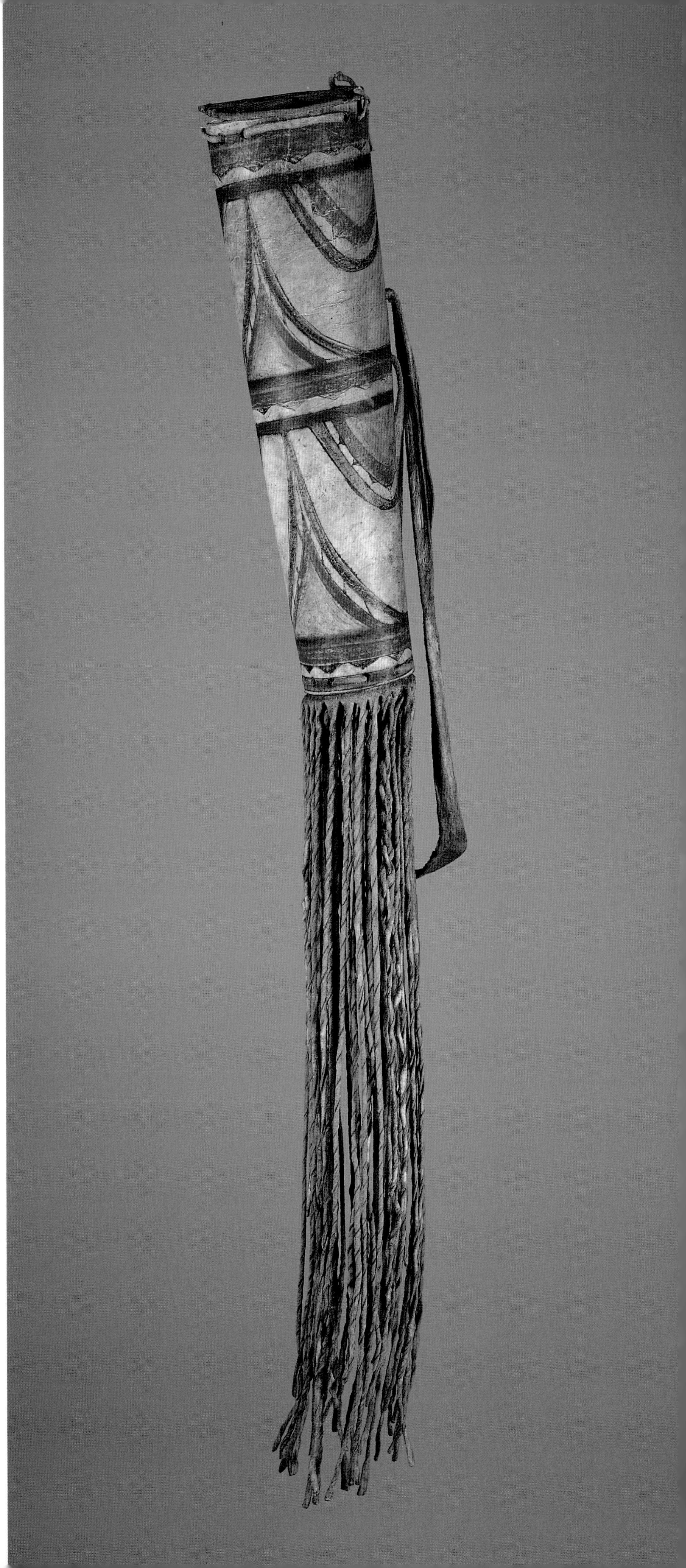

followed the same single-pair-single arrangement as the Cheyenne.

Kiowa cylinders are exceptional in the complexity of their compositions and in the precision and elegance of their painting. They are generally intended for headdresses and, therefore, are large in scale. The panel is often divided vertically into two parts and each side is painted with a contrasting design (pls. 42, 44), establishing a precarious and unexpected balance of diverse elements as the painting completely encircles the cylindrical form. Most compositions are banded horizontally on one or both sides; very few lack this feature. Those that are banded on one side only have an open field on the reverse, with a vertical configuration filling the space. The concept of a single, stepped figure emerging from the baseline (pl. 42) is rarely seen in parfleche imagery, but is a common feature of beaded designs executed on Kiowa pipe bags and small belt ponches. Inverted triangles with crescent forms (pl. 44)—one of the most prevalent features of Comanche cylinders—were also frequently used by Kiowa painters.

44 / **Kiowa cylinder, ca. 1875**

H 26 in., D 8 in. Rawhide, pigment

National Museum of the American Indian, Smithsonian Institution, 20/6424

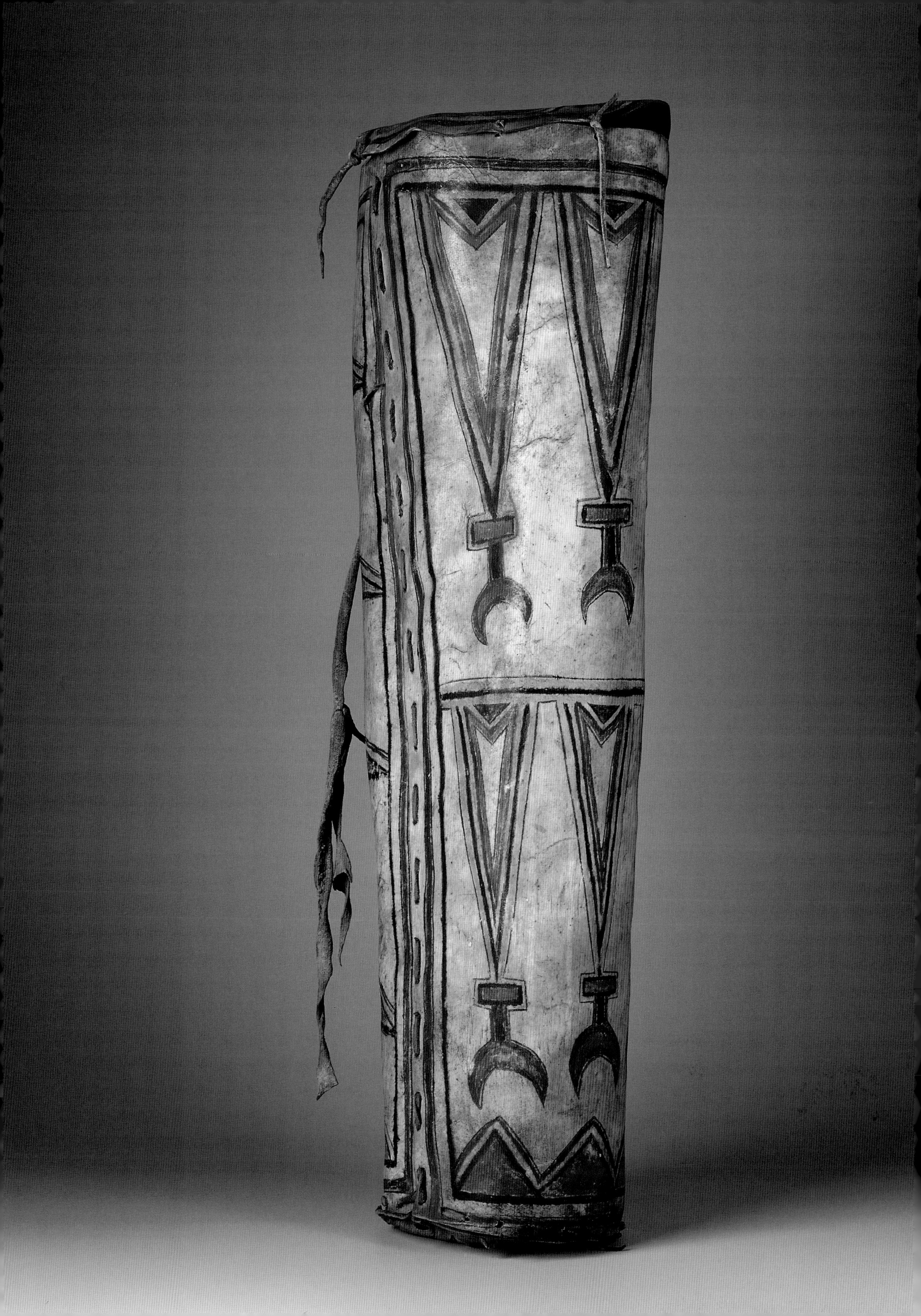

COMANCHE

Comanche parfleches are even fewer in number than Kiowa, which is surprising considering the size and historical importance of this tribe. Consequently, our knowledge is restricted by the small number of examples available for comparative study and further complicated by the fact that many Comanche parfleches are so similar to those of the Eastern Apache groups that it is difficult and sometimes impossible to differentiate them.

The great majority of parfleches known to have been collected from the Comanche are cylinders, and nearly all are painted with a variant of the same design (pl. 48). This consists of two, three, or four inverted triangles encircling the upper rim and a corresponding number of rectangular forms at the bottom. The triangles generally terminate in crescents although other motifs are sometimes substituted for this element, such as the stylized bear claws painted on the cylinder in plate 49. The sides of the triangles are usually bordered by a serrated edge of small black triangles or short, repeated lines, and the rectangular shapes below are similarly elaborated. On some examples, triangular or arching forms are substituted for the rectangles at the bottom.[6]

The finely painted case illustrated in plate 48 is unusual in its construction in that an undecorated piece of hide was added at the bottom to extend the length, but the superb painting is a classic example of Comanche style and composition. Many cylinders are fringed at the bottom in the manner of this piece, but others are not. This arrangement of fringe on the cylinder was common throughout the region and universally practiced by the Apache, Pueblo, and Ute. The method of attachment varied, but it was most typical for the fringe to be carefully sewn to the bottom rim of the case along the inside surface remaining below the recessed bottom disk. Another technique was to lace the fringe along the edge of the rim or sew it to the outside in such a way that its base flared slightly from the contour of the rawhide case.

The earliest parfleches collected from the Comanche were fringed flat cases. Variations of the composition painted on the Berlandier case (pl. 45) are found on three other documented Comanche parfleches, indicating that this configuration was commonly used. On one example it was aligned vertically but was identically structured with a central band bordered by four sweeping curves. The design ornamenting the case collected by Catlin (pl. 46) is organized quite differently, but also contains elements typically found in Comanche painting, specifically the inverted triangles and the alternating bands of light and dark bordering the image. This latter device is sometimes used as the top band on cylinders (pl. 48), but also appears as the central band in some compositions. This element was also used extensively by the Apache. It is notable that while Plateau artists often used a single row of light and dark blocks, they almost never doubled the band to create the

45 / **Comanche flat case, ca. 1830**

H 11 1/2 in. (not including flap), W 11 1/4 in.; height with fringe 24 in. Buffalo rawhide, pigment, native leather

Collected by Jean Louis Berlandier in Texas, 1828–51. Peabody and Essex Museum, Salem, Mass., E 3780

6. See the example illustrated in Morrow (1975: 110, upper left).

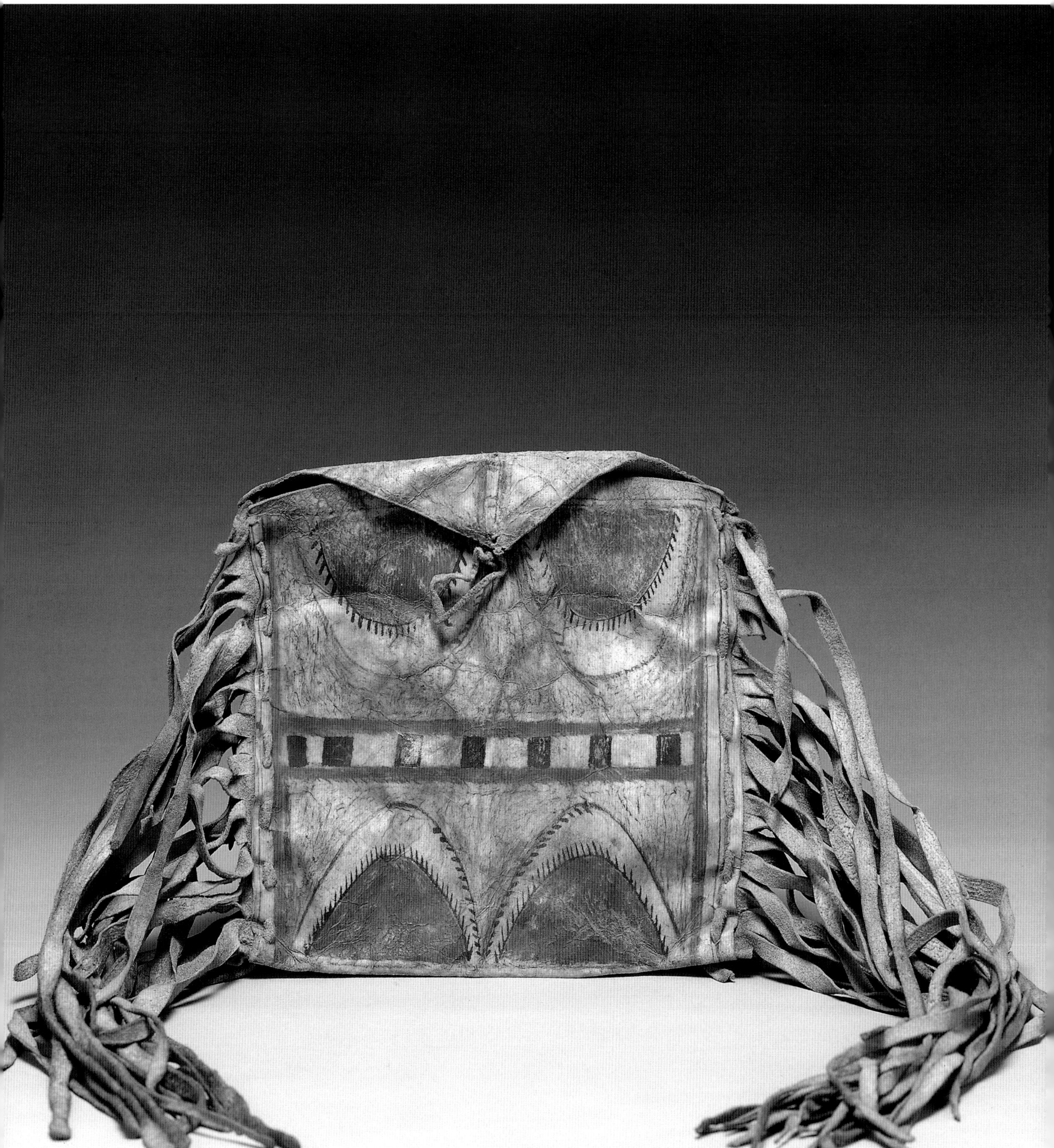

checkerboard effect favored by the Southwestern painters. The manner in which the edges within designs were conceived varied. Most paintings were rendered so that contours of major forms were outlined in black, with no linear separation of internal colors (pl. 48); others were simply drawn in color without black outlining (pl. 49), or incorporate it in only limited amounts. Often, a narrow, unpainted line was left between colors within the primary forms (pl. 46). The colors used were limited to red, yellow, blue and green, in addition to black outlining and smaller design elements, and many cases were painted with only two or three of these hues. It should be noted that, as a class, Comanche painting varies considerably in its degree of refinement, and in this respect differs from that of the Kiowa and Apache.

It is unknown if the Comanche ever produced the standard folded envelope, for none has been found in any collections. The only possible exception is one identified by Morrow (1975: 119) on the basis of its design. It features the same composition based on curvilinear elements described earlier, but other components equally suggest Apache origin. The Comanche apparently used a type of large, flat case (pl. 47), and may have preferred it over the envelope form. These cases, which were also made by the neighboring Wichita (pl. 8) and other Eastern Plains groups, are about the same size as a standard envelope but lack the capability of expansion. Only three examples of this type, all painted on the front side only, are known to have been collected from the Southern Plains. Of these, two were probably made by the same woman and are later examples collected at the turn of the century; however, another case dating from mid-century and collected from the Kiowa is identical in size and construction, and indicates that the type was used throughout the region during prereservation days as well.

46 / **Comanche flat case, ca. 1830**

H 10 1/2 in. (not including flap), W 10 in.; height with fringe 31 in. Buffalo rawhide, pigment, native leather

Accession records indicate that this case was probably collected by George Catlin and is of Comanche origin; Catlin visited the tribe in 1834; case accessioned by the Museum in 1884. National Museum of Natural History, Department of Anthropology, Smithsonian Institution, 73532

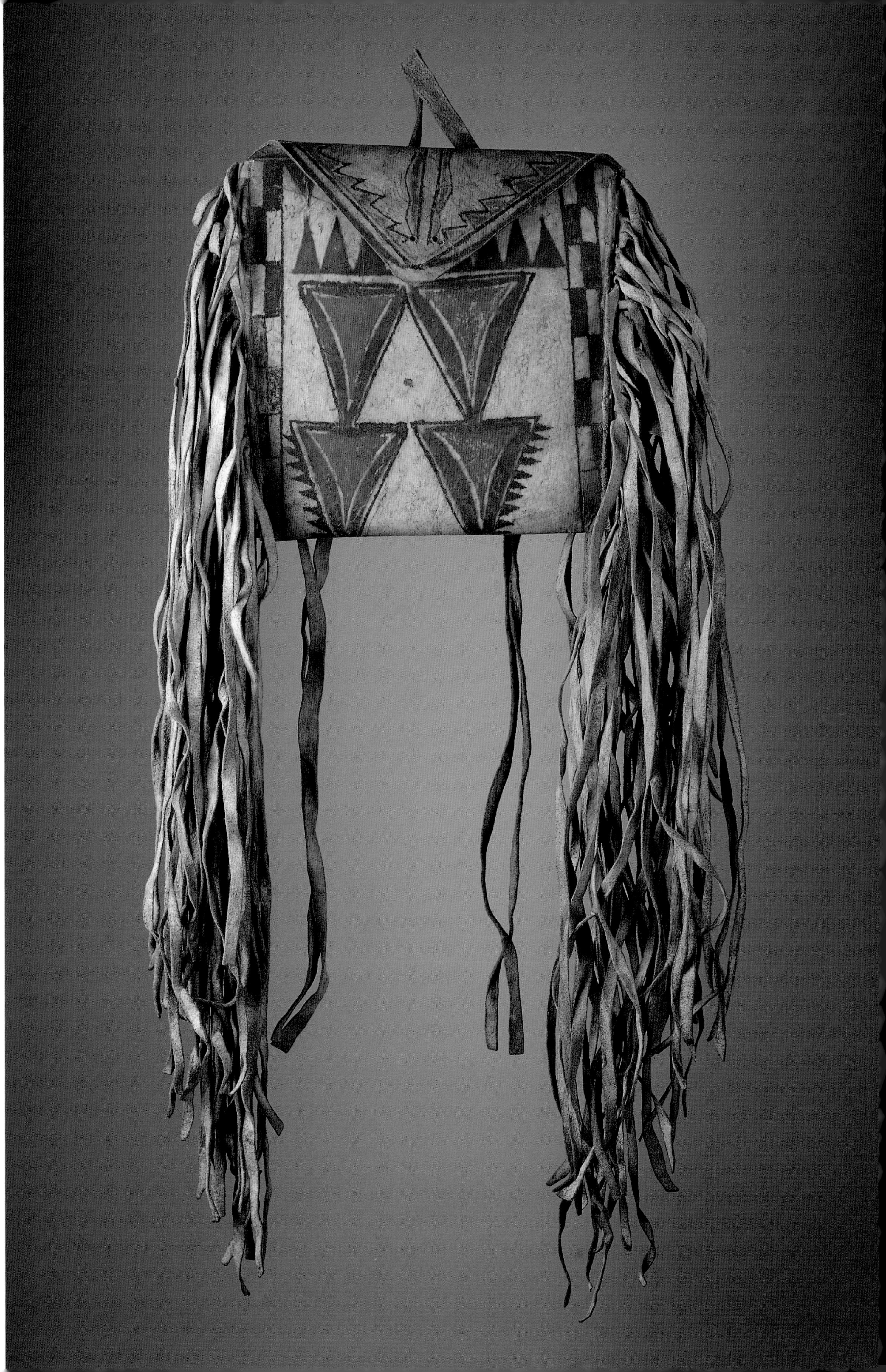

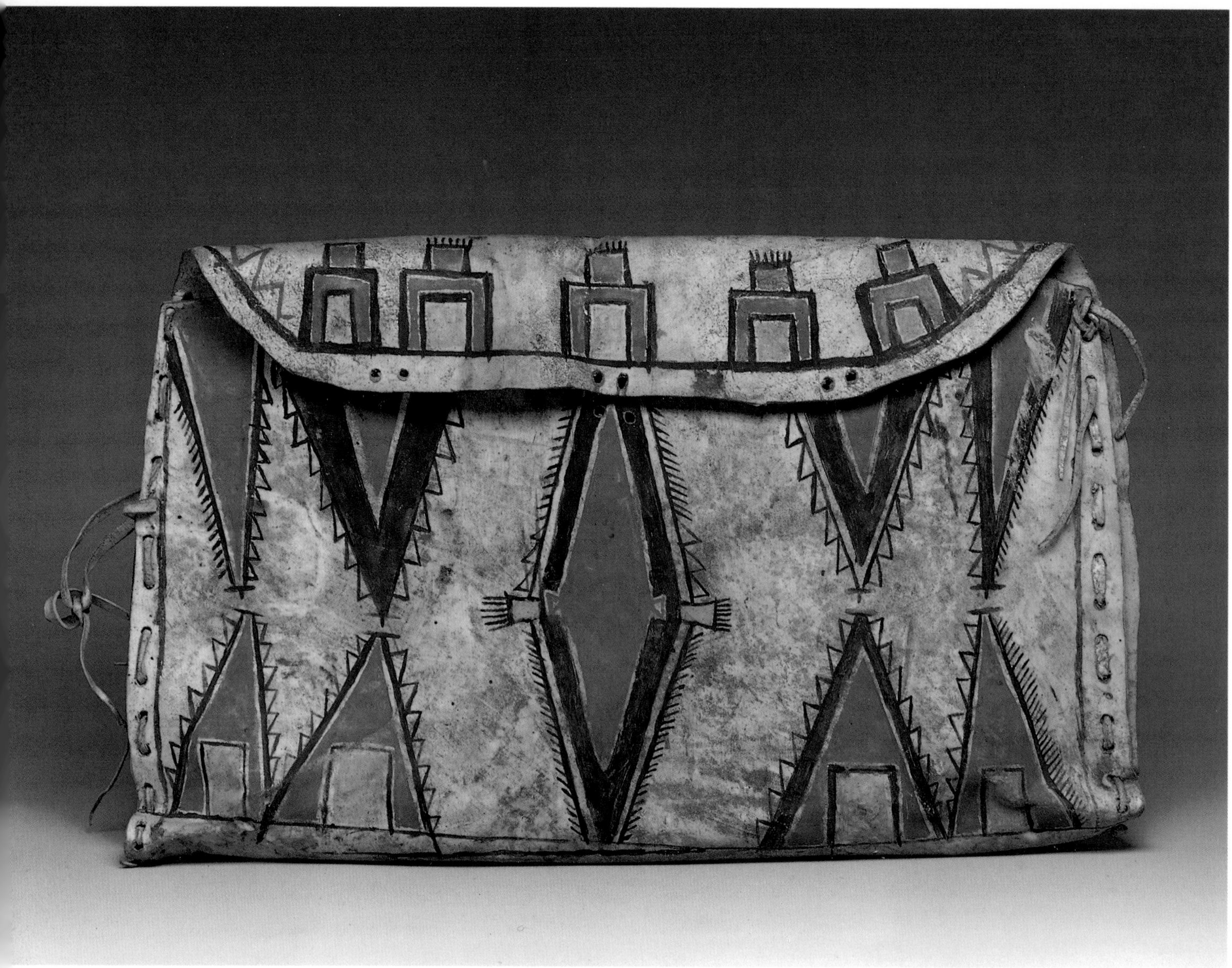

47 / **Comanche flat case, ca. 1900**

H 16 1/2 in. (not including flap), W 28 in. Rawhide, pigment

Collected by M. R. Harrington at Anadarko, Oklahoma, 1909. American Museum of Natural History, 50.1/4291

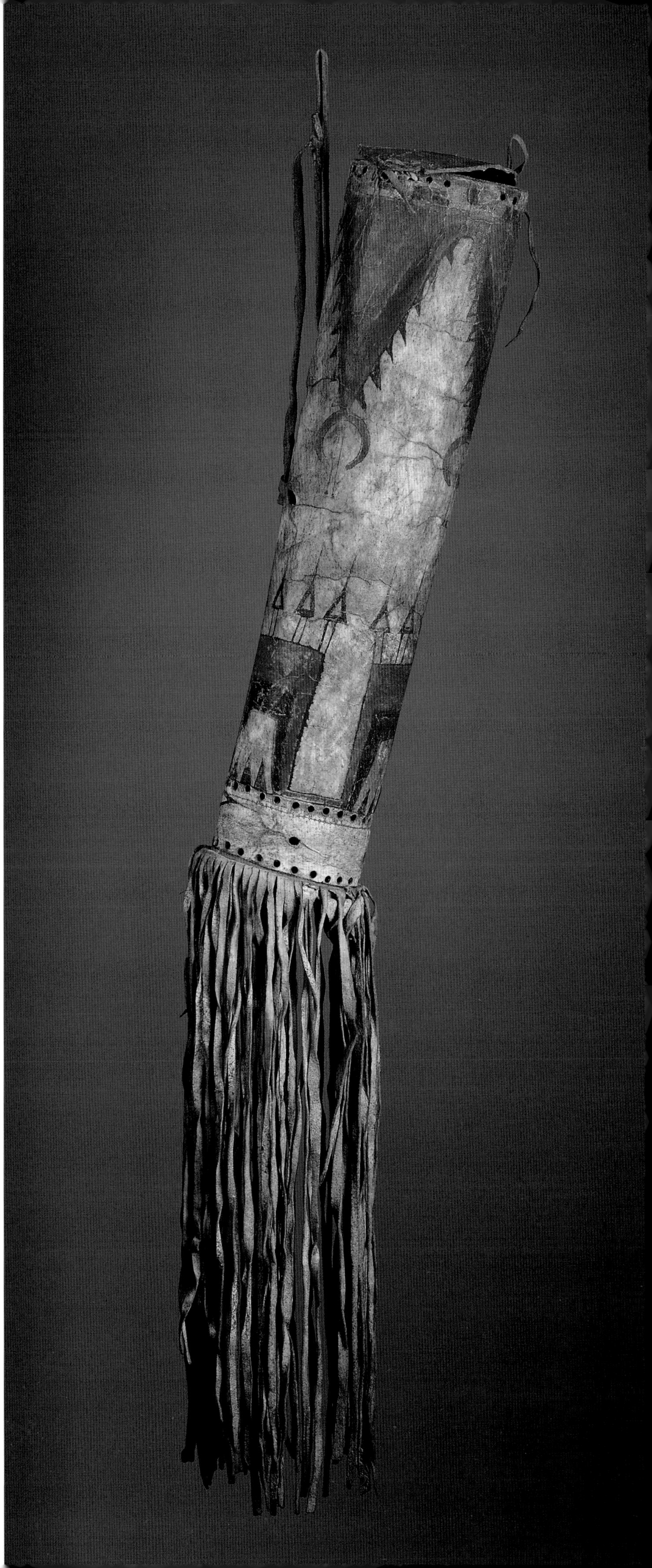

48 / **Comanche cylinder, ca. 1850**

H 22 in., D 4 1/2 in.; fringe 17 1/2 in. Buffalo rawhide, pigment, native leather

Accessioned as White Mountain Apache. National Museum of the American Indian, Smithsonian Institution, 19/3112

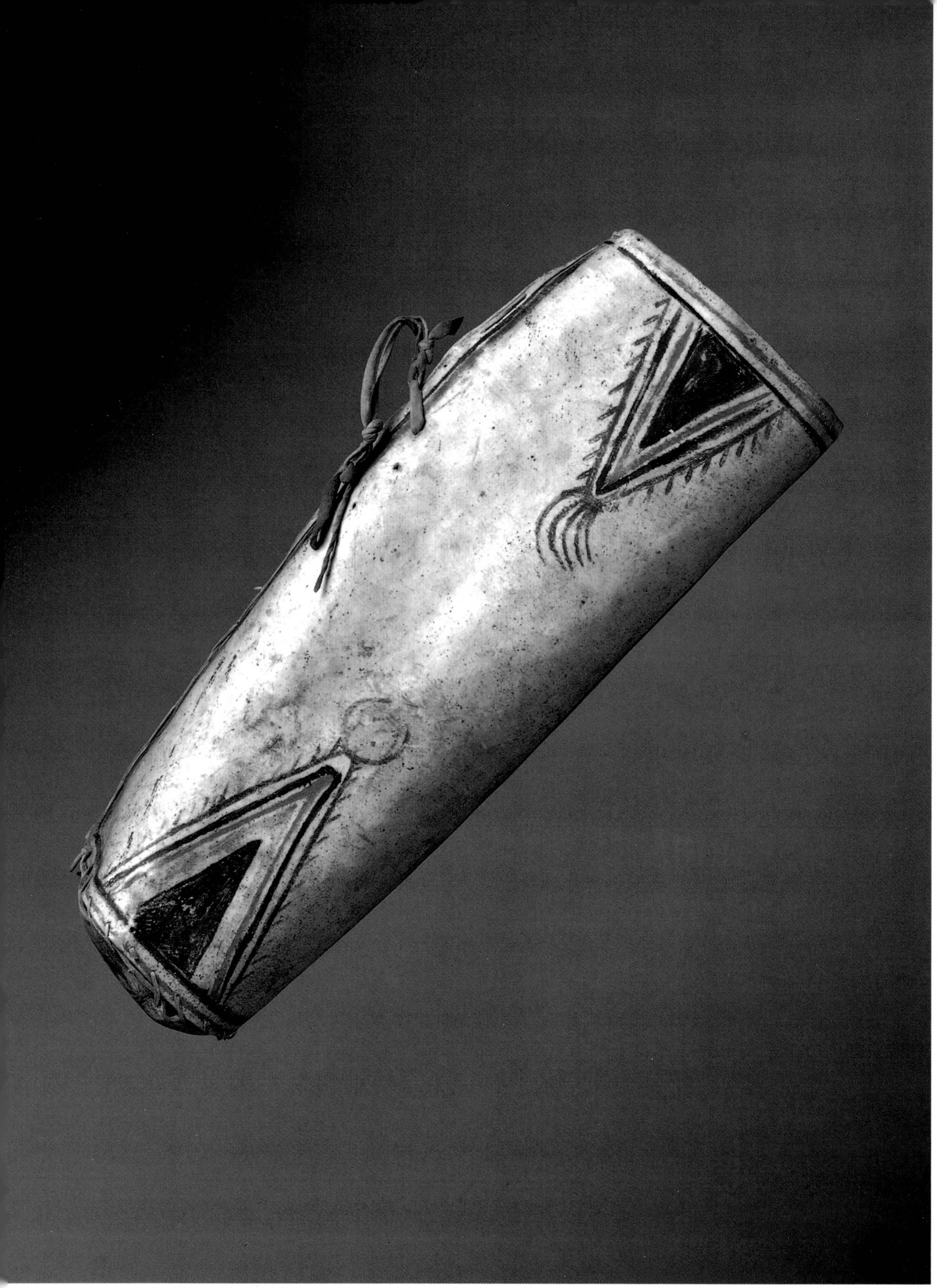

49 / **Comanche cylinder, ca. 1865**

H 19 1/4 in., D 5 1/2 in. Rawhide, pigment

Collected by M. R. Harrington in Oklahoma. National Museum of the American Indian, Smithsonian Institution, 2/1318

APACHE

The women of the Eastern Apache groups created one of the most distinctive traditions of parfleche in North America, yet little is known of its origin or evolution, or of the relationship between the different styles that were developed by the separate bands. Several Apache groups originally inhabited a large area of the Southern Plains bordering the Rocky Mountains, until they were either destroyed or displaced by the Comanche in the early eighteenth century. The surviving Mescalero and Jicarilla relocated into the mountainous areas of eastern New Mexico, while the Lipan retreated to southwestern Texas until joining with the New Mexican bands during the nineteenth century. These three groups remained in close proximity to the Southern Plains tribes, still venturing onto the Plains to hunt buffalo; they adopted Plains dress as well as other cultural traits and elements of material culture. Whether the original Plains-dwelling Apache manufactured parfleches before they acquired horses or later developed them through their association with the Southern Plains tribes in the 1700s is unknown, but by the last half of the nineteenth century they had established well-defined tribal styles.

The earliest Apache parfleches (pl. 51) bear a close resemblance to those of the Comanche from the same period (pls. 45, 46), almost to the point that they constitute a unified style. The two peoples were in continuous contact through warfare from their first encounters until the 1870s. Numerous captives were taken by both sides and material goods changed hands. This contact undoubtedly influenced parfleche production, resulting in a number of shared conventions in the painting and in the general design of the forms produced. Many of the specific elements that characterize Apache painting remain visible in Comanche work throughout the history of both traditions.

The greatest number of Apache parfleches in collections today are attributed to the Mescalero and Jicarilla, while very few examples have been collected from the Lipan and from the Chirachaua and Western bands.[7]

Little is known of Lipan artistic production because of this group's early displacement and the almost complete lack of documented pieces. The close association of the Lipan, the Mescalero, and the Jicarilla, and the inevitable influences occurring from sustained interaction, further obscures Lipan artistic traditions. Only two known parfleches are documented as having been collected from the Lipan: an exceptionally beautiful fringed case taken during a raid into Mexico (pl. 52) and another of the same period reportedly obtained in Texas ten to twenty years later. Both possess essentially the same features as others of the same type attributed to the Mescalero (pl. 53), raising the question of specific origin in spite of their collection history.

An extraordinary envelope without provenance, however, may very

7. Only one parfleche, an envelope, is known to have been collected from the Kiowa-Apache. It is consistent in style with those produced by the Kiowa, and is probably of Kiowa origin.

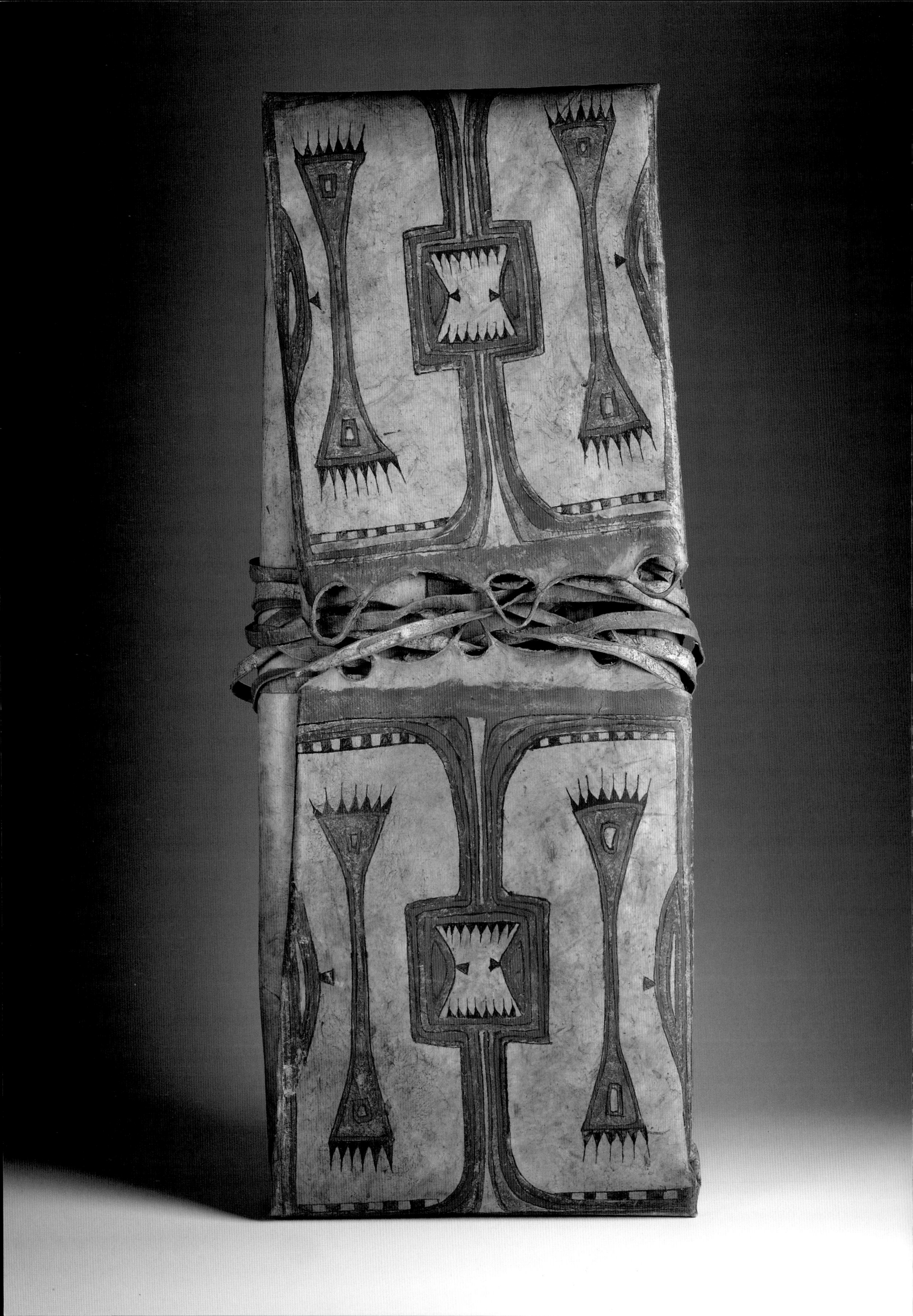

50 / **Lipan or Mescalero Apache envelope, ca. 1875**

L 41 in., W 15 1/2 in. Rawhide, pigment

American Museum of Natural History, 50.2/2554

well have been created by a Lipan artist (pl. 50). It is unquestionably of Apache origin, yet does not conform to any of the other known types in the organization of its stylistic elements. The painting is elegant and highly refined; it is comparable to the finest Mescalero work and reflects a similar sensibility. Also the bands of alternating black and white blocks and the incurving forms at the sides of the design are usually regarded as distinctive Mescalero elements. However, the compositional structure is organized in the conventional manner consistent with Jicarilla designs. The elongated black triangles are also associated with Jicarilla style, but their placement within the composition is reminiscent of Comanche or Mescalero types. Furthermore, the restraint of the composition, the delicacy of the forms, and the superb quality of the painting far exceed any documented Jicarilla work. The range of colors is different from those preferred by either Mescalero or Jicarilla painters, and each color within the design is separated by black outlining, a feature not found in the work of other Apache groups. The remarkable size and narrow proportion of this envelope is typical of both Jicarilla and Ute envelopes, and the wash of red ochre paint outside the delineated panel is a distinctive Ute trait, but the presence of painted side flaps is not consistent with the work of the Ute nor is the character of the painting. The fact that this remarkable parfleche reflects these other styles may indicate that they are descended from others of its type, that it exemplifies the Plains Apache tradition maintained by the Lipan until they were absorbed by the more numerous Mescalero and Jicarilla.

Mescalero women created a remarkable style of painted and incised envelopes unlike those made by any other tribe (pl. 54). The compositions contain precisely executed, intricate elements that extend from the folded ends of the flaps. At each end of the envelope is a wide band usually divided into eight rectangles, each filled with checkerboardlike squares of light and dark, crosshatching, or finely drawn parallel lines. In dramatic contrast to these solid blocks of pattern are delicate linear forms composed of pairs of lines, dots, and highly elongated triangles that project toward the center of the case. In some designs, the triangles are replaced by abstract feather forms or other slender geometric shapes. These elements emerge from stepped triangles attached to the baseline of the broad bands of pattern at the ends. Because no borders enclose the edges of the design, these linear elements appear to extend into an open, unpainted field, thus emphasizing their attenuation. The designs were first incised into the leather by cutting, not scraping, and were then painted. The colors are always the same: red, yellow, and green, with black outlining around the primary forms; linear elements, dots, and small triangles are drawn in both black and red. Colors within the major forms are not separated by line, but small unpainted areas are edged in either black or red as well.

The sensibility of these designs, particularly the end panels with their intricate patterns of red and black, is closely related to those adorning pieced leather traveling chests produced in Mexico during the colonial

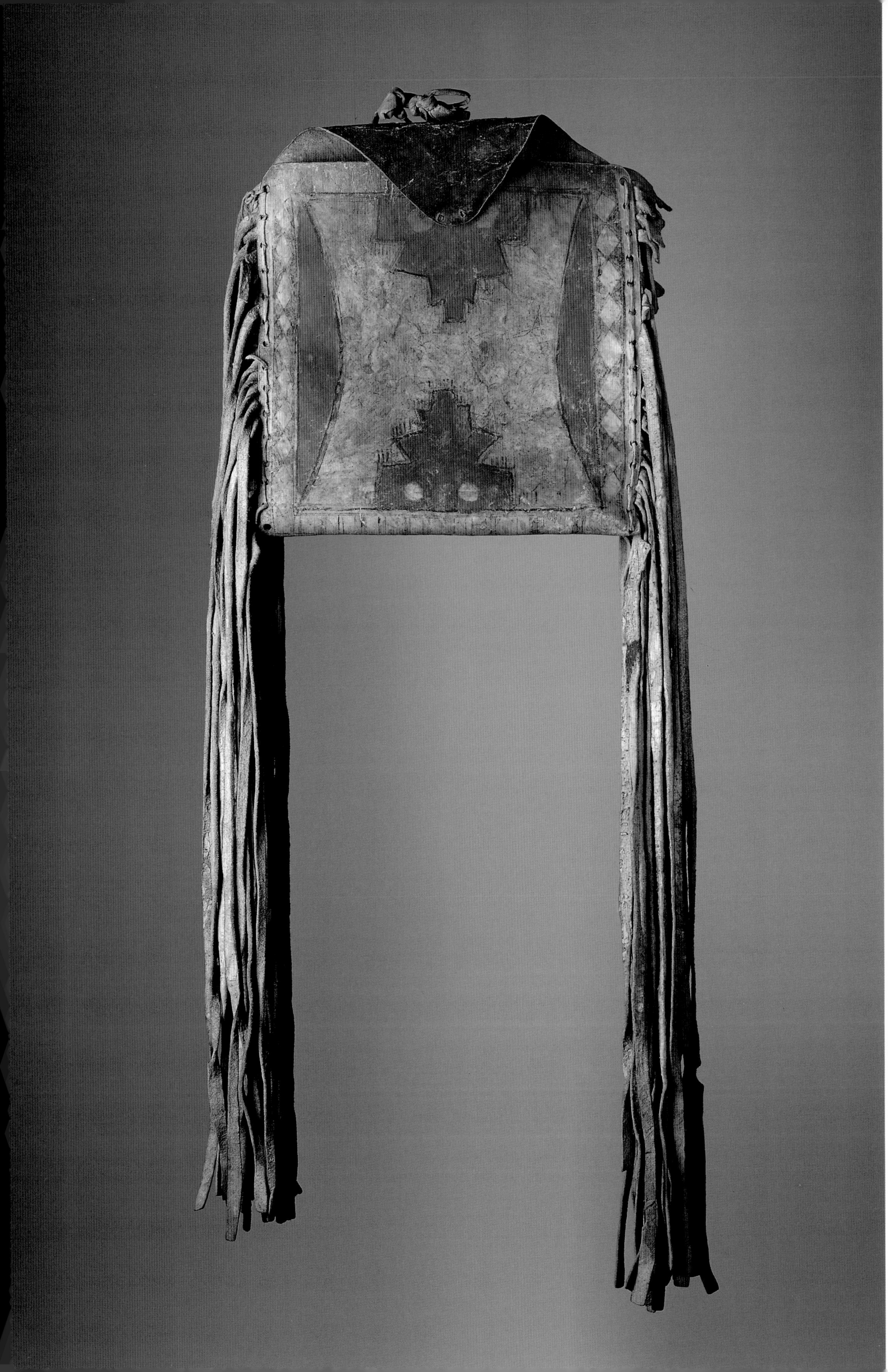

8. A superb Mexican chest of this type is illustrated in a recent exhibition brochure, *Sacred Land: Indian and Hispanic Cultures of the Southwest* (p. 14), published by the Taylor Museum of the Colorado Springs Fine Arts Center (1992).

9. See the unfolded Mescalero parfleche envelope (identified as a painted hide) illustrated in Mails (1974: 232), and the cylinder illustrated in Morrow (1975: 110, lower left). A related and interesting example is pictured in Lanford (1990: 43).

10. Only one Apache flat case is known—in the Chandler-Pohrt Collection—on which the entire design is finely incised.

period.[8] These and other examples of Hispanic leatherwork were common in New Mexico in the eighteenth and nineteenth centuries and clearly influenced Apache artists.

Mescalero envelopes are rather small with wide overlapping side flaps. Only the top one of these inner flaps was customarily painted. The designs consist of isolated circles with projecting lines that appear to be sun symbols, rectilinear forms arranged in a line, or a single band of integrated geometric elements. There is usually no decoration on the reverse sides of envelopes, although a particularly intriguing feature of this example is the presence of a stylized, elongated animal painted on the reverse side (reverse of pl. 54, p. 152). Possibly a wolf, it stands isolated below two diagonal lines. Its significance is unknown, but it is a startling and powerful image. Although uncommon, similar depictions have been found on other examples of Eastern Apache painting.[9] It is doubtful that they were intended to identify either the maker or owner of the object; rather, such figurative images probably had religious meaning and would, therefore, have been painted by men. Mescalero envelopes were made without tie holes, although some have a small slit in each flap for a thong. They were generally secured by wrapping long ties around the entire container.

While the designs of envelopes are essentially angular, the patterns on flat cases (pls. 51–53) and cylinders (pls. 55, 56) often contain strongly curving forms. Several of the cases include small circles in their compositions, either as unpainted elements within larger motifs or as floating devices on the flaps (pl. 53). The majority of flat cases are constructed with long, heavy fringe attached at the sides and occasionally a few of these fringes are wide-cut and serrated. The shape of the case itself is usually square or slightly vertical, and the closure flap is somewhat pointed. Most are painted without incising,[10] but the designs are no less intricate. Compositions are usually divided by a vertical band containing a series of triangles or some other geometric element, but other configurations were created as well. Borders vary; some consist of one or more lines of color, while others feature a band of alternating black and white squares, hourglasses, or diagonal bands. Some are painted on the reverse side with isolated motifs that are probably symbolic. The earliest Apache parfleches that have been preserved are flat cases, and they are painted only in red and green (pl. 51) like the works of all Southern Plains tribes from the same period.

Very few Mescalero cylinders have been collected. Like those of the Comanche and other Southwestern groups, the painting encircles the entire form, and fringe is attached around the base. The components of the design are generally consistent with other types of Mescalero parfleches but modified to fit the cylindrical shape effectively. The rawhide disks that cover the top are sometimes cut with projecting tabs, either to provide a means of attachment or for decorative purposes.

The Jicarilla Apache of northern New Mexico developed a separate tradition that is equally distinctive yet somewhat related in appearance

51 / **Lipan or Mescalero Apache flat case, ca. 1830**

H 12 3/4 in. (not including flap), W 13 3/4 in.; height with fringe 39 in. Buffalo rawhide, pigment, native leather

American Museum of Natural History, 50.2/4340

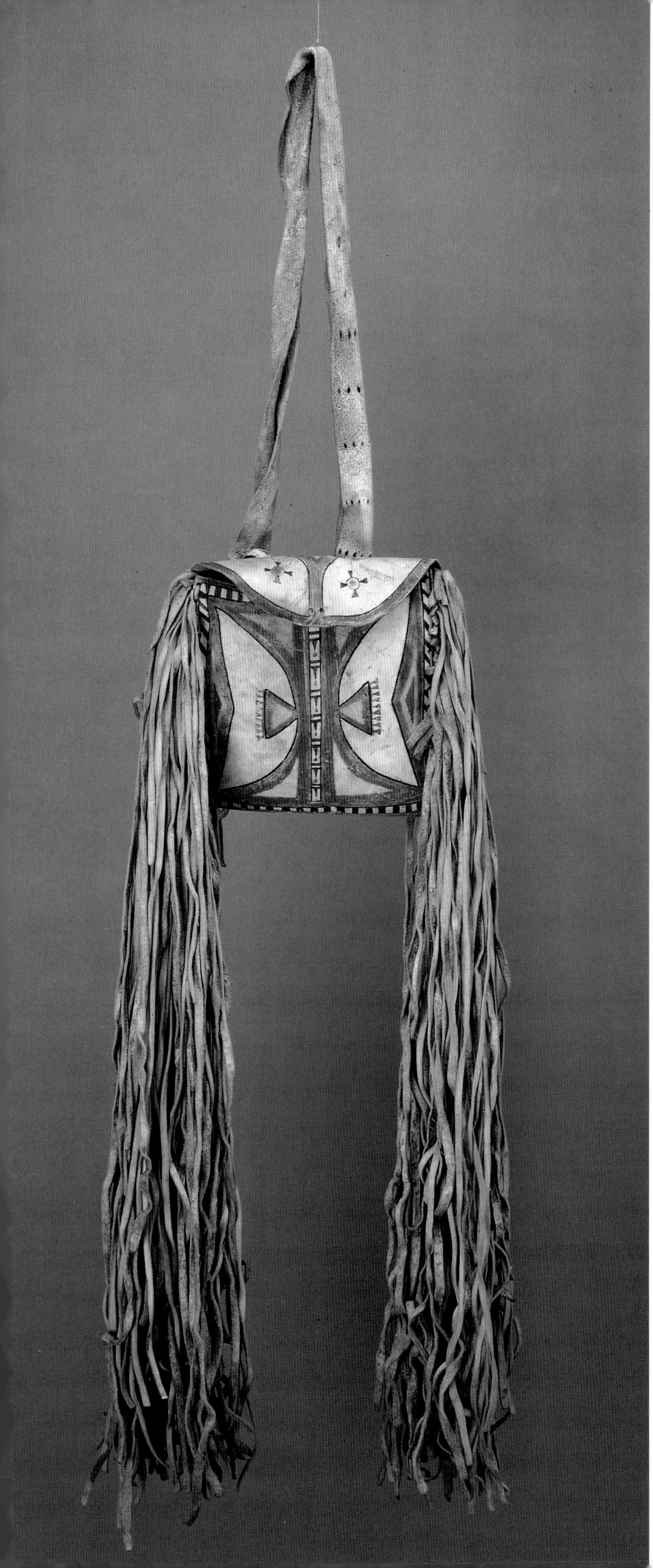

52 / **Lipan or Mescalero Apache flat case, ca. 1865**

H 10 in. (not including flap), W 10 in.; fringe 37 in. Rawhide, pigment, native leather

Taken at the Battle of Rey-Moliena, Mexico, by Capt. J. A. Wilcox, 4th Cavalry, during General McKenzie's raid on the Lipan Apache, May 19, 1873. Courtesy of the Trustees of the British Museum, London, 1954.W AM5.951

53 / **Lipan or Mescalero Apache flat case, ca. 1865**

H 10 in. (not including flap), W 9 3/4 in.; fringe 33 1/2 in. Buffalo rawhide, pigment

National Museum of the American Indian, Smithsonian Institution, 12/7565

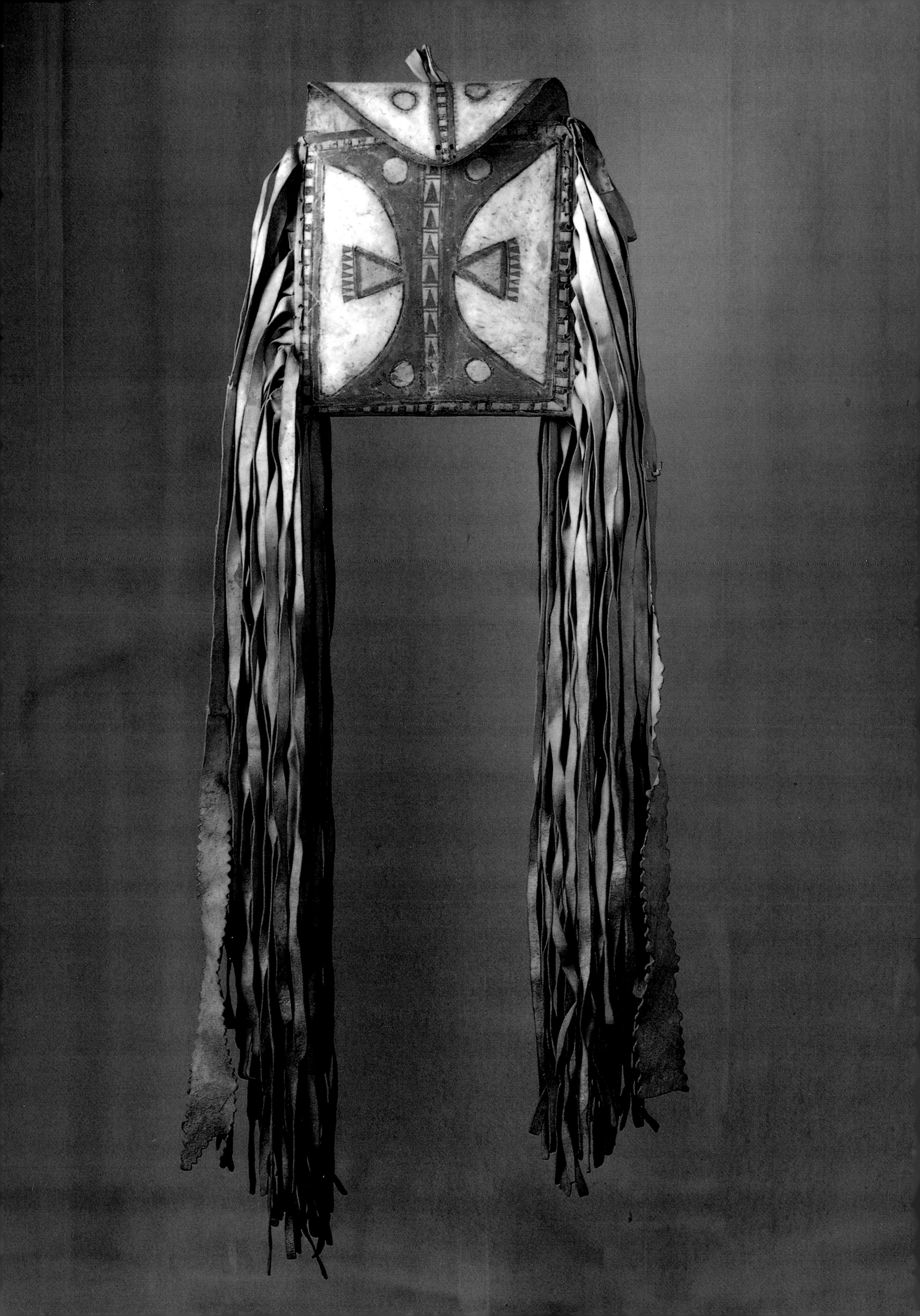

to one of the major stylistic types created in the Western Plateau region. The principal form found most frequently in collections today is the envelope (pl. 57). These are all exceptionally large and narrow, usually consuming most of a single hide and measuring from 34 to 40 inches in length. Compared to the style developed by the Mescalero, Jicarilla designs are unrestrained and loosely painted; their compositions reflect a lack of concern for precise delineation and symmetry, and possess a rather lyrical quality. Much of their effect is derived from the multitude of minute black triangles that edge the major forms and borders, establishing rhythms and activating the transition from painted to unpainted areas. The principal shapes are outlined in black; sometimes other small black units are incorporated within the image. Often small, unpainted circles, rectangles, or irregular shapes occur within the major motifs. Although the primary compositional forms are inherently angular, many are slightly rounded and softened by the character of the drawing.

Many compositions are structured with a large right triangle in each corner and a central configuration of triangles, rectangles, or diamonds. The unpainted area is always a significant component within the design. Colors used by Jicarilla women are often more varied than those appearing on Mescalero pieces. Red, yellow, and green are usually prominent, but sometimes blue or orange is included or substituted. It was also typical for Jicarilla painters to combine a pure, brilliant red with a deep, rusty red ochre in the same design. The borders of the compositions are

54 / **Mescalero Apache envelope, ca. 1875**

L 24 in., W 11 1/2 in. Incised rawhide, pigment

Collected at Taos Pueblo, New Mexico. National Museum of the American Indian, Smithsonian Institution, 3/5404

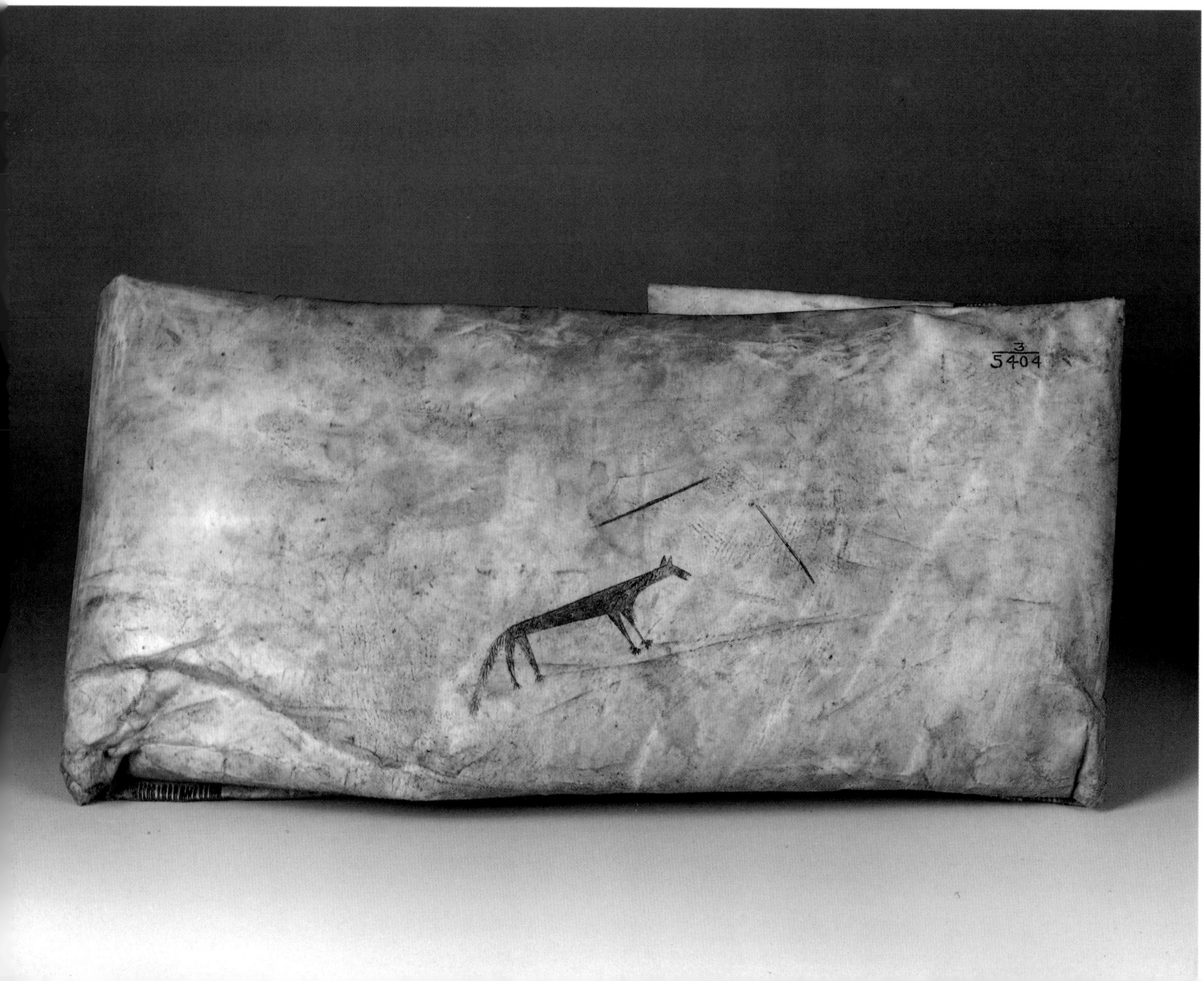

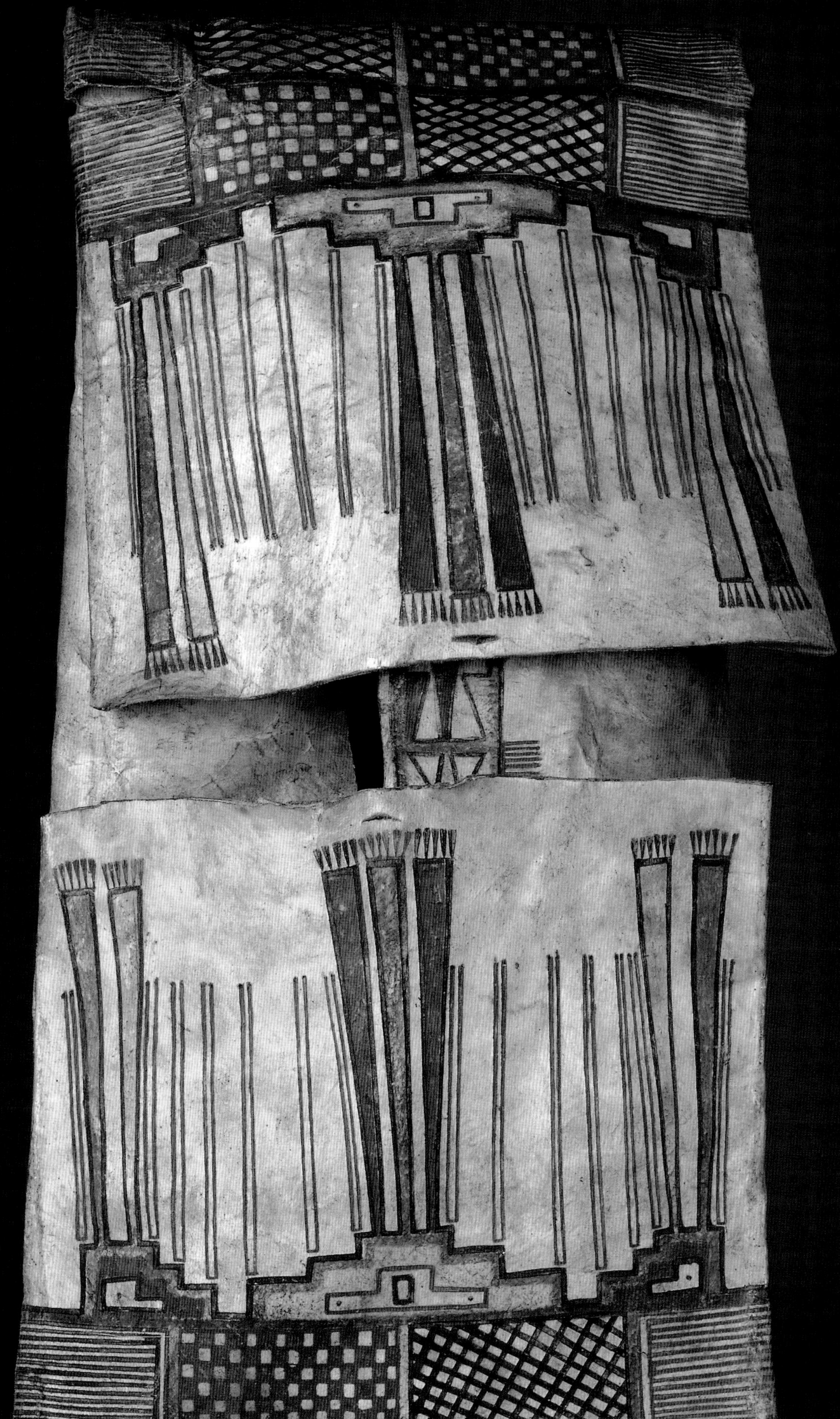

established by a single or double line of color, which usually extends into the design by enclosing motifs that lie along the edge. Side flaps are usually painted with designs that appear to have symbolic significance. Both flaps are painted but with disparate images, such as rows of geometric motifs, long bands joining circular forms, pictographic life forms, what appear to be celestial or directional symbols, zigzag lines, and short horizontal bands containing geometric shapes. This inner painting is consistently of a very different character from what appears on the outer flaps; it is clearly symbolic but its meanings are unknown. It is quite possible that most if not all of these images were created by men, in accordance with the designated roles of artists within Apache culture (Opler 1965: 379).

Jicarilla envelopes vary in the number of tie holes. Stake holes were sometimes incorporated for this purpose; other envelopes were closed by single or triple pairs or by the single-pair-single pattern. Fewer than a dozen of these envelopes are known to exist, so while comparatively rare, they are still far more numerous than Mescalero examples. In contrast, the most common Mescalero form to survive are flat cases, while Jicarilla examples of both flat cases and cylinders are very few.

The Chirichaua apparently used parfleches to some extent, as did some of the Western Apache groups, but they were a recent acquisition and there is conflicting information from informants as to whether parfleches were ever made by these peoples (Opler 1965: 378). The fact that a tradition of painted rawhide was maintained by the Chirachaua is supported by the existence of a number of elaborately decorated quivers (pl. 58). These are constructed from a single piece of rawhide with the addition of rawhide cutouts over red cloth, serrated rawhide bands at the center for the attachment of the shoulder strap, and a profusion of metal cones, all typical Chirachaua features seen on other types of objects. The designs are based on a repetition of triangles and zigzag lines, elements that are also found on other examples of Chirachaua painting, beadwork, leatherwork, and ritual items. The patterns consist of bands of color, some filled with contrasting triangles, repeated serrated bands of black triangles, and zigzag bands of multiple lines. The floral forms in the designs of the quiver in plate 58 are unusual. The black paint used on this quiver contains galina, a mineral that imparts a sparkle to the surface. It is typically found in the pigment used by Central and Western Apache groups.

With the exception of pieces obviously acquired in trade from other groups, the few painted parfleches collected from the Chirachaua, White Mountain, and Western Apache groups have little artistic merit. This suggests the possibility that the women of these bands never developed this art into an established tradition, and that the finely painted quivers may have been produced by men extending their own painting tradition to encompass this form.

55 / **Mescalero (?) Apache cylinder, ca. 1850**

H 17 3/4 in., D 4 1/2 in.; fringe 5 in. Buffalo rawhide, pigment

Collected at Taos Pueblo, New Mexico. Collection of Benson Lanford

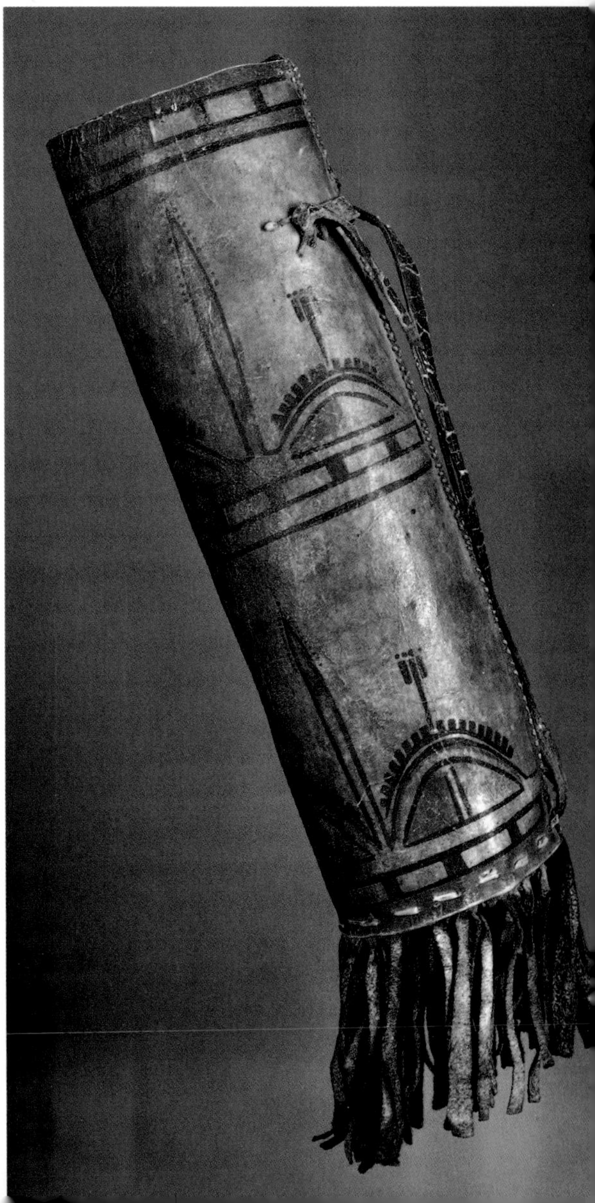

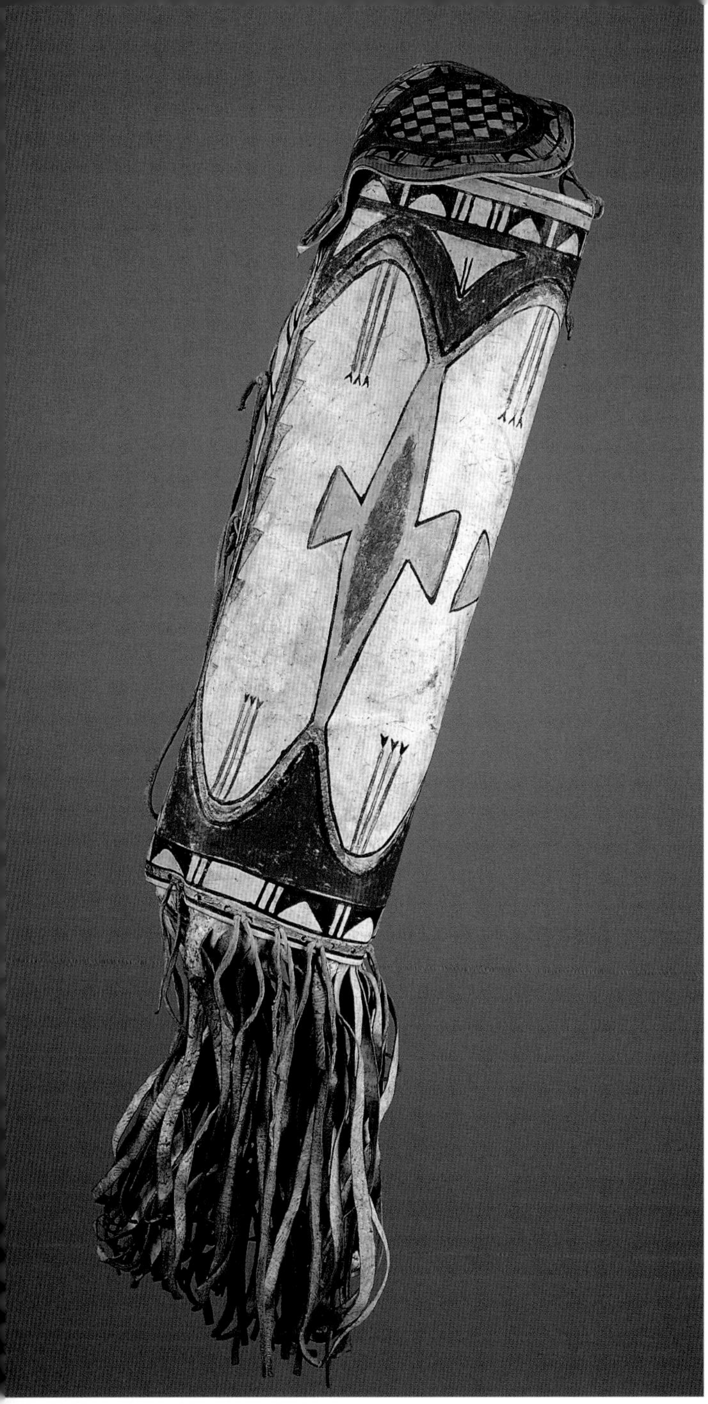

56 / **Mescalero Apache cylinder, ca. 1885**

H 20 in., D 6 1/2 in.; fringe 12 in. Rawhide, pigment, native leather

The Maxwell Museum of Anthropology, University of New Mexico, 74.1.18

57 / **Jicarilla Apache envelope, ca. 1880**

L 33 in., W 16 1/2 in. Rawhide, pigment

The Thomas Gilcrease Institute of American History and Art, 8926.101

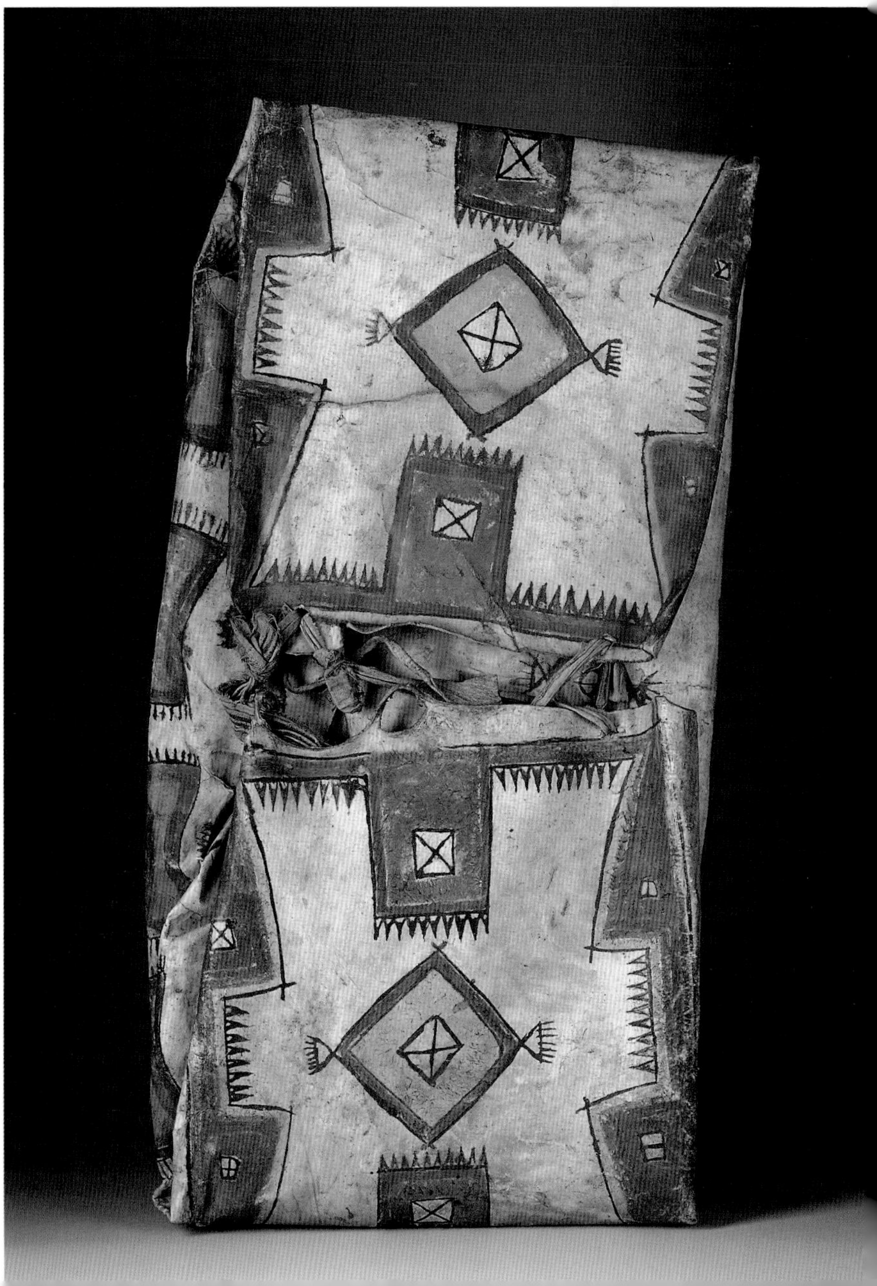

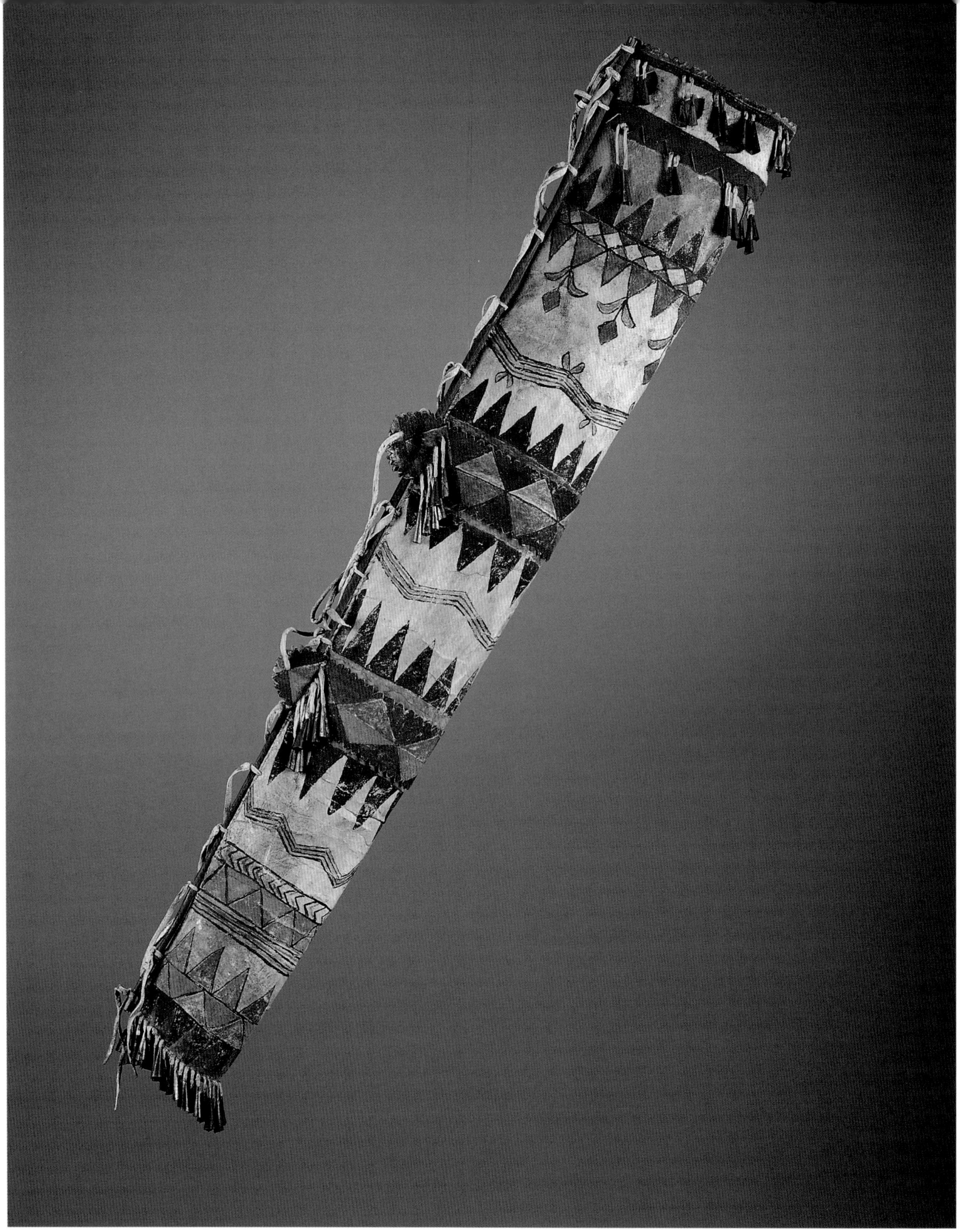

58 / **Chiricahua Apache quiver, ca. 1890**

H 34 1/2 in., W 6 in. Rawhide, pigment, native leather, metal cones, cotton cloth, wood

State Historical Society of Iowa, 2153

UTE

The Ute people inhabited an extensive intermontane region to the north of the Jicarilla Apache. The two groups were politically allied, and many of their artistic forms reflect their close association. Various arts of the Ute reflect styles of other tribes as well, but in construction their parfleches are most similar to those of the Jicarilla. Only six envelopes have been found that were collected from the Ute and also possess consistent, distinctive features; others are probably Plateau pieces acquired in trade and some are clearly of Sioux origin. All of those appearing to be of Ute manufacture were collected from the Northern, or Uintah, band.

Like Jicarilla examples, all but one of these envelopes were made from a single hide, are quite large, and are long and narrow in proportion (pl. 59). In some respects this is their most identifiable feature in that the painted compositions are varied and seem to have affinities with several other groups, including the Cheyenne/Arapaho, Plateau, Apache, and Shoshone.

It is difficult to characterize typical compositions with so few to compare, but they tend to be somewhat open and simple and a few are even composed without borders; others are bordered with a single line. Most designs are notable for their austerity and directness but none is quite so dramatic as the composition of the envelope in plate 59. The emptiness in its center is both unexpected and engaging, and is powerfully counterbalanced by the blocks of color in the corners. Major forms are outlined in black and colors within these motifs are often, but not always, separated by line as well. Most compositions include small black inverted triangles attached to primary elements. One of the most distinctive features is a "wash" of color applied outside the delineated design at the ends of the painted panels, extending to the ends of the flaps. This is usually painted in red ochre but has been rendered in blue on the envelope in plate 59. The Ute palette does not extend beyond red, yellow, blue, and green, plus the black units and outlining, and often only three of these colors are used. Side flaps were not decorated, in contrast to the envelopes of the Jicarilla. Two or three pairs of tie holes were most common, but stake holes sometimes served this purpose.

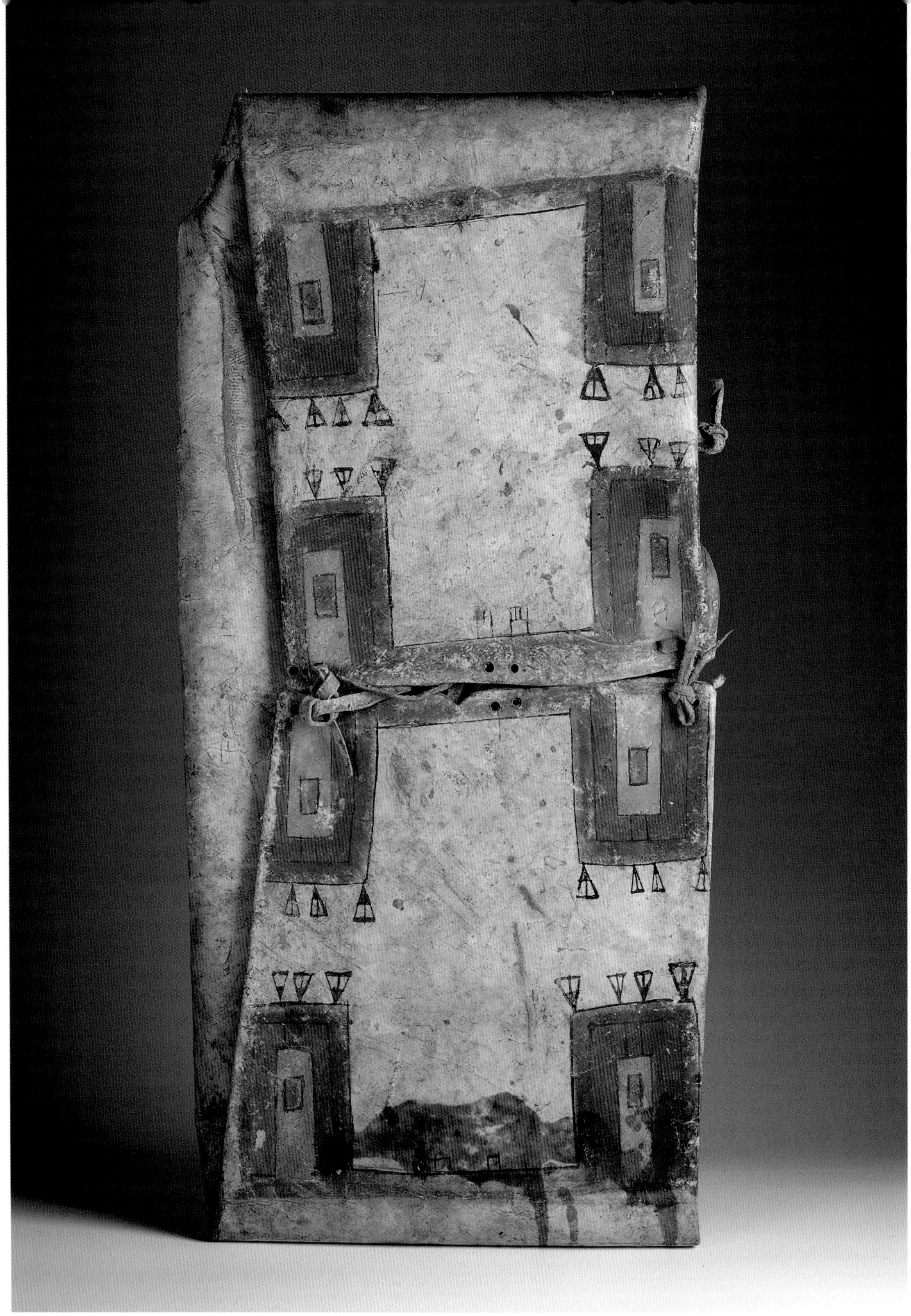

59 / **Ute envelope, ca. 1875**

L 36 in., W 16 in. Rawhide, pigment

Collected by Alfred L. Kroeber at Whiterocks, Utah, 1900. American Museum of Natural History, 50/1304

PUEBLO

Painting on rawhide assumed two forms among the sedentary Puebloan groups of the Southwest: shields that were constructed for war and ceremonial use, and parfleche cylinders made for the storage of religious objects. Although the use of shields in Pueblo cultures forms a long tradition extending from prehistoric times and is well described in the literature, little is known about the production and use of parfleches by these peoples. It seems certain that they adopted the form from the neighboring Southern Plains and Apache tribes with whom they traded and fought. This is evident from the basic similarity of construction and the fact that all of the known examples were collected from Rio Grande pueblos, whose inhabitants were in close and continuous contact with Plains and Apache groups.

Pueblo parfleches are rarely found in museum collections. A larger number have been purchased from Indian families in recent years and are now in private collections. It is also likely that a significant number remain in Indian possession, either serving their intended function or as heirlooms. Almost no mention is made of Pueblo parfleches in the literature except for a few references to undecorated containers (Hill 1982: 92), and their significance as artistic forms has remained almost unknown. However, surviving examples indicate that it was a well-established tradition among several Pueblo groups.

Two basic types were produced. The first are those of total Pueblo manufacture; fewer than ten of these are known, and they all vary somewhat in size, in details of construction, and in the elements and organization of their painted imagery. However, their characteristics are consistent enough that they are easily distinguished as a group from the Plains prototypes. There are significant differences in the way they were made and painted, as well as in their designs, which generally conform with those of other Pueblo ceremonial objects (pls. 60, 61). The most distinctive structural feature is the side seam, which is joined by extremely fine sinew sewing rather than the lacing methods of the Plains and Apache groups. Another identifying feature found on many is a fitted cap used to cover the top (pl. 61). These slightly domed caps are also finely sewn and were designed to fit down closely over the edge of the cylinder. Others are closed with a conventional disk or a flap that extends from the body of the cylinder. Pueblo cases vary greatly in size, ranging from less than 10 inches to more than 20 inches in length. They are fringed in the manner typical of Comanche and Apache cylinders, although a few are ornamented with a fine, secondary fringe as well. The thickness and length of the fringe as well as the method of attachment may be considerably different from one example to another, but on most it is painted with red or yellow ochre.

The painting techniques of Pueblo artists were different from traditional Plains methods and varied even among the different Pueblo painters. These differences in application, pigments, and sizing combine to create a wide range of surface qualities. Most parfleches were painted after they were constructed and, presumably, when the leather was completely dry. Many were first given a coat of white kaolin paint and then painted with colored pigments over this base surface in the same manner as wooden ritual objects, resulting in a matte surface. Others were apparently painted directly onto the rawhide and then heavily sized. Pueblo artists reportedly used peach juice as a sizing, which may account for the glossy surface and the darkened, yellowed appearance of the colors on many. Several may at some point have been overpainted with kaolin, which is now worn away leaving only small amounts on the surface or in the seams and cracks of the leather. A few were constructed with the napped surface to the outside, which was painted but never sized.

Some of the pigments used were the same varieties as those found on Plains pieces, but others were quite different. A few, in particular a deep red and dark red-brown, were transparent stains. A less intense orange and blue-gray appear to have this same quality. The paints on several pieces have aged or worn differently; for example, certain blues and yellows may have faded considerably, while the reds and brown/blacks remain vivid (pls. 61, 62).

All of these cylinders were made to contain fetishes, prayer sticks, feathers, and other religious objects, and the painted designs reflect this function. Most of these containers are covered with the iconographic imagery typical of Pueblo religious art, including stylized gods, kachinas and other sacred beings, terraced cloud forms, lightning, flowers, birds, animals, and other symbolic motifs (pls. 60, 61). These are often combined with a few geometric elements, generally at the top and bottom of the field. Other compositions are formed entirely of stepped geometric shapes. Many compositions are bordered by one or more bands of color or bands containing light and dark blocks. One remarkable painting (pl. 62) combines traditional motifs with a narrative depiction of a mountain lion in a tree, crouched to spring on an unsuspecting deer. The artist was undoubtedly influenced by Euro-American painting in his attempt to represent a more realistic space through overlapping forms, but the image itself may still have related directly to the contents of the case. The painting is reminiscent of similar portrayals in non-Indian style found on a few Pueblo pottery jars of the same period.

Because of the explicitly religious imagery on Pueblo parfleches, it may be assumed that they were painted by men in the same manner as other religious objects.

It was a common practice for Pueblo peoples to appropriate Plains and Apache parfleches for their own use, and the second type of Pueblo cylinder was created in this manner. The painted panels of both envelope flaps and flat cases were cut and formed into cylindrical shapes, fitted with top closures and fringed.[11] Usually there was some attempt to align the original painted design with the new form; however, some were

11. See Conn (1986: 118) for an example of this type of cylinder. It is clearly made from an envelope flap that, together with the style of fringe and traces of white kaolin paint, confirms its Pueblo origin.

60 / **Pueblo cylinder, ca. 1865**

H 21 in., D 4 1/2 in.; fringe 17 in. Buffalo rawhide, pigment, native leather

Possibly collected at Zia Pueblo, New Mexico. Denver Museum of Natural History, Crane American Indian Collection, 4803

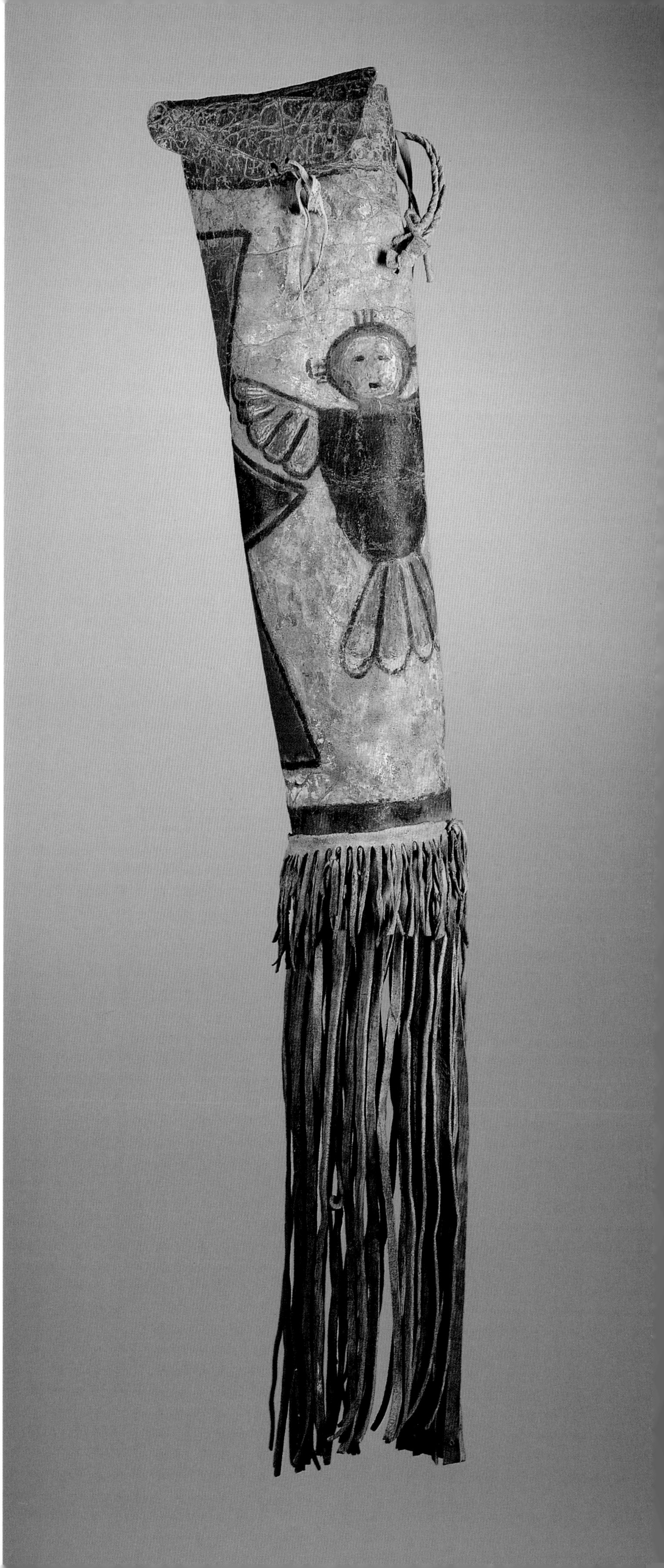

transformed much more effectively than others. Cases of this type were sometimes overpainted by their Pueblo makers, either by adding Puebloan images to the preexisting design or filling in areas with white kaolin or the ceremonial dark green paint sometimes seen on pottery used for ritual purposes. They are usually constructed by lacing with thongs in the traditional Plains manner rather than through sewing. This practice of recycling parfleches has resulted in the preservation of some very early examples of Southern Plains painting, in the same manner as those made into trunks by the Mesquakie.

61 / **Pueblo cylinder, ca. 1875**

H 9 1/2 in., D 3 1/4 in.; fringe 6 in. Rawhide, pigment, native leather

Private collection

62 / **Pueblo cylinder, ca. 1890**

H 15 1/2 in., D 4 1/4 in.; fringe 12 1/2 in. Rawhide, pigment, native leather

Collected at Cochiti Pueblo, New Mexico. Collection of William A. Miller

See other side of this cylinder on page 13.

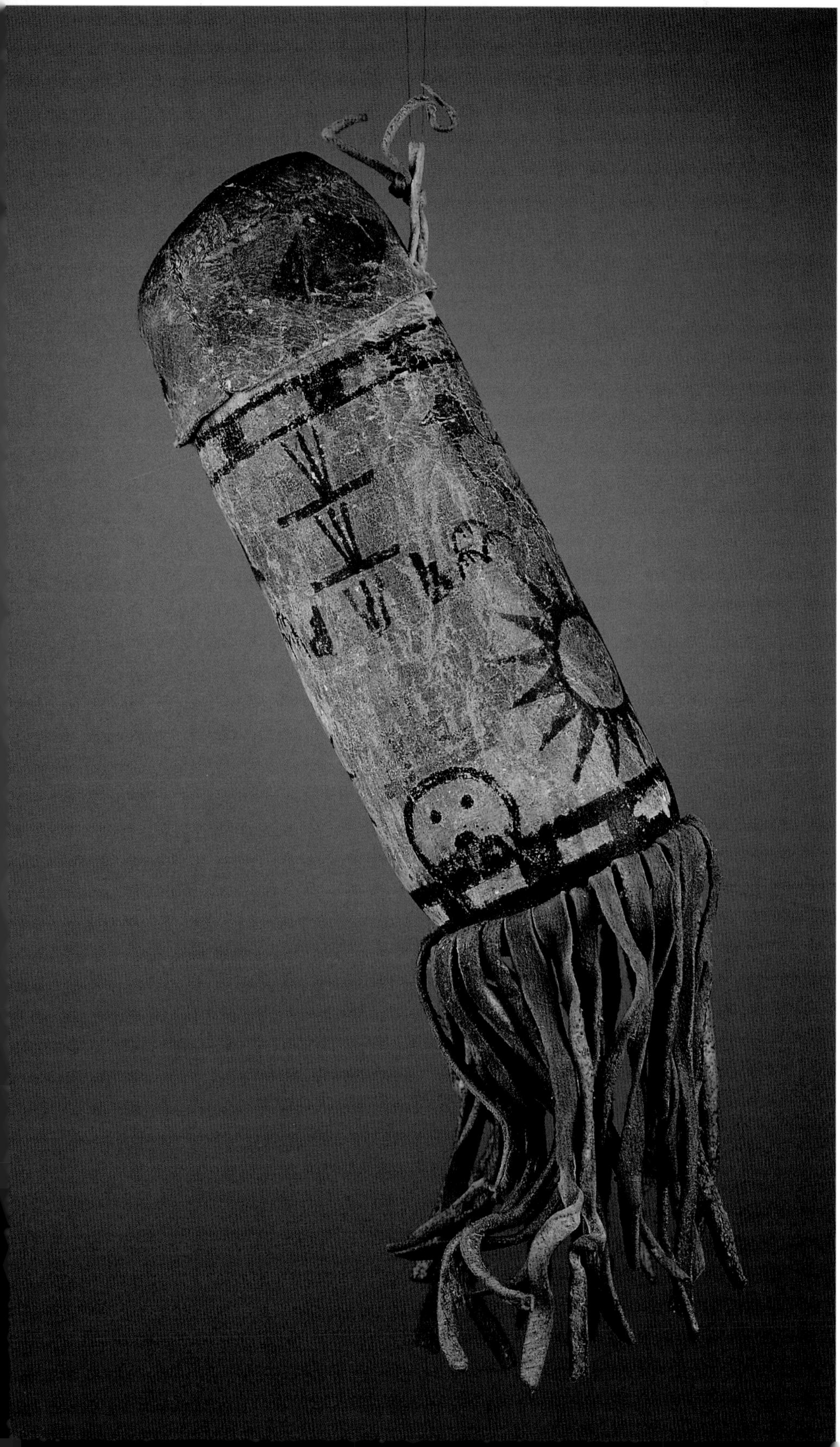

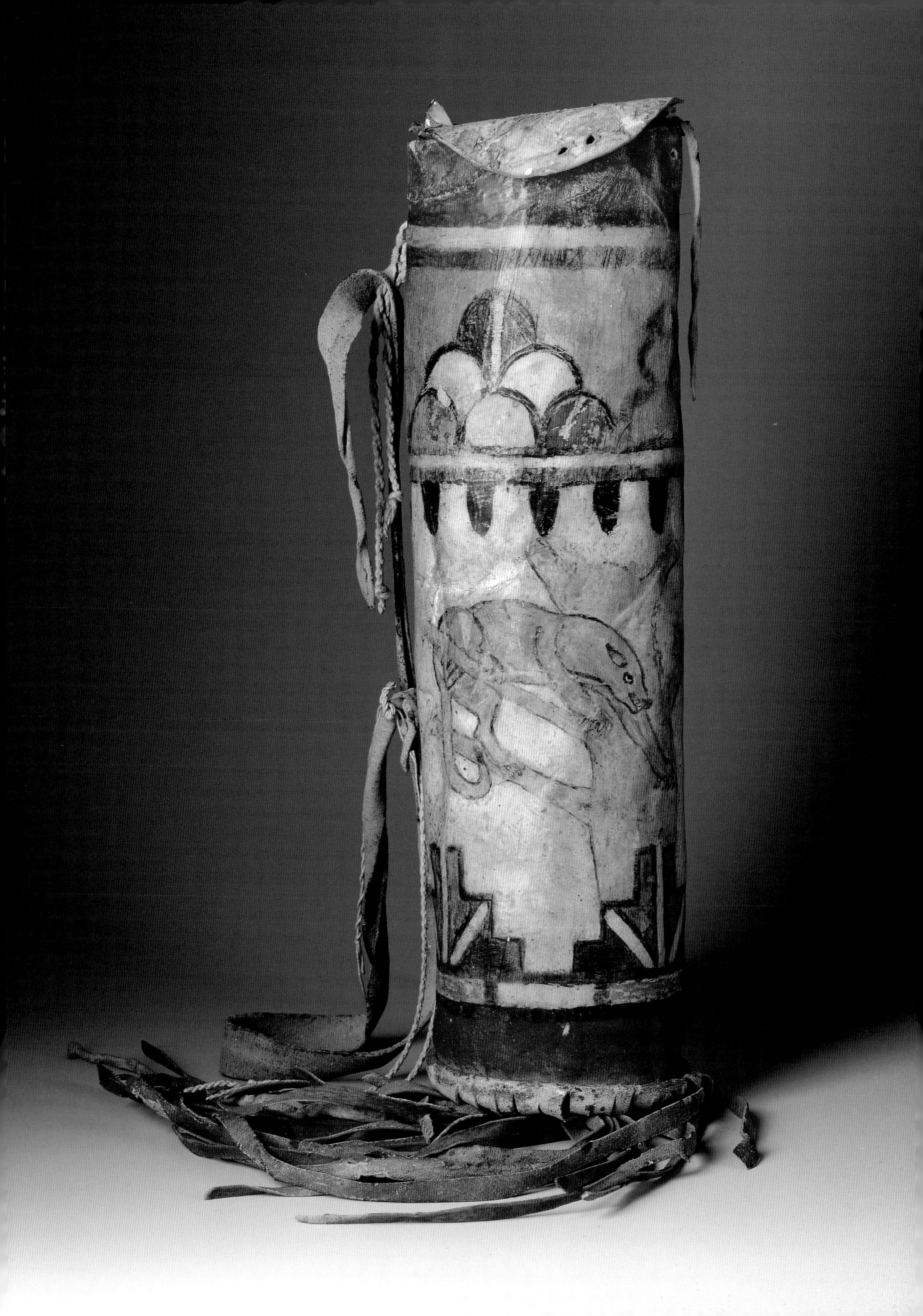

Northern Plains

GROS VENTRE, ASSINIBOINE, AND PLAINS CREE

The three tribes occupying the easternmost range of the Northern Plains were the Gros Ventre (or Atsina), the Assiniboine (who are known as the Stoney in Canada), and the Plains Cree. Although parfleches have been collected from all three groups, only those of the Gros Ventre may be recognized today as a well-defined tradition. Indeed, it is highly doubtful that the Cree ever produced painted rawhide containers in significant numbers, if at all. Only a few are attributed to this tribe through collection history and these clearly appear to be of Blackfeet manufacture,[12] undoubtedly acquired in trade or as gifts.

Fewer than ten envelopes have been located that are identified as having been collected from the various Assiniboine or Stoney groups, and more than half of these also appear to be of Blackfeet origin. The few others are painted in the differing styles of the Transmontane and Sioux. This situation—in which a very small group of parfleches collected from a single tribe (the Assiniboine), but reflecting a number of radically different styles, all of which are firmly documented as the prevailing styles of other tribes—raises the question as to whether any are actually of Assiniboine manufacture. It is quite possible that all were made by the women of other tribes and acquired in trade. If this is the case, we must acknowledge that we may never know for certain the manner in which Assiniboine parfleches were painted.

This seems to confirm Lowie's conclusion after collecting from the Assiniboine and Stoney in 1907 that there were too few available to permit a general description of style (1909: 23). He did record the symbolism associated with the design of one envelope obtained from the Stoney (pl. 67), which perhaps lends greater credibility to its purported Assiniboine/Stoney origin than exists for the others. However, it is known that Plains people often interpreted designs created by other artists, even those from other tribes, according to their own interests and beliefs, so it is possible that even this piece was created elsewhere. Also, it is but one example and may or may not be the most representative of Assiniboine style, especially when its construction and stylistic features are so consistent with and perhaps influenced by those of another tribe—in this case, the Northern Blackfeet.

In contrast, other small groups of parfleches acquired from a single tribe sometimes possess distinctive features that are present in most, if not all, of the examples collected, thereby defining the style and affirming their origin. For example, fewer than twenty-five parfleches are known to have been collected from the Gros Ventre people on the

12. See the envelope illustrated in Morrow (1975: 82).

63 / **Gros Ventre envelope, ca. 1865**
L 30 in., W 14 3/4 in. Buffalo rawhide, pigment
American Museum of Natural History, 50.2/4338

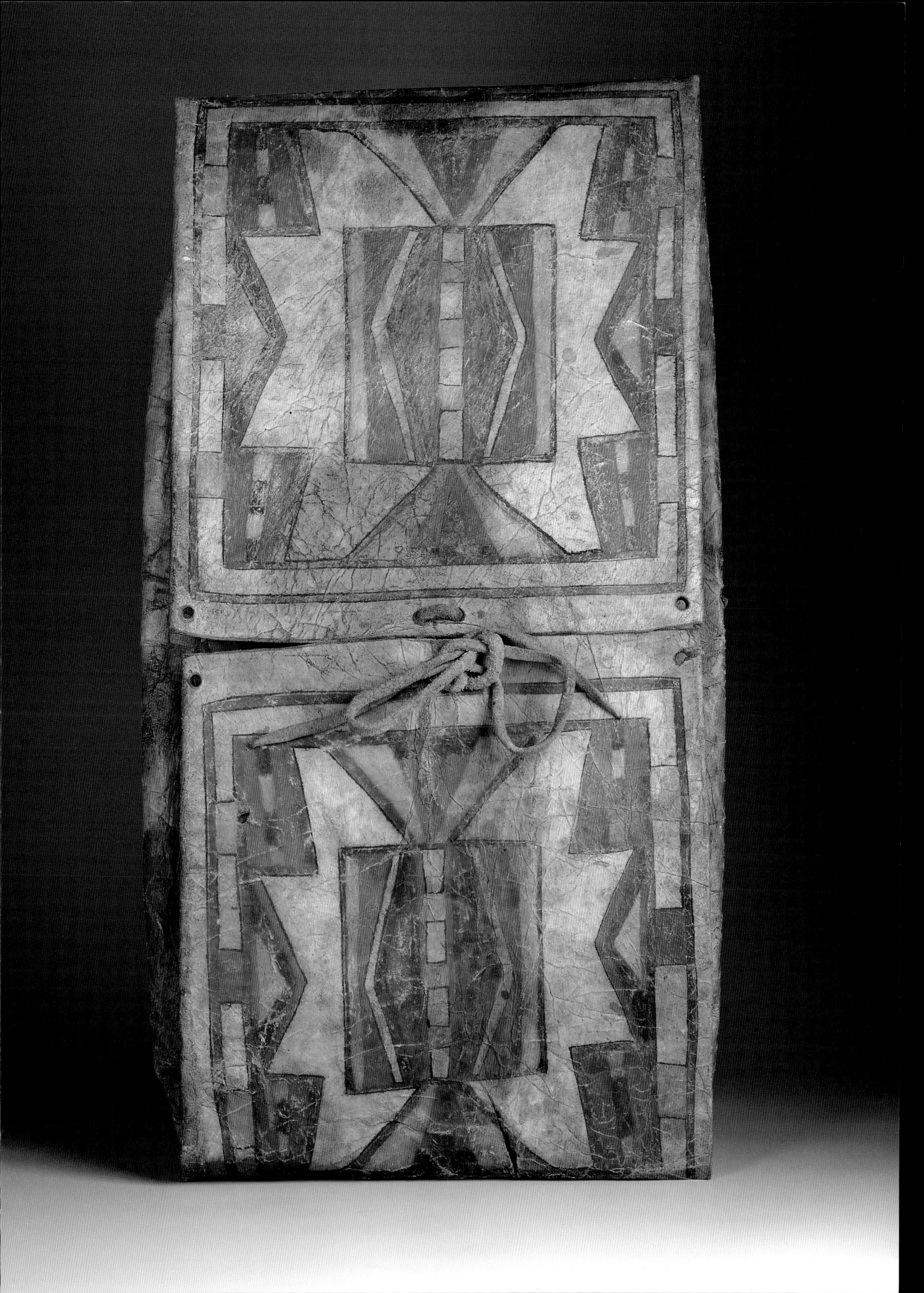

Fort Belknap Reservation, yet they constitute a stylistically unified body of works.

Gros Ventre parfleches can be identified by several interrelated elements within the painting. Perhaps the most prominent among these on many examples are the borders, which consist of two narrow bands of color, similar in form to those of the Blackfeet. However, Gros Ventre women often altered the coloration, sometimes transposing the colors of each band in the manner of the Kiowa (pl. 64); they painted others so that both bands were of one color along the sides of the panel, with a different color at the ends (pl. 65). In the remaining examples, the borders are of uniform color throughout (pl. 63), but still differ from the Blackfeet in other components. Specifically, most Gros Ventre designs include sequences of small blocks of color, either within the borders along the sides (pls. 63, 64), or within bands that form the central design elements (pls. 63, 65, 66). Occasionally, triangles are substituted for these blocks.

Another distinguishing aspect of Gros Ventre painting is the particular character of the black outlining. It was used only to separate painted and unpainted areas of the composition, never to separate colored shapes within the design elements as was the practice of the Central Plains tribes. Although this feature is seen in the work of other groups, in Gros Ventre designs this treatment had the effect of emphasizing the unpainted shapes within the composition, particularly the small rectangular forms adjacent to blocks of color, or the triangular negative shapes around painted triangles lying within unpainted rectangular spaces. The small units within the designs are colored, not black, as is usually the case with other tribes who used outlining; however, sometimes a series of black lines is used to divide unpainted areas of the border or central design (pl. 64). Black outlining is present in most early paintings, but was sometimes omitted in later pieces (pl. 66).

The color relationships found in Gros Ventre parfleche painting are often unusual and striking. While several are composed of the conventional combination of red, yellow, blue, and green, a number of others combine a pale brown and golden yellow with framing elements of darker blue and green (pl. 65). Others include a pale rose, almost a mauve, in combination with a soft native green.

The compositions tend to be complex and many are quite linear, with panels being subdivided both vertically and horizontally into well-balanced, gridlike fields encompassing triangular and diamond forms (pl. 65). Variations of the five-box design are seen (pl. 63) that may reflect the fact that the Gros Ventre and Arapaho were once united as a single tribe. Other compositions also bear a fundamental resemblance to those of the Arapaho, while a few reflect a strong Crow influence (pl. 64). Most are composed of both straightedged and curved forms, and are rather evenly balanced between painted and unpainted areas. The panels of envelopes are generally square or slightly rectangular. Side flaps are without painting, as is the reverse side. The hole

64 / **Gros Ventre envelope panel, ca. 1875**

H 16 in., W 14 3/4 in. Buffalo rawhide, pigment

Presented to Richard A. Pohrt by Cora Chandler of the Gros Ventre tribe, Fort Belknap Reservation, Montana, 1937. Collection of Richard A. and Marion D. Pohrt

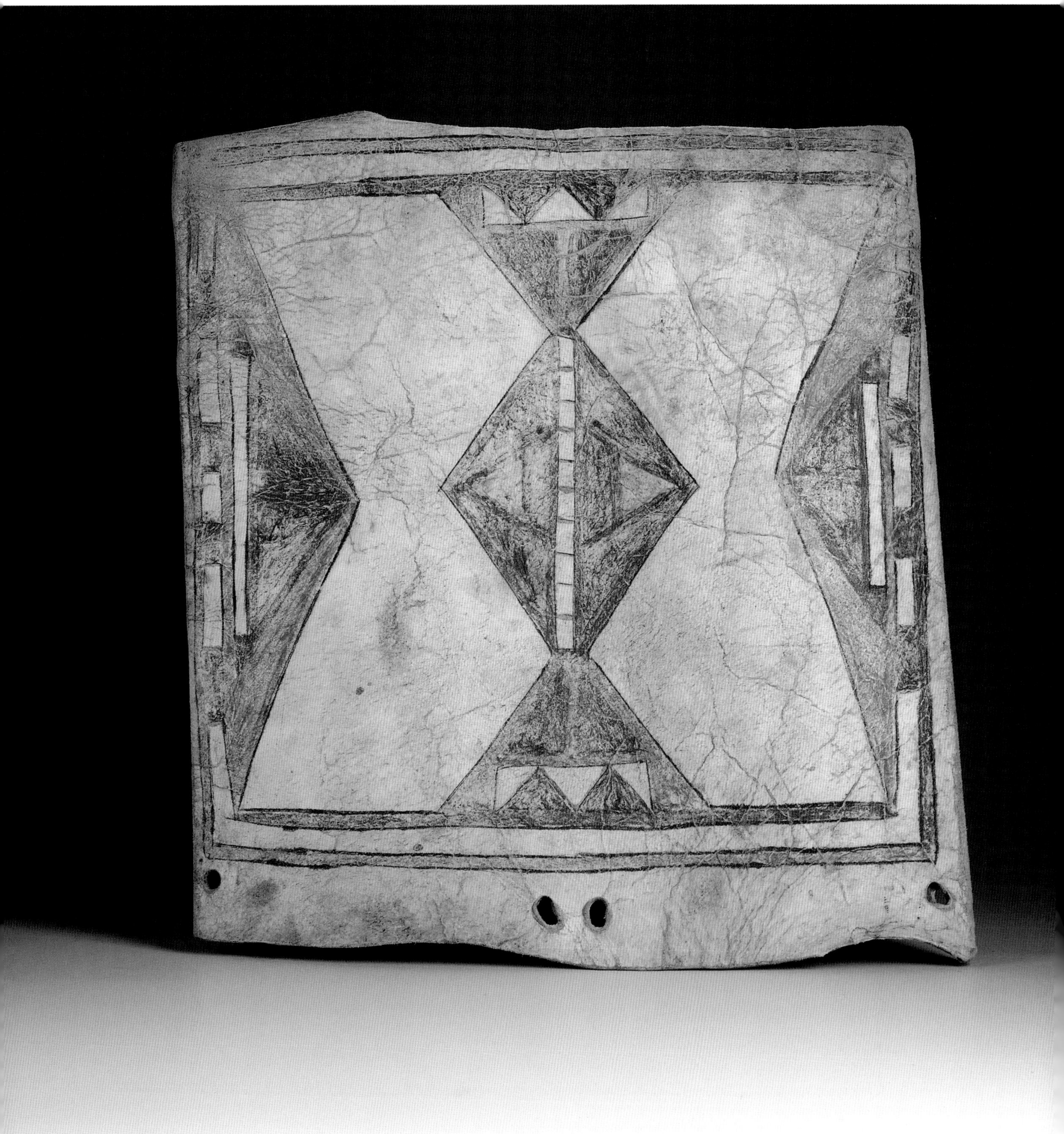

pattern on the outer flaps is traditionally single-pair-single, but a few are closed with three pairs.

Nearly all documented Gros Ventre parfleches are envelopes; only a few cylinders and flat cases are known. The latter are unfringed and identical in construction to those of the Sioux, with designs similar to those on envelopes. The cylinders are small and tapering and painted with designs that are related to those of the Crow.[13] The thongs that secure the case are long enough to provide a thin fringe, in the manner of Sioux, Crow, and Blackfeet cases of the same type.

65 / **Gros Ventre pair of envelopes, ca. 1885**

L 24 1/2 in., W 13 in.; L 24 3/4 in., W 13 in. Rawhide, pigment

Collected by William Wildschut from the Arapaho, Wind River Reservation, Wyoming. National Museum of the American Indian, Smithsonian Institution, 12/2153

13. An example of this type is illustrated in Kroeber (1908: 193).

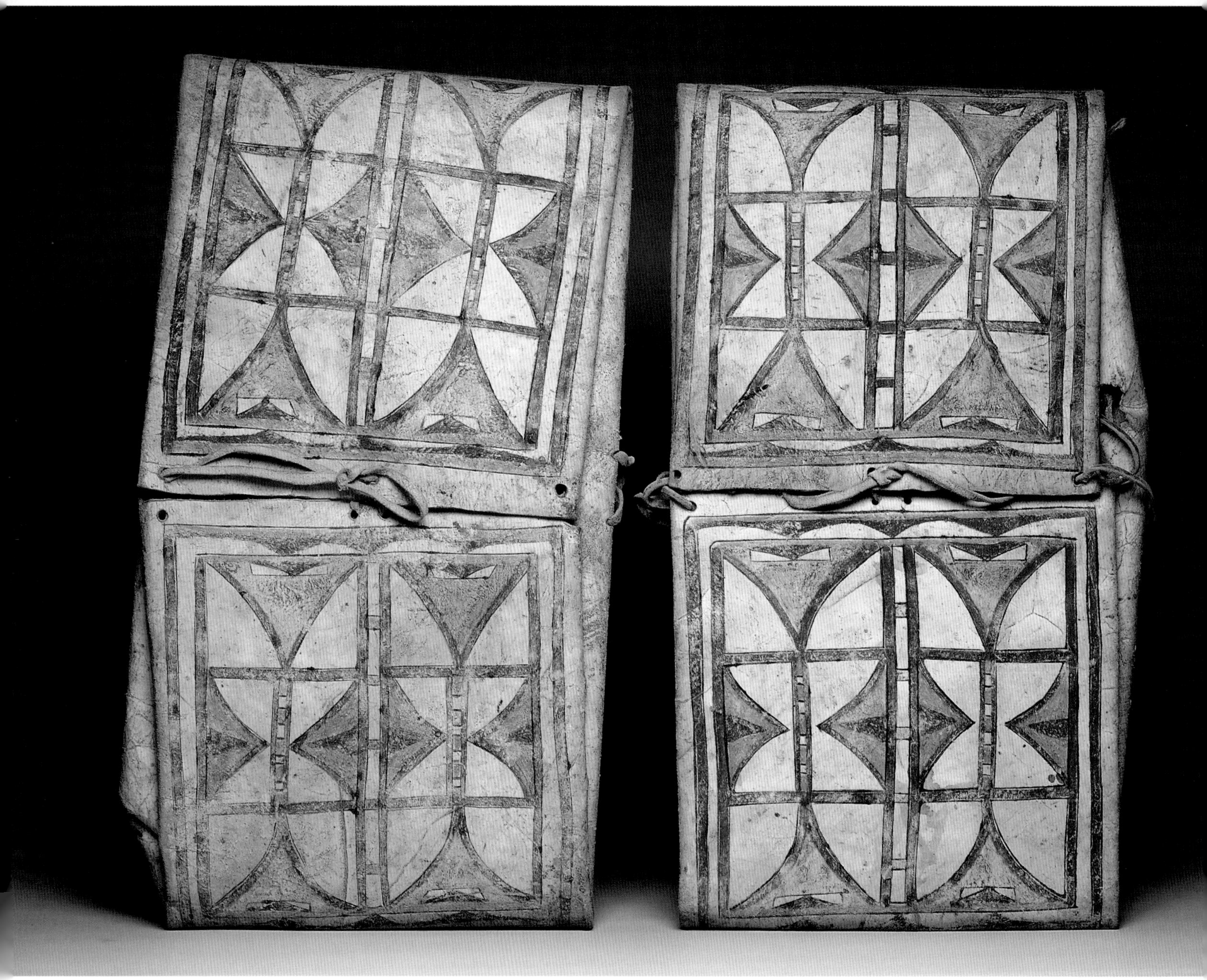

66 / **Gros Ventre envelope, ca. 1900**

L 27 1/4 in., W 13 3/4 in. Rawhide, pigment

Collected by Gilbert Wilson on the Fort Belknap Reservation, Montana, 1908. American Museum of Natural History, 50/7123

67 / **Assiniboine (?) envelope, ca. 1880**

L 22 in., W 13 1/2 in. Rawhide, pigment

Collected by Robert Lowie on the Stoney Reserve, Alberta, Canada, 1907. American Museum of Natural History, 50/6819

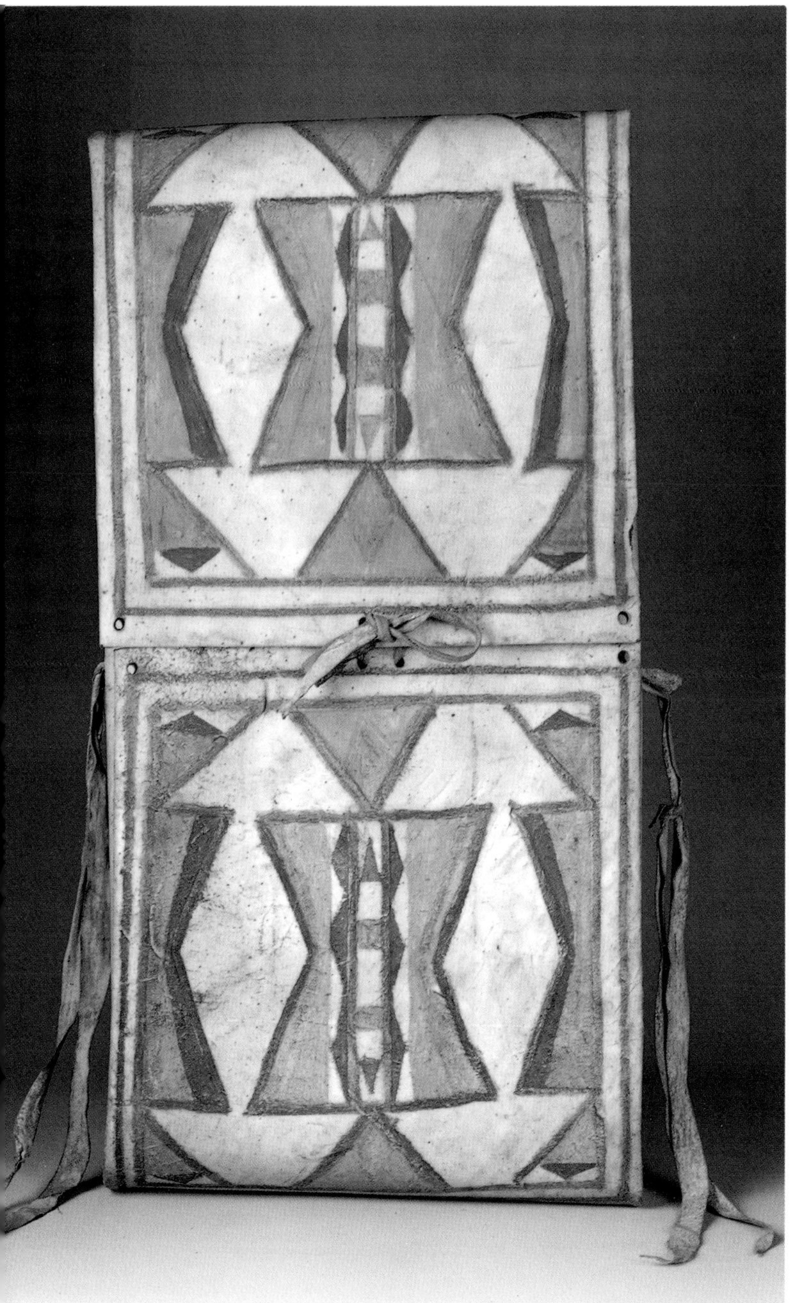

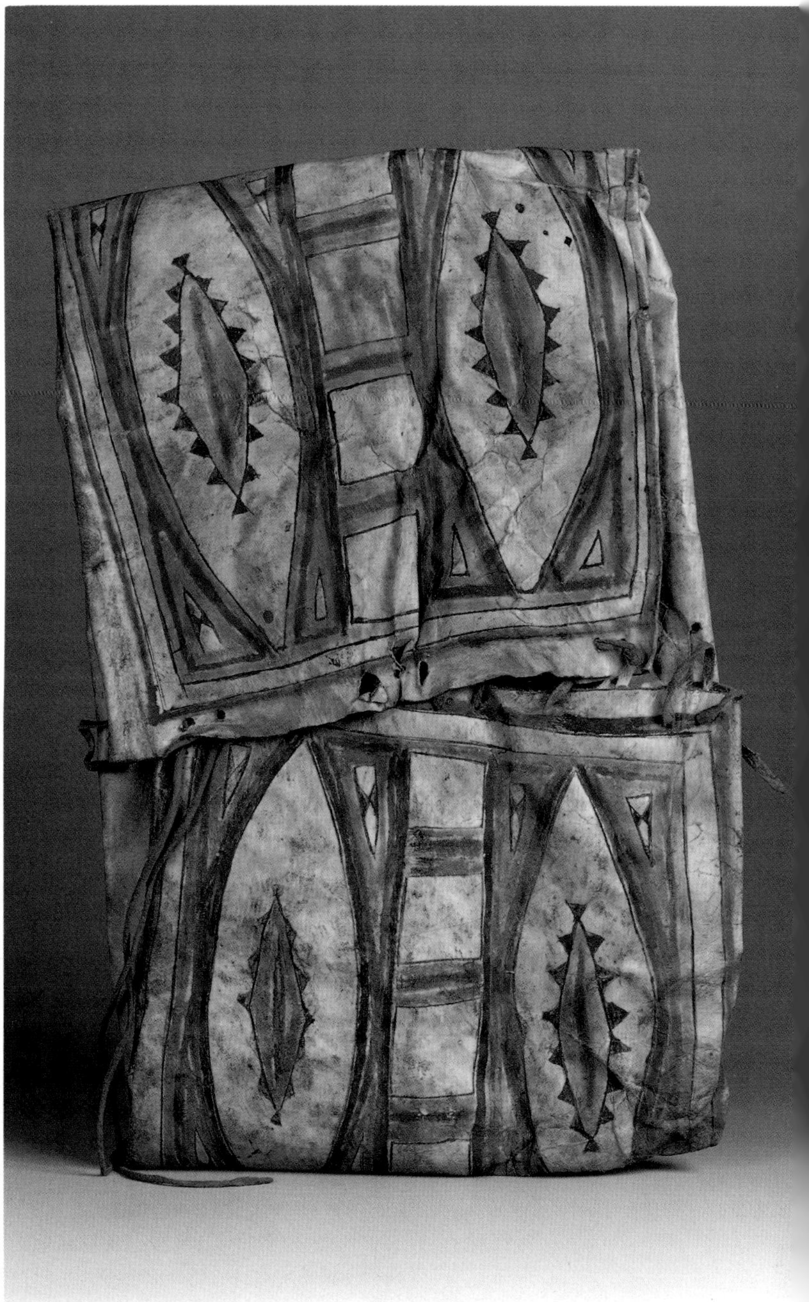

BLACKFEET

The largest and most powerful tribe in the Northern Plains was made up of the three divisions of the Blackfeet Confederacy: the Piegan, who were divided into northern and southern bands, the Blood, and the Siksika, or Northern Blackfeet. Although these groups were politically independent, they were closely allied and bound together by common cultural roots.

The parfleches created by the women of these divisions share many basic characteristics, but differ in a variety of details. A survey of Blackfeet collections suggests that there was a greater uniformity in style at an earlier date, with significant changes in the work of some groups during the last half of the nineteenth century. However, any conclusions from attempting to trace either the precise chronology or the exact nature of these changes must be tentative because of the lack of documentation and the continuous cultural exchange and trade in material goods, including parfleches, that took place between the three bands. While large numbers of Blackfeet parfleches may be found in collections today, relatively few have any collection history that indicates the tribal division from which they were obtained; and even when this information is available, there is no confirmation that the pieces were actually made where they were collected. At the same time, consistent differences in painting style are indeed apparent in many of the parfleches collected from specific divisions, enabling us to distinguish a distinct set of stylistic characteristics for each of the three groups. This allows us to identify a number of pieces, but it does not provide enough information to reconstruct fully the history of Blackfeet parfleche painting and classify all its various manifestations.

Apart from the variations in painting just cited, however, all Blackfeet parfleches share certain common features. Envelopes tend to be relatively small and compact, and are proportionally more square in shape than those from any other group. Even more distinctive, the outer flaps are trapezoidal in shape (pl. 73). Although this feature varies in degree—as may be seen in surveying the illustrations in this book—and was also used by the Sarci, Kutenai, and some of the Western Plateau tribes, it remains one of the surest indications of Blackfeet origin. All divisions used three pairs of holes to secure the outer flaps, and a single pair of holes was located at the center of each side near the crease. Loops of hide extended from these side holes, which were used in the Blackfeet method of tying the parfleche on the horse.

Blackfeet painting is somewhat difficult to describe in general terms because it varies so greatly in refinement and complexity. The most finely crafted pieces rival Cheyenne painting in their intricacy and delicate execution (pl. 77). At the opposite extreme are containers that are so loosely painted that a completely different effect is achieved (pl. 74). Some designs are exceedingly complicated, while others are so simple

68 / **Blackfeet (?) envelope, ca. 1840**

L 32 1/2 in., W 17 1/2 in. Rawhide, pigment

Collected by Count Armand Fouche d'Otrante during his travels in the Northen Plains region, 1842–44. Folkens Museum–Ethnografiska, Stockholm, 1854.2.10

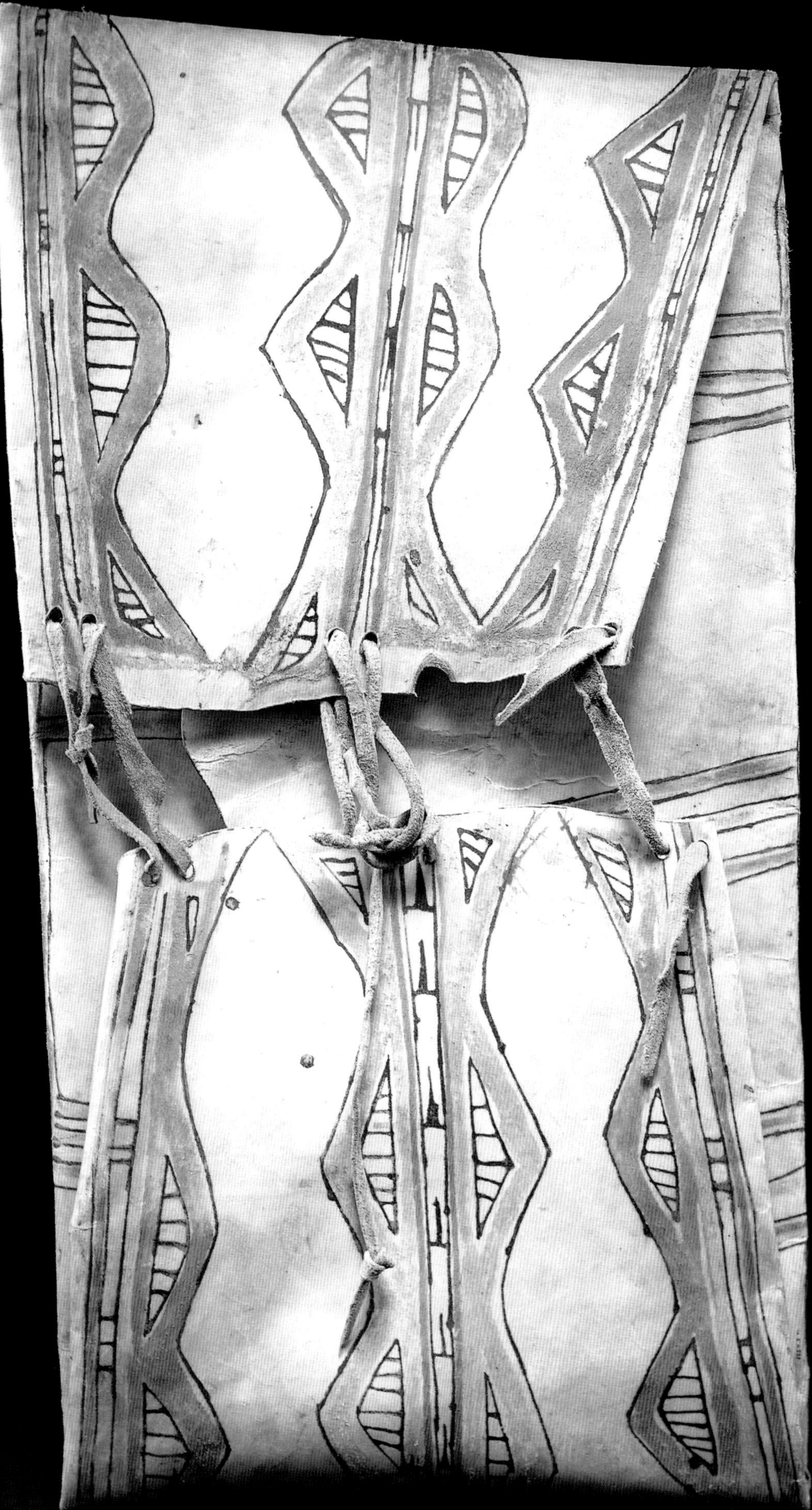

that they fail to sustain a viewer's interest beyond their initial impact.

Still, there are several discernable features in the painted designs that, like details of construction, transcend the stylistic variations of each division and unify Blackfeet painting as a whole. First, the images tend to be freely composed in both drawing and application of color—even the most refined possess a quality that is direct and expressive. Little concern for the exact symmetry found in many other traditions is apparent; instead, the paintings derive their sense of structure from the forceful, rhythmic quality of contour and line, and an overall balance of forms (pl. 71). Relatively large areas of unpainted hide were allowed to remain in many compositions, to the extent that this element sometimes functioned as a neutral background for the painted motifs (pls. 70, 77, 78); this was particularly true of those created by Blood women. Other artists chose to establish visually active, figure-ground relationships even while incorporating broad, unpainted spaces (pls. 68, 80).

A great variety of compositions were created or adopted from other tribes by Blackfeet painters, making it impossible to characterize a few configurations as classic designs as might be done with the Sioux and Cheyenne. Many of these included both curved and straightedged elements. Often the curving forms were combined with angular shapes in the most subtle manner, quietly animating the designs with an unexpected tension (pls. 69, 70); others are quite dramatic in effect (pl. 72). Compositions with a central figure were common (pls. 69, 80), as were those based on a two-part vertical division of the field (pls. 76, 78). Both usually incorporated diamonds, hourglasses, or a triangle-diamond-triangle configuration as primary elements. Other images were structured by dividing the field horizontally or vertically into three parts (pl. 73), or into four equal areas (pl. 72). Blackfeet women also produced their own interpretations of the five-box pattern of the Arapaho and the nine-box design so favored by the Transmontane groups. Other compositions were occasionally created that defy classification, such as the remarkable envelope pictured in plate 81. Another distinctive Blackfeet feature of composition is the transposition of colors within the overall configuration or central design elements (pls. 72, 80); this practice can be found in the work of all three divisions and during all periods.

The borders of Blackfeet parfleches consist of two narrow bands that are nearly always different in color. The area in between is sometimes left open and undecorated, or it may be filled in with diagonal bands, triangles, or rectangular shapes. When this is done, it is most common for one set of motifs to be used along the sides and another to be used at the top and bottom of each flap (pls. 72, 76). This type of border distinguishes Blackfeet envelopes from those of the Western Plateau groups that might be quite similar in most other ways (pl. 111).

Side flaps were almost always painted by the Piegan, usually with triangular designs or bands of color, while Blood women only occasionally

69 / **Blackfeet elliptical case, ca. 1840**
H 28 in., W 13 3/4 in. (not including fringe).
Rawhide, pigment, native leather

National Museum of the American Indian, Smithsonian Institution 6/5934

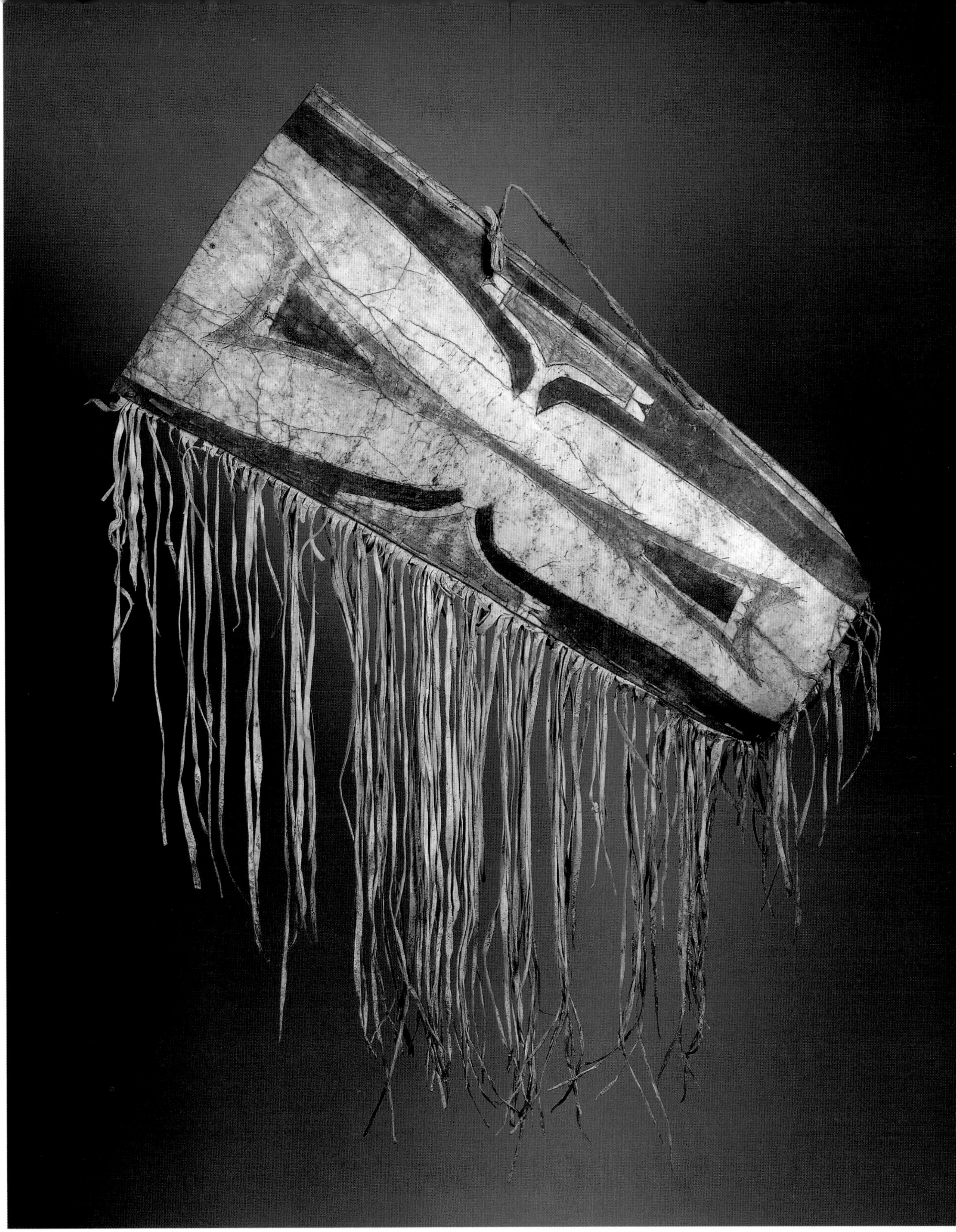

included this feature in their work. The Siksika generally preferred to leave the side flaps undecorated. This same variation is found in the presence or absence of painted bands on the reverse side. When the side flaps are painted, the designs extend from a base line that follows the edge of the envelope on the reverse, joining the painted panels adorning the outer flaps. On most Siksika and Blood envelopes, therefore, the backs of the containers are unpainted. On a very few envelopes and most flat cases, the reverse side is bordered by a single line of color framing the rectangular shape.

Blackfeet women seldom extended their range of color beyond the use of red, blue, yellow, and green, although unusual browns were sometimes substituted for a true red. Many paintings were even more restrained, being composed of only two or three hues in addition to black outlining. This was particularly true of those created by the Siksika and Blood, who tended to prefer a combination of red, yellow, and blue. In contrast, the Piegan generally incorporated all four colors into their designs, but even so the large areas of unpainted surface tend to lessen their effect. As a class, however, Blackfeet parfleches appear exceptionally rich in color because of the subtle differences in the pigments used, which result in a greater variation in the character of colors produced. Blackfeet women apparently continued to use natural pigments long after most tribes had completely adapted trade varieties. At the same time, they were creating large numbers of parfleches at the turn of the century, which were readily collected and preserved. The result is that the existing body of Blackfeet parfleches lacks the standardization of color found in the work of the Transmontane groups and Sioux, who were also producing in great numbers at the same time, and is often possessed of subtle and unexpected qualities. Of the three tribal divisions, the Piegan seem to have acquired trade colors first and utilized them most extensively, especially when they began to produce parfleches for the tourist trade associated with the opening of Glacier Park in 1910.

The sizing on Blackfeet parfleches varies greatly and affects the appearance of color. Some parfleches are so heavily sized as to appear varnished and yellowed, while others seem to be barely covered. Generally, the sizing is an obvious element, especially as it transforms the unpainted areas of hide within the design and unifies them with colored forms.

The major difference between parfleches of the three Blackfeet divisions is the method of painting and the resulting presence or absence of black outlining. The designs of all early Blackfeet parfleches were painted and then outlined in the manner described in the preceding chapter (pls. 68, 71, 77, 80). This approach was abandoned by the Piegan during the last quarter of the nineteenth century in favor of the second method described, in which the design was established by structural lines of color and then filled in with additional colors (pls. 74, 75). Dark blue was usually preferred for this element, but it was not uncom-

70 / **Blackfeet (Piegan?) envelope, ca. 1865**

L 27 1/2 in., W 16 in. Buffalo rawhide, pigment

National Museum of the American Indian, Smithsonian Institution 23/274

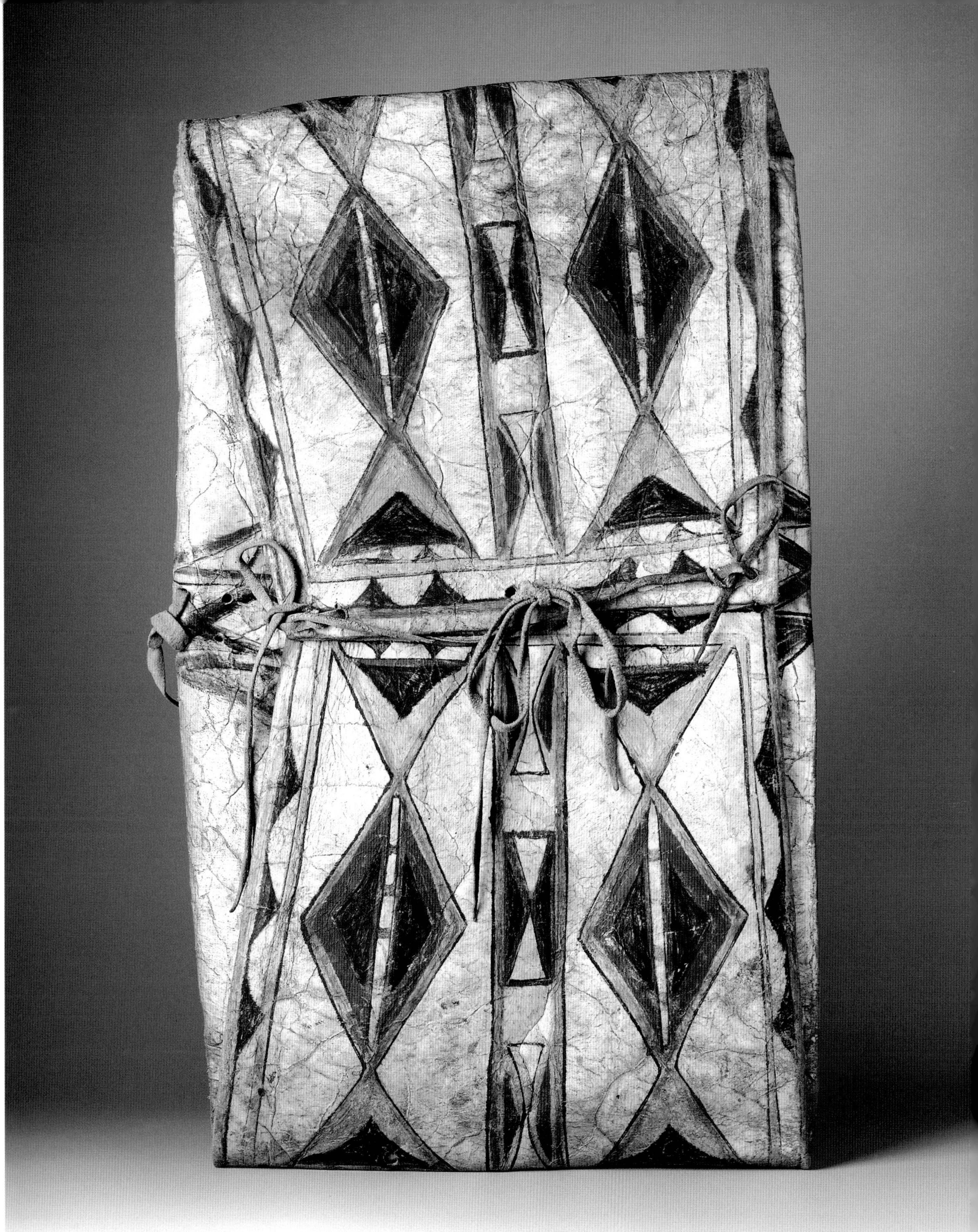

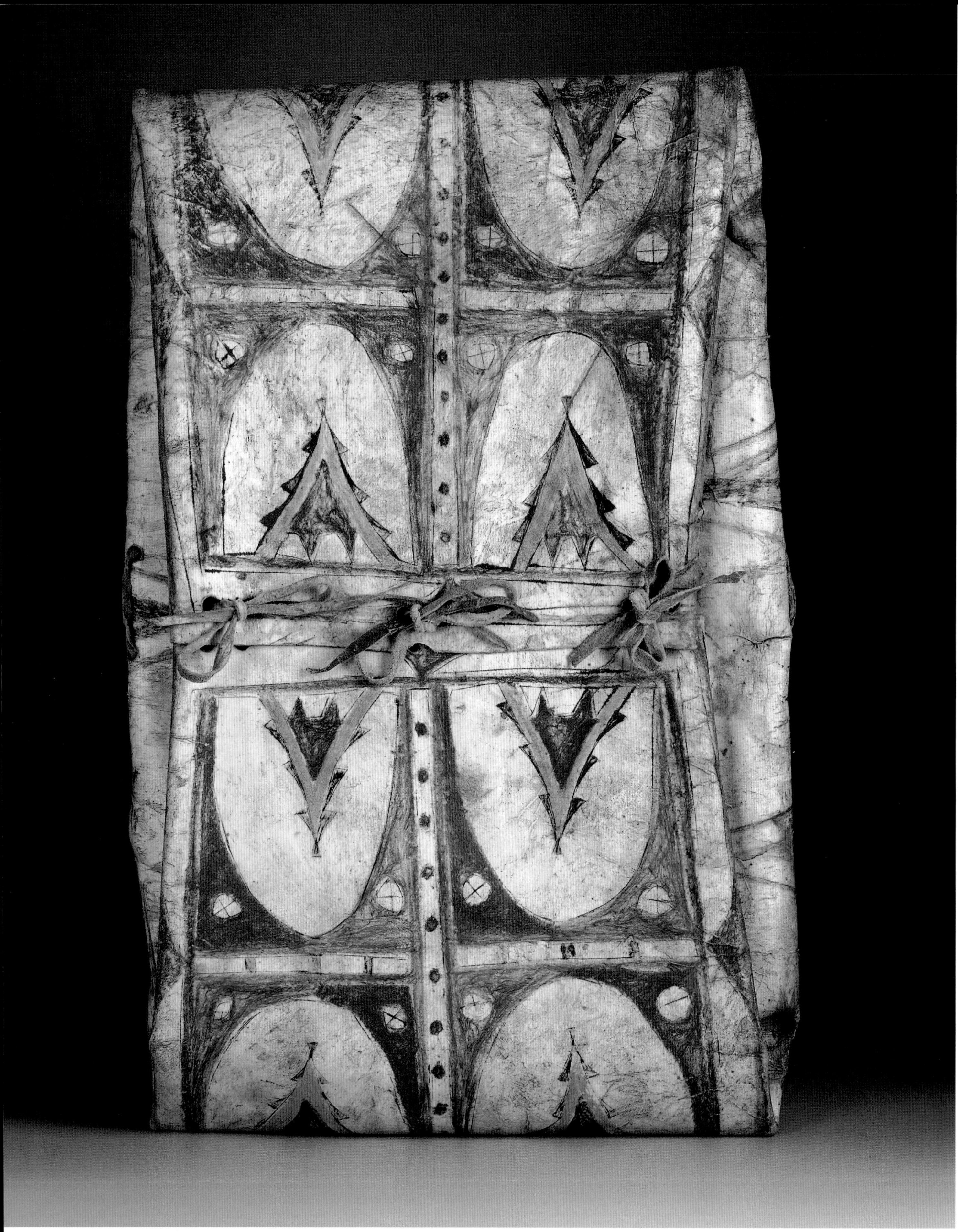

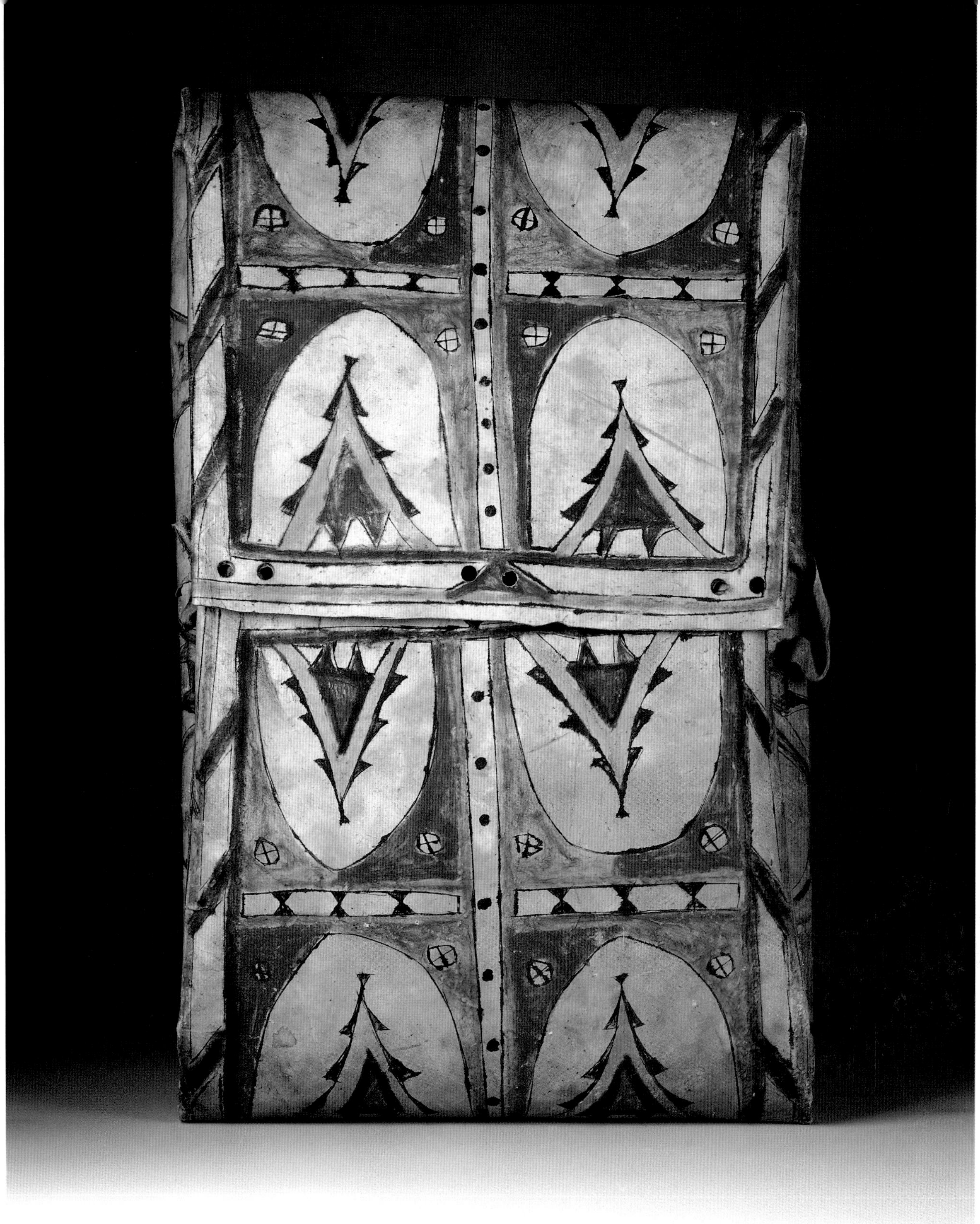

71 / **Blackfeet (Piegan?) envelope, ca. 1875**

L 27 in., W 16 1/2 in. Buffalo rawhide, pigment

Private collection

72 / **Blackfeet (Piegan?) envelope, ca. 1885**

L 25 1/4 in., W 16 in. Rawhide, pigment

Minnesota Historical Society, Museum Collections, Gift of Ann Winston, 8643/3

mon for two or even three different colors to be used for these structural lines within a single composition. The envelope illustrated in plate 73 is unusual in that the two styles are combined in its painting; the central figure is outlined while the outer forms and border are not. The Blood also adopted this style of painting but at a later date, probably during the early twentieth century. After this time, their parfleches are most easily differentiated from Piegan pieces by the lack of side-flap painting.

Blackfeet artists employed black outlining like the Gros Ventre; it was used only to separate the painted forms from the unpainted ground, never to separate colored areas within the major forms in the manner of Central Plains painters. Small black elements were incorporated by all three groups in conjunction with outlining, but were especially prominent in Blood designs (pls. 76, 77). The earliest Blackfeet paintings sometimes include a repetition of tiny black lines along the edges of major motifs.

The Northern Blackfeet maintained the greatest continuity of style throughout their history. They never gave up outlining and appear to have been the last of the three groups to adopt trade pigments. Surviving examples also suggest that Siksika envelopes were always small like those of the Blood people. In contrast, the earliest Piegan pieces are larger in scale, becoming smaller during the reservation period.

In addition to envelopes, all of the Blackfeet tribes produced large numbers of flat cases and cylinders in a variety of sizes. Many were constructed with elaborate fringe that was usually rather wide-cut, and it was common to further ornament containers of this kind with strips of red cloth attached along the seams (pl. 79). Most of the heavily fringed flat cases also had two pairs of flaring fringes suspended from the front surface (pl. 75); this very distinctive feature sets Blackfeet cases apart from those of the same type produced by the Western Plateau tribes, which are sometimes quite similar in other respects. More rarely, large flat cases with projecting ends that were essentially boat-shaped were produced.[14]

As mentioned earlier, a great many of these containers were made to store ceremonial items and sacred bundles. Several of this type are more or less entirely covered with red-ochre paint, to the extent that none of the original painted designs is visible.[15] This condition is the result of ritual procedures associated with the use of certain bundles. Over the years, the cases acquire successive layers of sacred color until their surfaces and fringe become a uniformly rich, dark red.

73 / **Blackfeet (Piegan) envelope, ca. 1890**

L 22 1/2 in., W 14 1/4 in. Rawhide, pigment

Attached label reads: "Blackfoot—Glacier Park—Browning, Montana." Collection of Michael and Sherry Maxwell

14. The frontispiece in Ewers (1955) pictures a large case of this type hanging from the saddle of a horse.

15. A number of these cases are pictured in Scriver (1990).

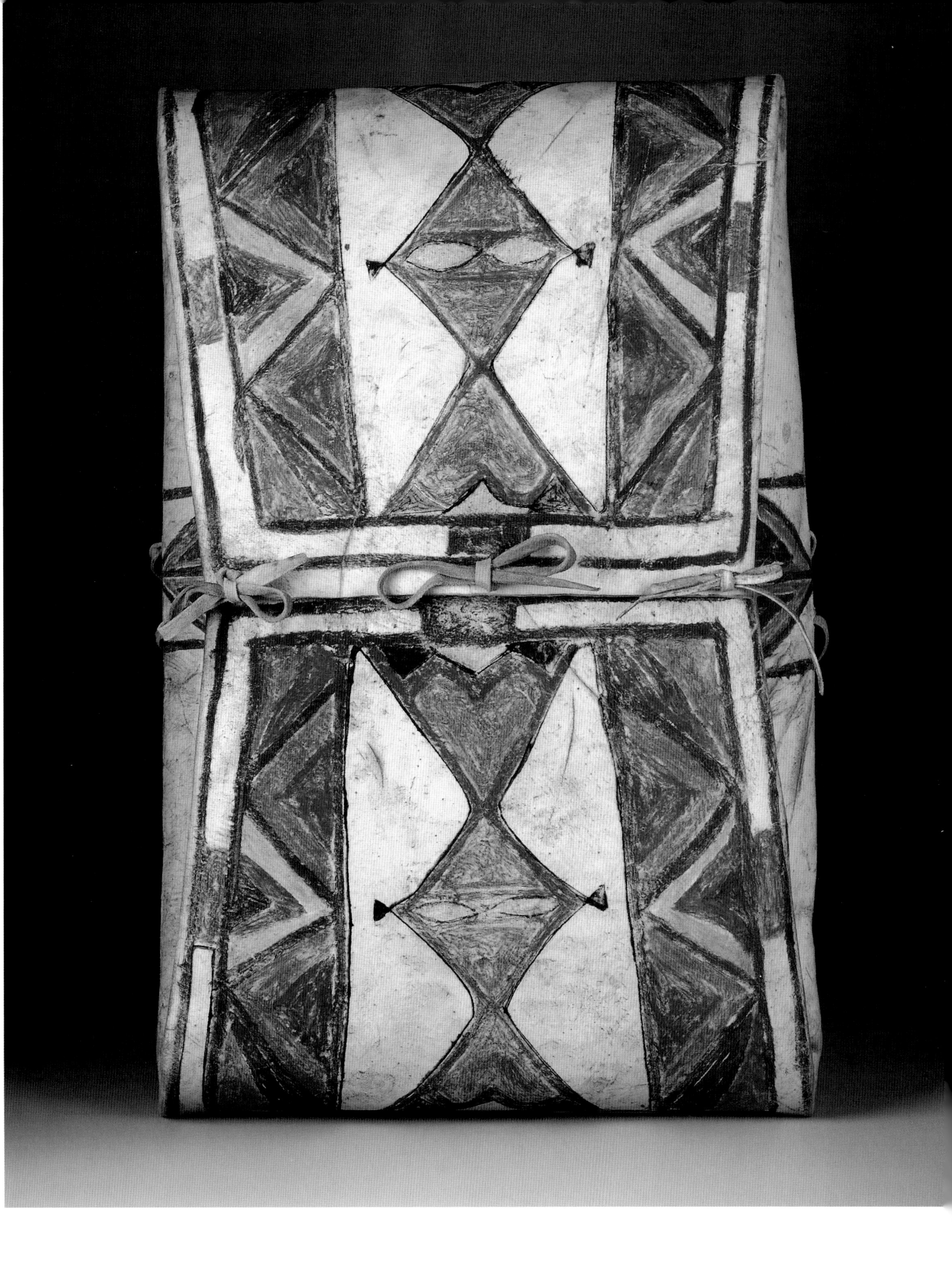

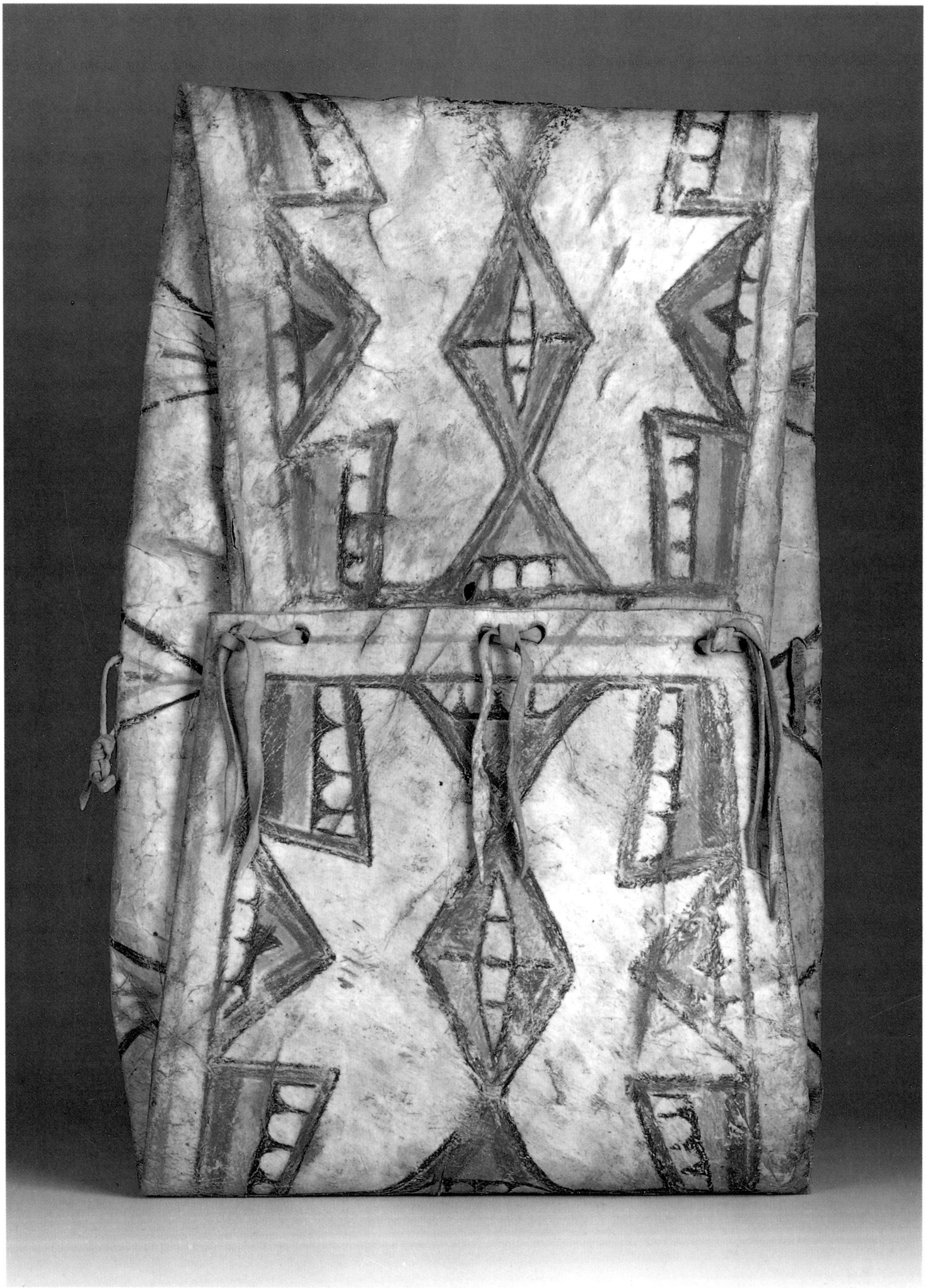

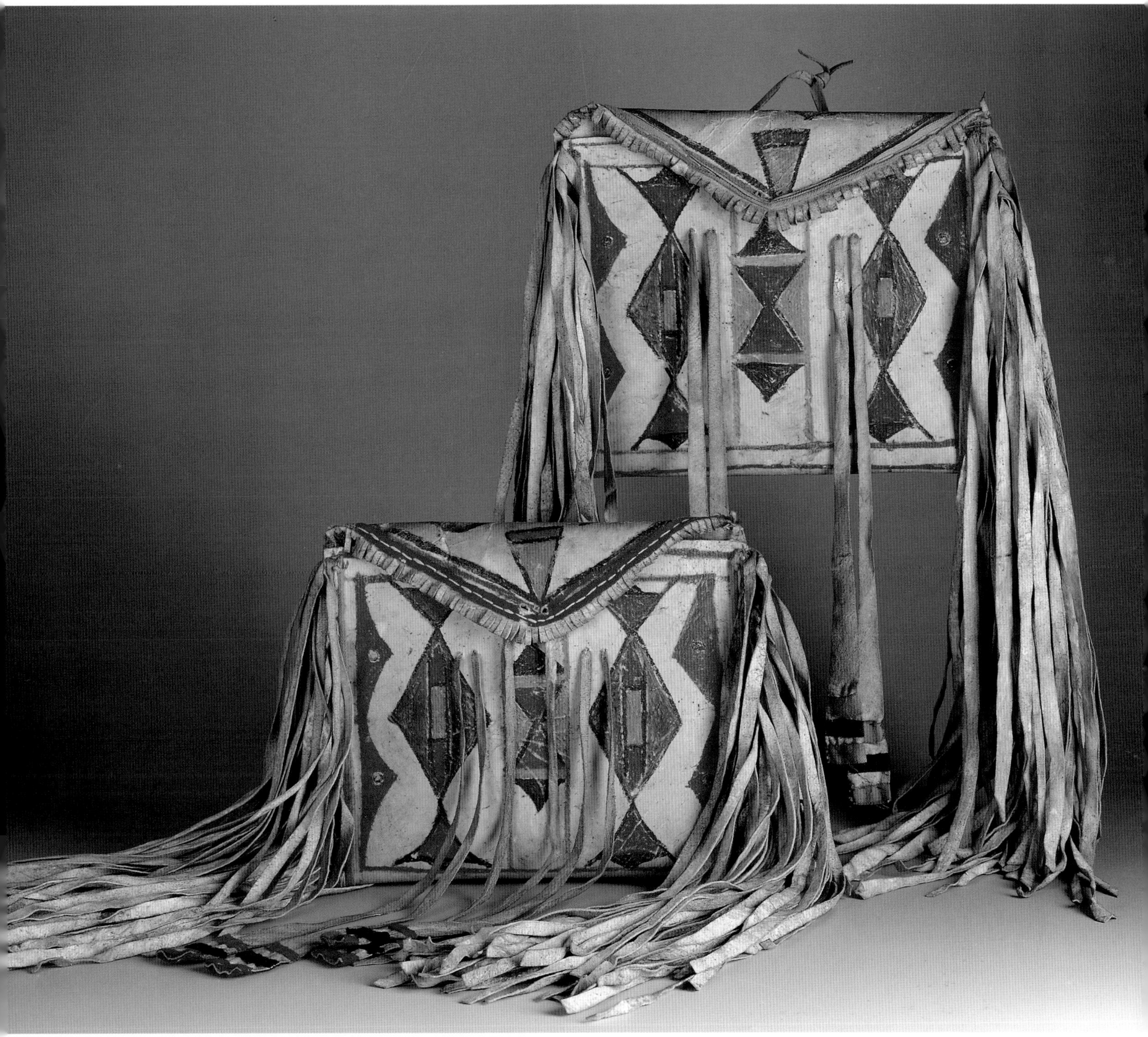

74 / **Blackfeet (Piegan) envelope, ca. 1890**

L 23 1/2 in., W 16 in. Rawhide, pigment

Private collection

75 / **Blackfeet (Piegan) pair of flat cases, ca. 1900**

H 10 in., W 12 1/2 in.; height with fringe 24 in.; H 10 in., W 12 3/4 in.; height with fringe 20 in. Rawhide, pigment, native leather, wool cloth

Collection of William A. Miller

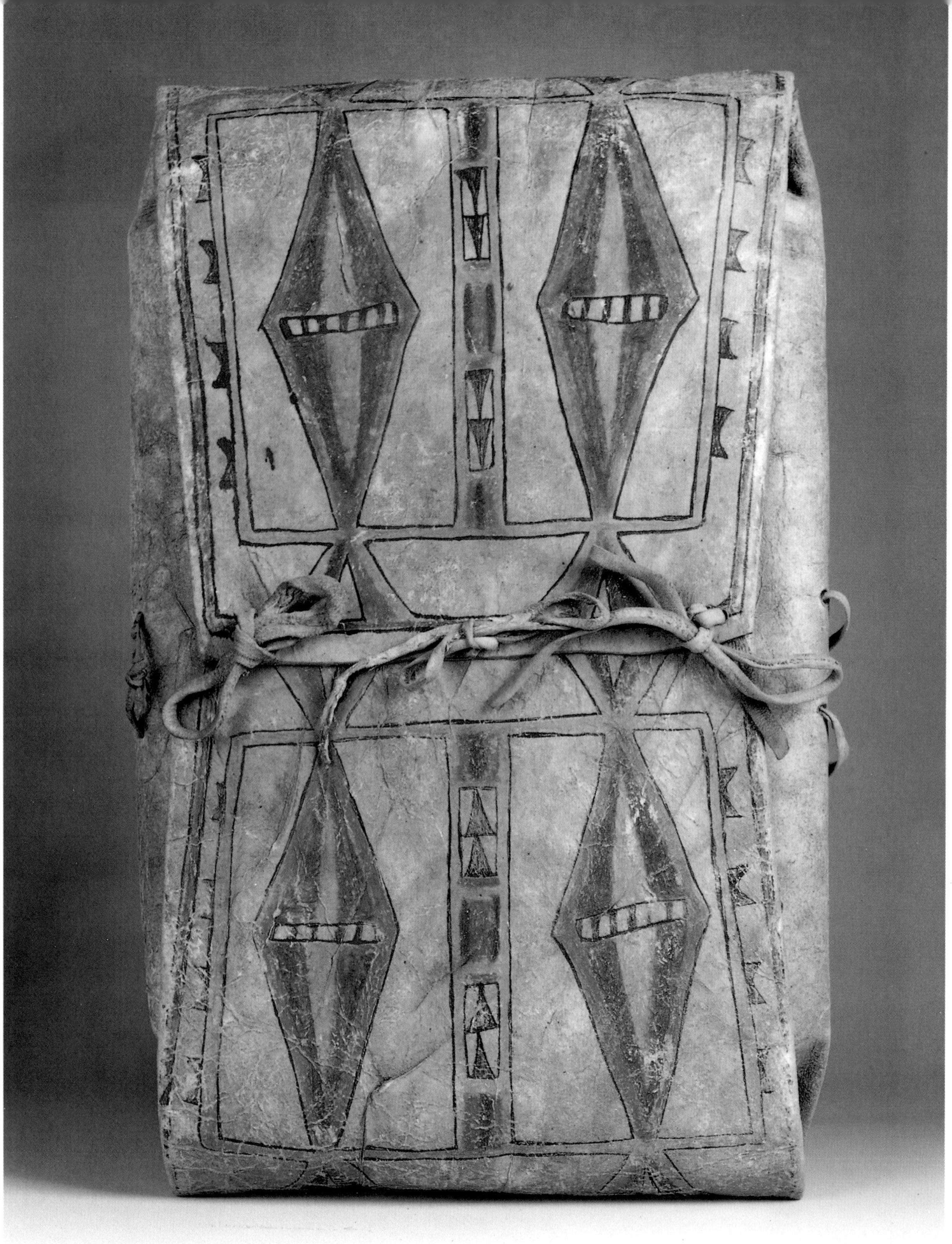

76 / **Blackfeet (Blood) envelope, ca. 1875**

L 22 in., W 13 in. Rawhide, pigment

Collection of Kenneth and Barbara Canfield, Santa Fe

77 / **Blackfeet (Blood) envelope, ca. 1885**

L 21 in., W 14 in. Rawhide, pigment

The University Museum, University of Pennsylvania, Philadelphia, 29-47-184

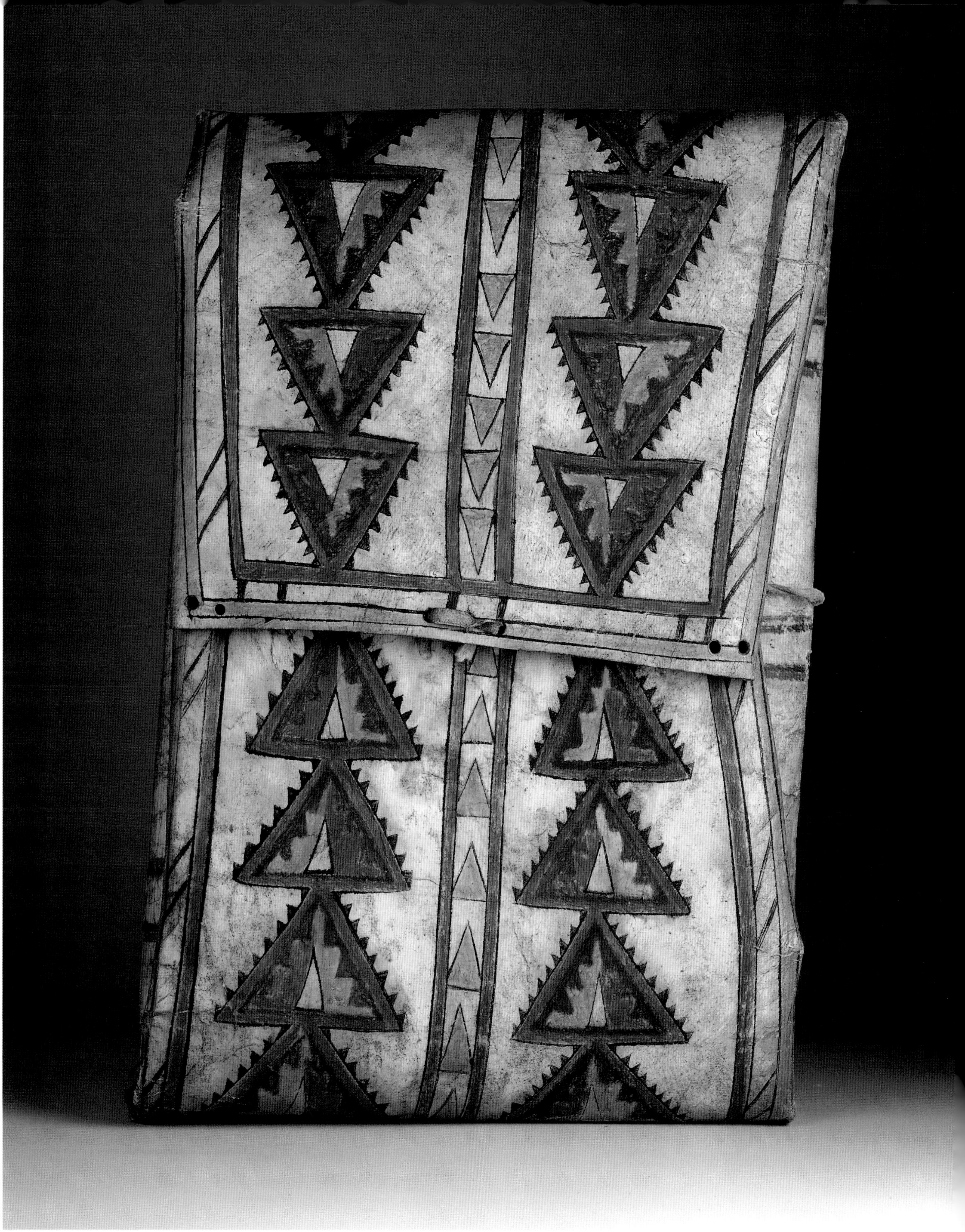

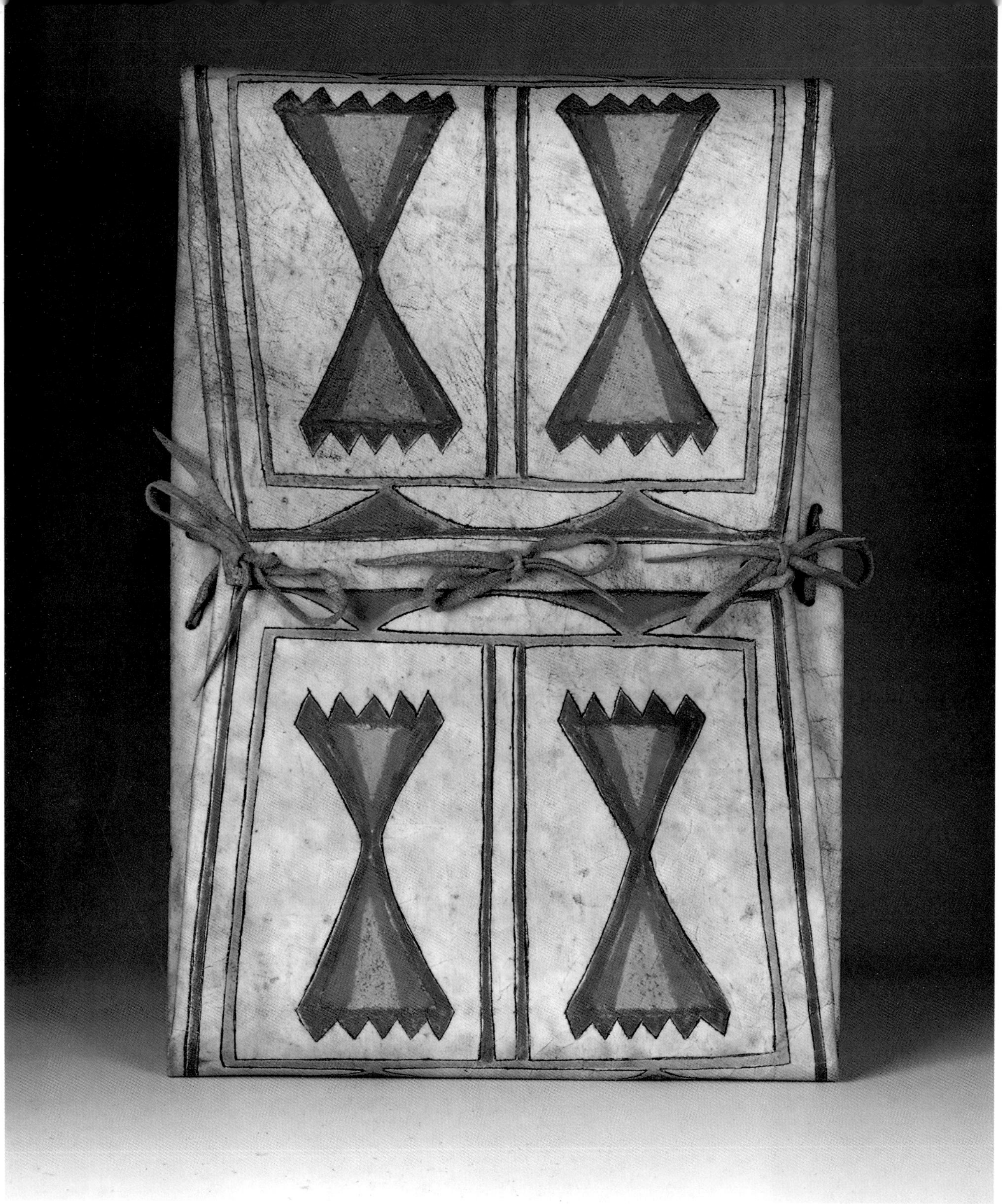

78 / **Blackfeet (Blood) envelope, ca. 1900**

L 24 in., W 16 in. Rawhide, pigment

Collected by Clark Wissler in Northwest Territory, 1903; matching envelope in the collection of Staatliche Museen, Museum für Völkerkunde, Berlin. American Museum of Natural History, 50/4416

79 / **Blackfeet (Blood?) cylinder, ca. 1890**

H 24 in., D 6 1/4 in.; fringe 20 in. Rawhide, pigment, native leather, wool cloth

The University Museum, University of Pennsylvania, Philadelphia, 45-15-838

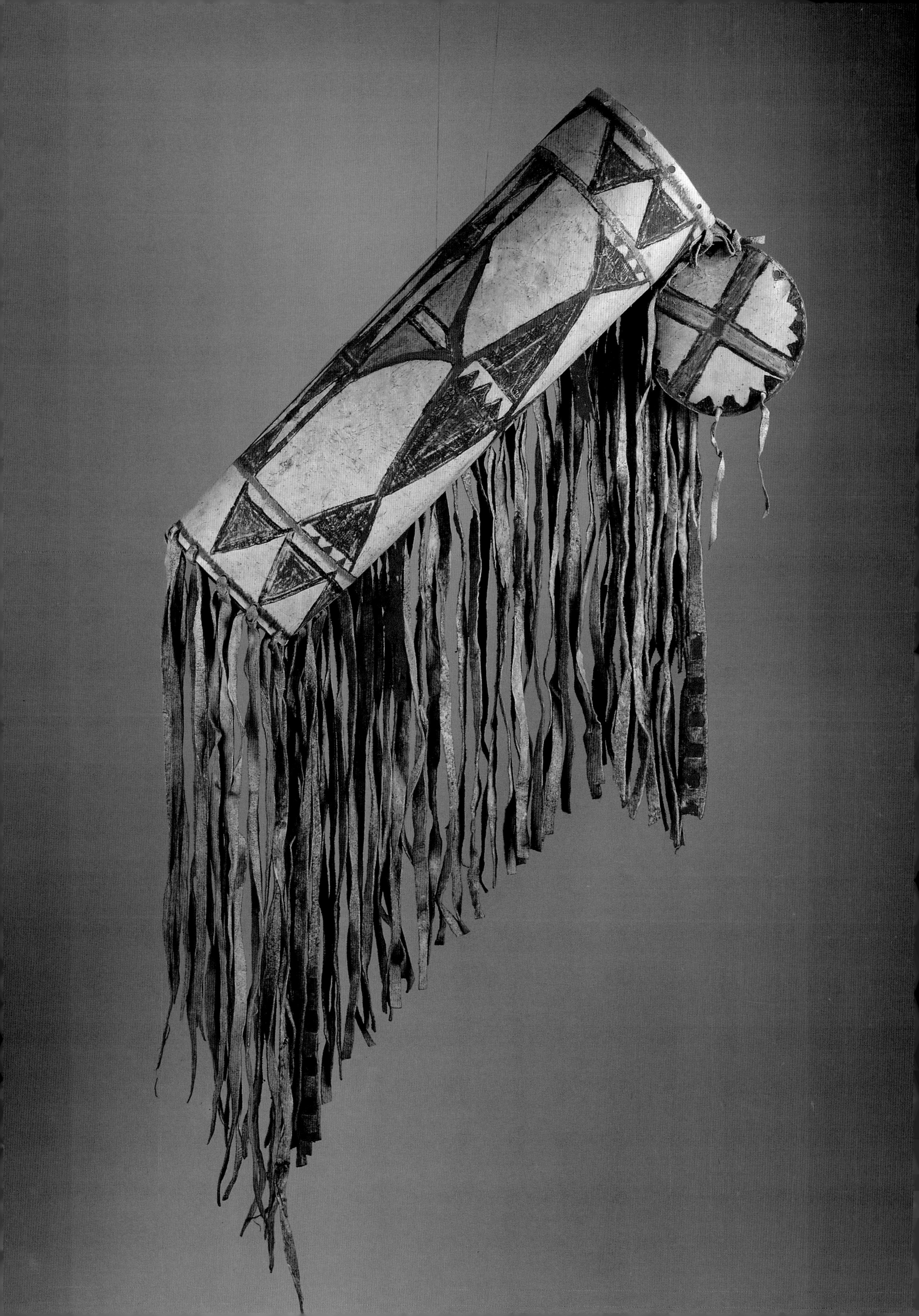

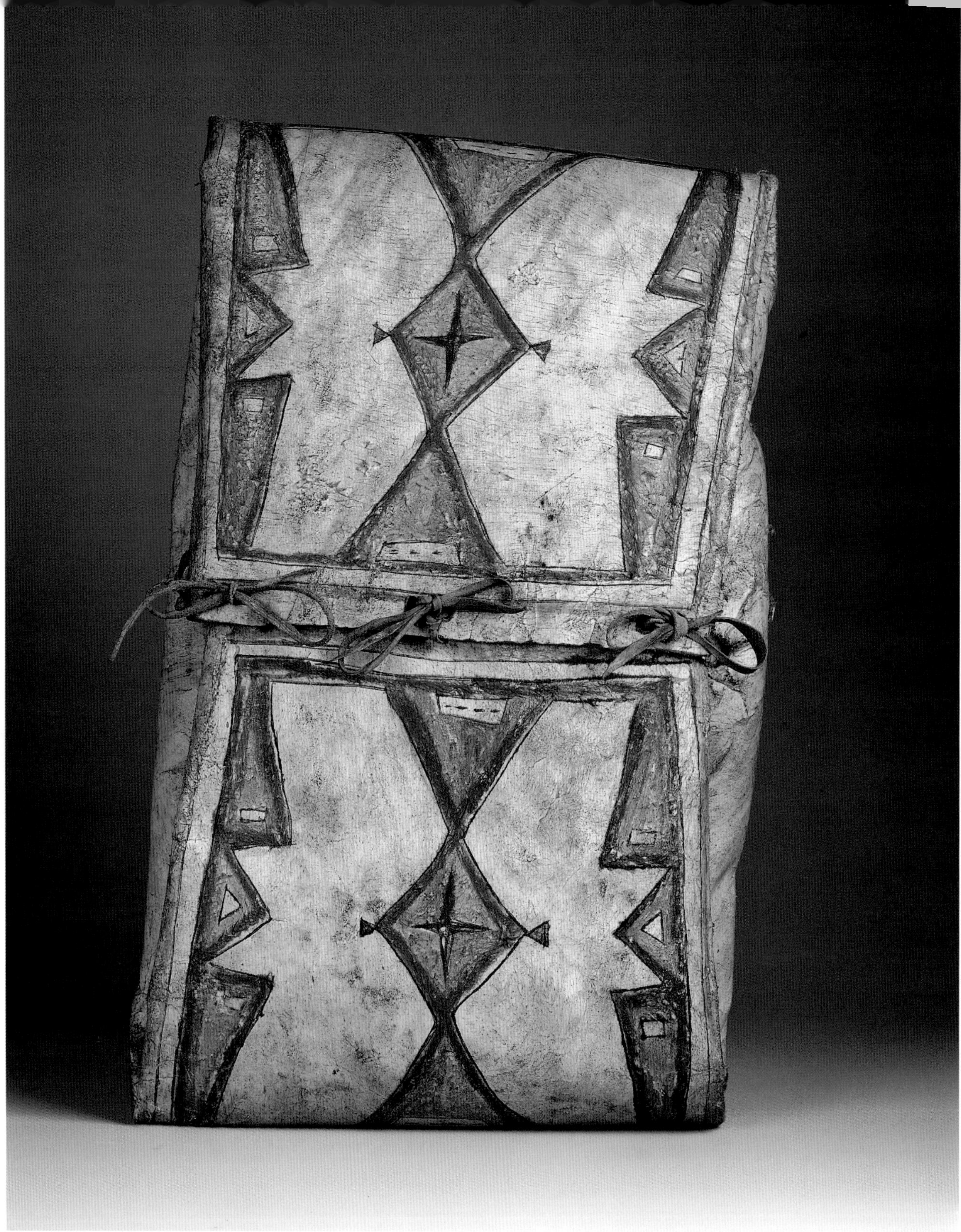

80 / **Blackfeet (Siksika) envelope, ca. 1875**

L 22 in., W 13 in. Rawhide, pigment

Collected by P. E. Goddard from the Sarci, 1905. American Museum of Natural History, 50/5959

81 / **Blackfeet (Siksika or Blood) envelope, ca. 1890**

L 21 1/2 in., W 13 3/4 in. Rawhide, pigment

Collection of Glenbow Museum, Calgary, Alberta, AF 5313

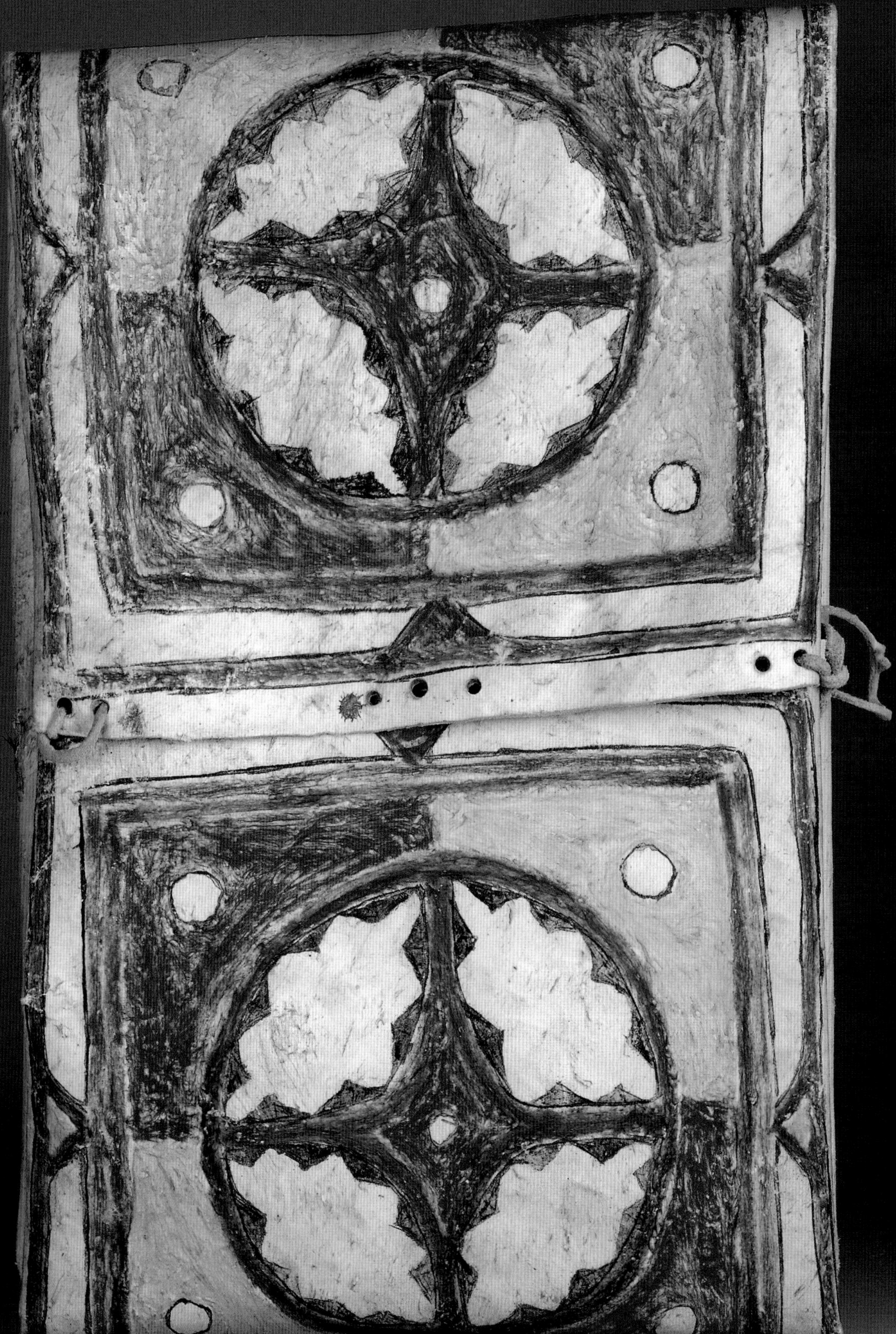

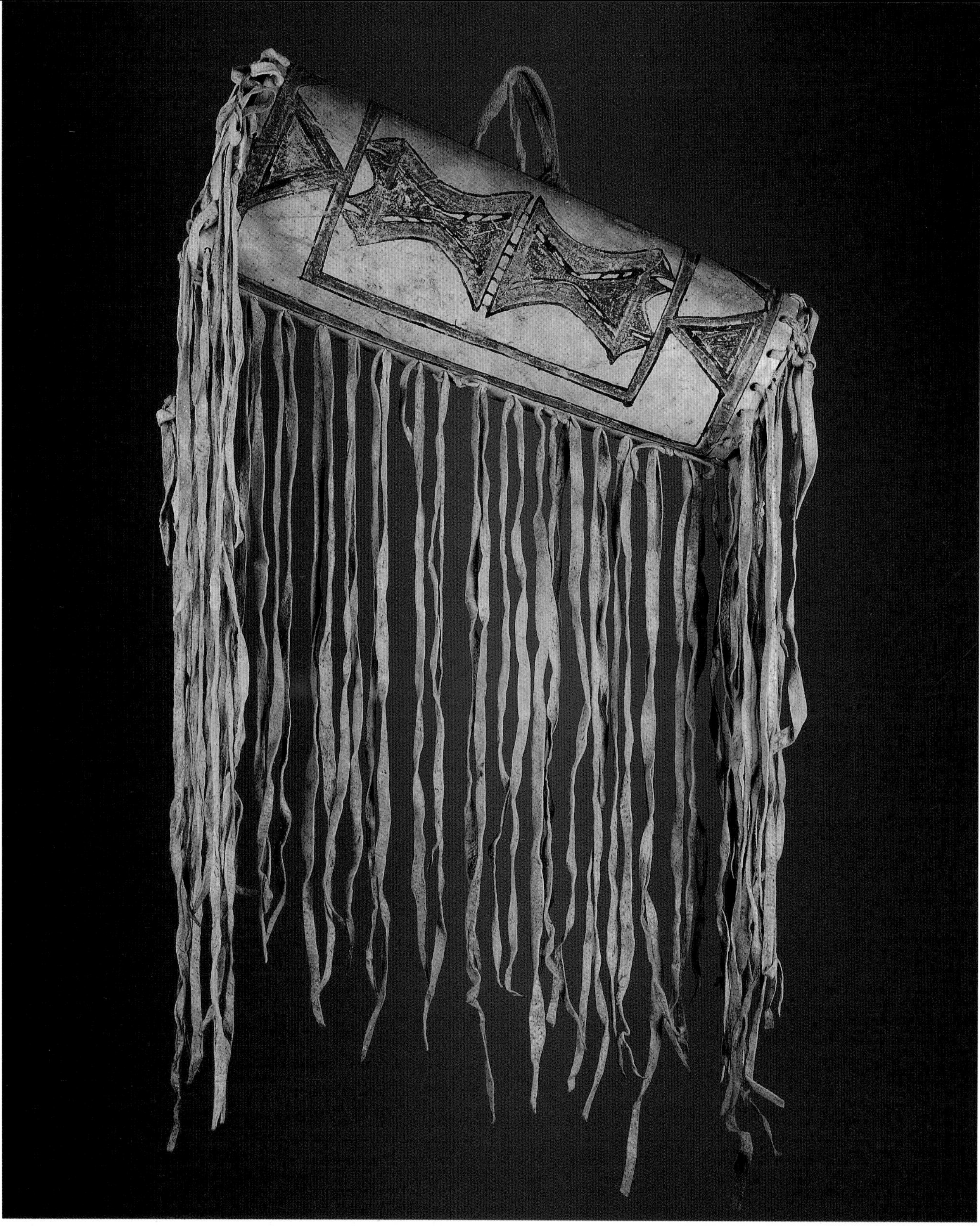

82 / **Blackfeet (Siksika) cylinder, ca. 1880**

H 16 in., D 5 in.; fringe 21 in. Rawhide, pigment, native leather

Collection of Glenbow Museum, Calgary, Alberta, AF 1166A

SARCI

The Sarci were a small tribe closely allied to the Blackfeet, who occupied the territory to the northwest of the Siksika. They were culturally similar to the Blackfeet, and the few parfleches collected from them are indistinguishable from Blackfeet examples; they possess all of the defining Blackfeet features and reveal none that would set them apart. Indeed, these parfleches may be of Blackfeet origin obtained in trade by the Sarci, or else Sarci painting was so heavily influenced by their dominant neighbors that their parfleches are stylistically identical.

The majority of parfleches attributed to the Sarci tend to be rather loosely painted and without black outlining in the manner of Piegan pieces (pl. 83). The remaining examples are similar to the parfleches of either the Siksika and Blood, or the Western Plateau, their stylistic diversity reinforcing the probability that they were acquired directly from those groups. Certainly a tribe so small and unified would not concurrently maintain three or four distinct styles. Undoubtedly the Sarci produced parfleches of their own, but it is impossible at this time to identify them with assurance.

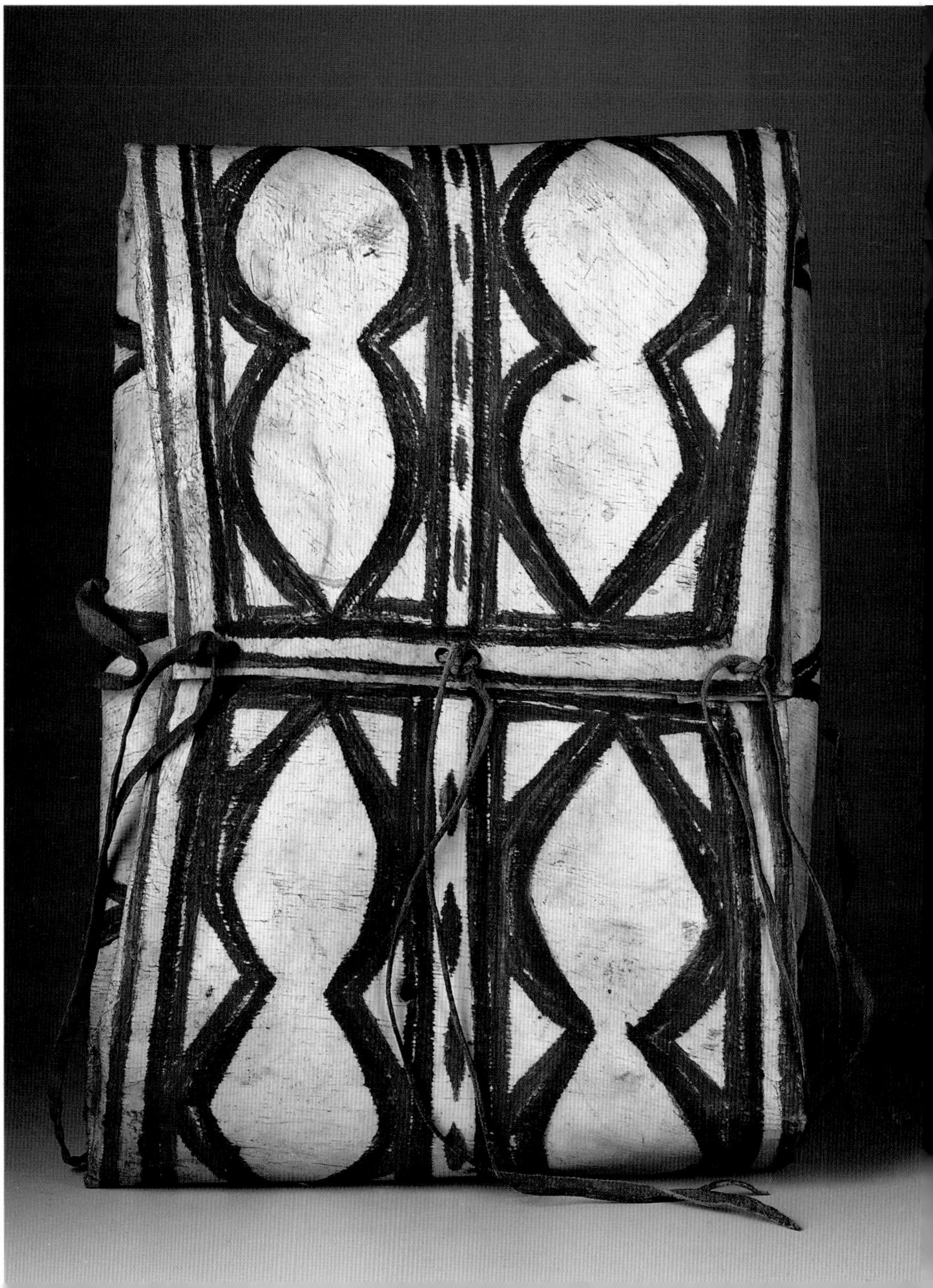

83 / **Sarci (?) envelope, ca. 1890**

L 24 1/2 in., W 16 1/2 in. Rawhide, pigment

Collected by Clark Wissler in Northwest Territory, 1903. American Museum of Natural History, 50/4399

KUTENAI

The Kutenai inhabited the intermontane region of the northeastern Plateau in Alberta and the United States. Although the different bands occupied this area throughout the nineteenth century, their traditions indicate that they were originally Plains people. It is probable that they were driven to the western side of the Rocky Mountains by the Blackfeet at the beginning of the nineteenth century or earlier. They subsequently divided into Upper and Lower divisions, the Upper band being significantly influenced by the Plains buffalo hunting culture. Stylistically their parfleches reflect this continuous association with the Northern Plains peoples, and for that reason they are included here rather than as a part of the Plateau region. Indeed, they appear to be the link extending Blackfeet parfleche traditions to the Yakima and Columbia River tribes of the Western Plateau.

A small number of Kutenai parfleches have been preserved, yet they comprise a highly recognizable style and unified body of works. It is remarkable that such a small tribe should develop one of the most distinctive styles and retain it in spite of surrounding influences. That it was sustained over a long period is evident in comparing pieces painted during different times (pls. 84–86). Most surviving pieces are envelopes, although two side-fringed cases are known.

Kutenai parfleches are distinguished by their visual complexity. The principal forms within compositions are freely and expressively drawn, in sharp contrast to the sense of finely detailed intricacy established by the minute brown/black triangles and lines integrated throughout the design. Even these elements, however, assume differing progressions and point in various directions, contributing to an all-pervasive movement and energy. Compositions are constructed of running diamonds, triangles, bands, and curvilinear forms—all combining with the smaller units to create a complex interplay of visual rhythms that vary in scale, interval, and direction. The side flaps are painted with images that are equally complex but contrasting in pattern, thus intensifying the richness of the total form. An early, documented pair of envelopes (pl. 84) features side flap designs that appear closely related to the incised and painted rock art of the region. They are covered with a multitude of meandering abstract configurations, beyond precise interpretation yet highly evocative.[16]

The envelopes are constructed like those of the Blackfeet, with trapezoidal flaps and three pairs of holes, but lacking the pairs of holes at the sides. On the oldest examples, stake holes serve for the ties. They differ in proportion, however, being somewhat longer in relation to width. Full-size envelopes are large, although a number found in collections were made for children and are correspondingly small.

Some compositions are reminiscent of Blackfeet designs, including the transposition of color. Borders on the earlier pieces are formed by a

16. Lanford (1980, 1984) has analyzed the close relationship existing between the geometric designs of painted parfleche and beadwork produced by the Transmontane peoples. It is interesting to note the similar affinity between the unusual side-flap designs painted on this Kutenai pair of parfleches and the freely drawn, beaded designs embroidered on the early Plateau double saddle bag illustrated in Conn (1986: 161).

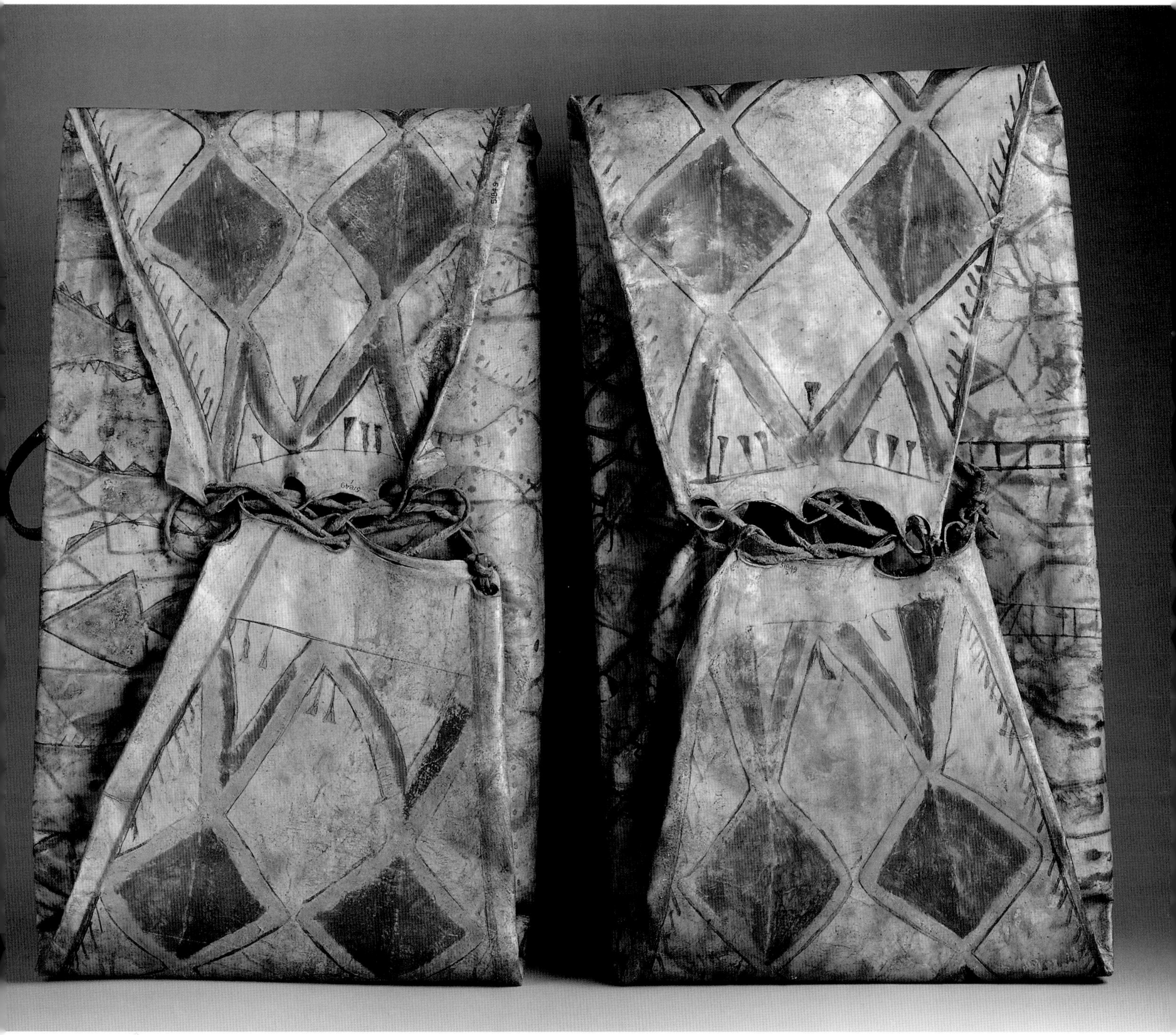

84 / **Kutenai pair of envelopes, ca. 1850**

L 30 in., W 17 in.; L 29 in., W 17 in. Rawhide, pigment

Collected by George Dorsey at St. Eugene Mission, Montana, 1897. Field Museum of Natural History, Chicago, 51849

single line, while later examples are made with two narrow lines of color enclosing an unpainted area filled with groups of opposing diagonal lines. The predominant colors in designs are red, yellow, and blue, although the old native green and rusty red were used on several even after trade colors were readily available (pl. 86). All of the primary forms are outlined in black, and lines may or may not be used to separate colors within. On the earlier pieces, the paint is rather thinly applied and some colors have such a translucent quality that surface and color fuse into an image seemingly filled with light and space (pl. 85).

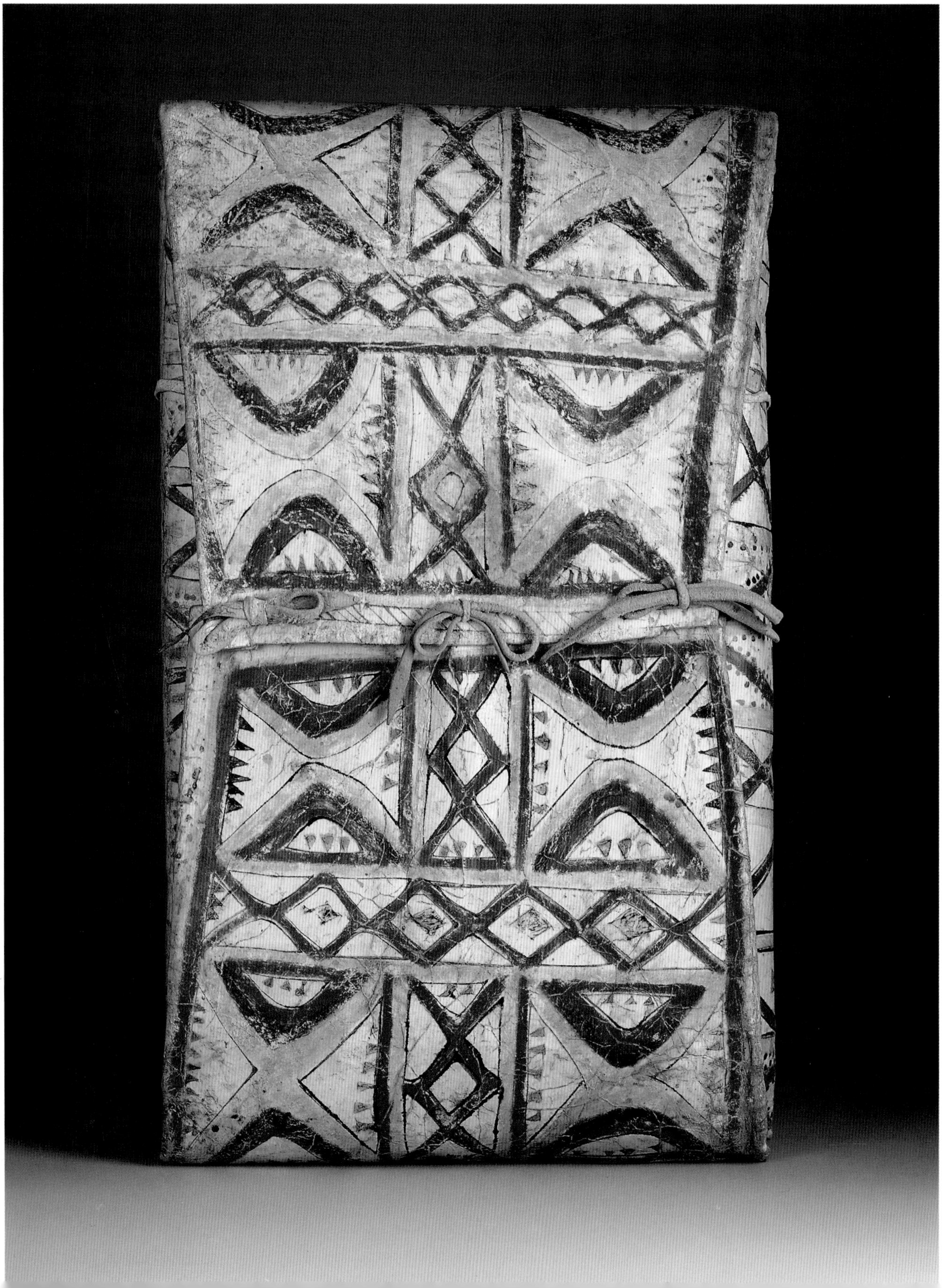

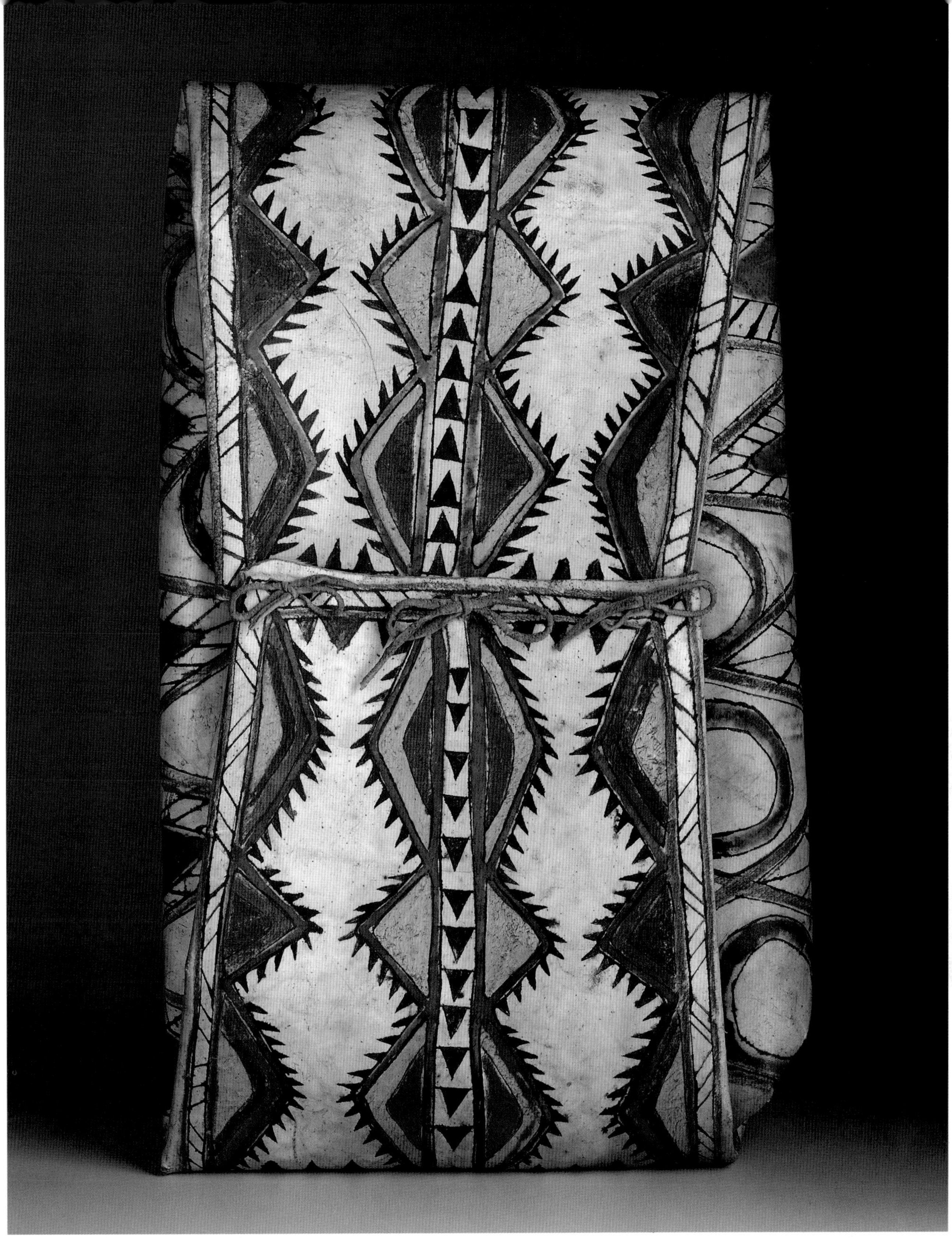

85 / **Kutenai envelope, ca. 1875**

L 27 in., W 17 in. Rawhide, pigment

Private collection

86 / **Kutenai envelope, ca. 1900**

L 25 in., W 14 in. Rawhide, pigment

Collected by Alfred L. Kroeber, 1900. American Museum of Natural History, 50/1364

Transmontane

It has been the common practice in the study of American Indian cultures to divide North America into geographic regions known as "culture areas," based on the fact that each area was inhabited by tribes that were fundamentally similar in their ways of life. Thus, the culture areas of the Plains, Plateau, and Great Basin have traditionally been viewed as distinct and separate. It has long been recognized, however, that there existed considerable cultural exchange among certain tribes of these regions through the diffusion of horses, extensive trade relations, and political alliances. One manifestation of this interrelationship was the development of an artistic style during the nineteenth century based on common aesthetic concepts. It encompassed particularly the production of beadwork and painted rawhide, establishing a close affinity in the imagery created through the two mediums, and transcended both cultural differences and geographic boundaries.

This tradition was first identified as "Crow style" on the assumption that it had originated with that tribe and spread to the Plateau and Basin groups. It was later called "Crow-Intermontane," acknowledging that the style extended to both sides of the Rocky Mountains. Most recently, however, it has been designated Transmontane (Conn 1986: 128), suggesting a more complex origin and intertribal development, and affirming its production over a wide, geographically varied range. The principal tribes who sustained the Transmontane tradition included the Crow of the Northern Plains, the eastern and northern Shoshone groups inhabiting the northeastern Great Basin, and several Eastern Plateau tribes, including the Nez Perce, Flathead, and Cayuse. The style also influenced the tribes inhabiting the Western Plateau in varying degrees, extended southward to the Ute, and may even be discerned in the compositions of the Blackfeet and Gros Ventre.

The distinguishing features of Transmontane parfleche painting are generally consistent throughout the region, and are closely identified with those developed by the Crow. The similarities are so great, in fact, that the parfleches from all the tribes within the area might be classified as a single group. Although specific traits certainly existed in the work of different tribes, they are difficult to discern at this time because of the interrelationships of these groups and the lack of meaningful documentation. This is particularly true in trying to separate the parfleches of the Crow, Nez Perce, and Shoshone, whose work is most closely related. Large collections have been obtained from each of these tribes, but each one contains works from the other two groups; the objects are mixed together and none is documented according to its maker, only where it was collected. A much smaller number of pieces have been acquired from the Bannock, Flathead, Cayuse, and other Eastern Plateau peoples; the same difficulty exists in attempting to identify their works, compounded by the small number of objects available for comparative study.

In acknowledging the basic similarities in the painting of these groups, the extensive exchange that resulted in the dispersal of each tribe's work into the hands of the others, and the limited value of collection data, a precise tribal identification is usually tentative and often impossible. However, certain predominant features may be recognized in composition or painting style that appear to be associated with specific groups; these are especially visible when a significant concentration of works possessing these characteristics have been collected from a single tribe. The following discussion, therefore, is based on such observations and is intended to reveal the individual conventions established and maintaned by the major groups.

CROW

The Crow probably produced the greatest number of parfleches of all the Transmontane tribes. They maintained a very high level of production during the final quarter of the nineteenth and well into the twentieth century and, although few envelopes that date before 1870 have survived, there is every reason to believe that they were manufacturing significant numbers prior to that time. A survey of collections today indicates that the body of parfleches documented as having been collected from the Crow, and which are also stylistically consistent, is extremely large. This includes standard envelopes as well as other types of containers associated with religious life.

As indicated, a description of Crow parfleches also serves to describe and identify the basic features of those produced by the Shoshone and Nez Perce. Crow envelopes are relatively long and narrow in overall proportion, and are closed with a single pair of tie holes in the outer flaps. Their compositions are bold and angular, being constructed of elements that are straightedged and precisely drawn; they are most often based on a large diamond (pls. 88, 90, 92) or hourglass (pls. 91, 93) shape as the central element on each flap, although in many paintings these are commonly integrated with rectangular forms. Other common compositions feature rectangular shapes as principal elements, or incorporate a complex of geometric forms. On most envelopes the two panels combine visually to form a single configuration across the full expanse of both flaps.

The designs were formed by a linear framework of dark blue line. The principal elements were first defined, then divided and subdivided to create a complex image within the pictorial field. The resulting shapes were then filled in with additional colors to complete the painting. The outlines of primary forms often vary in width, tapering from a wide base to a sharp point along the length of the line. These expanding lines are one of the most dramatic features of the style; they inevitably animate the composition, visually expanding and spreading their energy throughout the surrounding space.

The borders of painted panels of envelopes and most other types of cases were established by a single line of dark blue adjoining an outer line of green, quietly containing the image, yet allowing the design to expand to the very edges of the object. More rarely a single line of green or some other color might be used, but this is usually on a medicine container where the standard conventions might not apply. No painting was ever done on the side flaps or reverse sides of envelopes, unlike some Plateau examples that might be considered similar in other ways.

The coloration of most surviving Crow parfleches is strong and visually dynamic. Dark blue, a vibrant red and yellow of equal intensity, and a pale to medium green and turquoise blue of the same value are combined in most compositions. This preference appears to have been well established by 1860, and was maintained into the twentieth century, although a deep orange is sometimes seen in pieces dating after 1900.

The earliest Crow parfleches, which are all containers for sacred objects and date from the mid-nineteenth century or earlier, are painted in a more restrained but no less dramatic manner; most are visionary and pictographic, and feature a black image floating on a red ground (pl. 95) or on one that is unpainted. Geometric designs from this period were apparently composed of heavy black structural lines enclosing areas of red in conjunction with additional red shapes delineated by fine black outlining.[17] This double use of black was replaced by the dark blue structural lines that are synonymous with classic Transmontane painting sometime after 1850, and the element of thin black outlining disappeared completely from Crow work.

The Crow also have an early tradition of incising, and many of the most finely executed examples have been collected from them (pls. 88, 89). The designs that were created by cutting and scraping the dark epidermal layer of buffalo hide are essentially identical to those produced with paint; the individual elements and their overall organization maintain the precise angularity and classic structure that characterize Transmontane style. The remarkable visor with its drawing of horses (pl. 87) is the only known figurative example in this technique, and it is directly related to the pictographic rock art found throughout Crow country as well as to the images painted by men on robes, shirts, and tipis.

In addition to standard envelopes, the Crow produced a variety of flat cases, cylinders, and boat-shaped containers to house bundles composed of sacred objects. Unlike the other Transmontane tribes, the Crow people possessed several types of medicine bundles in great numbers, and an exceptionally large quantity of these objects was collected in the early twentieth century and well documented as to their origin and use.[18] That most were acquired together with their parfleche cases provides some sense of the correlation between the classes of medicine bundles and the types of cases made to contain them. For example, most war bundles were kept in unfringed cylinders, although some were contained in unfringed flat cases of either square or boatlike shape. Most rock medicine bundles were kept in square flat cases, but a few are found

87 / **Crow (?) sunshade, ca. 1850**

L 17 in., W 12 1/2 in. Incised buffalo rawhide, pigment

Collected at Fort C. F. Smith, Montana, in the 1860s; this object is cut from the painted panel of an envelope flap, the fragmentary design on the reverse side indicating that the original parfleche was of Gros Ventre or Blackfeet origin. Collection of Richard A. and Marion D. Pohrt

17. Only one parfleche believed to be of Crow origin with geometric designs and dating about 1850 or before has been located. It is a double flat case in the collection of the Staatliche Museen, Museum für Völkerkunde, Berlin, and illustrated in Hartman (1873: no. 58). A cylinder collected from the Crow, and of comparable age, appears to be painted in the same manner but is so worn that very little of the design remains for study. Still, it helps confirm the presence of this early style. It is in the collection of the National Museum of the American Indian, Smithsonian Institution.

18. The largest collection of Crow medicine bundles, now in the collection of the National Museum of the American Indian, Smithsonian Institution, was assembled by William Wildschut between the years 1918 and 1927. Numbering more than 260, it comprises the largest collection of sacred bundles from any Plains tribe to be preserved (see Wildschut 1975).

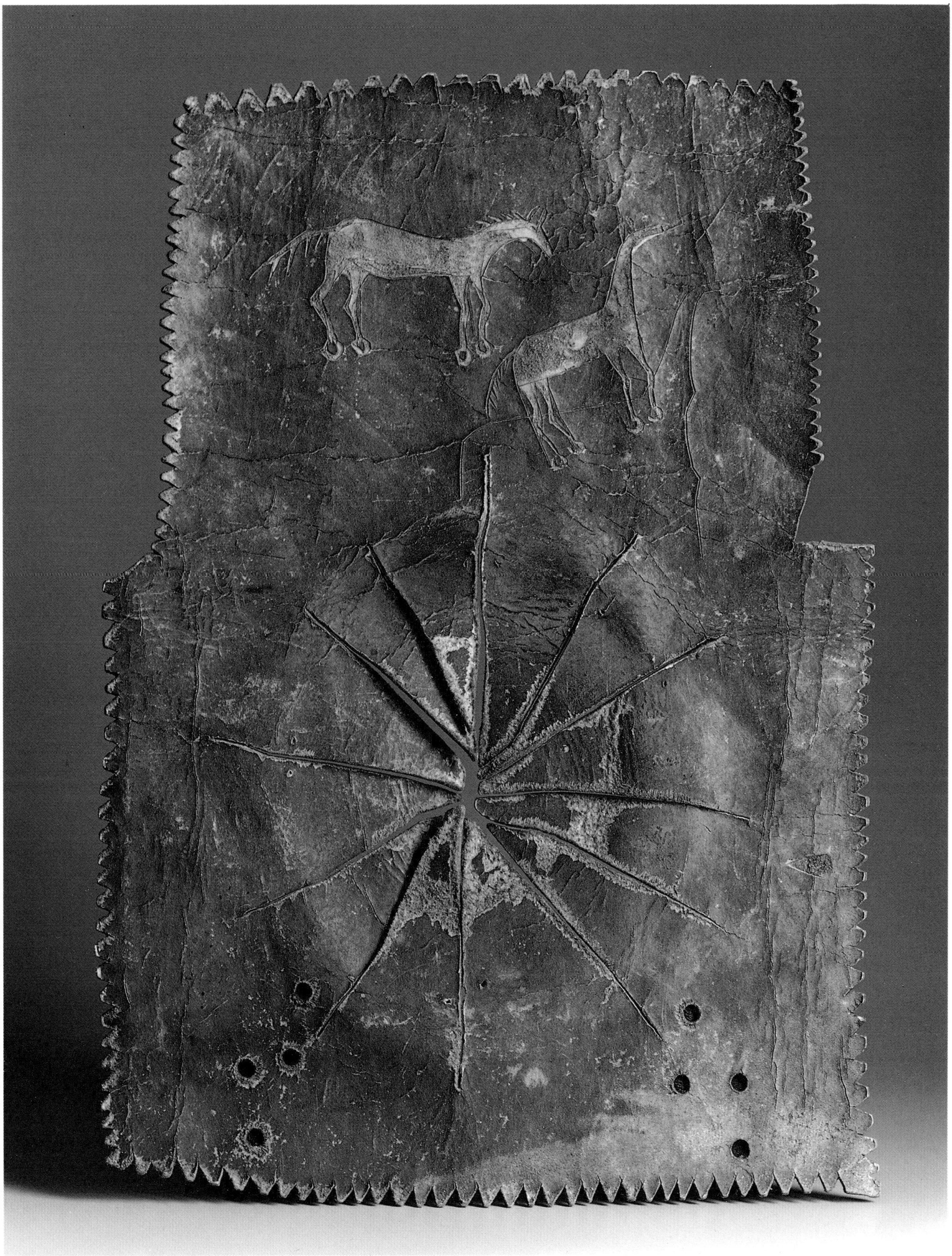

in either cylinders or boat-shaped cases. Sun-dance bundles are usually associated with boat-shaped cases, although some were collected in cylinders. Most tobacco bundles were contained in soft leather bags, yet a few may be found in parfleche cylinders or wide rectangular cases. It would appear that there was a general tendency to house the different types of bundles in parfleches of a specific kind, but practices varied, perhaps in accordance with the vision from which the bundle originated.

Four distinct types of flat cases were produced for sacred objects. The most elaborate were composed of two attached cases, tied so that one container hung directly above the other when the entire assemblage was suspended from the saddle (pl. 94). The larger, primary case was square in proportion with exceptionally long fringe and a closure flap that was usually ornamented with trade cloth and bead embroidery. The smaller case was always boat-shaped, with a shorter fringe and trade cloth and bead decorations at the side seams. It is interesting that, unlike other kinds of medicine bundle containers, none of this type has been collected with complete contents; in fact, nearly all are empty. A number of the larger flat cases with fringe, but without the addition of a smaller case, also appear in many collections today.

Unfringed flat cases of varying sizes and proportions were also made in large numbers. Most were nearly square or slightly rectangular in shape, and the majority were made with triangular flaps. Most were also finished with one or two colors of trade cloth along the seams. The case illustrated in plate 96 is typical of this type, although the addition of the attached feather case is unusual. A smaller number of rather large, horizontal flat cases are found in collections and represent a distinct type as opposed to smaller cases made for utility purposes. The fourth type of flat case produced was boat-shaped; the contour of the upper edge was cut in an inverted curving or triangular shape so that the ends projected upwards (pl. 95). Unlike other kinds of flat cases where the use might be in question, these were reserved exclusively for sacred use. Although the form was also produced to a very limited extent by the Arapaho and Blackfeet, it is mainly associated with the Crow. Some examples that are components of double cases have been collected from the Nez Perce, but these may be of Crow origin. Apparently large numbers of this type were made, for several are found in collections today.

A variety of cylinders were also produced. The most common were unfringed (pls. 97, 98), but large numbers ornamented with long, heavy fringes were created as well. These are fundamentally the same in appearance and construction as those produced by the Nez Perce (pl. 110) and Shoshone (pl. 103) with only minor differences in the compositional elements of the painting.

88 / **Crow envelope, ca. 1850**

L 31 1/2 in., W 14 in. Incised buffalo rawhide

Possibly collected by Herman Haupt, Jr., at Crow Agency, Crow Reservation, Montana. American Museum of Natural History, 50.2/6201

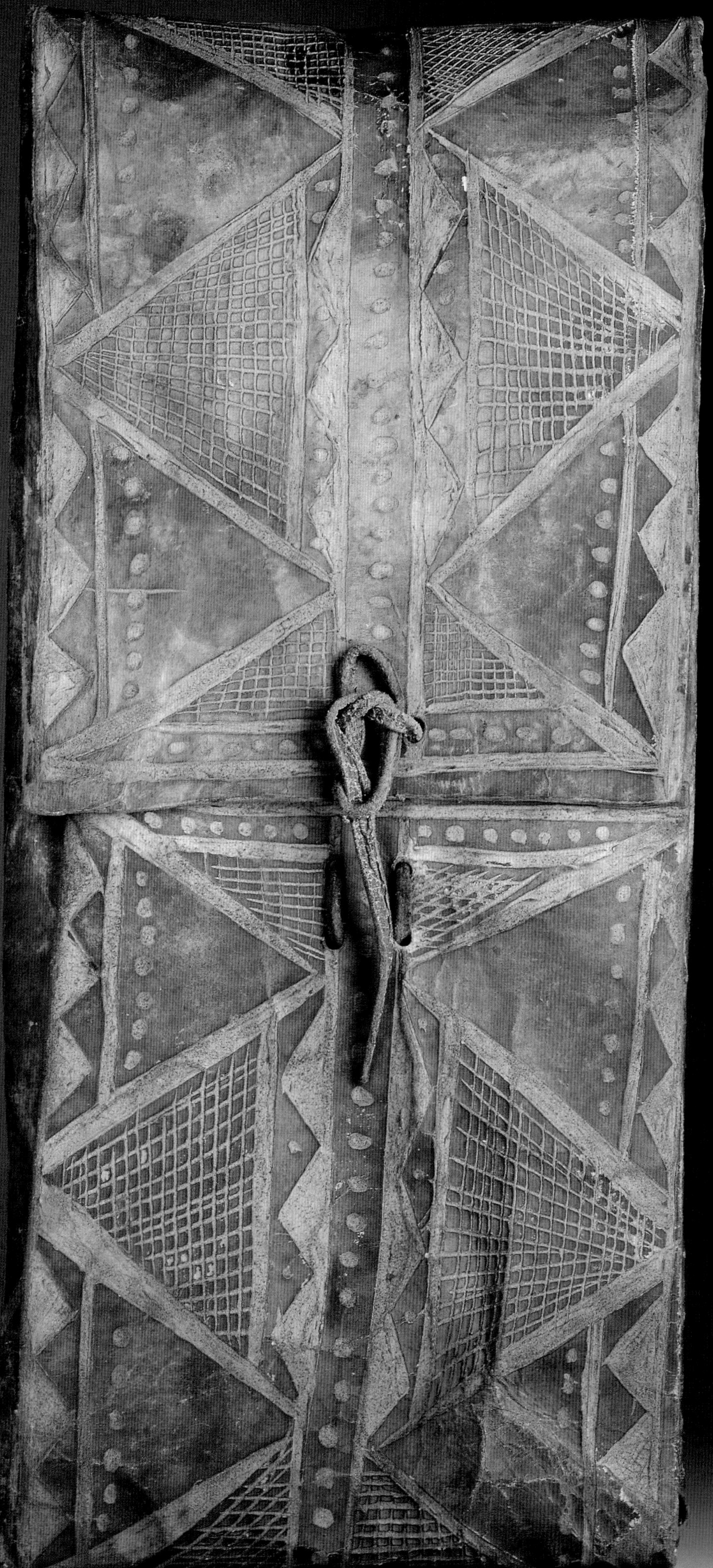

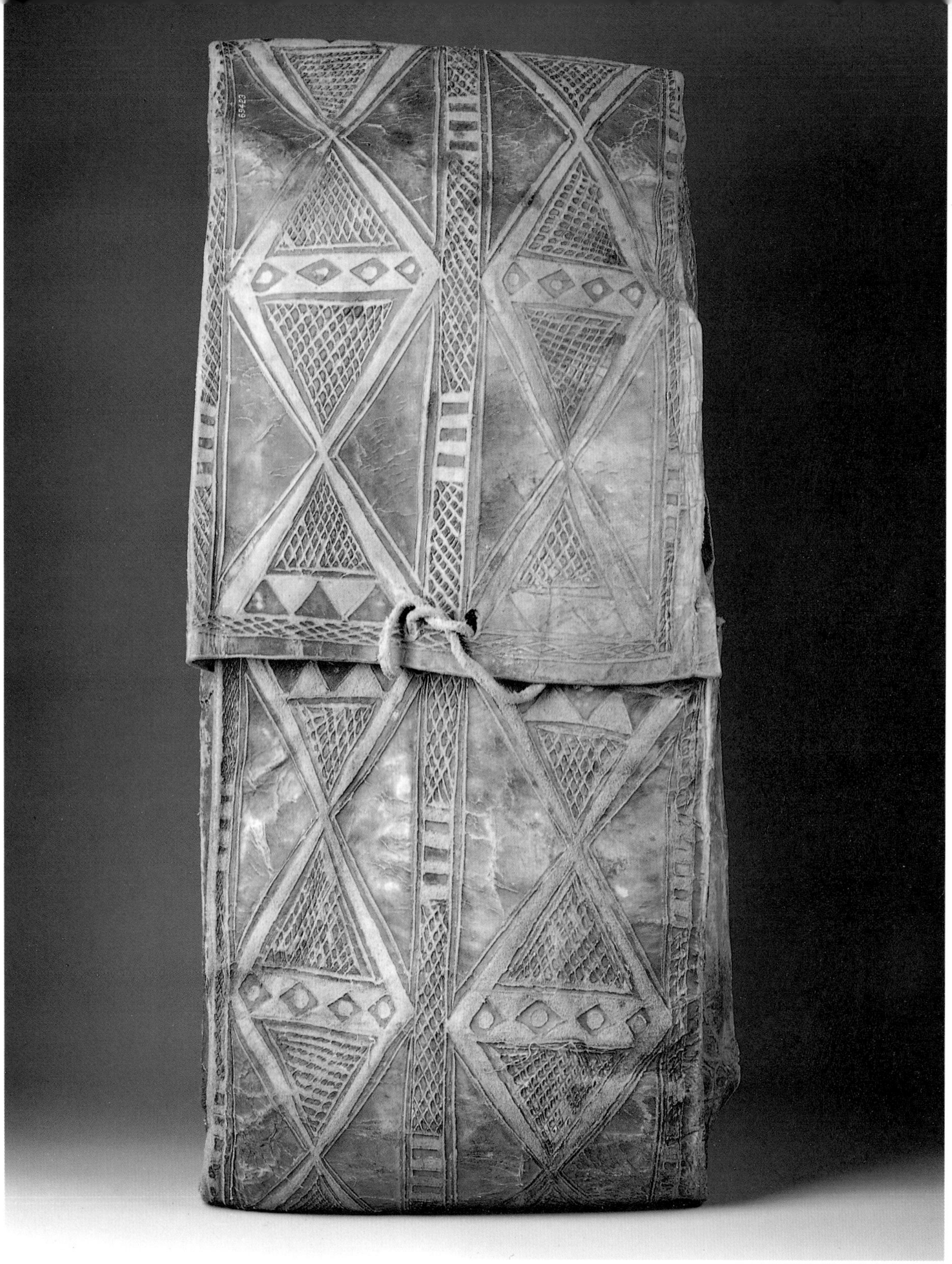

89 / **Crow envelope, ca. 1850**

L 29 in., W 12 1/2 in. Incised buffalo rawhide

Collected by S. C. Simms at Pryor, Crow Reservation, Montana, 1901; matching envelope formerly in the collection of the Field Museum and now in the collection of the Denver Art Museum. Field Museum of Natural History, Chicago, 69423

90 / **Crow envelope, ca. 1875**

L 29 in., W 13 1/2 in. Buffalo rawhide, pigment

Accessioned as Cheyenne; matching envelope in the collection of the National Museum of Natural History, Department of Anthropology, Smithsonian Institution. National Museum of the American Indian, Smithsonian Institution, 11/4249

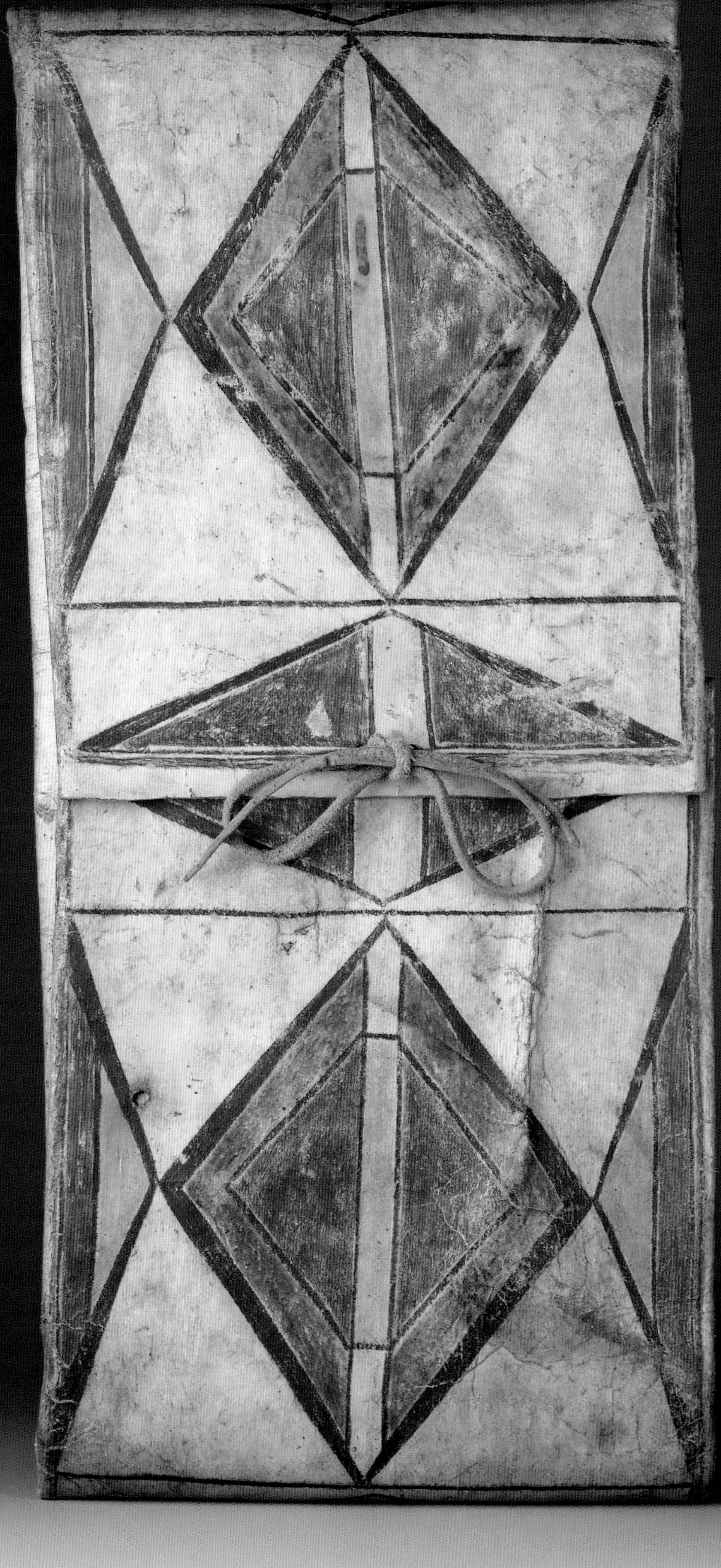

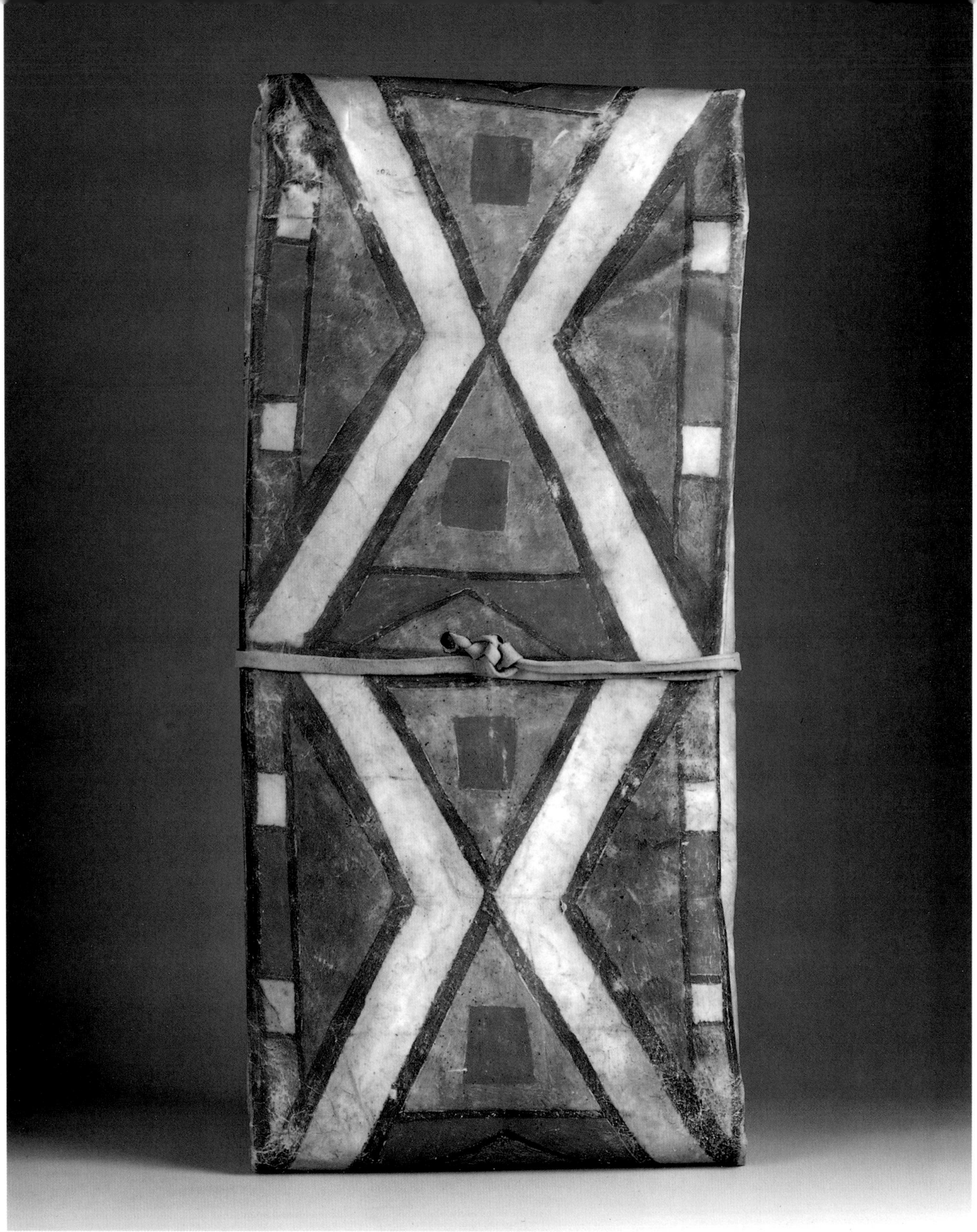

91 / **Crow envelope, ca. 1885**

L 27 in., W 12 1/2 in. Rawhide, pigment

Collected at Lodge Grass, Crow Reservation, Montana. Collection of Kenneth and Barbara Canfield, Santa Fe

92 / **Crow envelope, ca. 1890**

L 28 1/2 in., W 12 in. Rawhide, pigment

Collection of Kenneth and Barbara Canfield, Santa Fe

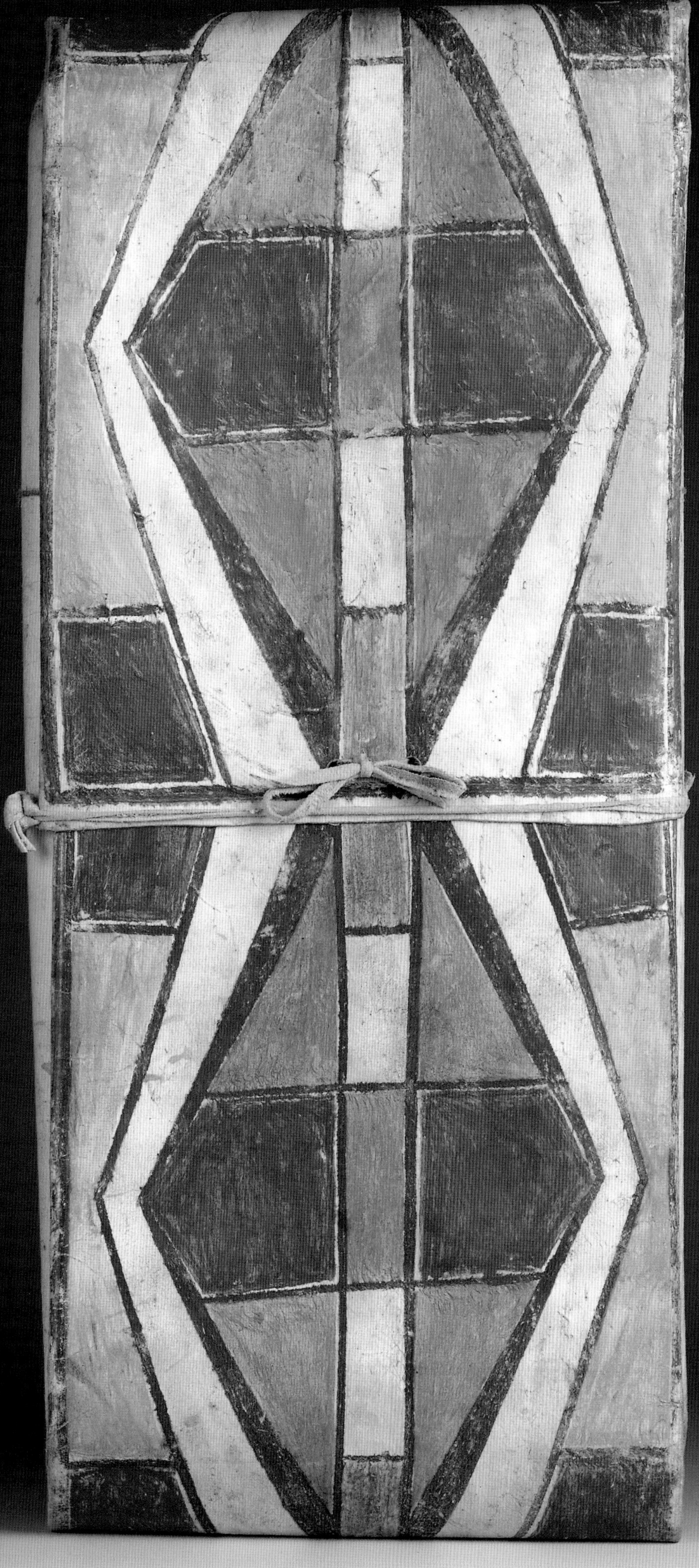

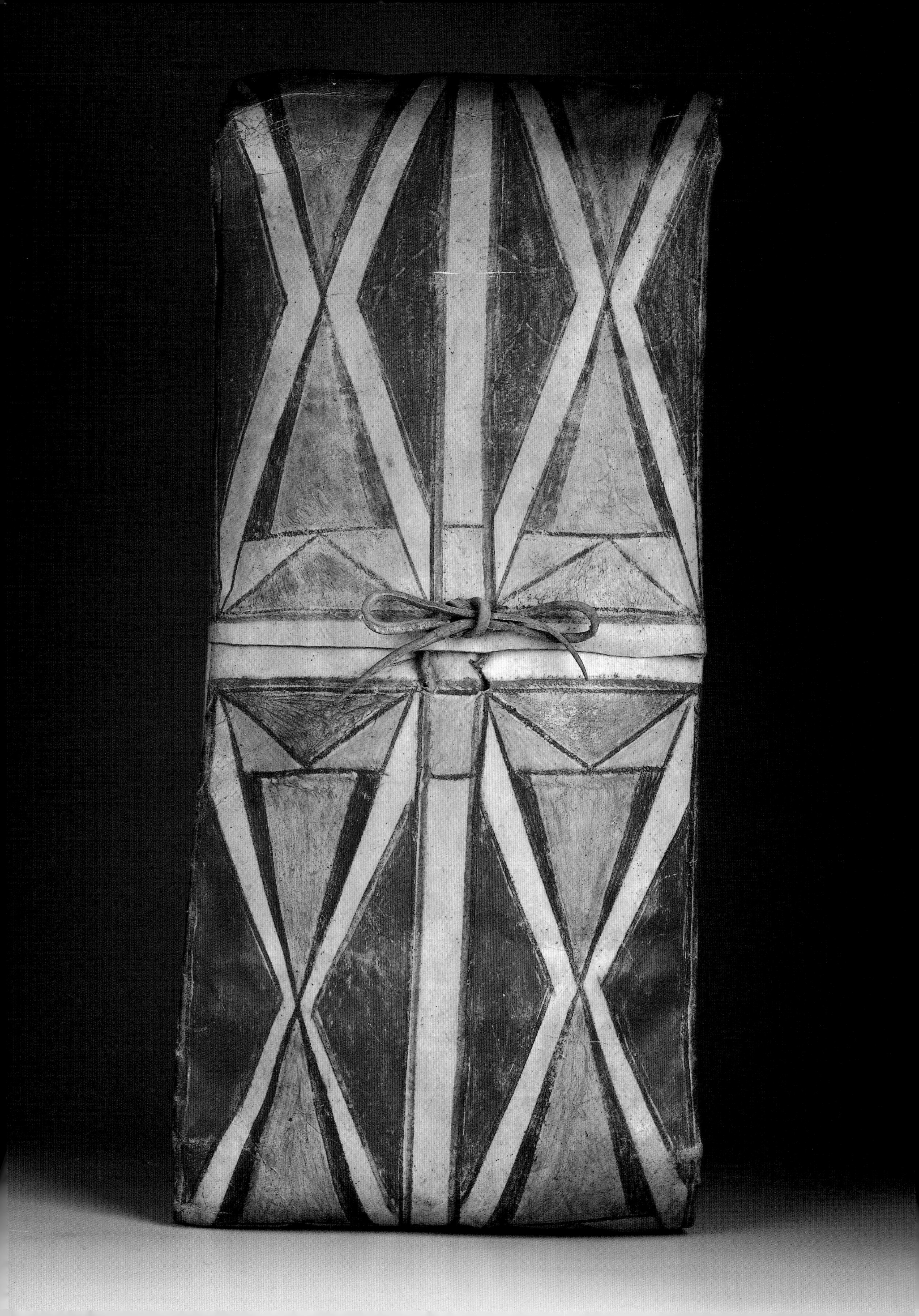

93 / **Crow envelope, ca. 1890**

L 27 in., W 12 1/2 in. Rawhide, pigment

Collected by Earnest E. Murray of Billings, Montana, before 1926. The University Museum, University of Pennsylvania, Philadelphia, NA 10681

94 / **Crow double flat case, ca. 1875**

H 3 1/2 in., W 10 in. and H 9 3/4 in. (not including flap), W 10 in.; height with fringe 43 in. Buffalo rawhide, pigment, native leather, wool cloth, glass beads

National Museum of the American Indian, Smithsonian Institution, 20/7702

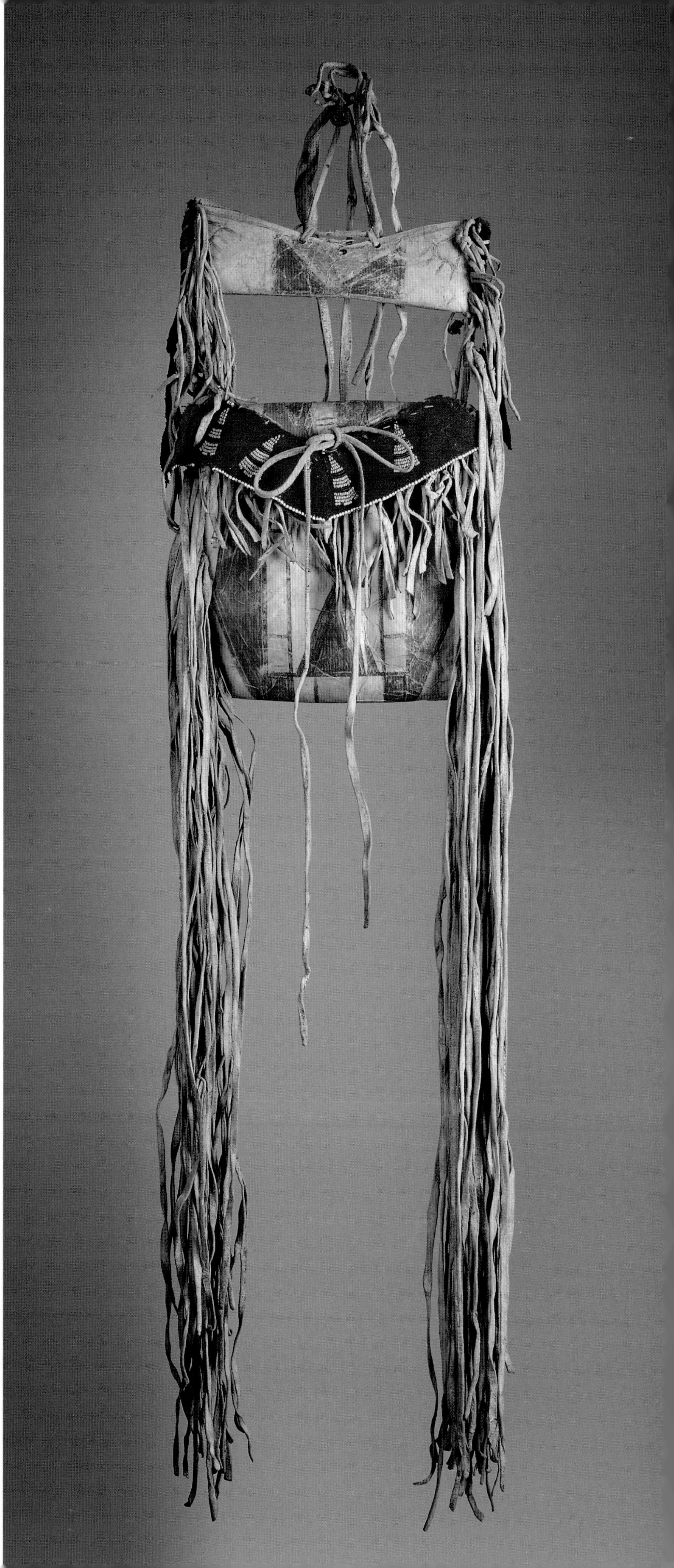

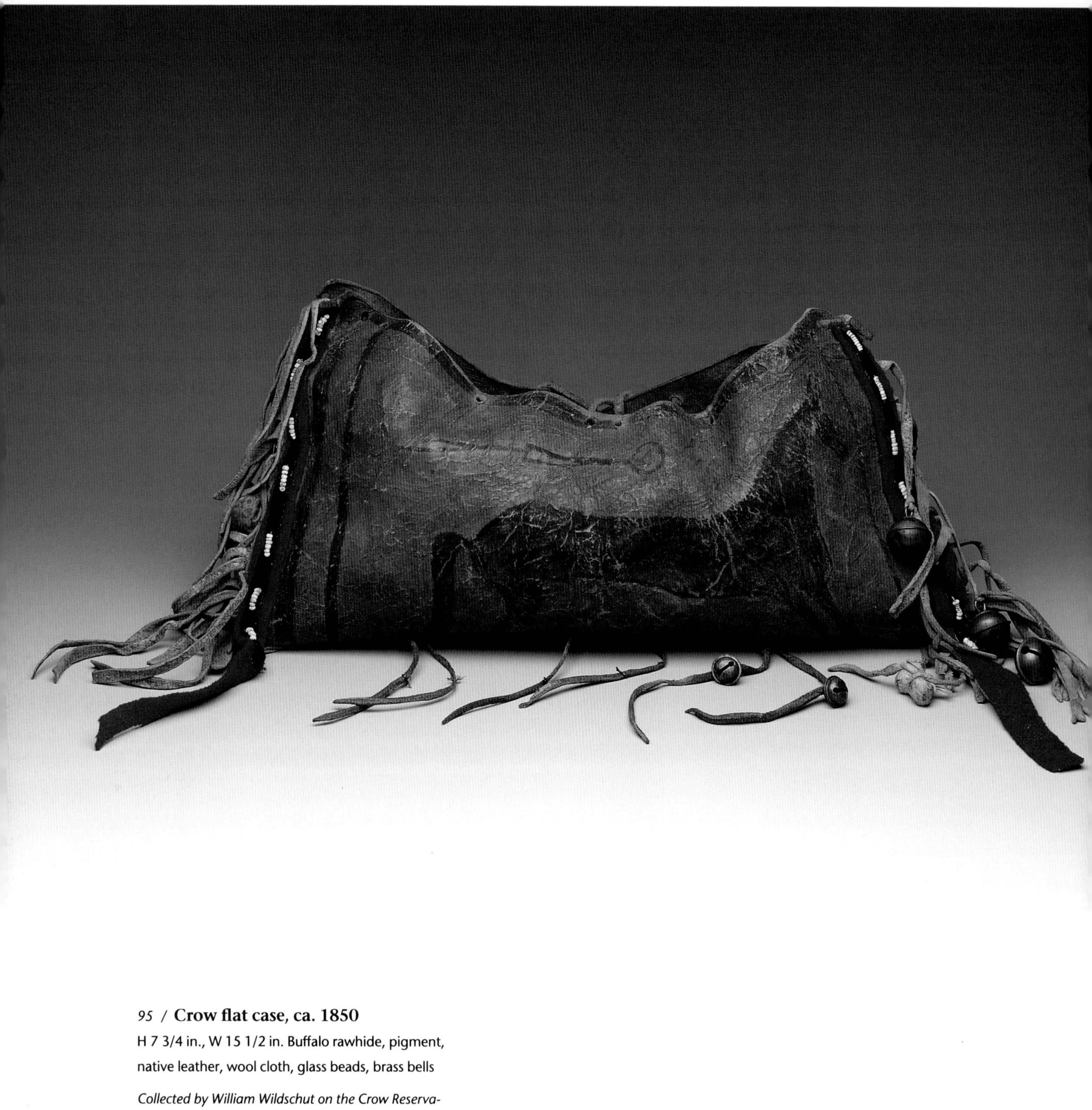

95 / **Crow flat case, ca. 1850**

H 7 3/4 in., W 15 1/2 in. Buffalo rawhide, pigment, native leather, wool cloth, glass beads, brass bells

Collected by William Wildschut on the Crow Reservation, Montana. National Museum of the American Indian, Smithsonian Institution, 13/5312

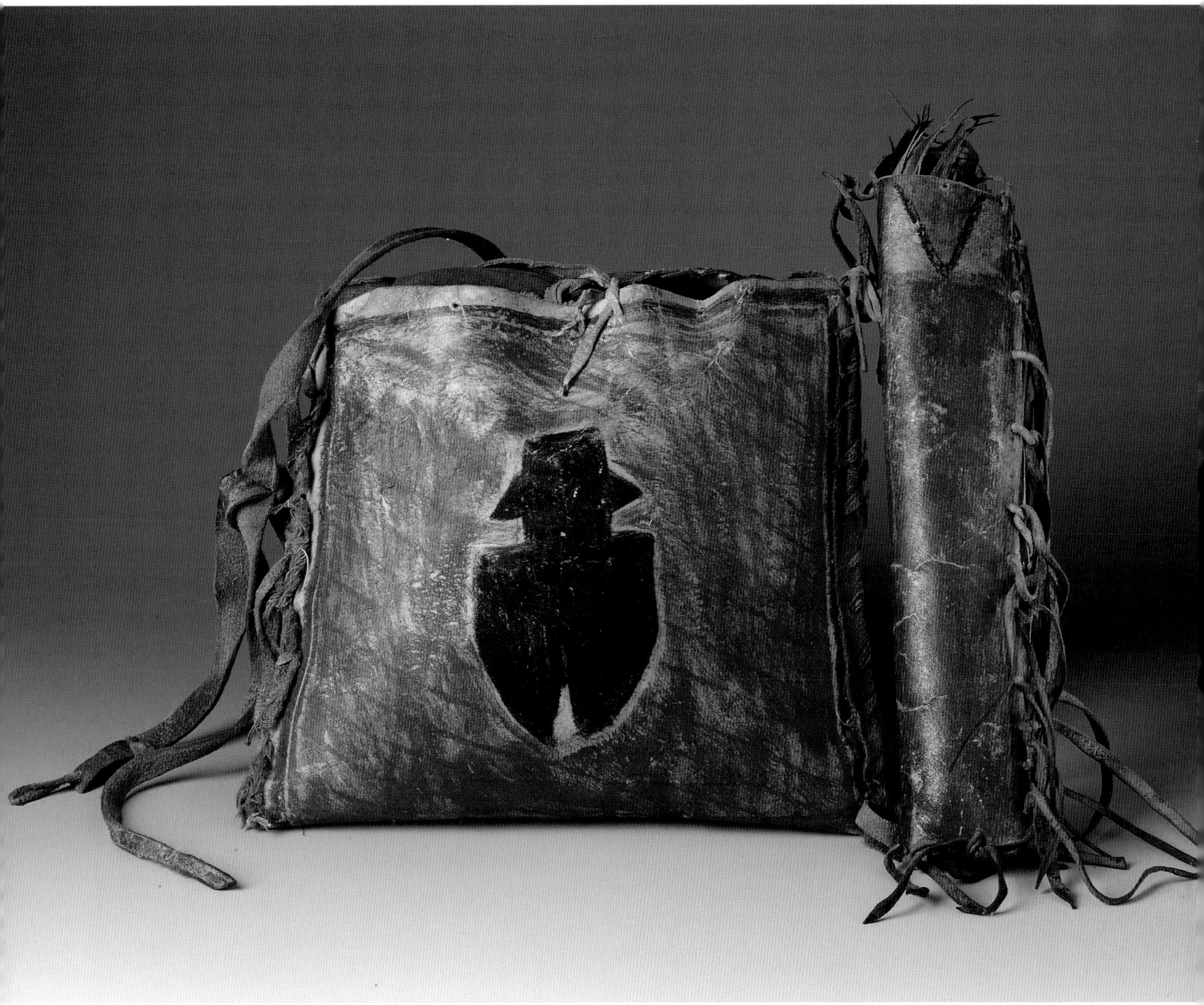

96 / **Crow flat case and attached elliptical case, ca. 1860**

H 8 1/2 in., W 10 in. and H 11 in., W 2 1/4 in. Buffalo rawhide, pigment, native leather, wool cloth

Purchased by Albert Green Heath from Big Lake. Logan Museum of Anthropology, Albert Green Heath Collection, Beloit College, 31.136

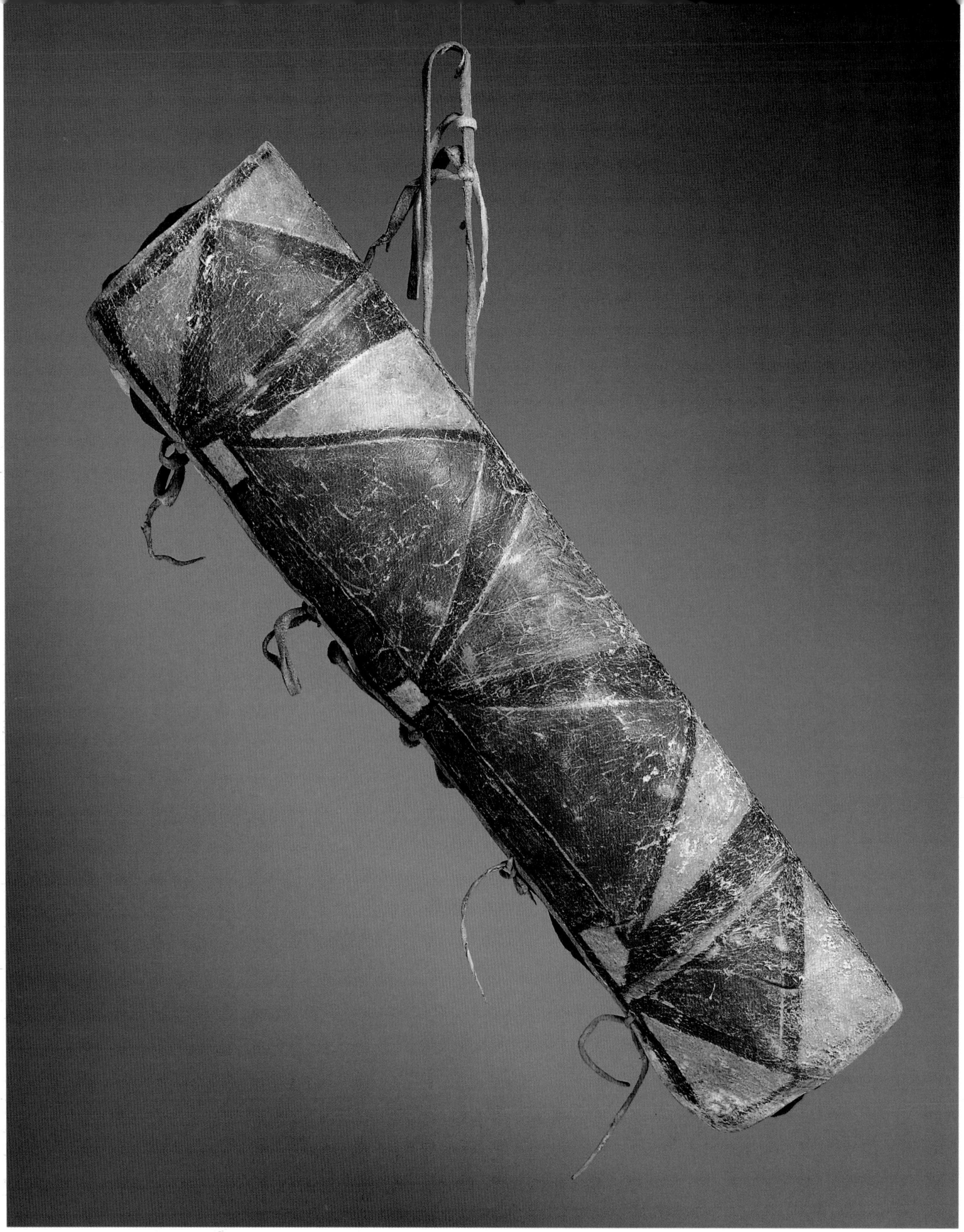

97 / **Crow cylinder, ca. 1875**

H 23 1/2 in., D 5 1/2 in. Rawhide, pigment

Belonged to Big Forehead; collected by William Wildschut. Field Museum of Natural History, Chicago, 110682

98 / **Crow cylinder, ca. 1885**

H 22 1/2 in., D 5 3/4 in. Buffalo rawhide, pigment, wool cloth, glass beads

Collection of Michael and Sherry Maxwell

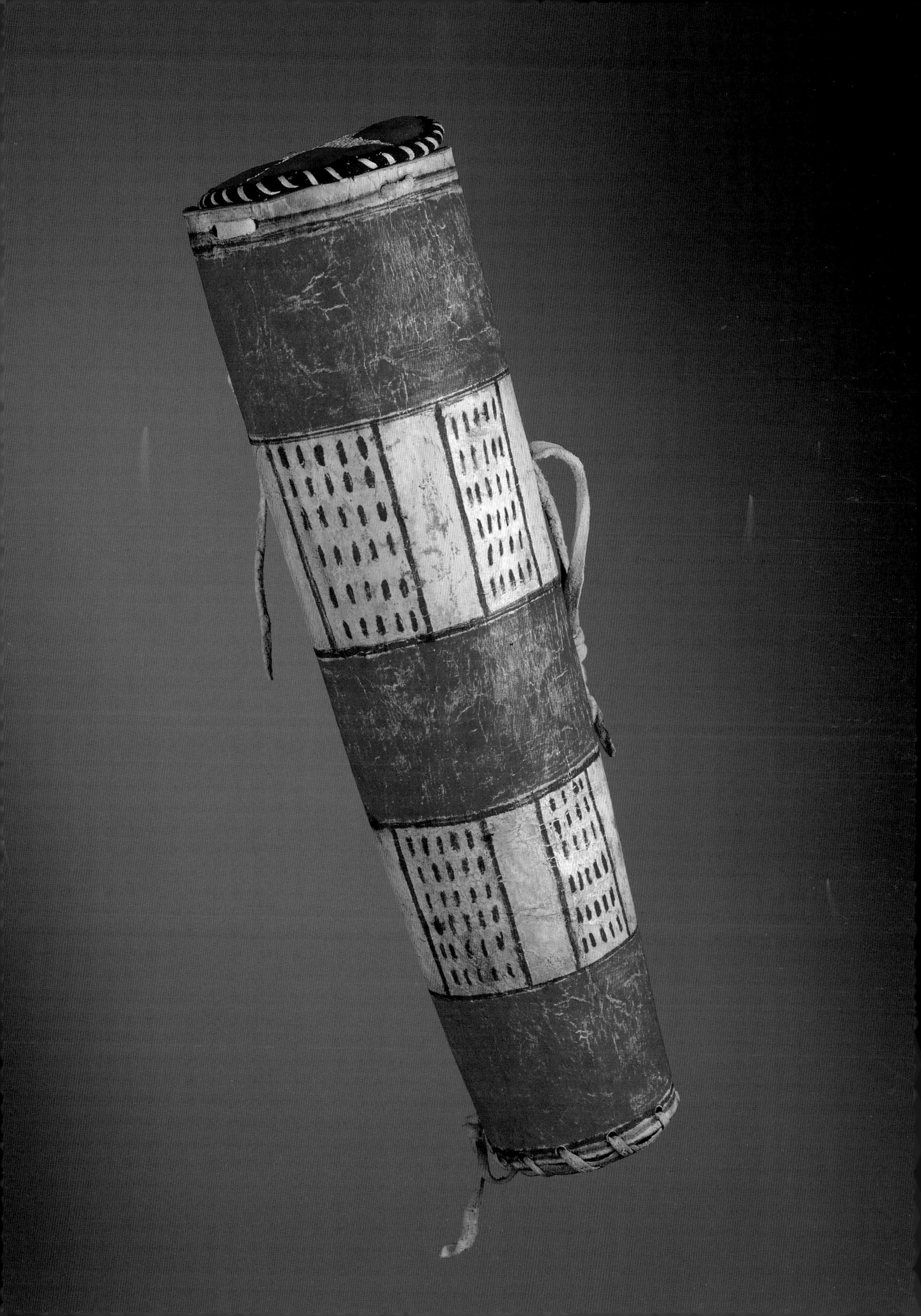

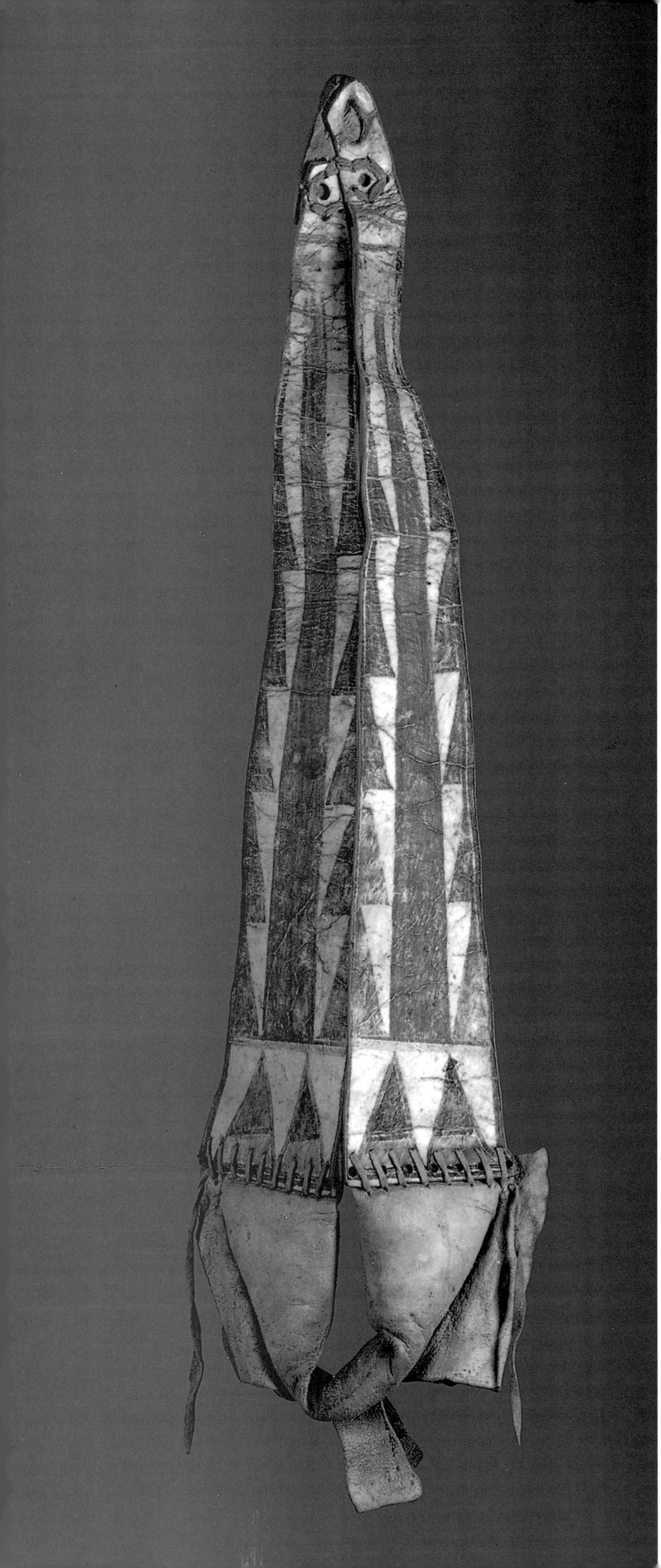

99 / **Crow crupper, ca. 1875**

L 32 in., W 9 1/4 in. Buffalo rawhide, pigment, native leather

Collected by George Dorsey for the Fred Harvey Company, 1903. Courtesy of The Carnegie Museum of Natural History, Pittsburgh, 2418-96

100 / **Crow saddle ornament, ca. 1890**

Two attached panels, each H 18 in., W 24 3/4 in.

Rawhide, pigment

Collected by George Dorsey for the Fred Harvey Company, 1903. Courtesy of The Carnegie Museum of Natural History, Pittsburgh, 2418-96

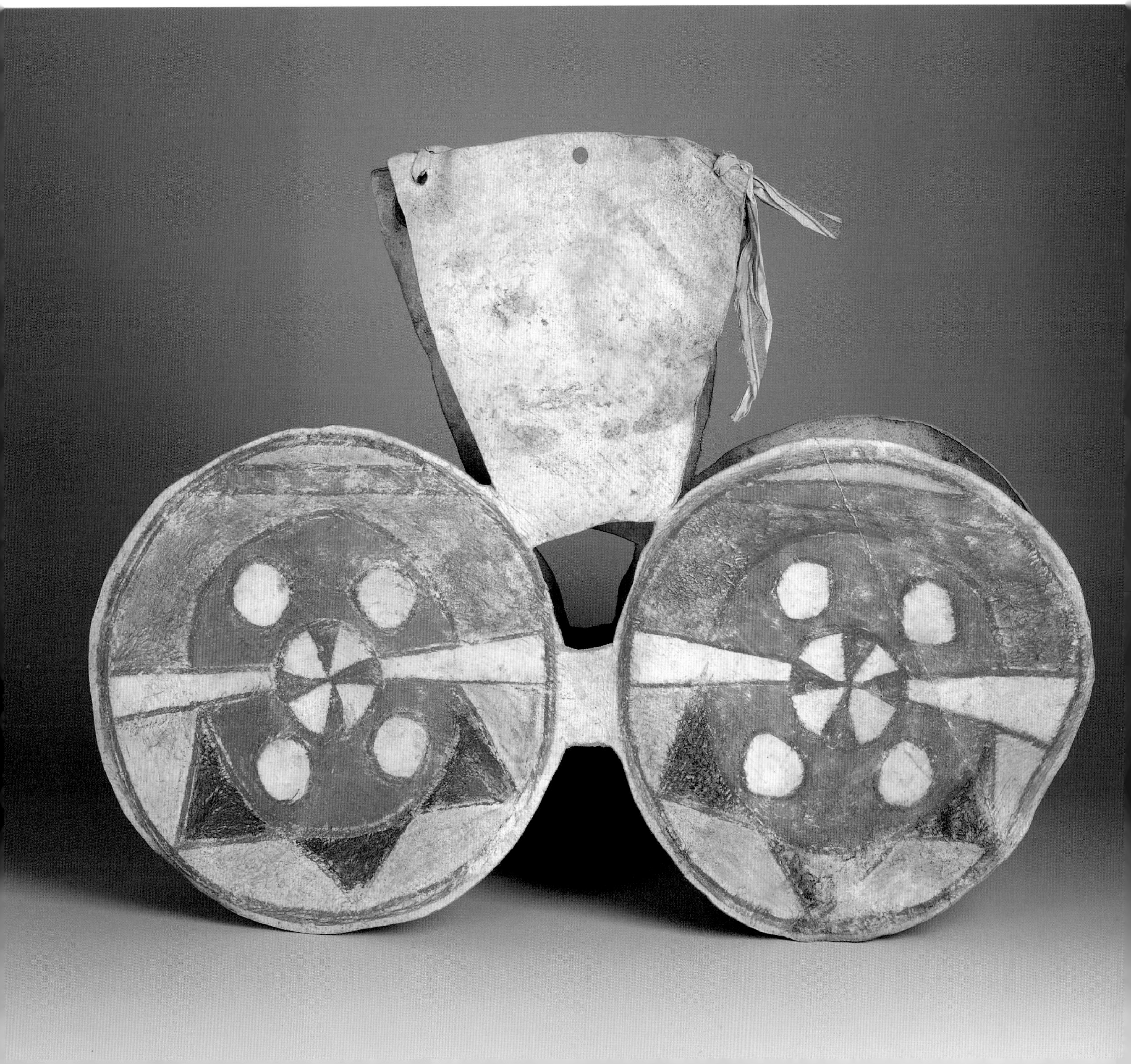

SHOSHONE

Shoshone parfleches appear to differ from those of the Crow primarily in the compositions that were favored; as indicated, the character of the painting itself and the elements that make up the designs are identical. One configuration often seen is based on a three-part vertical division of the field (pl. 102). The outer panels are painted symmetrically so that they are perceived as very wide borders along each side of a narrow central field. An earlier example (pl. 101) is conceptually similar, in that the central area of the composition is also broken into three vertical bands and subdivided in such a way that positive and negative hourglass shapes occupy the center panel. There is also an affinity between the broad bands at the top and bottom of the design on the older envelope, and the comparable bands at the sides of many later examples. This three-part composition was also used by the Crow, but to a more limited extent.

Another feature seen on many Shoshone envelopes is unbroken blocks of color at the corners (pl. 102). This element probably derives from another predominantly Shoshone composition known as the nine-block. In this configuration the field is broken by two vertical and two horizontal linear divisions, creating nine rectilinear spaces with the center block being the largest (pl. 107). This design had a wide distribution throughout the Transmontane area; it was especially favored by the Wind River Shoshone, but was also used extensively by the Nez Perce and other Plateau groups. The Crow adopted it as well. A variety of other Transmontane compositions were created by variations based on this configuration. Additional designs are also attributed to Shoshone women, but it is unknown how typical they might be. Many seem quite similar to others collected from the Bannock, Crow, and Eastern Plateau groups.

Envelopes attributed to the Shoshone tend to be shorter in proportion than classic Crow examples. The borders are essentially the same, but often the outer line is a turquoise blue rather than green, which may be a Shoshone trait. Most Shoshone parfleches in collections are envelopes, but the few cylinders and flat cases that have survived indicate that the Shoshone were also fond of heavily fringed containers (pl. 103) constructed and painted like those made by the Crow and Plateau tribes.

101 / **Shoshone envelope, ca. 1875**

L 26 in., W 12 1/2 in. Buffalo rawhide, pigment

Collected by F. M. Covert. National Museum of the American Indian, Smithsonian Institution, 1/237

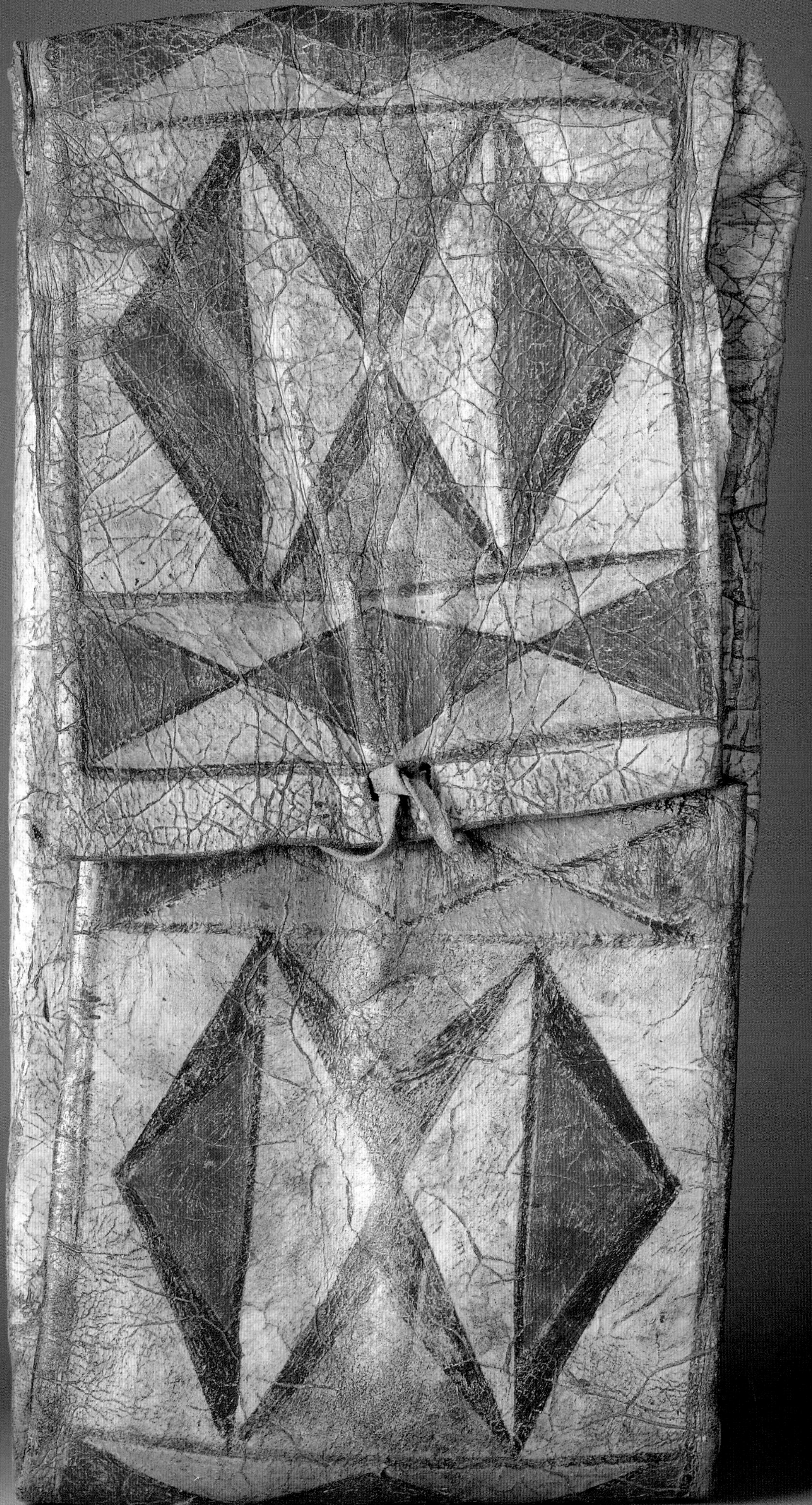

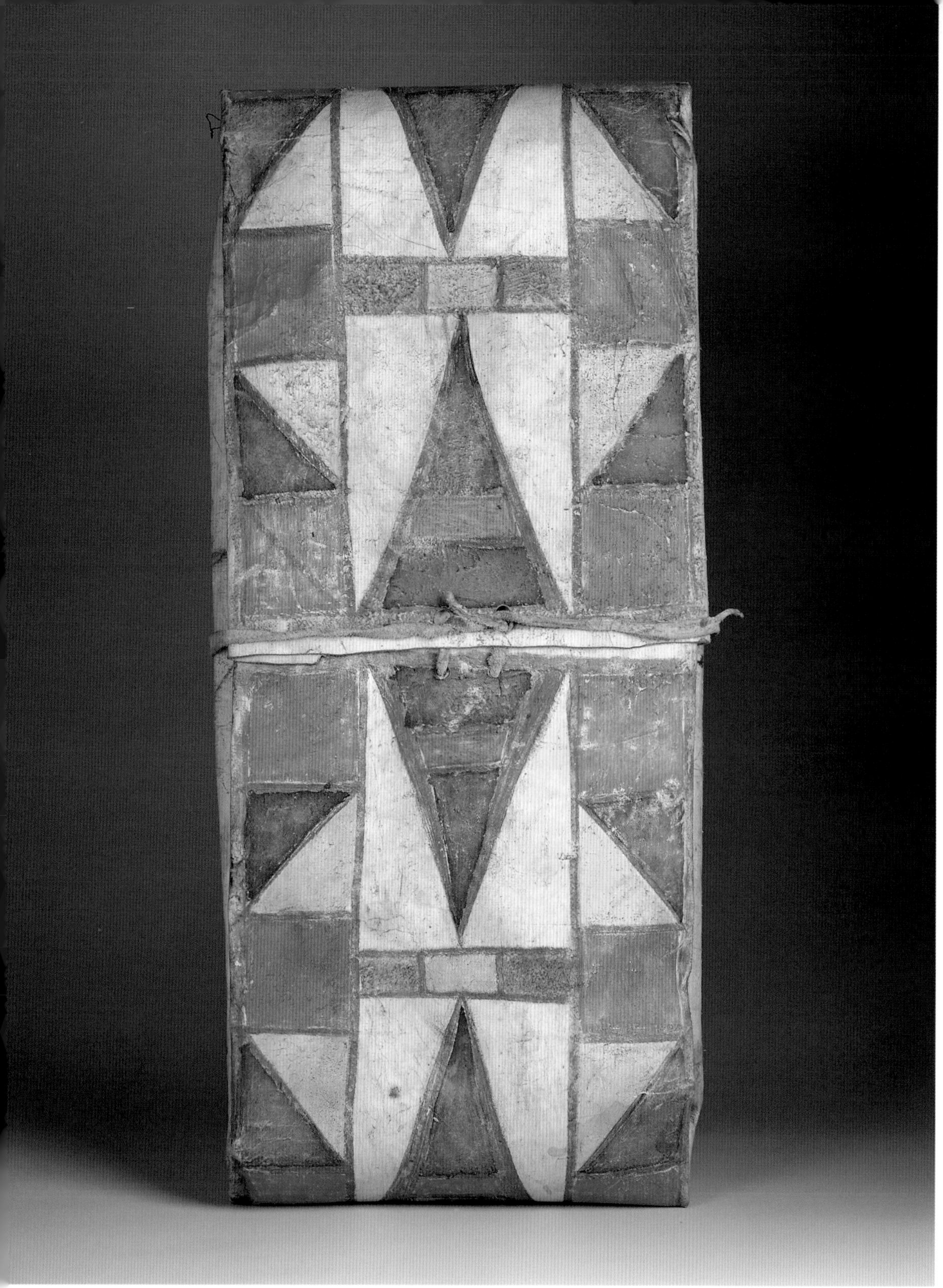

102 / **Shoshone envelope, ca. 1890**

L 28 in., W 12 in. Rawhide, pigment

Collected by Alfred L. Kroeber on the Wind River Reservation, 1900. American Museum of Natural History, 50/1126

103 / **Shoshone cylinder, ca. 1890**

H 21 1/2 in., D 6 in.; fringe 29 in. Rawhide, pigment, native leather, wool cloth, glass beads

Collected by George Dorsey on the Wind River Reservation, 1900. Field Museum of Natural History, Chicago, 60773

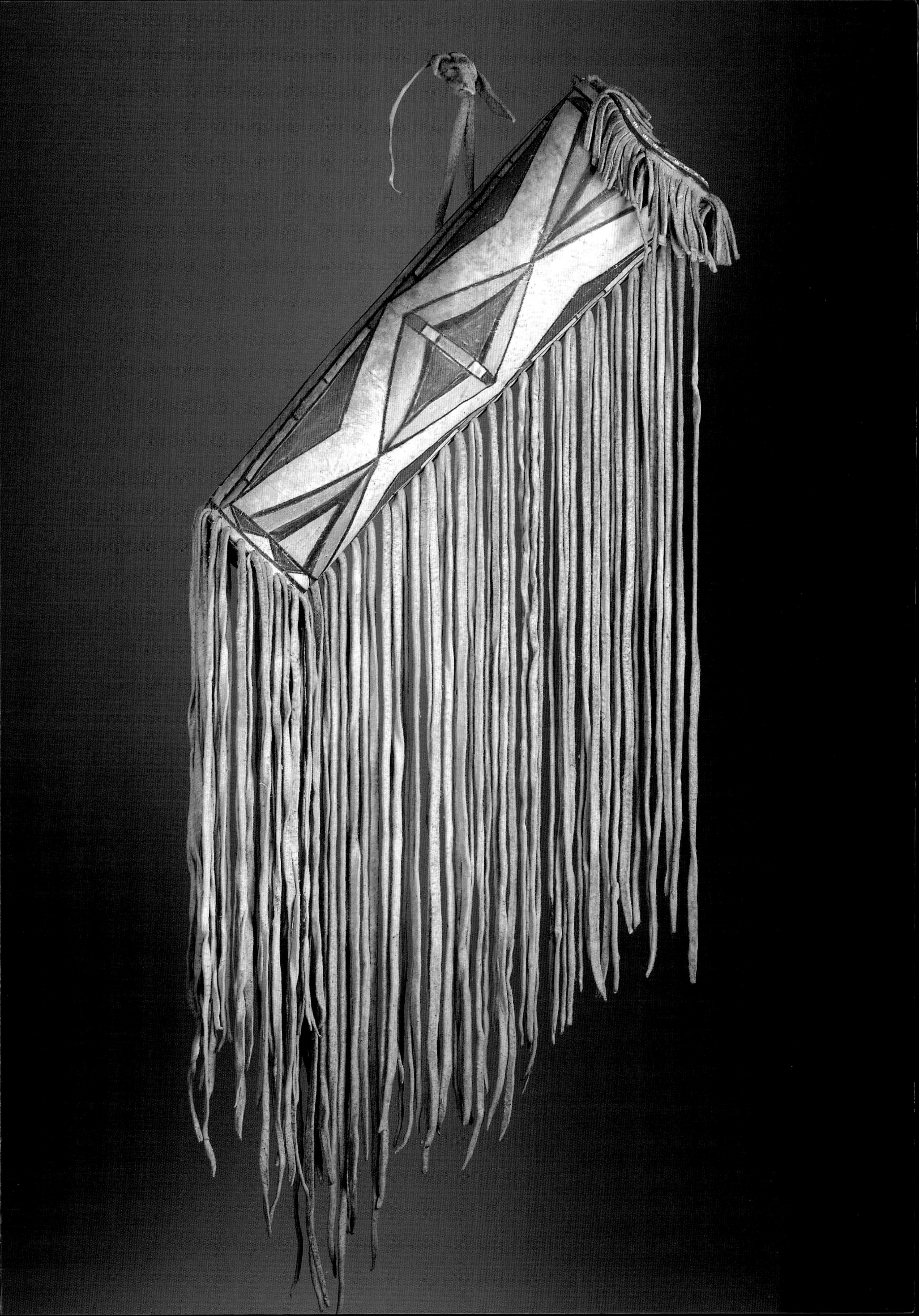

EASTERN PLATEAU

The parfleches of the Nez Perce may be considered representative of all Eastern Plateau groups in that the works collected from this tribe are generally typical of those obtained from the Flathead, Çayuse, Coeur d'Alene, and other Eastern bands. While there were undoubtedly distinct variations developed within this area based on the traditions of individual tribes or on different time periods, it is impossible to reconstruct their origins today. Extensive trade and intermarriage, with the resulting exchange of material goods and aesthetic concepts, produced a blending of tribal styles and a dispersal of objects throughout the region.[19] This activity has occurred for generations, to the extent that collection history has little bearing on the origin of any piece or its formal characteristics. Another reason to focus on the Nez Perce is that the great majority of parfleches collected in the region were acquired from these people; relatively few have been obtained from other groups. Even when highly distinctive parfleches are collected from these smaller tribes, such as the Flathead envelope illustrated in

19. The cultural complexity of the Plateau region is well documented in Ruby and Brown (1986).

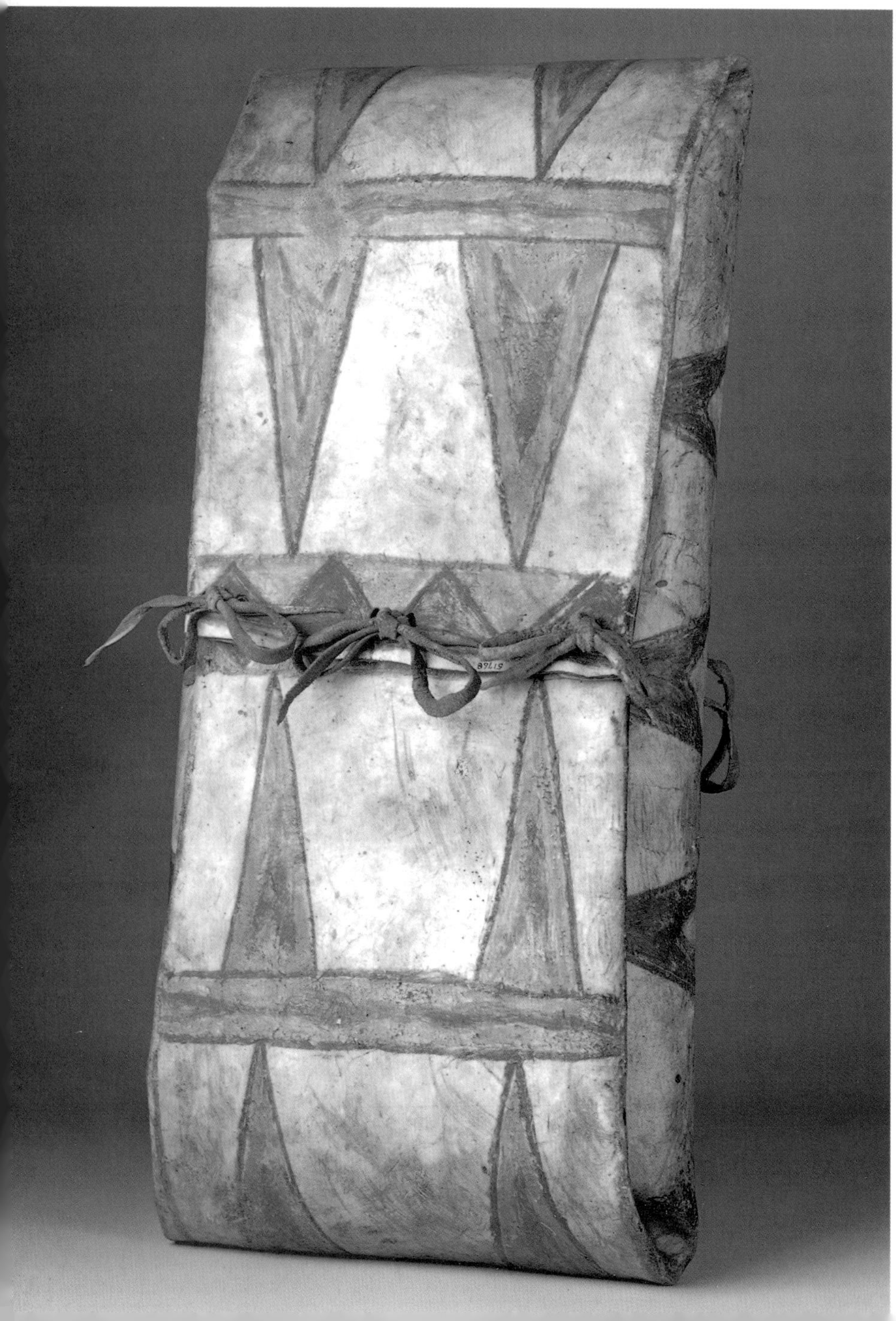

104 / **Flathead envelope, ca. 1885**
L 26 in., W 12 in. Rawhide, pigment

Collected by George Dorsey on the Flathead Reservation, Montana, 1897. Field Museum of Natural History, Chicago, 51768

105 / **Eastern Plateau envelope, ca. 1885**
L 28 in., W 13 in. Rawhide, pigment

Private collection

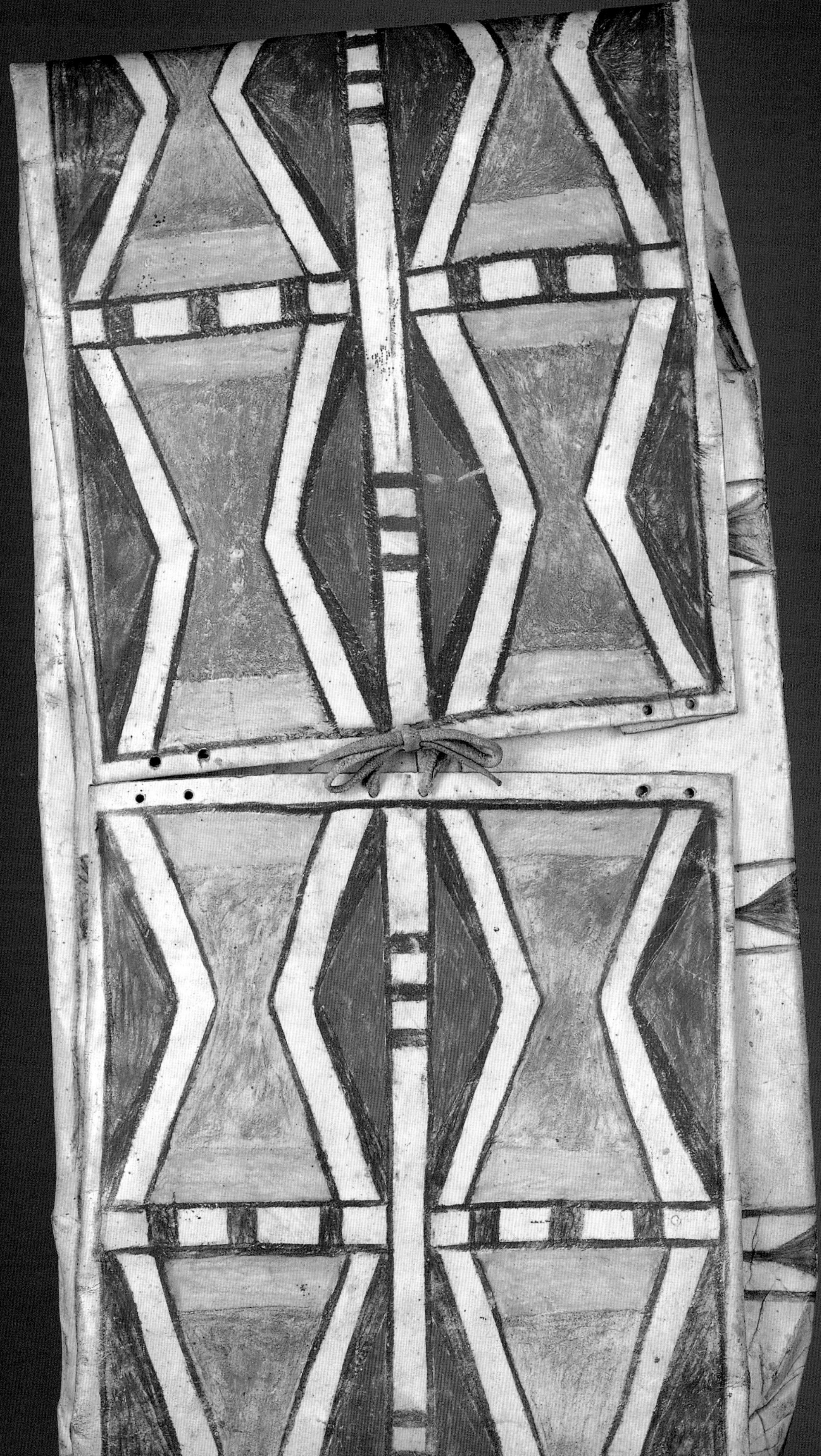

plate 104, there exists no sizable body of works for comparison and it is unknown if such a piece is characteristic of the tribe's style or reflects instead the innovation of an individual artist. Therefore, a larger group of parfleches, such as those from the Nez Perce, tends to render a more visible pattern of characteristics.

There appear to be two influences present in Eastern Plateau parfleche production: that which may be identified as Crow and, by extension, Shoshone; and that which reflects a more general pan-Plateau sensibility, perhaps emanating from an earlier regional style or resulting from continuous interaction with Western Plateau groups. The first undoubtedly stems from the close bond of friendship between the Crow and Nez Perce, and their continuous exchange of goods over a long period. The Nez Perce, as well as Flathead and Cayuse, regularly ventured onto the plains to hunt buffalo, often visiting and trading with the Crow and Shoshone. Many parfleches were acquired from these tribes in this manner, and their presence surely had an impact on the work of Plateau women. In fact, it must be assumed that some of their parfleches are indistinguishable from Crow prototypes; others, however, include features that serve to identify their Plateau makers.

For example, most Nez Perce envelopes—like those of the Shoshone—tend to be slightly shorter and wider in proportion. Even more revealing is the use of multiple colors in the structural lines that form the designs (pl. 107). Borders are usually a single line, rather than two, and are sometimes different in color from those used to define the inner shapes. Some compositions include elements that may be considered typical Plateau devices, such as a central band filled with diagonal bars or shapes that are outlined in a second color (pl. 109). Other designs that resemble Crow painting in every other way lack the tapering lines synonymous with that tribe's work (pl. 106). In construction, Plateau envelopes executed in Transmontane style are identical to Crow and Shoshone examples, with a single pair of tie holes and comparable technical quality in the preparation of the rawhide. None has side flap decoration or painting on the reverse side.

Other envelopes collected in significant numbers from Eastern Plateau tribes appear stylistically different from those deriving from the Transmontane tradition. Although they utilize similar straightedged forms and possess the same complexity, the distribution of elements is more dispersed and there is less concern for precision in the drawing (pls. 105, 108). Structural lines are often rendered in more than one color, and not all divisions of color within the designs are bordered by these lines. The color relationships within the paintings are less standardized than those of the Crow style, and many designs are almost completely covered with paint. The borders consist of a single line of color. Side flaps are often painted, and a line is sometimes used to delineate the back of the parfleche. Two or three pairs of tie holes may be used rather than a single pair. Finally, the character of the hide, sizing, and paint surface vary considerably with different pieces.

106 / **Eastern Plateau envelope, ca. 1890**

L 27 1/4 in., W 12 1/4 in. Rawhide, pigment

Matching envelope, collected on the Crow Reservation, Montana, in the collection of the Buffalo Bill Historical Center, Plains Indian Museum, Cody, Wyoming. Collection of Kenneth and Barbara Canfield, Santa Fe

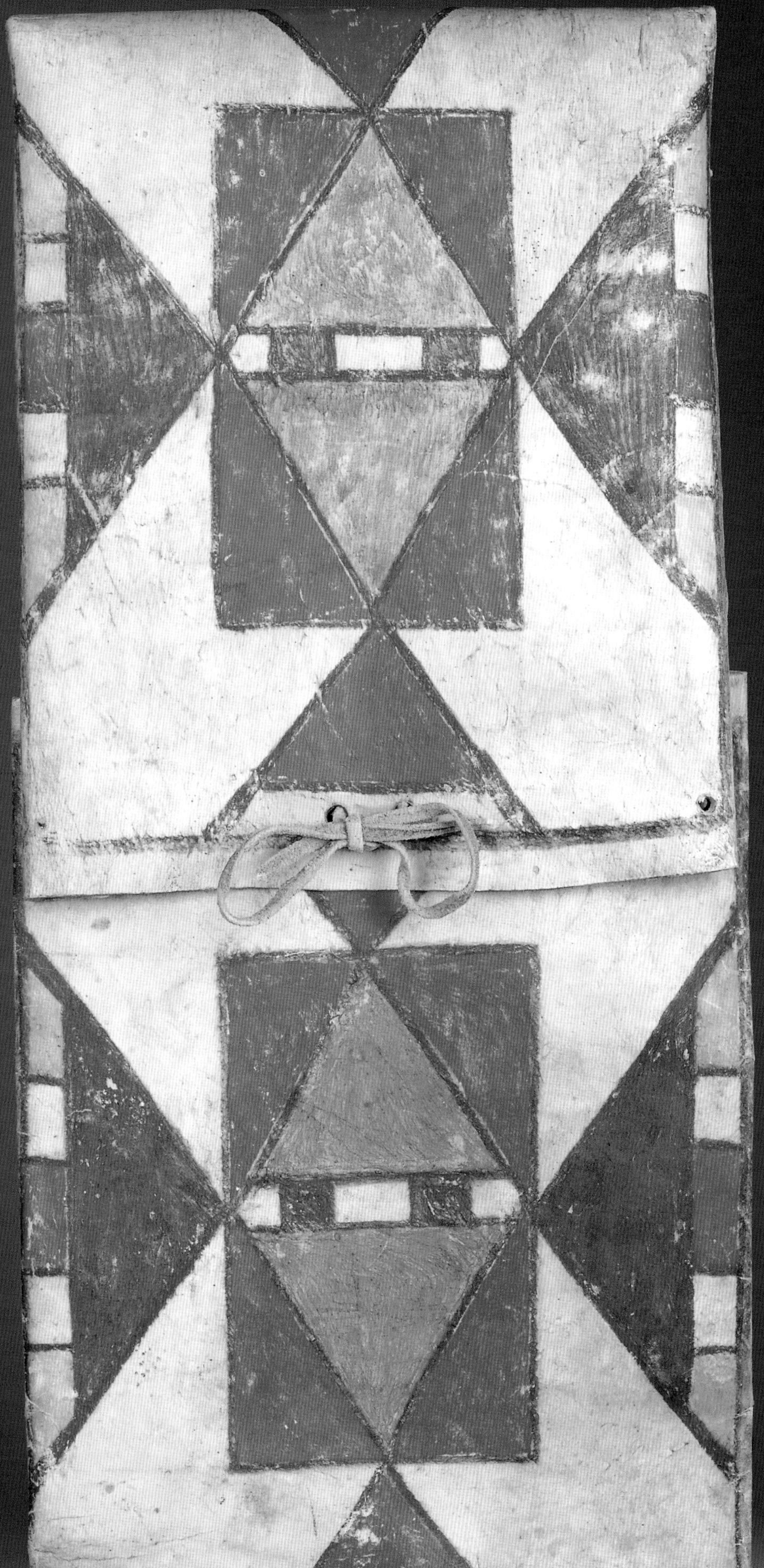

This latter group shares many similarities with a number of parfleches collected from various Western Plateau tribes, particularly from the Yakima at the turn of the century (pls. 119, 120), but also the Umatilla and Warm Springs peoples. This serves as a reminder that while the Eastern Plateau tribes maintained their Transmontane traditions, they were also actively sustaining a centuries-old relationship with the Western tribes of the region. The Nez Perce, Cayuse, and Flathead functioned as middlemen in an extensive trade network that linked the Plains tribes with those of the Columbia River basin. The same dynamic of trade, intermarriage, political alliances, and cultural exchange previously described characterized this interaction, and encouraged the diffusion of material goods and artistic styles throughout the entire Plateau area. This activity probably intensified during the reservation period as different tribes were located together. For example, after they were combined on the Umatilla Reservation in northeastern Oregon, the Umatilla and Wallawalla maintained a close association with the tribes in the Warm Springs Reservation to the west, while the Cayuse maintained their close ties with the Nez Perce to the east (Ruby and Brown 1986: 260). Undoubtedly, many parfleches produced by the Western tribes subsequently came into the possession of the Eastern groups through this and similar exchanges, influencing their rawhide paintings to varying degrees during different periods. Transmontane pieces passed to the West with similar effect.

This active exchange and the resulting influences that remained throughout the nineteenth century reinforce the possibility that a more unified style of painting may have been practiced by all Plateau tribes before the Eastern groups adopted so many aspects of Plains culture and assumed their part in the development of the Transmontane style. Evidence suggests that Crow/Shoshoni influence manifested itself most fully in Eastern Plateau painting after 1850. Indeed, the oldest pieces collected from and attributed to the Nez Perce and Flathead are much closer in appearance to those typically produced by the Columbia River groups. It seems likely that a very early Plateau style developed in the eighteenth century in response to the aesthetic concepts of several Plains cultures as parfleches from a variety of tribes found their way to Plateau peoples along with the diffusion of horses. As Plains parfleche designs were appropriated by Plateau tribes and modified according to their own artistic traditions, a number of stylistically related types must have emerged concurrently. These undoubtedly continued to evolve slowly through cultural exchange within the Plateau and periodic influences from the outside. Ultimately, it would appear that this tradition was sustained in the Western Plateau, while the Transmontane aesthetic increasingly defined the work of the Eastern groups.

The Nez Perce and other Eastern Plateau groups did not possess the kinds of sacred bundles held by the Crow and Blackfeet, but produced both flat cases and cylinders of the same general type. The side-fringed cases were similar in most respects to those of the Crow; however, all

107 / **Nez Perce envelope, ca. 1890**

L 29 in., W 13 1/2 in. Rawhide, pigment

Private collection

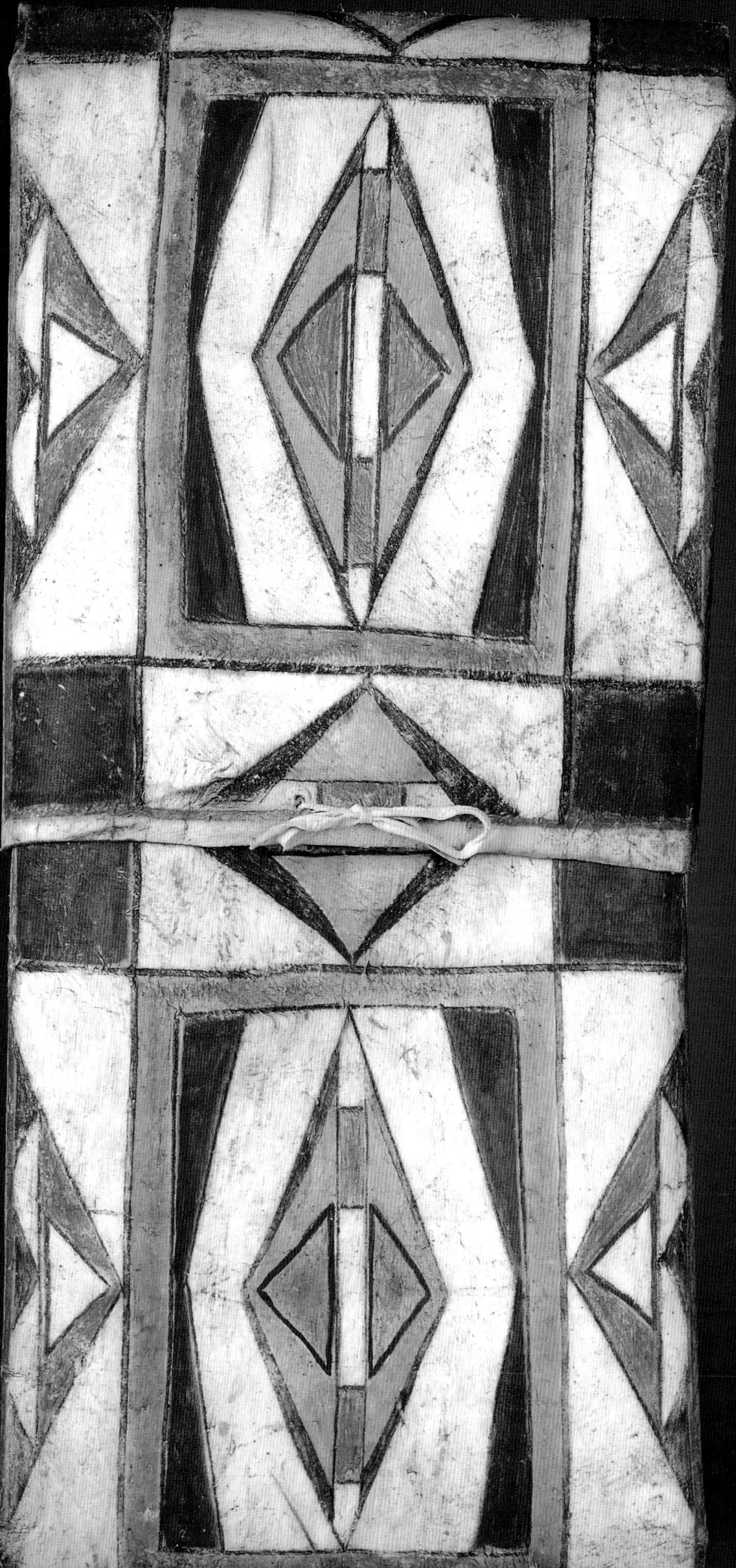

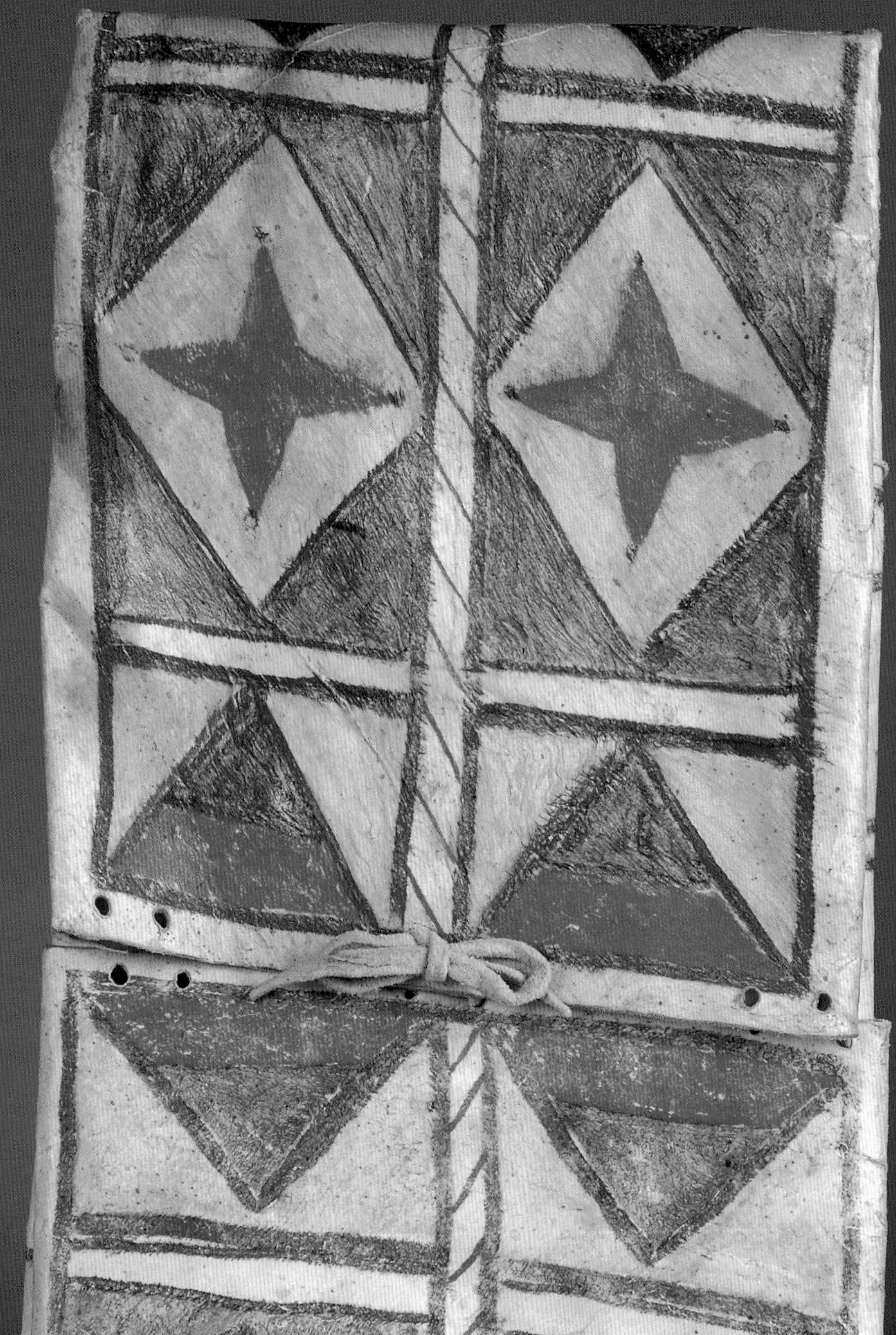

108 / **Eastern Plateau (Nez Perce?) envelope, ca. 1900**

L 16 3/4 in., W 8 3/4 in. Rawhide, pigment

Collected on the Nez Perce Reservation, Idaho. Private collection

109 / **Nez Perce pair of envelopes, ca. 1910**

Each L 29 in., W 12 1/2 in. Rawhide, pigment

Collected on the Nez Perce Reservation, Idaho. Private collection

of the known Plateau cases were painted exclusively with geometric designs. None of the vision-inspired images sometimes seen on Crow medicine cases appears, although there were a number of exceptionally beautiful cylinders made (pl. 110) in the Crow style. It is probable that most of these were initially made to contain the elaborate, Plains-style feather bonnets worn by Eastern Plateau warriors, while later examples were created for parade purposes.

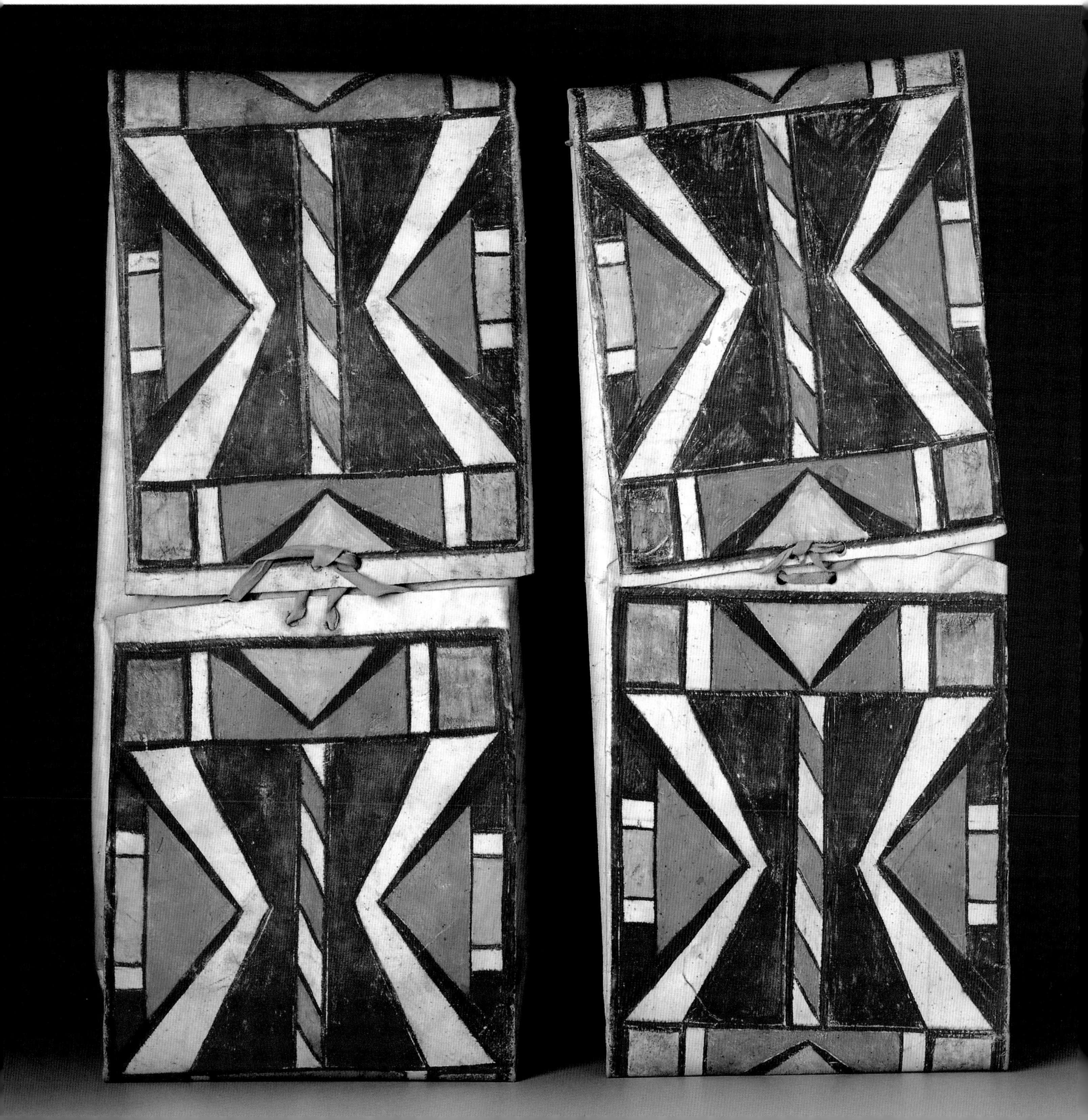

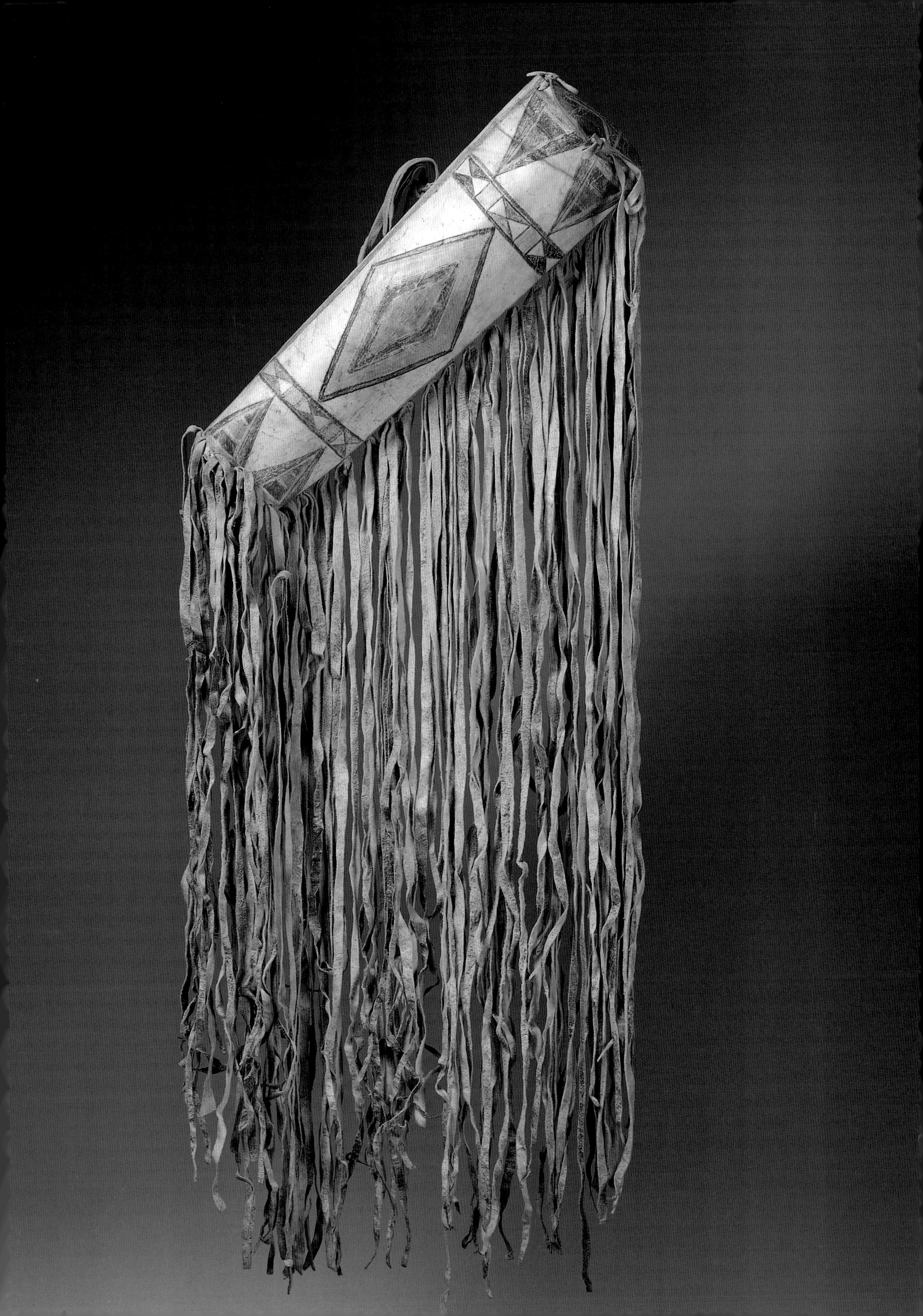

Western Plateau

The Plateau region extends from the Rocky Mountains in the east to the Cascades on the west, and from the upper reaches of the Fraser River in the north southward to the edge of the Great Basin in what is now Oregon. A multitude of tribal groups inhabited the area, sustaining themselves through fishing, gathering wild foods, and hunting. This region was perhaps the most culturally diverse of any on the continent. The social and political structures, religions, economic activities, and social customs varied considerably, as did the manners of dress, housing, and migration patterns; all reflected the cultures bordering the Plateau including the Plains, Northwest Coast, California, Great Basin, and Subarctic. The Columbia and Fraser River systems facilitated trade throughout the entire Plateau region, and The Dalles on the Columbia River thrived as one of the most important trade centers in Western North America, bringing together peoples, material goods, and cultural influences from all the adjoining regions.

The introduction of the horse into the area in the early eighteenth century initiated a number of significant changes in the patterns of many Plateau societies. As discussed in the foregoing section, this new influence most dramatically affected the Eastern Plateau tribes inhabiting western Montana, Idaho, and eastern Washington and Oregon, who adopted many features of Plains culture, but it extended to the Western groups living in Western Washington and Oregon as well. By the second quarter of the nineteenth century, many Plateau tribes had developed large herds of horses, thus greatly increasing their mobility. The active production of parfleches was adopted as a part of this complex. Even prior to that time, they were undoubtedly present in the Plateau as a result of trade, and must have been made by several groups.

There were three centers associated with parfleche production in the Western Plateau region, based on the numbers that have been collected; all were located in the grasslands of the Columbia River basin. First were the tribes located on the Warm Springs Reservation, including the Wasco who originally inhabited the south bank of the Columbia River near The Dalles, and the four divisions of the Tenino. Second, and to the north, were the Yakima, who shared their reservation with the Klikitat and small numbers of Wishram displaced from The Dalles region. Finally, to the east on the Umatilla Reservation were the Umatilla proper, the Wallawalla, and the Cayuse. Parfleches were also collected from tribes on the Colville and Spokane reservations, but not in significant numbers.

A number of stylistically distinct types were created by these peoples during various periods, but it is impossible to trace these production patterns today because there exists no substantial basis for assigning individual tribal designations. Parfleches were freely traded throughout the

110 / **Nez Perce cylinder, ca. 1880**

H 20 1/2 in., D 5 in.; fringe 36 in. Buffalo rawhide, pigment, native leather

Collection of Kenneth and Barbara Canfield, Santa Fe

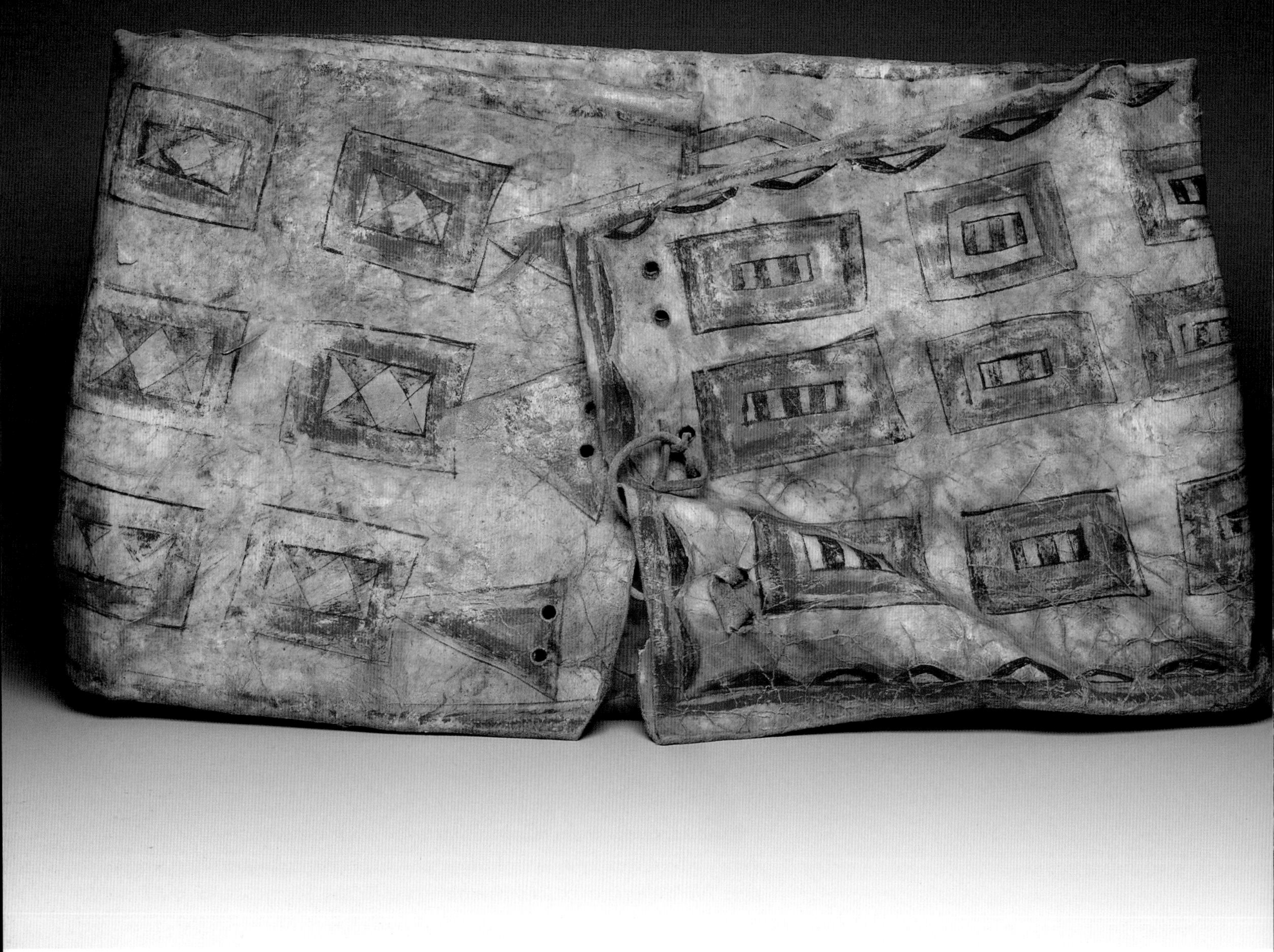

111 / **Western Plateau envelope, ca. 1830**

L 29 in., W 15 1/2 in. Rawhide, pigment

Collected by T. T. Waterman on the Warm Springs Reservation, Oregon. National Museum of the American Indian, Smithsonian Institution, 10/7540

112 / **Western Plateau (Umatilla?) envelope, ca. 1860**

L 23 in., W 14 in. Incised buffalo rawhide, pigment

Collected from the Sioux; one of a pair; this envelope is nearly identical in its design to an older, conventionally incised envelope collected from the Umatilla, also in the Lanford collection (see illustration, page 55). Collection of Benson Lanford

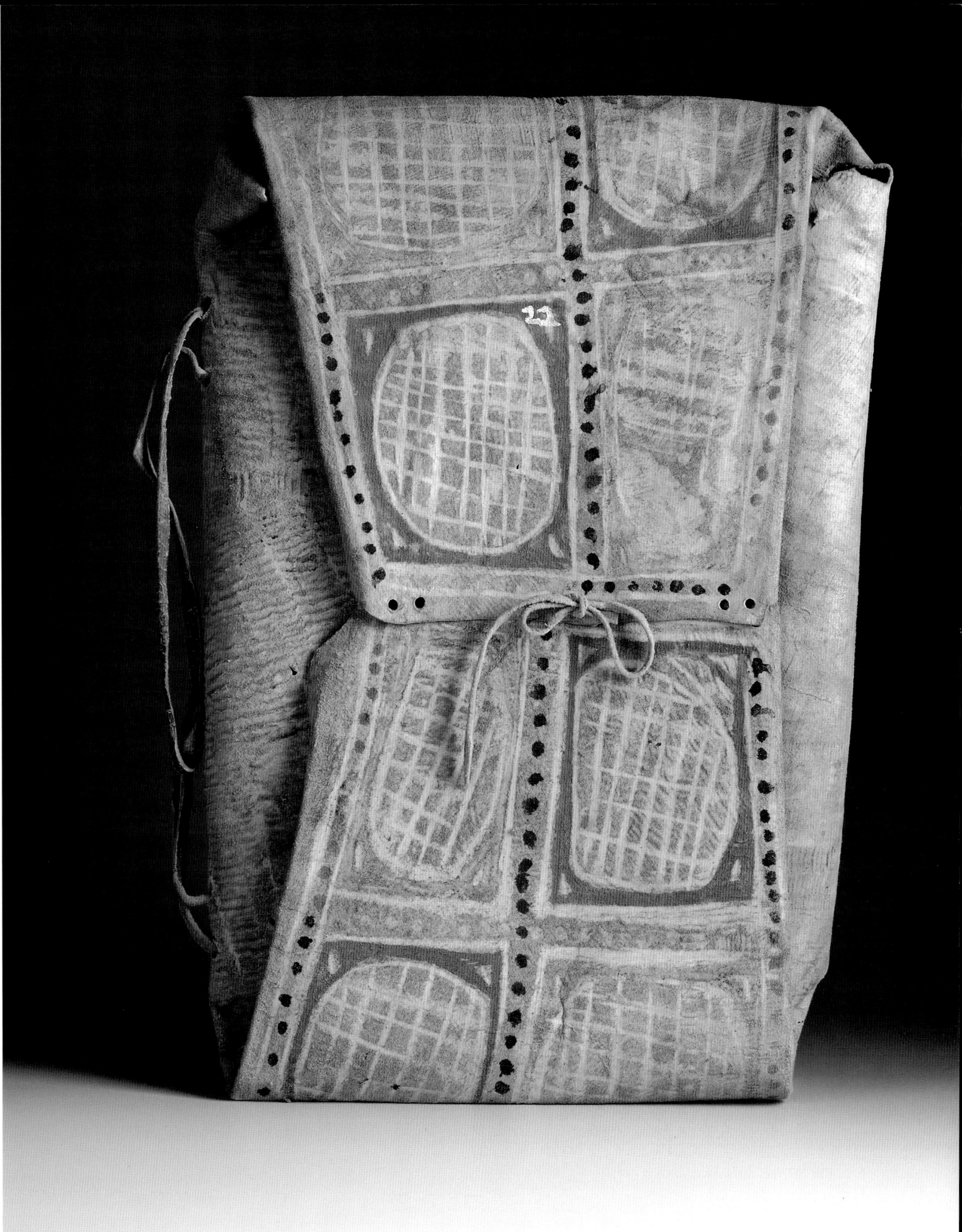

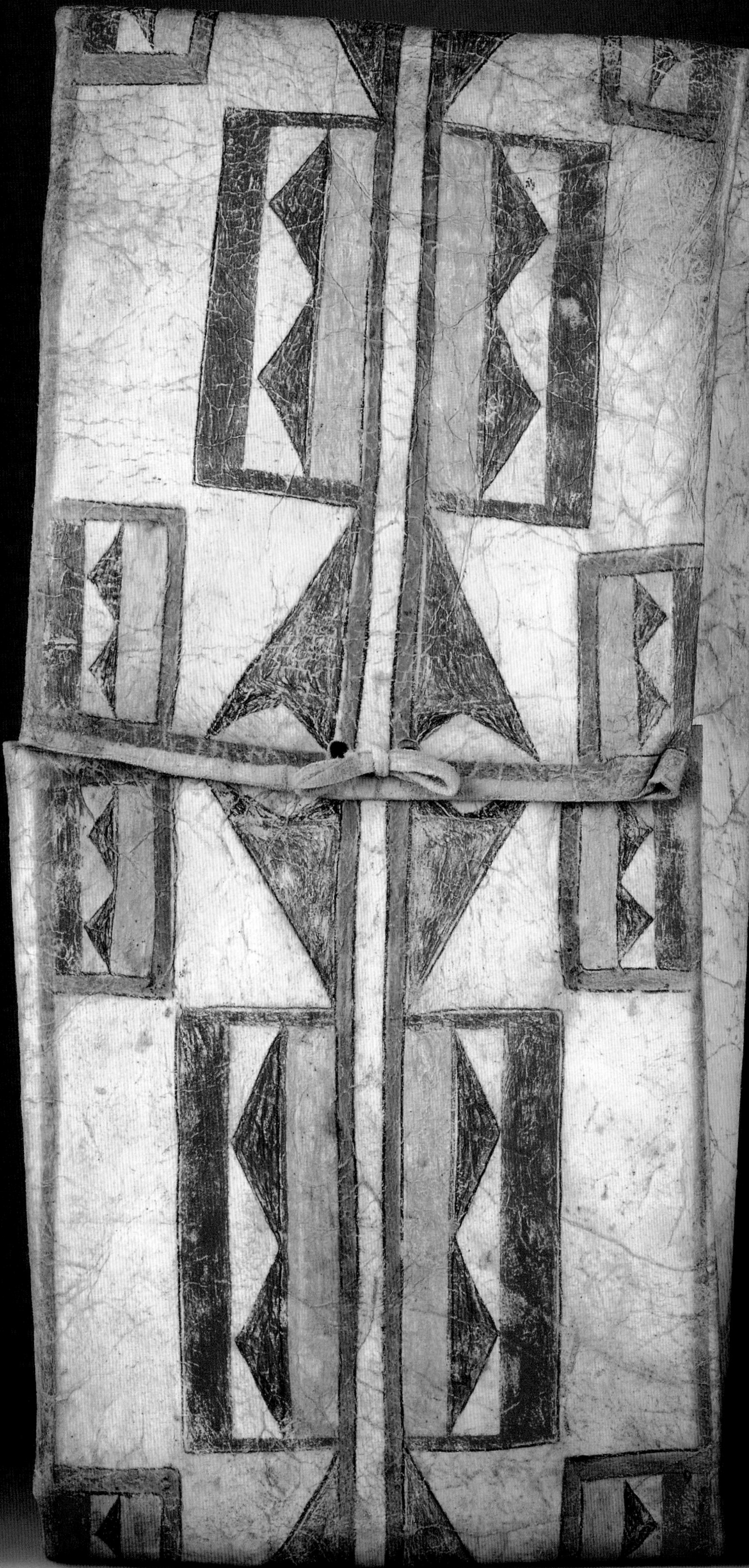

113 / **Western Plateau envelope, ca. 1865**

L 27 3/4 in., W 12 3/4 in. Buffalo rawhide, pigment

Collected on the Warm Springs Reservation, Oregon. Collection of Continental Insurance, courtesy Douglas Drake Gallery, New York, 1250

region, to the extent that all types were almost equally dispersed among all the tribes by the time substantial collecting had begun. With this trade occurred the continuous exchange of design concepts, so that any design developed by one group was very likely to have been appropriated by others. Intermarriage compounded this dynamic, as did reservation settlement. And, typically, no parfleches were obtained with the identities of their makers. The result is bewildering. A survey of collections today reveals a number of types, some quite distinct and others created as stylistic variants, all collected from Western Plateau groups in such numbers that their production in the region is assured, but all of questionable tribal origin.

For example, an envelope of classic Plateau design (pl. 113) collected from the Warm Springs Reservation and documented as such might have been made by either a Wasco or Tenino woman, or by a woman of one of the other Tenino divisions—Wyam, Tyigh, or Dockspuse; it also might have been made by a woman from another tribe, such as Umatilla, married into one of the Warm Springs groups but maintaining her own traditions; or it could have been made at a different location and traded to the Warm Springs family from whom it was collected, as envelopes of this type have been acquired from the Umatilla, Wallawalla, Flathead, Nez Perce, Cayuse, and others.

At the same time, most envelopes with this design have been collected from the Warm Springs Reservation. Such concentrations of stylistic types are the best, and only, indication of tribal or subregional production that exists today. The examples of Western Plateau parfleches illustrated here, therefore, reflect the diversity found within the region, but each represents a type acquired in sufficient numbers to suggest an established tradition. Together, they represent what must be considered the components of a regional style.

A number of envelopes of an unusual type and all of great age have been collected from the Warm Springs Reservation (pl. 111). Together with envelopes that are adorned with the five-block pattern and a number of flat cases, they represent one of the earliest traditions in the Western region. All are large and wide, and most are constructed with trapezoidal flaps and three pairs of tie holes, suggesting strong Blackfeet influence. The majority are made of buffalo hide that has been heavily sized. Their most distinctive feature, however, is the disparate designs of their outer flaps. Unlike parfleches that reveal slight differences in their designs as a result of the artists' casual omission or inclusion of minor elements, these images were intentionally varied as an aesthetic decision. Although the designs on each flap are closely related in their individual components and character of painting, the configurations formed by the elements are structured differently. The compositions themselves usually include both curving and straightedged forms; and geometric shapes that are typically drawn in an angular fashion, such as triangles or diamonds, are often slightly rounded in contour. Black outlining is incorporated throughout the paintings to define

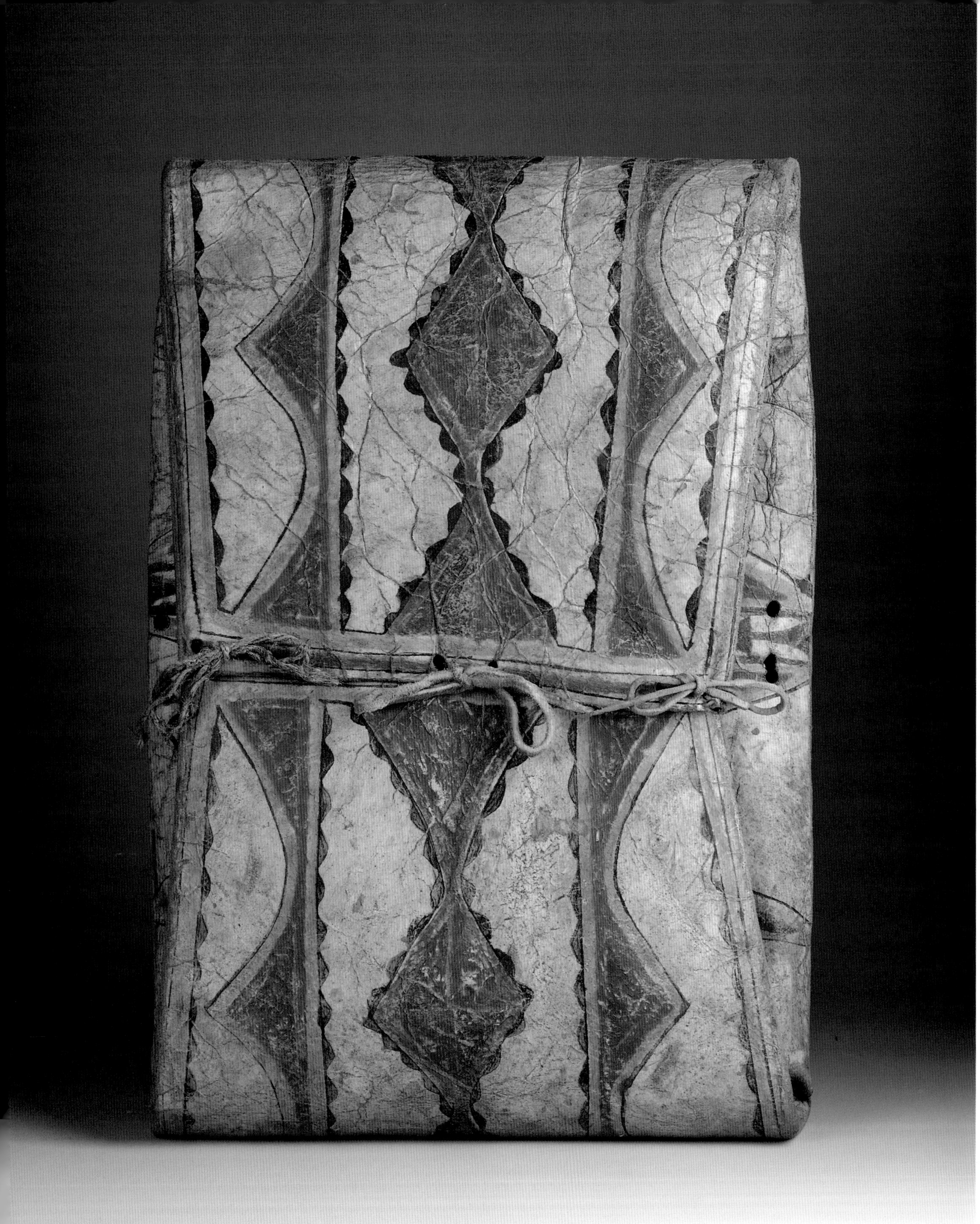

114 / **Western Plateau (?) envelope, ca. 1870**

L 20 1/2 in., W 14 in. Rawhide, pigment

Collected by E. C. Miller on the Yakima Reservation, Washington, 1913. American Museum of Natural History, 50.1/7201

major forms, separating painted and unpainted areas and sometimes color divisions within shapes. The handling of this line is forceful and expressive, imparting a sense of tension and movement. Numerous black elements are usually included, and the contours of primary motifs and borders are often scalloped or edged with triangles. The side flaps are usually painted with fairly elaborate designs. Even though most of these parfleches appear to date prior to 1860, a full range of color is used, setting them apart from Plains pieces of the same period. Included in most paintings are reds, ranging from brilliant, pure varieties to dull rust-colored hues, yellow, a very dark blue, pale green, and a golden orange. Most are probably of native origin. It is this phase of Plateau painting that most closely resembles Jicarilla Apache parfleches in painting style and, to a lesser extent, those of the Kutenai and Blackfeet.

Blackfeet influence is apparent in several parfleches collected from Western Plateau groups. These include pieces obtained from the Umatilla and Yakima in addition to those found at Warm Springs. The compact proportions, trapezoidal flaps, and compositional conventions that distinguish these containers suggest that a Northern Plains influence may have passed to the tribes of the Columbia basin through the Kutenai and other small bands occupying the northeastern Plateau.

One very interesting example of this type is decorated with a highly unusual technique (pl. 112). The envelope has been constructed so that its outer surface is formed of the flesh side of the hide, roughly scraped to produce a napped surface. The artist first created her design by scraping through the nap to the smooth, hard surface beneath, and then heightened the effect with paint. No other parfleche utilizing this technique has been found, but a conventionally incised envelope bearing a nearly identical design was collected from the Umatilla (see p. 55). It is one of several incised containers collected from Plateau groups, indicating that the technique, sometimes attributed to the Crow alone, was widespread. While a few were collected from the Nez Perce, most have been obtained from the Warm Springs peoples. Some are composed of straightedged forms, but a number incorporate the curving shapes often found in Western painting. Even the angular designs, when they appear, are distinctly Plateau in character, rather than Crow, and the majority are constructed with trapezoidal flaps.[20]

If a single composition may be thought to represent the Western Plateau region, it would be the five-block pattern. As indicated, this is one of the oldest Plains designs and is found throughout the Plateau, but it is especially associated with the Western groups in collections today and was certainly one of their most traditional patterns. The finest of these paintings, like the envelope illustrated in plate 113, possess a monumental sense of scale deriving from their architectural structure, clarity of form, classical balance, and simple, understated rhythms. Lines of varying width coalesce into rectilinear shapes that are counterbalanced against the restrained, yet dynamic, movement of repeated tri-

20. See Penney (1992: 170) for an example of this type. An excellent example of an incised envelope with curvilinear designs is illustrated in Morrow (1975: 47).

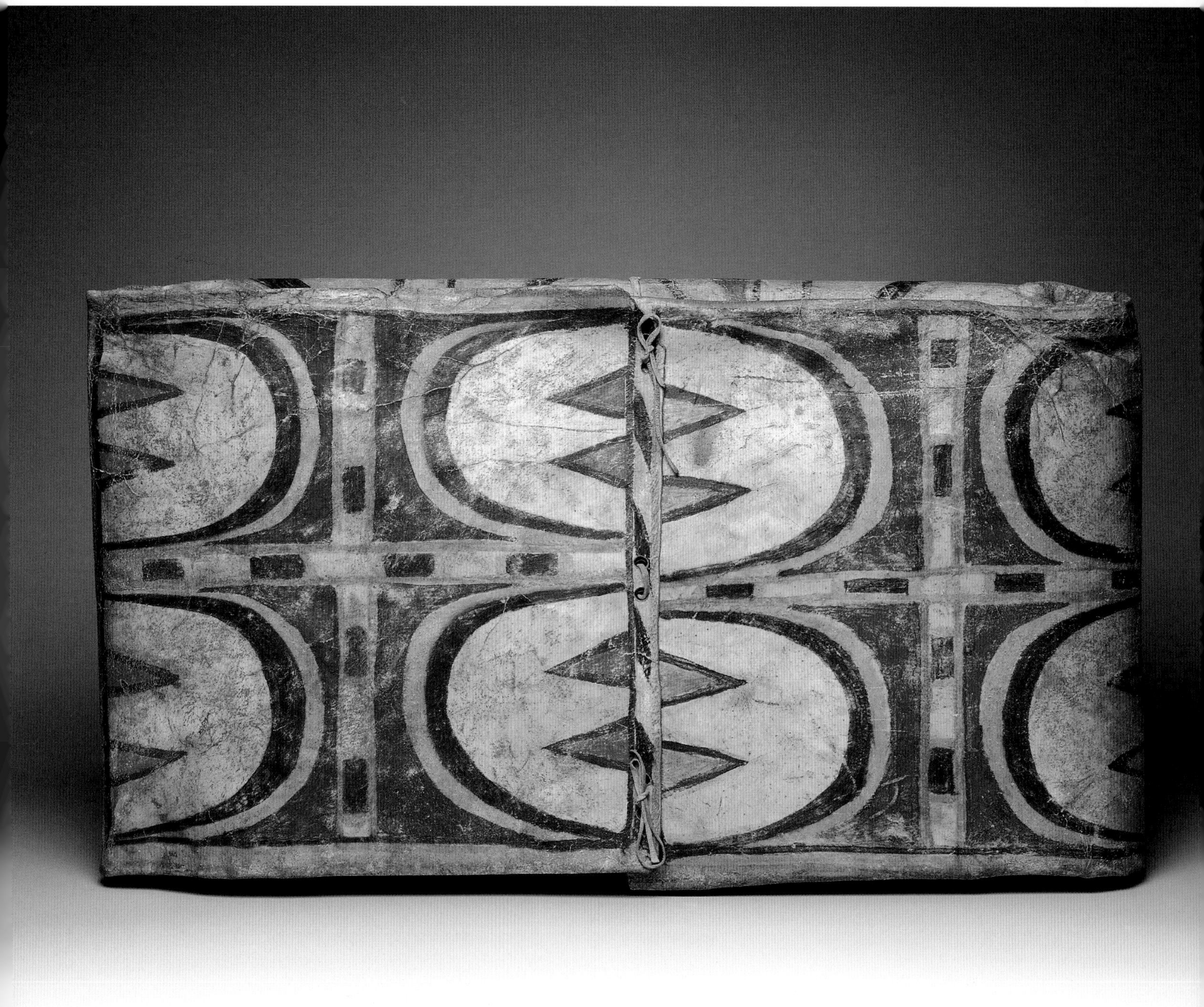

115 / **Western Plateau envelope, ca. 1880**

L 28 1/2 in., W 15 1/2 in. Rawhide, pigment

Private collection

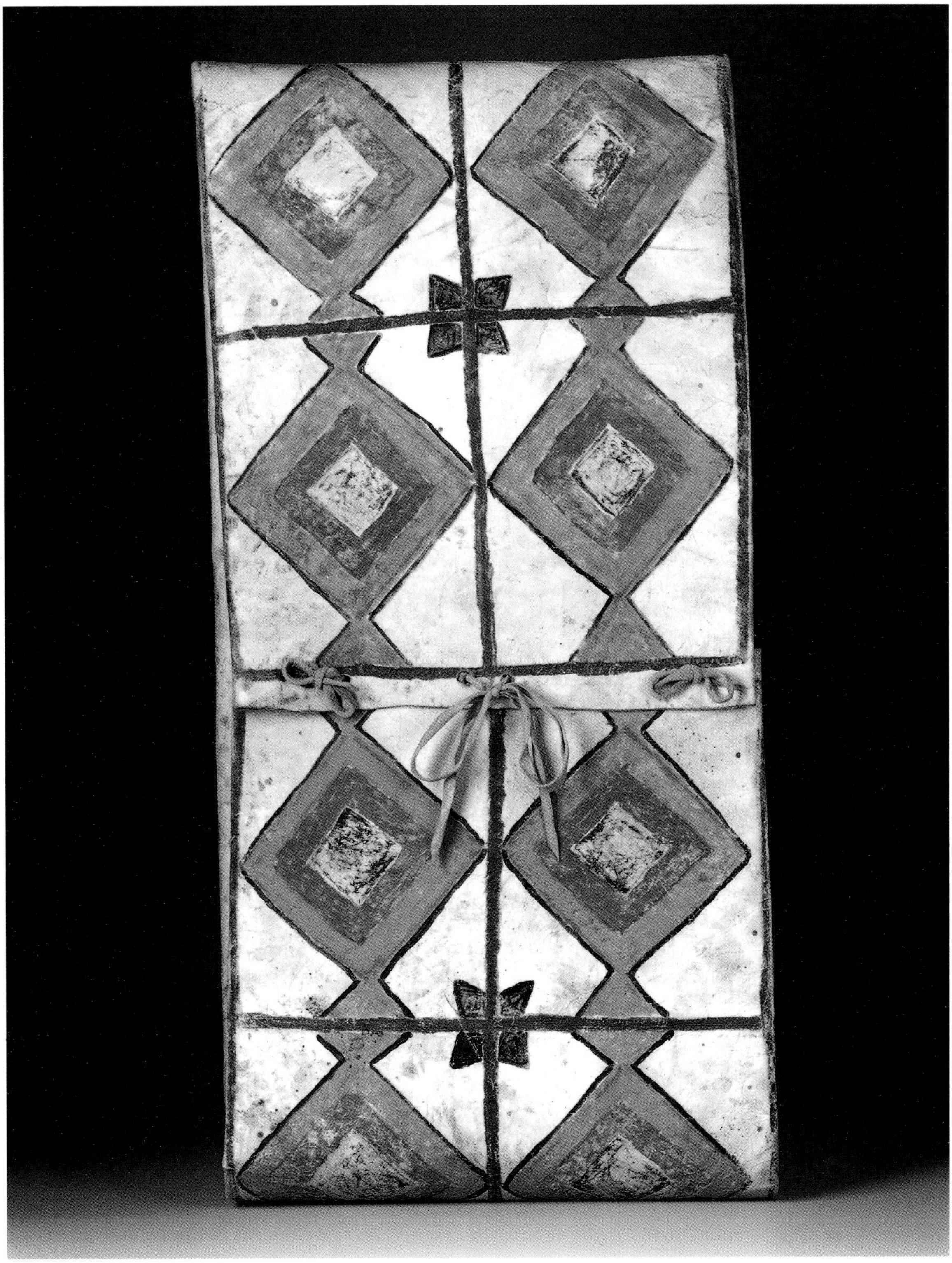

116 / **Western Plateau envelope, 1890**

L 29 in., W 14 in. Rawhide, pigment

Collection of Eliot and Jeanne Nusbaum

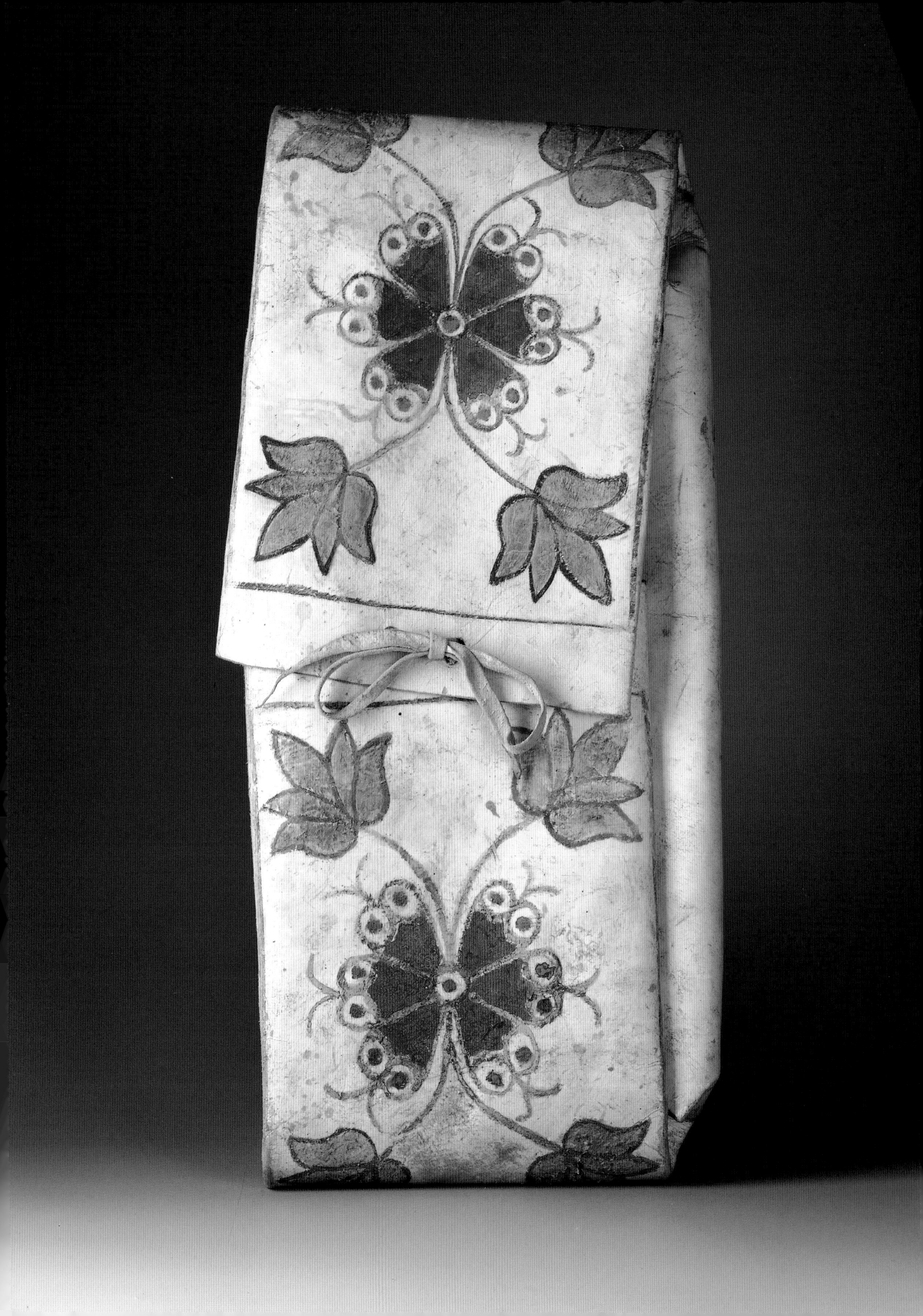

117 / **Western Plateau envelope, ca. 1900**

L 26 in., W 10 1/4 in. Rawhide, pigment

Collected on the Warm Springs Reservation, Oregon. Private collection

angles. The drawing is always direct and powerful in effect, infusing the image with a linear activity held in check by the solidity of the blocklike forms. Nearly all have an open band running through the center of the composition, striking against the angularity of the design. The border of the panels consists of a single line, usually rendered in a soft native green that is also used in the interior structure of the painting. This native pigment was retained in paintings even when the remaining colors, consisting of red, yellow, blue, and dark green, were trade varieties. The side flaps are usually undecorated, either in keeping with their Plains prototypes or suggesting an Eastern Plateau origin, but the number of tie holes might vary from a single pair to three pairs. The structural lines within the designs are of varied width and color, and are occasionally so finely rendered that they function visually as true outlining; however, these lines are always dark blue or dark green, never black.

Some early parfleches have been collected on the Yakima Reservation that closely mirror Northern Blackfeet painting and construction (pl. 114). The single element that sets them apart, suggesting that they are likely Plateau interpretations of the Blackfeet type rather than pieces acquired in trade, is the extensive use of black scalloping within the design. This feature is a predominant element in Western Plateau painting and appears during all periods (pls. 111, 118, 123). Of all the phases of Plateau painting that reflect Blackfeet style, these early examples from the Yakima are the closest in appearance. They are limited in number and may represent a concentrated period of production.

Many Western parfleches are painted with sweeping curvilinear forms. One dramatic composition of this type (pl. 115) is powerfully balanced with opposing curves set within a linear framework. This design, in which the panel is divided into four equal divisions with a semicircular, arching shape in each, is known as a classic Western Plateau type, but also appears in Blackfeet (pl. 71) and Kutenai (pl. 85) painting. It probably occurs among Eastern Plateau groups as well. Curved designs were favored by Western Plateau women into the twentieth century (pl. 118), and remain one of the most distinctive features of the region.

Another type of parfleche frequently collected from the Western tribes, but occasionally found among the Eastern groups is illustrated in plate 116. These parfleches are composed so that the unpainted hide functions as a true background upon which angular motifs are painted. Even though designs of this kind are well balanced and visually dynamic, they lack the complex figure-ground integration typical of Transmontane painting. This pictorial separation of figure and ground is especially enhanced when the hide is rendered extremely white through its processing, as in this example. It has also been intensified by heavy black outlines surrounding the diamonds, which are typical of this style, and contrasting dark green lines that divide the panels. A comparable example of this style is the cylinder illustrated in plate 124.

Floral images (pl. 117) are very unusual in parfleche painting and

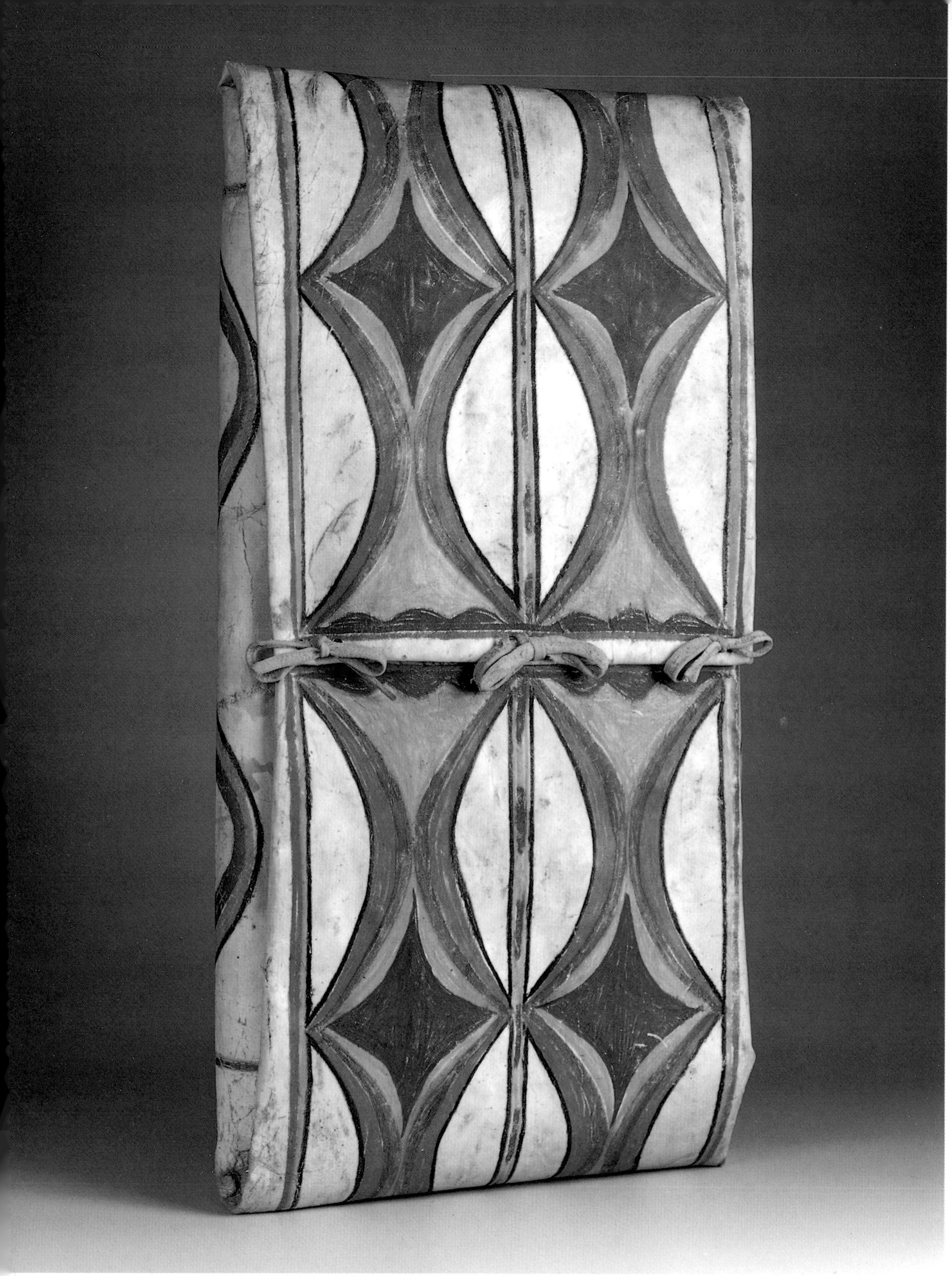

118 / **Western Plateau envelope, ca. 1910**

L 28 1/2 in., W 14 1/2 in. Rawhide, pigment

Collected on the Warm Springs Reservation, Oregon. Collection of Continental Insurance, courtesy Douglas Drake Gallery, New York, 1277

119 / **Yakima envelope, ca. 1900**

L 27 in., W 15 in. Rawhide, pigment

Collected on the Yakima Reservation, Washington, 1901. Field Museum of Natural History, Chicago, 69096

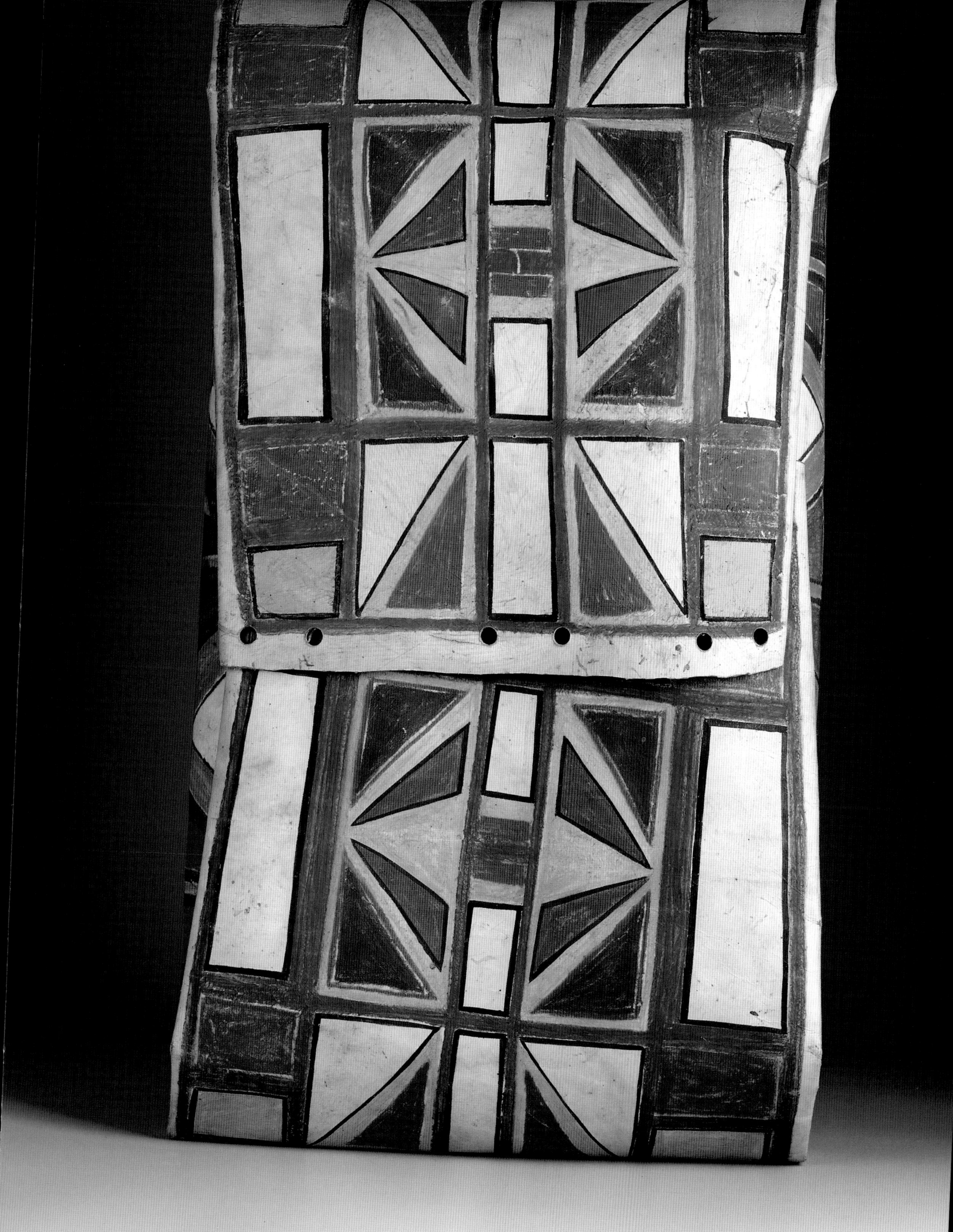

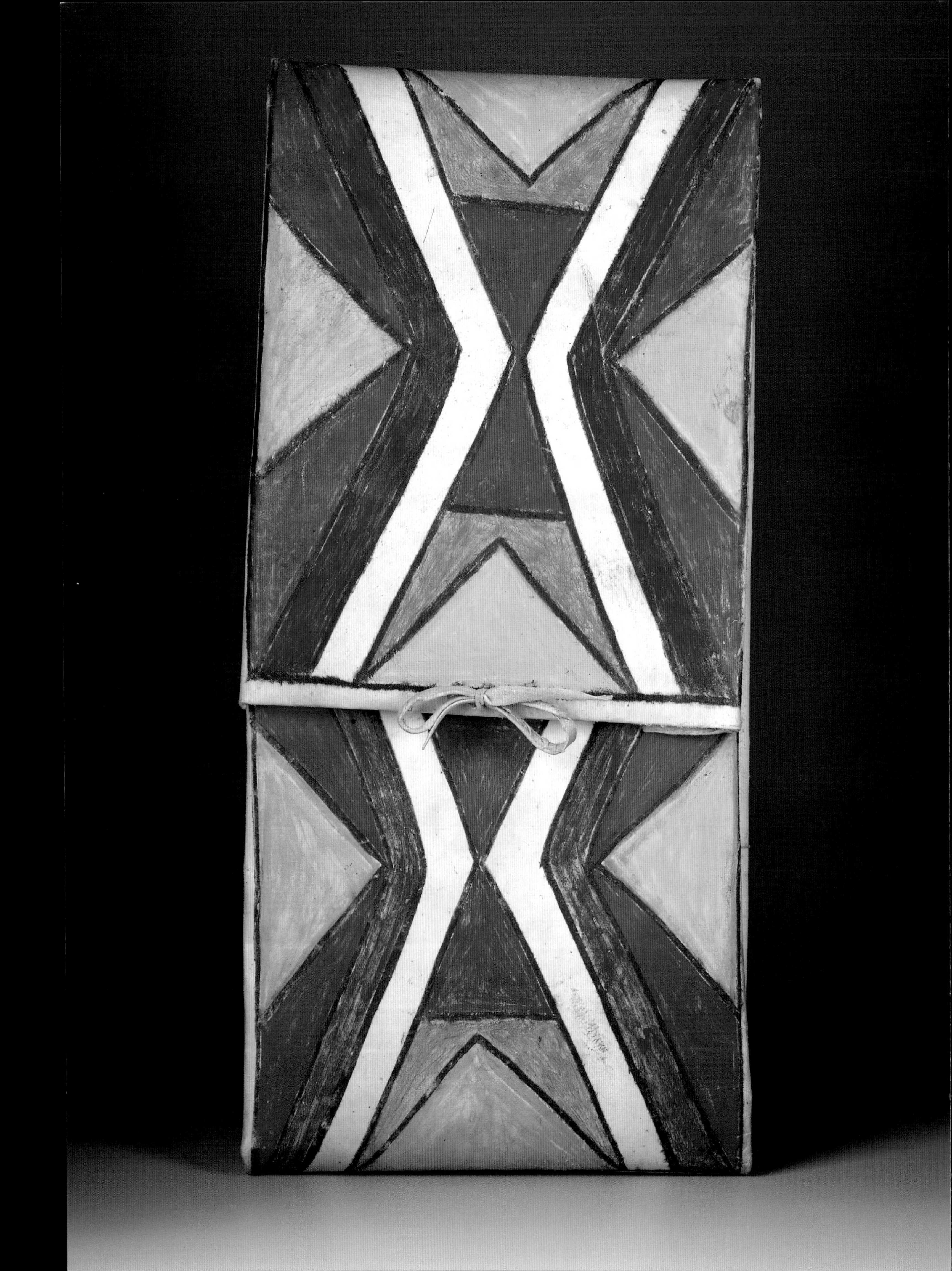

120 / **Yakima (?) envelope, ca. 1900**

L 26 1/2 in., W 12 1/4 in. Rawhide, pigment

The University of Iowa Museum of Art, 1986.58B

are a late development. However, it is not entirely surprising that they appear, considering the extensive use of floral designs in Plateau beadwork. During the same period they also became a popular device on woven corn husk bags, another major Plateau art form. Only four of these floral envelopes are known; all are composed with a single blossom at the center of each flap, surrounded by scrolling leaves, but all were painted by a different hand. At least one was collected from the Crow, who were also incorporating floral images into their art at this time, but the others are associated with Plateau groups. The only other group to experiment with floral designs were the Sioux, who used them on a few of their later pieces.[21]

Toward the end of the nineteenth century, a powerful geometric style was developed by the Yakima and possibly the Klikitat who shared their reservation. It is characterized by exceptionally bold design, strong, saturate color, and heavy black outlining used selectively within the composition to control color relationships and intensify unpainted shapes (pl. 119). Most have trapezoidal flaps and three pairs of tie holes, thus sustaining the Blackfeet influence seen in earlier pieces, and finely painted designs on the side flaps, echoing Kutenai work in concept. A related group of parfleches that are stylistically similar are probably of Yakima origin as well. They are equally powerful in the force of their compositions and use of color, but feature rectangular shaped flaps and Eastern Plateau designs, and incorporate structural lines of dark green throughout the painting (pl. 120), omitting the use of black.

The Western Plateau tribes have a great tradition of side-fringed cases, and an exceptionally large number have been collected. Most show considerable age and some are among the earliest pieces to have survived from this region (pls. 121, 122). Approximately thirty-five cases of this type have been examined by this researcher, but several others are known to exist. Of the group examined, more than twenty were collected from the Warm Springs or Yakima reservations, suggesting a Western Plateau origin for many of those without collection history. In contrast to Plains cultures, whose cases of this type are usually associated with ceremonial life, Plateau peoples used them to store and transport a variety of religious and secular possessions. None has been collected with its contents intact, but informants relate that many were used to carry medicinal items. In later years, side-fringed cases were commonly used as parade objects, in keeping with the customs of the Transmontane and Northern Plains tribes.

These fringed cases are identical in construction to those produced by Plains and Southwestern tribes, and there is also a close resemblance in many of the painted designs to those created by other groups. However, the shape of Plateau cases is particularly distinctive; all are horizontal in format, and for many this feature is quite pronounced (pl. 123). Most Plains cases of this type are nearly square or slightly vertical, especially those from the Southwest that are most easily confused with Plateau pieces. Only Blackfeet fringed cases are sometimes horizontal

21. See the examples illustrated in Morrow (1975: 225) and Porsche (1987: 42).

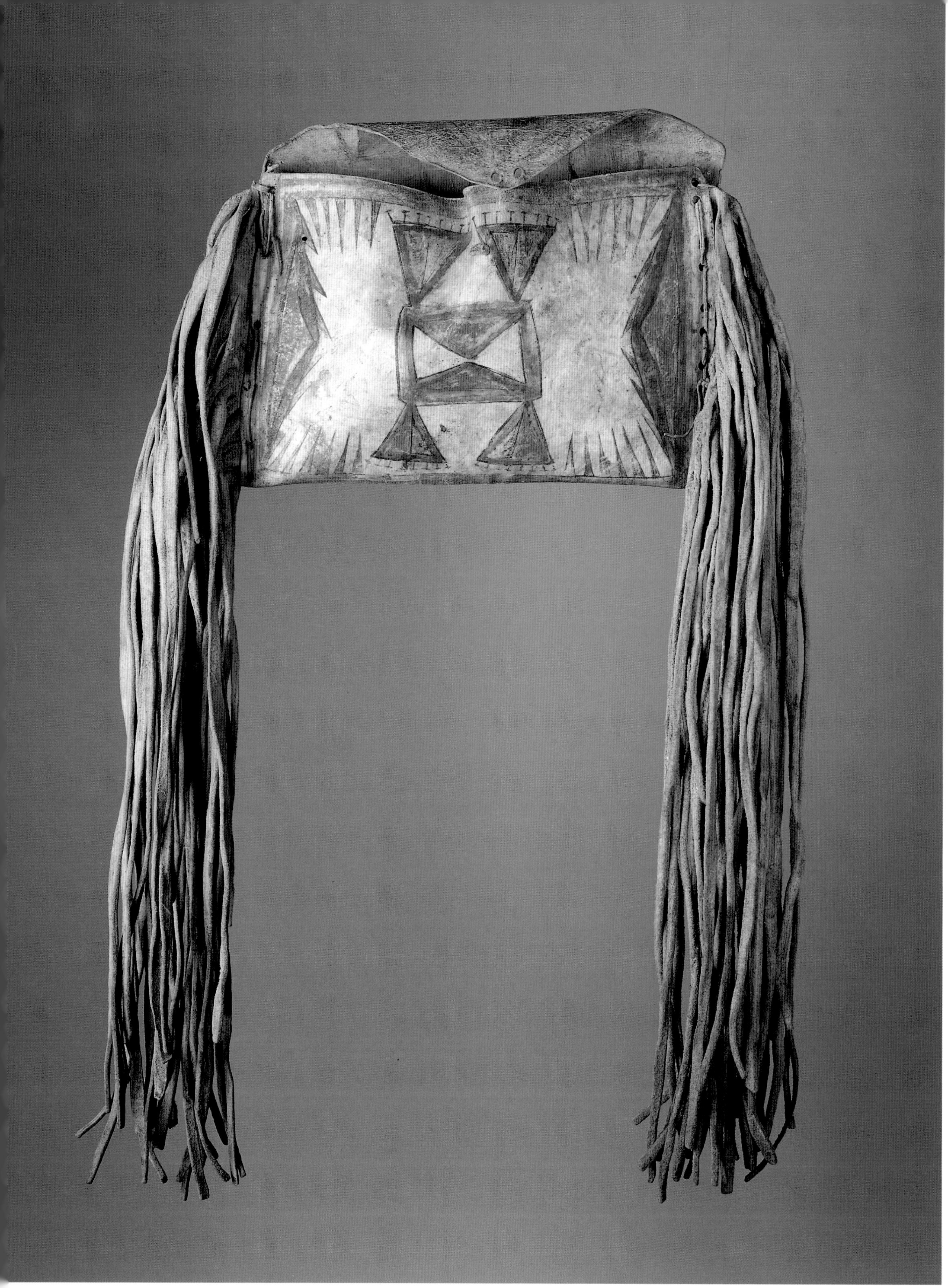

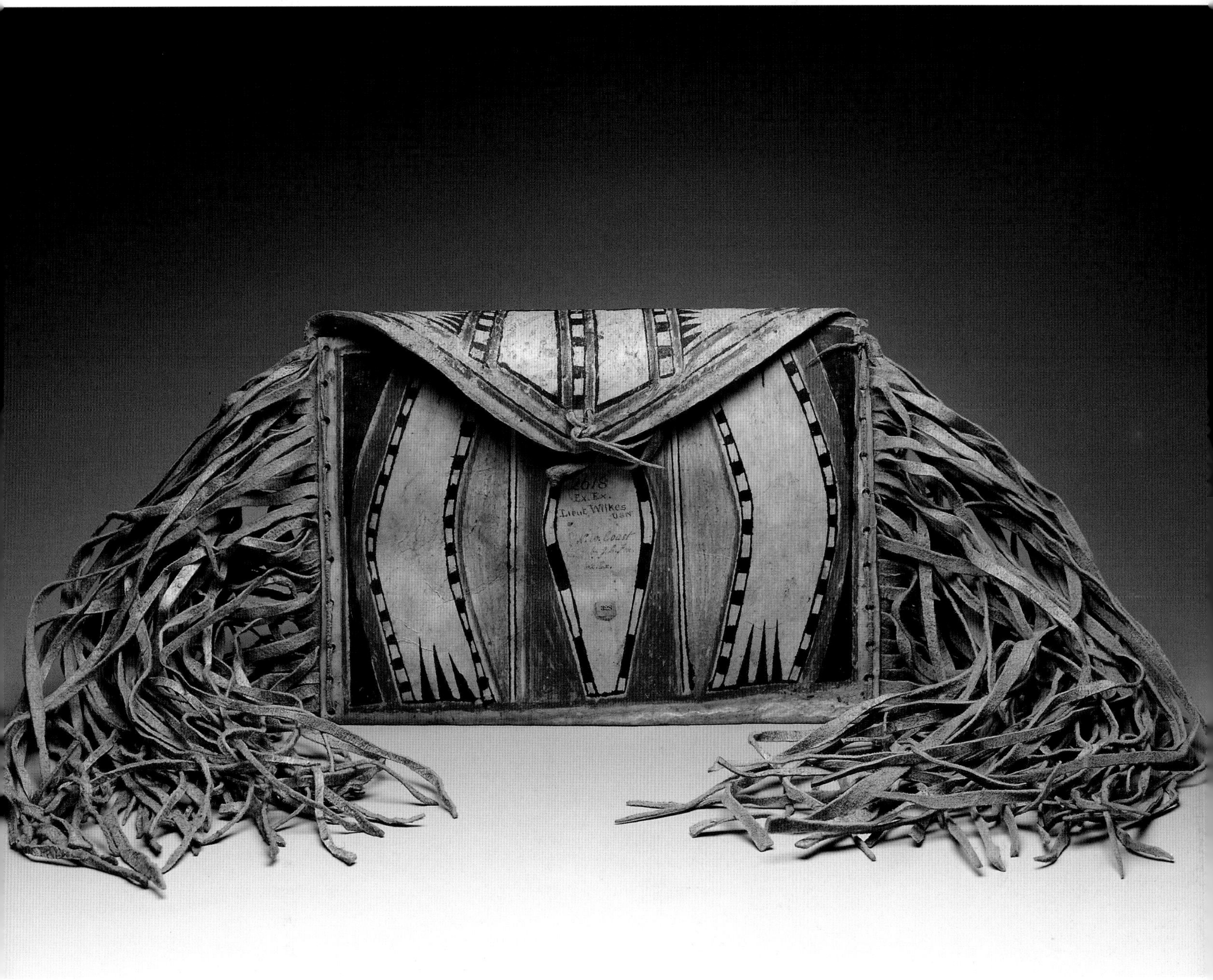

121 / **Wasco (?) flat case, ca. 1830**

H 9 in. (not including flap), W 14 in.; height with fringe 31 in. Buffalo rawhide, pigment, native leather

Collected by Fred Harvey at The Dalles, Washington, 1905. Field Museum of Natural History, Chicago, 86520

122 / **Western Plateau flat case, ca. 1835**

H 10 in. (not including flap), W 15 in.; height with fringe 23 in. Buffalo rawhide, pigment, native leather

Collected by J. L. Fox of the Wilkes Expedition at Fort Vancouver, Washington, 1841; probably presented to him by representatives of the Hudson's Bay Company. National Museum of Natural History, Department of Anthropology, Smithsonian Institution, 2618

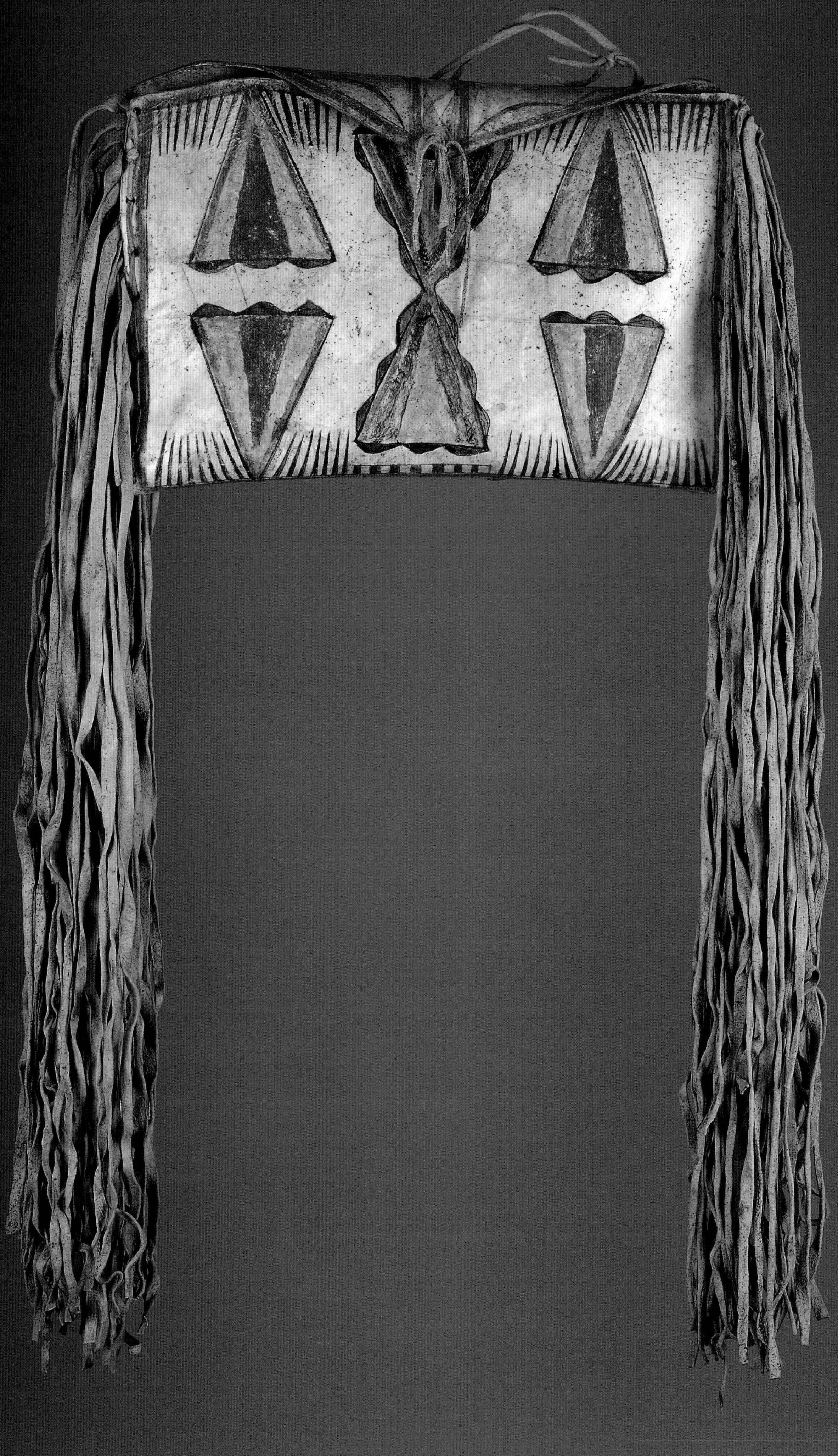

123 / **Western Plateau flat case, ca. 1860**

H 9 in. (not including flap), W 14 1/2 in.; height with fringe 28 in. Buffalo rawhide, pigment, native leather

Collection of Michael and Sherry Maxwell

in shape, but not to such an extreme degree, and they differ enough in other details to be easily identified.

A variety of compositional formats were created, but nearly all were delicately outlined and contained intricately drawn elements in brown/black. Narrow bands containing black hourglasses, diagonal lines, or alternating blocks of black and white were integrated into many compositions, often as border elements but also as a part of the central design. Many also possessed a particularly striking feature: rows of sharp, highly elongated triangles projecting from the top and bottom borders of the panel, filling the open spaces between the larger design elements. These triangles, described by some writers as painted "fringe," also appear in the designs of the Kutenai (pl. 85), Apache (pls. 50, 57) and Comanche (pl. 46), but are usually not so long and slender as those drawn by Plateau artists. Still, the resemblance is often very close and parfleches of all these tribes are often misidentified as originating from one of the others on the basis of this element alone. The central motifs of Plateau cases were constructed of some combination of triangular, diamond, hourglass, or rectilinear shapes, although some designs contained gently curving forms. These major elements were often edged with black scallops or repeated triangles, again duplicating the styles of the Kutenai, Southern Plains, and Apache.

Although the affinities in style between the Blackfeet, Kutenai and the Western Plateau are direct and to be expected, there is no clear explanation for the close relationship with the Southwestern groups. That so many of the defining elements in Plateau painting are also present in the work of the Eastern Apache and Southern Plains groups is a mystery. The two peoples are geographically separated by more than 1,500 miles, with no direct contact through trade or warfare. However, the style is archaic. It may have originated in the Southwest and passed to the Plateau with the horse in the 1700s, where it was preserved in varying degrees throughout most of the nineteenth century; or it may have been carried from the Basin adjoining the Plateau by the Comanche when they migrated into the Southern Plains from the northwest. It seems more likely that the style originated in the south, however, based on the similarity of its elements with those found in Hispanic leatherwork, which was an extremely early influence.

Cylinders (pl. 124) are comparatively rare in Western Plateau collections, suggesting that they were never produced in the numbers created by Transmontane groups. Still, they were a well developed part of their parfleche tradition during the last decades of the nineteenth century, and continued well into the twentieth as parade items. It would appear that they used Transmontane examples as a model in that the construction and general appearance are the same; however, the specific features of the painting style and compositional structure are consistent with other types of Western Plateau parfleches.

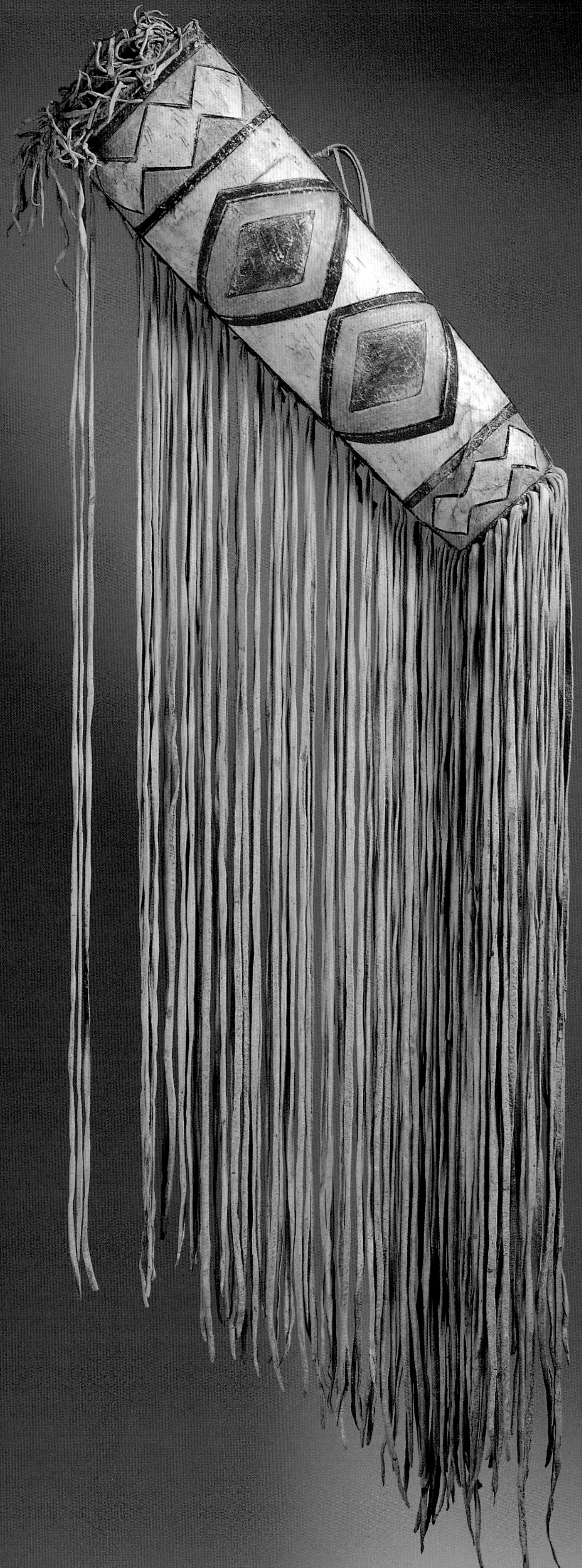

Symbolism and Associative Meanings

It is often assumed that Native American objects with no direct ritual function are secular and purely decorative, without spiritual association. Yet, a perceptive view of most traditional Indian cultures reveals a variety of fundamentally united world views in which religious thought was all pervasive. Few aspects of life existed outside the spiritual realm and, to some extent, all artistic expression functioned as an embodiment of religious belief. In addition to ceremonial items, this pattern of thought extended to the production of many utilitarian objects that incorporated the makers' aesthetic decisions and expressive intent. In fact, many of the most profound Native American art forms were created through the formal elaboration of functional objects. While serving what might be regarded as mundane purposes, these forms simultaneously communicated both an intellectual and an expressive content, transmitting the personal vision of the artist and the aesthetic traditions of the culture. Recognizing this, one may begin to understand the significance of parfleche painting, both for the makers and for those whose lives were enriched by their work.

It is impossible to present a truly comprehensive explanation of content in parfleche painting or concisely describe its various manifestations because so little information was recorded from nineteenth-century informants who could have provided that insight. The tradition and its artists slipped away too quickly. And what we do know of this subject has been filtered through the inquiries of a very few researchers working with a small number of tribes. While their contributions are highly significant and enlightening, they are also limited and biased by the perspective of their times and disciplines.

We also recognize through subsequent studies that the various ways symbolism functioned within the great diversity of parfleche-making cultures—the subtle structuring of layered meanings and the manner in which concepts were expressed and understood—is a complicated and sometimes controversial subject. Perhaps the greatest difficulty faced by these researchers was expressed by Kroeber (1900): "The whole question of [decorative] symbolism is intimately bound up with religion. I do not think that it can be thoroughly studied without having gained the confidence of the Indians in regard to their religion." Thus, for an outsider to have examined thoroughly the meanings associated with parfleche designs would have required several conditions: First,

124 / **Western Plateau cylinder, ca. 1890**

H 20 1/4 in., D 5 1/2 in.; fringe 35 in. Rawhide, pigment, native leather

Collection of Benson Lanford

an extensive knowledge of the tribe's religion and mythology; second, the complete trust and confidence of informants who could provide information; third, a sufficient command of the language to enable the researcher to grasp subtle shades of meaning as they were explained; and, finally, adequate time to pursue the study in depth.

Unfortunately, such ideal conditions seldom, if ever, existed. By the turn of the century, most tribes were rapidly undergoing tremendous cultural change, with the result that many traditional art forms were either significantly evolving or disappearing altogether. There was simply too much needing to be saved and not enough time for those skilled researchers working under difficult conditions to accomplish the task. And the oral traditions of the native peoples did not long preserve concepts that were intrinsic to lost art forms. Those concepts evolved in relation to cultural and artistic change, and were thus embodied in alternate forms which continued to be produced.

What results is a fragmentary body of knowledge. While a number of intensive studies were made that focused on selected aspects of Plains life and material culture, other features were described only in the most general sense. Early references to parfleches fall somewhere in between. Probably because parfleches were so essential to the nomadic way of life practiced by the tribes who possessed them, anthropologists usually focused on their construction and function as storage containers. The painted designs were regarded as secondary and decorative. Most early studies that did describe the paintings avoided the issue of content altogether. Scholars attempted instead to analyze the structural elements of the designs and systems of composition in an effort to assign tribal characteristics or to identify features that were common to all.[1] Only Kroeber's concentrated study of the Arapaho (1907) dealt specifically with symbolism in parfleche imagery;[2] but others (e.g. Wissler 1904; Boas 1927) discussed parfleches within more extensive analyses of decorative art and symbolism in Indian culture, and these, together with Kroeber's work, provide important insights into the various kinds of meanings that were expressed.

It is generally understood that no fixed, universally recognized symbolism existed in parfleche painting; rather, it varied greatly according to tribal tradition and individual preference. Among some tribes a single motif or a commonly used, conventionalized design in its entirety evoked a specific set of associations for all members of the group. For example, Sioux women often utilized the diamond or designs which featured the diamond as the principal element to symbolize the turtle or the breast of a turtle (pl. 13) (Wissler 1904: 241, 257). The great significance of this association is reflected in the belief that the turtle is intimately connected with women's sacred power, having influence over conception, birth, the period of infancy and the functional diseases and disorders of women (ibid, 241). Thus, these parfleche designs embody the ever-present concerns surrounding the principal role of women in Sioux culture. It is not surprising that this motif was

1. See Kroeber 1908: 169–179; Lowie 1909: 23–24 and 1922: 277–89; Spier 1925 and 1931.

2. See, specifically, Kroeber's "Decorative Art," pt. 1, pp. 36–150 (1902).

extended to a variety of beaded objects as well, such as cradles, women's leggings and navel amulets. Crow women also employed a diamond as the central element in many of their designs (pl. 90), but endowed it with a different meaning. They associated this motif with the sand lizard, which they regarded as a talisman; its highly stylized image functioned as a visual prayer for safety, health, and long life. Its protective power was also invoked in the diamond-shaped navel amulets made for children.

According to Weltfish (1965: 261), the Pawnee, in contrast to surrounding Plains tribes, often painted their parfleches with celestial symbols representing the sun, the moon and its rays, the darkness of night, the stars (pl. 9), and the emerging light of dawn.[3] Such imagery derives from Pawnee cosmology and undoubtedly referred to a complex set of beliefs which would have been central to the lives of everyone in the tribe. Representations of four-pointed stars occasionally appear on Plains and Plateau parfleches (pl. 108)[4] and, although their specific meaning was never recorded, were surely intended to connote religious associations. The use of this symbol was widespread throughout much of North America; sometimes rendered as a Maltese cross, it usually represented the morning star, an important element in the ceremonial life of many tribes.[5] It has been found incorporated into the parfleche designs of the Northern Blackfeet, Arapaho, Cheyenne, Mesquakie, Pawnee, Sauk, and Nez Perce and Western Plateau peoples, but was probably used by other groups as well.

Designs and colors were always sacred and talismanic among the Cheyenne, and the creation of parfleches was traditionally regarded as sacred work (Grinnell 1923, vol. 1, 168). All women's arts, including quill embroidery, the painting of robes and parfleches, and feather ornamentation, were under the direction of societies, or guilds, called The Selected Ones. Elderly women in these guilds were specialists in their respective arts and possessed the spiritual prerogative and knowledge to guide initiates. They transmitted the secret meaning of the designs and maintained the strict rules governing the use of designs, their formal organization, and the arrangement of colors (ibid; Powell 1977: 36). This powerful tradition accounts for the great continuity of artistic style and technical excellence that characterize Cheyenne parfleches from all periods.

The Mesquakies reportedly painted many of their trunks with designs that were associated with clan identity (Morrow 1975: 226), thus referring to the religious origins of the tribe and its related political and social structure.[6]

Other religious associations pertaining to the origins of parfleche design are revealed in the traditions of the Arapaho and Sioux. The oldest and most distinctive Arapaho patterns (pls. 32, 33) were created by the mythic Whirlwind Woman, also known as First Woman, a sacred being believed to be the first woman on earth (Kroeber 1907: 110). It was she who first instructed Arapaho women in all the phases of parfleche-

3. Welftish also states that such designs were painted only by those with the necessary religious qualifications.

4. See the Arapaho case illustrated in Feder (1965: pl. 34).

5. Parfleches with the morning star design should be seen within this larger context rather than associated specifically with Ghost Dance doctrine.

6. Some contemporary tribal elders and religious leaders had reservations regarding this; others expressed the opinion that the symbolism of trunk paintings may have extended even beyond clan identity to include various concepts of Manitou power.

making and painting. Other designs were revealed to women directly through their dreams, and this was also regarded as an emanation from the spirit world.

Wissler (1904: 247) notes that Sioux women often dreamed their designs as well and that such experiences were attributed to Double Woman, the feminine culture heroine of that tribe. In addition to other mystical functions, this supernatural being guided women in their creative work, and her appearance in their dreams was regarded as a great blessing. A design originating in this way was always considered the work of Double Woman herself; once it was dreamed and painted by the recipient, it might be copied by other women, but its sacred source and associative meaning were always acknowledged. Double Woman was usually described as one of twin sisters, who were tied or fastened together by a cord, and their image sometimes appears in Sioux beadwork and quill embroidery (Maurer 1992: 158–61). Although the full extent of her manifestations is not well understood outside Sioux culture,[7] we know this mythical being played an important role in the supernatural life of these people and in the creation of parfleches. In describing Double Woman's relationship to Sioux women's art, Wissler (1904: 247) also suggested the depth of associative meanings conveyed by the paintings:

> Now, it seems that a dream design is, after all, not so much a distinct type of design as an illustration of the manner in which Dakota philosophy accounts for the origin of the present styles of decorative art. It is sufficient evidence that these traditional 'holy women' are still an active force in the development of art; and this, in connection with the other traditions of their power and the unreal aspects of art, tend to give every design a vague symbolic background.

Wissler wrote this in 1904, based on primary research. Seen within the context of what we now understand regarding the depth and complexity of Sioux religious traditions, we may assume that the designs were not "vaguely" symbolic to the Sioux themselves. These conventionalized images were an iconic expression of profound belief and a visualization of the ever-present sacred powers which guided their lives.

The symbolism associated with parfleche design could also be highly personal. This practice of attaching individual meaning was most fully described by Kroeber in his study of the Arapaho, but other references indicate that it was widespread among other tribes as well. Kroeber found that although all the women of the tribe used the same basic vocabulary of design elements and adhered to compositional structures defined by tribal style, each artist assigned her own meanings to her designs. The same motifs could therefore be used by numerous artists to express a variety of ideas. For example, he noted that a diamond might be used to represent a person, an eye, the navel, a lake, a star, a turtle, a buffalo-wallow, a hill, life or abundance (*hiiteni*), or the interior of a tent (Kroeber 1907: 144; also Boas 1927: 103). He also explained that these same

7. See Wissler (1912: 92) for a brief discussion of the Double Woman cult.

significations might be represented by different motifs as well, so that a person might be symbolized not only by a diamond, but by a small rectangle, triangle, square, cross, dot and line, as well as by a rudely realistic design (ibid.).

The result was that nearly identical designs could convey very different meanings and an accurate interpretation of an image depended upon the explanation of the maker. A specific example based on one of the oldest and most distinctive Arapaho designs (pl. 32) will best illustrate the character of this symbolism. In 1903 George Dorsey recorded the meaning of a parfleche made by a different woman but bearing essentially the same image as this envelope:[8]

8. Taken from George Dorsey's notes accompanying objects collected for the Fred Harvey Company in 1903, including the parfleche described, which is now in the collection of the Carnegie Museum of Natural History, Pittsburg, cat. no. 31-79-308.

> Six rows of colored designs represented the whole appearance of the earth (rough). Two white lines traversing two center designs denoted the paths of the sun and moon. White and blue lines at edge of the parfleche means the "Ocean" and horizon. Blue paint, the sky; red paint, the earth; green paint, the grass; white field, water. This parfleche denotes the winter season.

The content of another parfleche painting by yet another maker, with the same design and differing only in minor details, was recorded by Kroeber (1907: 108–9):

> . . . the triangles represent tents. Strictly, the equilateral triangles and the pairs of right-angled triangles represent tents; but the four blue right-angled triangles at the corners of the design, half of a tent. Their colors denote the colors (red, yellow, blue, or green, but not black) with which tents were formerly painted. The design is longitudinally trisected by two white stripes which represent paths. Black dots in them are coyote-tracks. These stripes are edged on one side by red, and on the other by blue; these colors denote night and day, and, because night and day are opposite, are on opposite sides of the white stripe. The blue lines enclosing the whole design represent tent-pegs. The white stripes which they enclose are rivers; the red and yellow stripes which they enclose are camp-sites. The small squares in the corners of the design are the ends of the earth (*haneisa biitaawu*). The white areas within the design, consisting each of a high narrow trapezoid surmounted by an equilateral triangle, represent women. This design (i.e., style of design) was first made by the mythic cosmological character, Whirlwind-Woman.

Kroeber further illustrated three additional cases with compositions nearly identical to those just described, each with its own equally individualized meaning (1907: 118, pl. 21).

Kroeber's work has sometimes been discounted on the assumption that his informants were simply telling him what he wanted to hear—that they invented meaning when none was originally intended—in order to please, or at least not disappoint, the researcher. In fact, Kroeber was well aware of this dynamic in pursuing his work, and this critical understanding was clearly expressed in a letter to Franz Boas recounting his efforts (1900):

With the Arapaho at Wind River I was very successful. I obtained information on ornamentation as fully as could be desired, and what improved its value was that it was given readily in most cases. Some of the information was corroborative of that which I secured last year, and much was new. The general character of the symbolism is the same; but there are differences, due to varying habitation and to the relative unimportance of the ghost-dance in the north. There is comparatively less beadwork and much more painted rawhide in Wyoming, so that in the latter I found a practically untouched field.

With my work among the Shoshonean tribes I am dissatisfied. I concentrated my attention in symbolism and ornamentation—with the Shoshone and Bannock entirely, with the Utes largely—and I do not think the results were good. The great body of my information is unreliable. The Shoshone tribes are very different from the Arapaho in disposition. They are, more approachable and friendly, but far more secretive. I usually got information with but little urging, which with the Arapaho was always a criterion of its value, and for some time this disposed me to consider it true. But later reflection and tests convinced me that much of it may have been deliberate lies. The real trouble is the lack of certainty. A small part of the information is surely correct and some is obviously worthless; but the great body of it is doubtful. Of this much, possibly all is all right, but it is impossible to tell with certainty whether or not it is reliable. Not being altogether satisfied with the Shoshone and Bannock results, I determined to concentrate my money and time on the Utes. But I did not fare much better. I was nearly three weeks with the Uinta Utes, and made every effort to get information on religion and ceremony, but failed completely; and this is I think sufficient to discredit the information I received in regard to ornamentation.

The whole question of symbolism is intimately bound up with religion. I do not think that it can be thoroughly studied without having gained the confidence of the Indians in regard to their religion. I got into the wrong habit last winter of treating it as a purely aesthetic matter. Consequently I think that the plan of visiting several new tribes in a short time was not a good one. This was especially the case with the Shoshone tribes, both because of the existing lack of information concerning their religion and their markedly reticent disposition.

I have looked over my Arapaho notes to compare them with those from the Shoshone, Bannock and Utes. The comparison only confirms me in the belief of the complete validity of the former and the unreliability of the latter.

As suggested by the previous descriptions, many Arapaho designs are symbolic representations of the world or of the specific landscape in which the tribe and animals lived. These images often included their camps and trails as well, portraying tangible and familiar surroundings. Sometimes, however, a mythic world, represented by the four directions or the sacred hoop, or big wheel (*baaxoti*), a ceremonial symbol of the earth or universe, was interpreted through these forms (Kroeber 1907: 116). The practice of adorning parfleches with depictions of the land and sky has also been recorded among the Shoshone, Crow, Kutenai, Thompson and Sioux, and was probably common with many other tribes as well.[9] Other Arapaho designs embodied the abstract principles of life-force and abundance (Kroeber 1907: 143, 149); this, too, must have extended to other groups.

It also seems inevitable that the Plains people would associate the

9. Boas 1927: 97 (for the Shoshone); Wildschut 1975: 29 (for the Crow); Kroeber 1908: 175 (for the Kutenai); and Morrow 1975: 43, 131 (for the Sioux). For the Thompson Indians, descriptions of parfleche designs by James A. Teit of specimens in the collection of the Canadian Museum of Civilization: cat. nos. 11-C-228 (VI-M-562) 5; 11-C-362 (VI-M-560) 3; 11-C-363 (VI-M-561) 4.

parfleche with the buffalo. Filled with food and the material possessions essential for life, the containers must have recalled the sacred animal from which these necessities were obtained. Weltfish (1965: 191) describes large Pawnee parfleches 2 1/2 feet long by 1 1/2 feet wide and a foot deep designed to hold the thinned and dried meat of a whole buffalo. In the most basic and tangible sense, this arrangement of meat wrapped in its own hide evokes the physical substance of the living animal.

Some parfleche designs may also represent the buffalo or even refer to its anatomy in much the same manner as the "box-and-border" designs painted on women's robes depicted the animal's internal structure. This reference is suggested by the extensive use of the hourglass, triangle, and diamond as the central figure in many parfleche compositions. Boas (1927: 119) noted that the buffalo was represented pictorially by an hourglass-like shape or, in its most abbreviated, abstract form, by a simple rectangle. This association extending to parfleche painting seems especially plausible considering the great number of parfleche designs based on hourglass configurations and, accepting the accuracy of Boas's statement, this reference would be further reinforced by the rectangular shape of the envelope itself. Ewers (1939: 10–11) also recorded that the elongated hourglass shapes that form the central motifs on womens' painted robes with "border-and-hourglass" patterns are often "elaborated in such a way as to approach a schematic representation of the buffalo," and that this "is the nearest approach to the representation of life forms to be found in any of the geometric-design patterns." It is interesting to note that the particular Comanche robe that Ewers used to illustrate his statement featured a central motif containing other significant elements as well (see illustrated robe, p. 252). While essentially an elongated hourglass in its outermost contour, the motif specifically represented the buffalo's body by a central diamond joined at two of its opposing points by triangles, thus forming the triangle-diamond-triangle configuration, one of the most common of all parfleche designs (pls. 70, 73, 80).

Hourglass forms, as well as triangles and diamonds, also were used as abstract depictions of vertebrae in various types of Plains pictorial representation. One of the most explicit depictions of this convention is recorded in the portraits of Plains men by Bodmer and Kurz.[10] Both artists portrayed warriors whose chests and arms were elaborately ornamented with tattoos or painted images. The designs usually feature a central band filled with these repeated motifs running from the base of the man's throat down the center of his chest, an apparent visualization of the spine even when symbolizing other concepts as well. In the same manner, many parfleches have a narrow central band filled with one of these three geometric elements or simple blocks running the full length of the envelope, suggesting a spinal column and conceptually transforming the rectangular case into the body of the animal (pls. 41,

10. See Bodmer 1984, particularly the portraits of Tukan Haton (p. 187), Mahchsi-Nihka (p. 303), Addih-Hiddisch (p. 315), and an unidentified male (p. 317). See Kurz 1937: pls. 10, 16, 37, and 41.

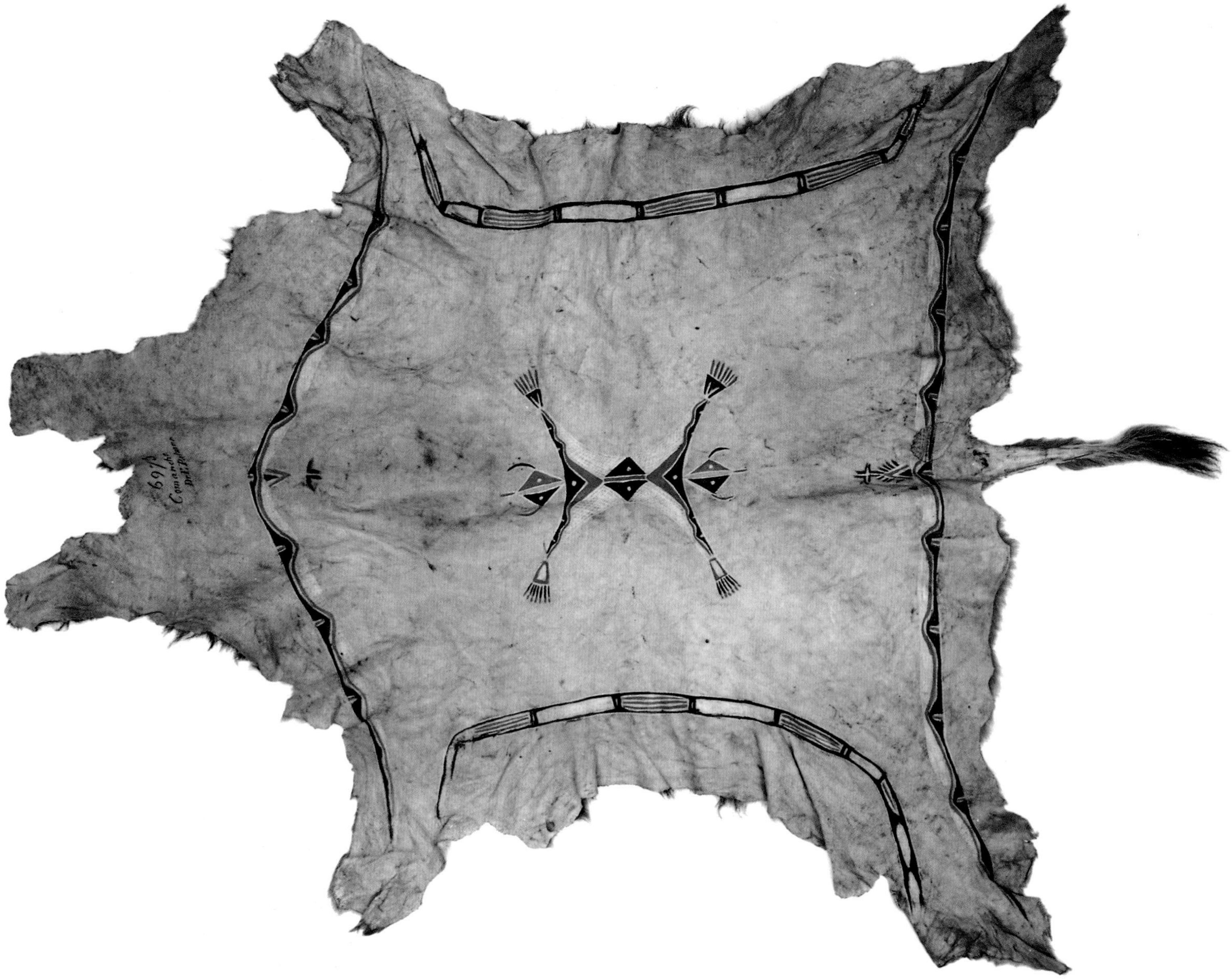

70, 86).[11] At least one researcher recorded this association. In his description of the design of a Sarci envelope, Edward Sapir documented that the center band running the length of the design was called "*mi na wusa,* vertical column, spine."[12] The use of these motifs appearing within center bands is often expanded to form the entire design, so that the whole pattern consists of hourglasses and diamonds (pl. 105) or repeated triangles (pl. 77) held in place by a linear structure.

Color symbolism sometimes functioned in the same manner as design motifs in that it could be used according to the intentions and interpretation of the individual artist. Several tribally recognized systems of color symbolism have also been recorded, where specific colors are consistently associated with sacred helpers, the four directions, life-force, the seasons, or other ceremonial aspects of life.

To understand the full relationship between image and idea in parfleche painting, it is important to recognize that not all artists were equally interested in symbolic content. Some women were undoubt-

11. Evan Maurer made this significant observation in his study of Plains Indian painting, and I am indebted to him for suggesting that I explore it in my own research.

12. Taken from Sapir's catalogue description of the design on a parfleche in the Canadian Museum of Civilization, cat. no. V-D-273.

edly far more sensitive and thoughtful in utilizing the spiritual traditions of their tribe and the expressive potential of their own ideas. Other women apparently were satisfied and wholly engaged by the formal issues of the painting alone; the images they painted had become so conventionalized that they could be constructed without thought or intended meaning. In such cases, the original symbolism may have been forgotten and lost, while the design itself persisted. Teit (1930: 57) indicates that some Plateau tribes adopted their designs along with the parfleche itself from other tribes, and copied them without knowing their significance. It is also probable, however, that many women told researchers that they produced designs "just to be pretty" in order to avoid discussions about their work, either because of reticence or the assumption that explanations would not be understood. That this factor should not be underestimated is clearly revealed in historian Frank Linderman's foreword to his biography of Pretty Shield, a medicine woman of the Crow tribe, written in 1932 (1972: 9)

> Throughout forty-six years in Montana I have had much to do with its several Indian tribes, and yet have never, until now, talked for ten consecutive minutes directly to an old Indian woman. I have found Indian women diffident, and so self-effacing that acquaintance with them is next to impossible. Even when Indian women have sometimes acted as my interpreters while gathering tribal legends they remained strangers to me.

Whatever the case, this variance of artistic intent is clearly described by Kroeber, Boas, Wissler, and others in their studies of Plains decorative arts and symbolism. The confusing point is that all artists—whatever their intentions—used the same conventionalized design elements, composite forms, and compositions dictated by their tribal style. Paintings intended to represent tangible objects, specific scenes or incidents, abstract concepts, or sacred associations were indistinguishable from paintings intended as purely formal and decorative exercises without meaning.

Perhaps because the motivation of the artists and the purpose of the paintings are never explicit, there has been a tendency in recent years for many writers to classify all parfleches with the latter group. This is unfounded. All evidence indicates that some form of symbolic content was prevalent in the parfleche painting of most tribes during the prereservation years, while those works without meaning are typically associated with the loss of traditions and the final period of production.

Finally, we must consider that the greatest measure of content is, after all, not always in the explanation of the artist. It emerges most directly—like music—beyond words, through the intrinsic power of the image and its hold on the heart and mind. These paintings were inseparable from the world view of their makers, formed from their collective experience and cultural role as women; from the details of their daily lives and the richness and love of family life and tribal associations; from the invisible spirit forces that filled their world and the profound religious traditions that sustained their inner, sacred lives; and from their intimate relationship with nature and the sweeping, monumental landscapes and incomparable light of the American West which was their home. All of this was somehow given tangible form in these paintings, through an intuitive expressive power transcending time and cultural boundaries.

A separate and remarkable class of parfleches, which is extremely rare and seldom mentioned in the literature, was painted with images that were inspired by sacred visions. These mystical paintings represent the spiritual forces revealed to men during their vision quest, a process of prolonged fasting, meditation, and physical suffering through which an individual sought spiritual guidance and blessings. They adorned cases that held medicine bundles originating from visions, representing either the principal spirit-helper embodied within or depicting some aspect of the vision itself. For example, the extraordinary Crow war bundle case illustrated in plate 95 portrays the mythic black horse that appeared to the owner in his vision, transmitting knowledge and sacred power. Another Crow cylinder, described by Wildschut (1975: 53, fig. 19), was painted with a red crescent moon and triangles representing sharp-pointed, fleecy clouds recalling the time of night when the vision was seen.

Stylistically, these paintings closely correspond to the images depicted by men on shields. This is not surprising considering that both expressions emanate from the same source and serve a related purpose. In at least one instance the identical image was used on both objects. This tradition was noted by Harrington (1972: 117) in his discussion of the Buffalo Medicine bundles of the Kiowa. He described the design on the parfleche case of a healing bundle consisting of a yellow circle with a blue central spot and border, floating on a background of reddish earth paint. He then stated that "such circles are emblems of the Buffalo Doctors, whose shields bore the same design."

Visionary designs on parfleches are of three types. The most dramatic are those paintings that depict sacred beings in a representational manner (pls. 31, 95). A variety of life-forms and objects might be represented, including humans, buffalo, horses, birds, dragonflies, lizards, turtles, lightning, the sun, the moon, stars, and rainbows. Very few of these cases have survived and it seems likely that they were always exceedingly rare.

In the paintings of the second group, abstracted images are used to represent life-forms and other elements of supernatural power. These are distinguished by motifs that, though abstract in varying degrees, are never part of the established, conventionalized designs that define a given tribal style. Rather, they are specifically symbolic of the vision and were painted as they were revealed through that source. A Crow medicine case bearing the images of a single buffalo track floating against a red on red, diagonally banded field (pl. 96) is representative of this type. Two cylindrical cases collected by Kroeber from the Arapaho also illustrate this type (pl. 40 C, R); the highly abstracted designs represent buffalo, spirit-persons, buffalo skulls, and sweat houses. All are depicted as essentially horned figures, a device universally connoting sacred power in Plains iconography. Kroeber (1907: 134) recorded the designs of one as representing the acquisition of supernatural power, especially of control of the buffalo, by the owner of the case. He also noted the presence of inverted crescents in the designs of Kiowa cylinders (pl. 44) that he felt might be related in their meaning. Another Arapaho case for sacred objects (pl. 39) bears a totally abstract design whose meaning was never recorded, but its unusual curvilinear composition based on the sacred number four implies its visionary origin. The power of the painting and presence of the object are further enhanced by the thin layer of sacred red paint that covers the entire case. Other pictorial devices seen on parfleches of this group include pictographic forms such as highly stylized horse tracks, often used in combination with geometric motifs.[13]

13. See Conn (1982: 87, pl. 99) for an excellent example of this kind of design.

The third type consists of cases that are painted with the standard elements and compositions of a tribal style, but that are still intended to represent some aspect of a vision or dimension of a sacred power. For example, a Crow boat-shaped case that housed a Sun Dance bundle was painted in typical Crow designs said to represent the mountains, the earth, the sky and the rainbow (Wildschut 1975: 29, fig. 3). The sacred association of these designs is never explicit; rather, the function of the case suggests the content of the painting. The designs on a Crow cylinder containing another sacred bundle (pl. 97) probably function in this way.

The representational images of the first group and, to some extent, the abstract and pictographic depictions of the second, were of a type traditionally painted by men. While it may be impossible to ever know for certain, the parfleches that bear these designs are quite probably the result of a collaborative effort between a man and a woman. It is doubtful that a man would have possessed the technical skills necessary to produce a fine parfleche, and it is equally doubtful that a woman would be asked to render such a powerful image not belonging to her, adopting an unfamiliar style in accordance with the instructions of the vision's owner. It is more likely that the woman prepared the hide to the point that it was ready to paint, at which time the man came forward to execute the image. Following the painting, the woman would have completed the various steps to finish the case. In some instances both may have completed different parts of a single painting, the woman delineating the border and other geometric motifs, the man rendering the representational elements. It is also possible that, on some occasions, women may have produced images by instruction, although the sureness and expressive power of the finest paintings seem to reflect the profound intensity born of the artist's personal religious experience. The greatest number of visionary cases have been collected from the Crow, but others of this type have been obtained from the Arapaho, Cheyenne, Kiowa, Comanche, and Sioux. It is also possible that the Apache parfleches noted earlier (p. 152) should be considered part of this tradition.

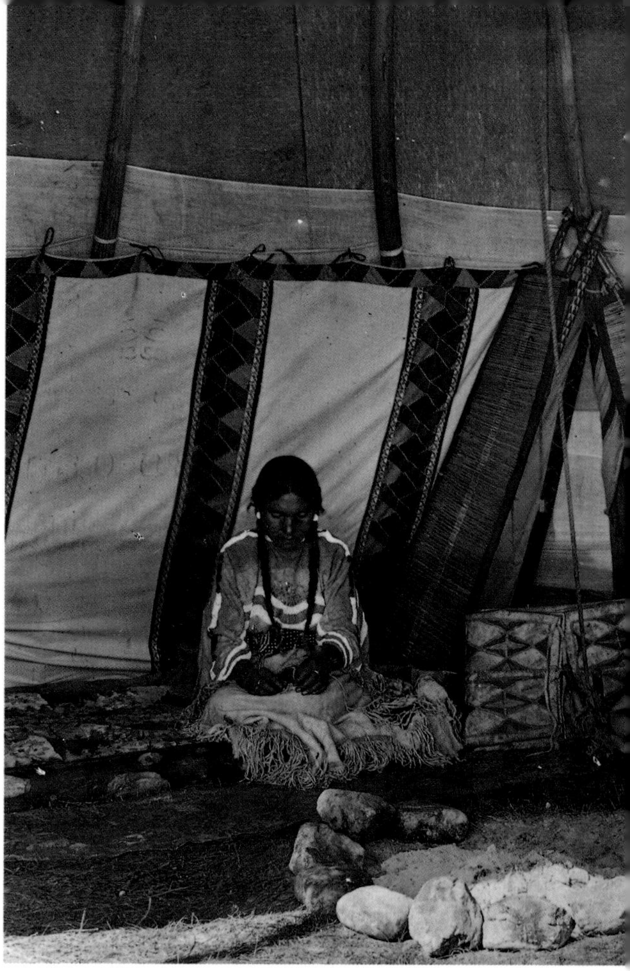

In contrast to symbolism and associative meaning in parfleche painting is the practice of giving names to designs and specific motifs. "Named" designs do not function as symbols or convey ideas; rather, they are descriptive terms used to identify common motifs and patterns (Wissler 1904: 233–39). They provided artists with a practical vocabulary, allowing them to describe the elements of their compositions for purposes of discussion. Consequently, the names had to be generally acknowledged and understood within the tribal group or at least by the artist's immediate circle, and each tribe formed its own set of terms. Names such as "arrowhead," "pointed," "flying geese," and "feather" were typical (Douglas 1934: 43); those taken from life forms were not intended to represent the objects named, rather they were applied because of their resemblance to the completed design. An interesting and recent example of this practice was recorded by Morrow (1975: 42). She noted that an old Sioux design had been renamed the "bridge" design, because it reminded the women of a bridge across the Missouri River. When the design was originated there were no bridges of this type; the new name was adopted, probably in the 1920s or '30s, because the structure had become a common reference for all the women living in the area at that time. Although the full extent of the use of named designs has not been recorded, it was undoubtedly a widespread practice throughout the parfleche-making regions.

In addition to the meanings conveyed through the painted designs, the very presence of parfleches communicated a variety of impressions to other members of the community. Numbers of finely painted parfleches stacked within the tipi or hung from the horses during camp movements reflected the industry and material well-being of the family (Wissler 1904: 256). They indicated that the men were ambitious and capable providers, and that the women had shared this responsibility in gathering wild foods and preparing the quantities of dried meat obtained through the hunt. They were visible proof that the family was well-ordered and well-provisioned, both for their own needs and for those less fortunate whom they might help support through their generosity. Most significantly, they also revealed the accomplishment and artistic skill of the women who possessed the ability to create such beautiful objects.

During prereservation times, the greatest public display of material wealth, including all the parfleches owned by each family, occurred during camp movements. These were essentially formal occasions, and provided families with the opportunity to enhance their prestige through the exhibition of beautiful possessions and the display of shields and other ceremonial objects. The social importance of this tradition was demonstrated by the continuation of elaborate equestrian parades during the early reservation period. These events were a common feature

Interior of Mad Wolf's tipi, Blackeet, ca. 1900. His daughter, Strikes On Both Sides, sits near a large parfleche envelope propped against backrests. Photograph by Walter McClintock. Courtesy Beinecke Rare Book and Manuscript Library, Yale University

*"With Her Proudly Decked Horse." This portrait of a Cayuse woman depicts the elaborate horse trappings typically displayed by Transmontane women during camp movements and equestrian parades. Fringed parfleche cylinders hang from *a saddle that is draped with a blanket with beaded strip and beaded bandolier bag. A fringed saddle bag hangs behind the decorated saddle. Photograph by Edward S. Curtis. Courtesy Edward E. Ayer Collection, The Newberry Library.*

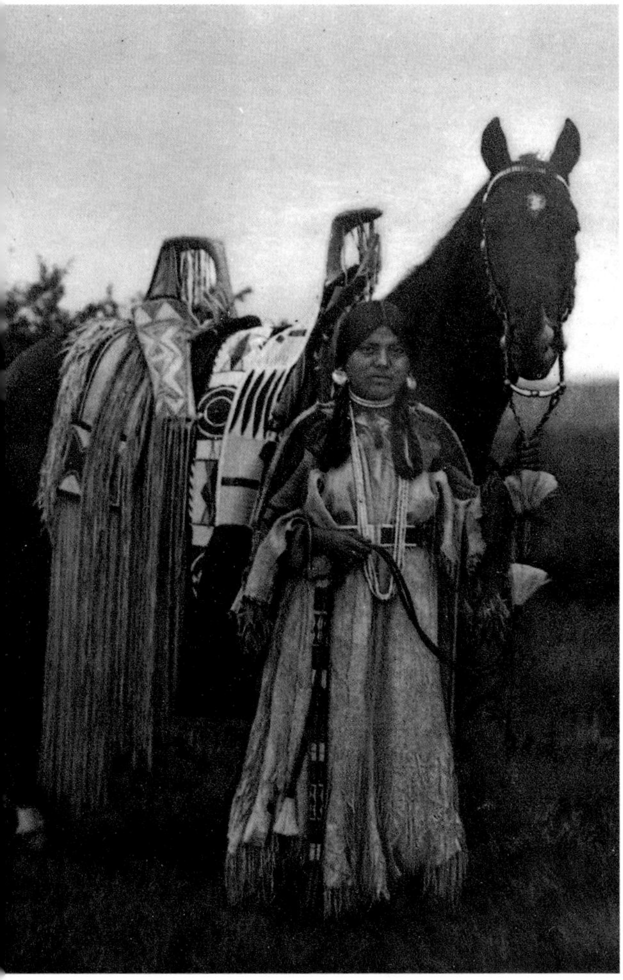

of every significant social or ceremonial gathering, such as the Sun Dance, Fourth of July celebrations, tribal powwows, and great intertribal events such as the Crow Fair in Montana and the Pendleton Roundup. Many parfleches produced during this era were intended more as ornaments for the horses than as functional containers. The expansion capacity of these later envelopes was diminished even while they continued to be beautifully painted, and the secularization of medicine cases occurred at this time. These elaborately fringed cases hung empty at the horses' sides, but symbolized the spiritual blessing and religious prerogatives associated with the ownership of sacred bundles and recalled the practice of women adorning their horses with the ceremonial regalia of their male relatives.

During these early reservation years and well into the twentieth century, as the tribes were undergoing dramatic cultural changes, older Indians invariably associated the parfleche with the richness and integrity of the old way of life. Long after the tribes were permanently settled and rawhide containers were no longer needed as utilitarian objects, they were still highly valued as aesthetic forms and symbols of traditional culture. They continued to be made and used as parade items, particularly by the tribes of the Northern Plains and Plateau regions, and were often used as decorations in traditional lodges during ceremonial occasions. They remained an important part of the wedding ceremonies of many Plateau tribes. On these occasions, parfleches filled with blankets, shawls, trade cloth, and other gifts were presented to the bride's family, while beautiful corn husk bags filled with dried foods were given to the relatives of the groom. They were regarded among many tribes, particularly the Sioux, as one of the most appropriate and valued gifts to be presented at giveaways, and many were made specifically for that purpose.

Even when parfleches no longer served these symbolic functions, beyond the time when they were publicly displayed as objects of prestige and cultural identity, many were preserved by Native American families as treasured heirlooms, to be handed down as a way of remembering, of honoring, the makers and their history as a people.

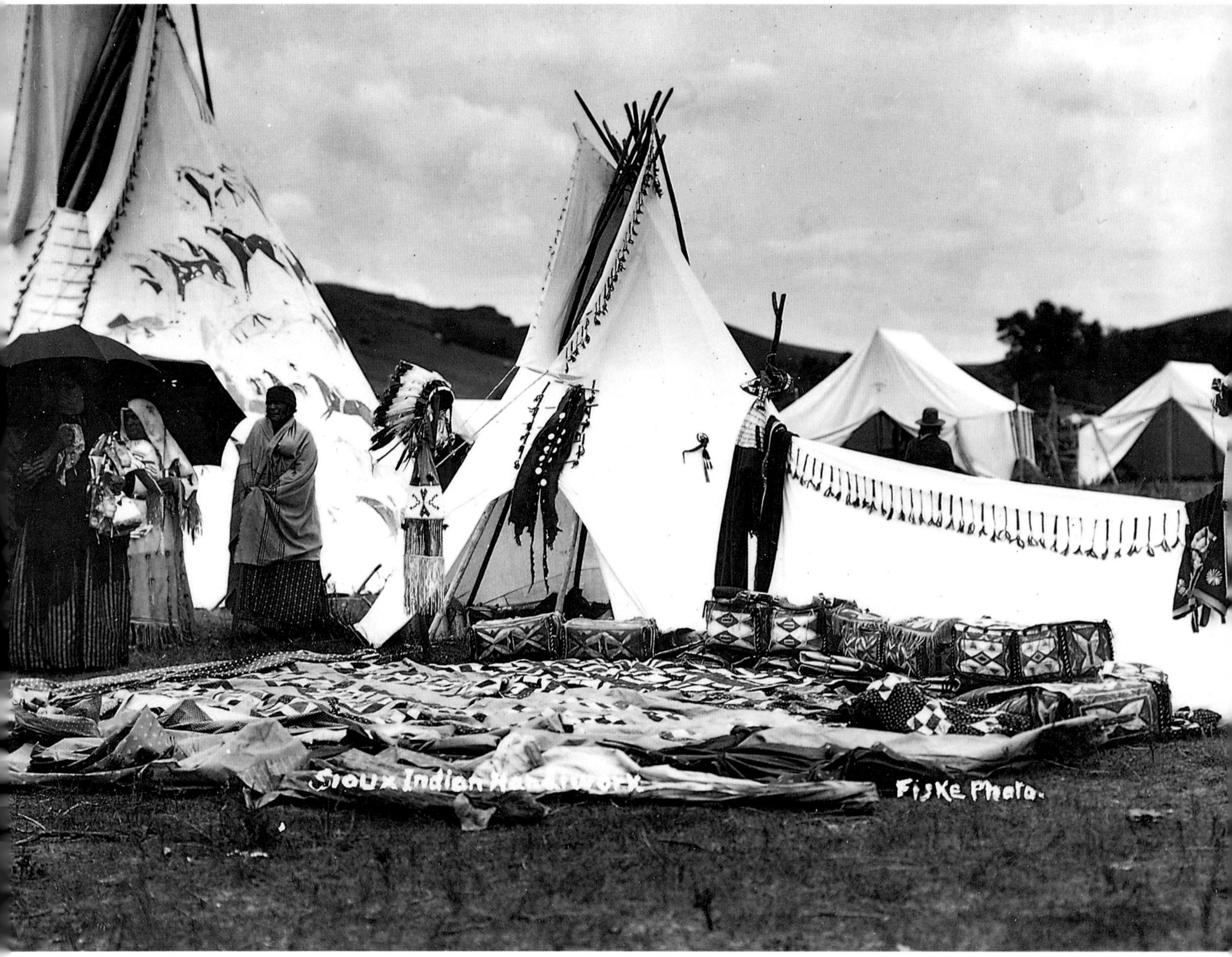

"Sioux Indian Handiwork." Photograph by Frank Fiske, Fort Yates, North Dakota, 1900–10. Several pairs of parfleche boxes and envelopes are visible in this group of items assembled for a Sioux give-away on Standing Rock Reservation. Also included are quilts, ceremonial clothing, beaded pipe bags, a headdress, and a tipi liner. Courtesy State Historical Society of North Dakota.

Bibliography

Barbeau, Marius

1960 *Indian Days on the Western Prairies.* National Museum of Canada Bulletin No. 163, Anthropological Series No. 46. Ottawa.

Bates, Craig D.

n.d. *Parfleches of the Crow and Plateau Peoples.* Unpublished manuscript.

Batkin, Jonathan

1990 "A Rare Apache Medicine Bag." In *Eye of the Angel,* ed. David Wooley, pp. 47–50. Northhampton, MA: White Star Press.

Beltrami, G. Costantino

1828 *A Pilgrimage in America.* London. (Reprinted Chicago: Quadrangle Books, 1962).

Berlandier, Jean Louis

1969 *The Indians of Texas in 1830.* Edited by John C. Ewers. Washington, D.C.: Smithsonian Institution Press.

Blish, Helen H.

1967 *A Pictographic History of the Oglala Sioux.* Lincoln: University of Nebraska Press.

Boas, Franz

1955 *Primitive Art.* New York: Dover. (Originally published Oslo: H. Aschehoug, 1927).

Bodmer, Karl

1984 *Karl Bodmer's America.* Introduction by William H. Goetzmann, annotations by David C. Hunt and Marsha V. Gallagher, artist's biography by William J. Orr. Omaha, NE: Joslyn Art Museum; Lincoln: University of Nebraska Press.

Brunius, Staffan

1990 "North American Indian Collections at the Folkens Museum-Ethnografiska, Stockholm," *European Review of Native American Studies* 4(1): 29–34.

Canfield, Kenneth

1988 "Plains Abstractions," *Art and Auction* 11(3): 196–201.

Catlin, George

1841 *Letters and Notes on the Manners, Customs, and Conditions of the North American Indians.* 2 vols. London: George Catlin.

Cincinnati Art Museum

1976 *Art of the First Americans.* Cincinnati: Cincinnati Art Museum.

Coe, Ralph T.

1976 *Sacred Circles: Two Thousand Years of North American Indian Art.* London: Arts Council of Great Britain.

Conn, Richard

1979 *Native American Art in the Denver Art Museum.* Denver: Denver Art Museum.

1982 *Circles of the World: Traditional Art of the Plains Indians.* Denver: Denver Art Museum.

1986 *A Persistent Vision: Art of the Reservation Days.* Denver: Denver Art Museum.

Curtis, Edward S.
1907–30 *The North American Indian.* 20 vols. Cambridge and Norwood, MA: The University Press (vols. 1–5) and Plimpton Press (vols. 6–20).

Densmore, Frances
1918 *Teton Sioux Music.* Smithsonian Institution, Bureau of American Ethnology Bulletin 61. Washington, D.C.

Deutsches Ledermuseum
1976 *Indianer Nordamerikas: Katalog Heft 4.* Offenbach, Germany: Deutsches Ledermuseum.

Dockstader, Frederick J.
1973 *Indian Art in America.* New York: Promontory Press.

Douglas, Frederic H.
1934 "Symbolism in Indian Art and the Difficulties of its Interpretation." *Leaflet 61.* Denver: Denver Art Museum.
1936 "An Incised Bison Rawhide Parfleche." *Material Culture Notes,* No. 6. Denver: Denver Art Museum.
1936 "Parfleches and Other Rawhide Articles." *Leaflet 77–78.* Denver: Denver Art Museum.

Douglas, Frederic H., and Rene d'Harnoncourt
1941 *Indian Art of the United States.* New York: Museum of Modern Art.

Dunn, Dorothy
1968 *American Indian Painting of the Southwest and Plains Areas.* Albuquerque: University of New Mexico Press.

Ewers, John C.
1939 *Plains Indian Painting: A Description of an Aboriginal American Art.* Palo Alto: Stanford University Press.
1945 *Blackfeet Crafts.* United States Department of the Interior, Bureau of Indian Affairs. Washington, D.C.
1955 *The Horse in Blackfoot Indian Culture.* Smithsonian Institution, Bureau of American Ethnology. Bulletin 159. Washington, D.C.
1982 "Artists' Choices," *American Indian Art Magazine* 7(2): 40–49.
1992 "A Century of Plains Indian Studies," *American Indian Art Magazine* 17(4): 36–47.

Ewing, Douglas C.
1982 *Pleasing the Spirits.* New York: Ghylen Press.

Feder, Norman
1965 *American Indian Art.* New York: Abrams.
1965 *American Indian Art Before 1850.* Denver: Denver Art Museum. Summer Quarterly.
1967 *North American Indian Painting.* New York: The Museum of Primitive Art.
1978 "Pawnee Cradleboards," *American Indian Art Magazine* 3(4): 40–50.

Feest, Christian F.
1980 *Native Arts of North America.* London: Thames and Hudson Ltd.

Fehrenbach, T. R.
1974 *Comanches: The Destruction of a People.* New York: Alfred A. Knopf.

Galante, Gary
1979 "The Painter: The Sioux of the Great Plains." In *The Ancestors: Native Artisans of the Americas,* ed. Anna Curtenins Roosevelt and James G. E. Smith, pp. 1–21. New York: Museum of the American Indian.
1980 "Crow Lance Cases or Sword Scabbards," *American Indian Art Magazine* 6(1): 64–73.

Galante, Gary
1984 "East Meets West: Some Observations on the Crow as the Nexus of Plateau/Upper Missouri River Art," ed. F. Dennis Lessard. In *Crow*

Indian Art: Papers Presented at the Crow Indian Art Symposium, pp. 49–60. Mission, SD: Chandler Institute.

Gibbs, Peter

1982 "Duke Paul Wilhelm Collection in the British Museum," *American Indian Art Magazine* 7(3): 52–61.

Gilman, Carolyn, and Mary Jane Schneider

1987 *The Way to Independence.* St. Paul: Minnesota Historical Society Press.

Grinnell, George B.

1923 *The Cheyenne: Their History and Ways of Life.* 2 vols. New Haven: Yale University Press.

Hail, Barbara

1980 *Hau, Kola!: The Plains Indian Collection of the Haffenreffer Museum of Anthropology.* Brown University, Studies in Anthropology and Material Culture, vol. 3. Providence: Haffenreffer Museum of Anthropology.

Haley, James L.

1981 *Apaches: A History and Culture Portrait.* Garden City, NY: Doubleday and Company, Inc.

Harrington, M. R.

1972 "Kiowa Buffalo Medicine Bundles," *Indian Notes* 8(4): 114–27. New York: Museum of the American Indian, Heye Foundation.

Hartmann, Horst

1973 *Die Plains und Prärieindianer Nordamerikas.* Berlin: Staatliche Museen Preussischer Kulturbesitz, Museum für Völkerkunde.

Henry, Alexander, and David Thompson

1897 *New LIght on the Early History of the Greater Northwest.* Edited by Elliott Coues. New York: Harper. (Reprinted Minneapolis: Ross and Haines, 1965).

Hill, W. W.

1982 *An Ethnography of Santa Clara Pueblo, New Mexico.* Edited and annotated by Charles H. Lange. Albuquerque: University of New Mexico Press.

James, Edwin

1823 *Account of an Expedition from Pittsburgh to the Rocky Mountains, Performed in the Years 1819–1820.* Vols. 14 and 15 of *Early Western Travels,* ed. R. G. Thwaites. Cleveland: Arthur H. Clark Co., 1905.

John, Elizabeth A.

1975 *Storms Brewed in Other Men's Worlds: The Confrontation of Indians, Spanish, and French in the Southwest, 1540–1795.* College Station: Texas A & M University Press.

Kroeber, Alfred L.

1900 Letter to Franz Boas, dated August 28, Academy of Sciences, San Francisco. Archives, American Museum of Natural History, New York.

1907 "The Arapaho." *Bulletin of the American Museum of Natural History* 18, pts. 1, 2, and 4 (1902–7).

1908 "Ethnology of the Gros Ventre." *Anthropological Papers of the American Museum of Natural History* I, pt. 4.

Kurz, Rudolph Frederick

1937 *The Journal of Rudolph Frederick Kurz 1846–1852.* Translated by M. Jarrell; edited by J. N. B. Hewitt. Smithsonian Institution, Bureau of American Ethnology Bulletin 115. Washington, D.C.

Lanford, Benson L.

1980 "Parfleche and Crow Beadwork Designs," *American Indian Art Magazine* 6(1): 32–39.

1984 "Beadwork and Parfleche Designs." In *Crow Indian Art: Papers*

Presented at the Crow Indian Art Symposium, pp. 7–14. Mission, SD: Chandler Institute.

1990 "Apache Dress in the Derby Collection." In *Eye of the Angel,* ed. David Wooley, pp. 40–45. Northhampton, MA: White Star Press.

Larpenteur, Charles

1933 *Forty Years a Fur Trader on the Upper Missouri: A Personal Narrative of Charles Larpenteur, 1833–1872.* Edited by Paul L. Hederen. Chicago: Lakeside Press.

Laubin, Reginald and Gladys Laubin

1971 *The Indian Tipi: Its History, Construction and Use.* New York: Ballantine.

Lessard, F. Dennis

1980 "Crow Indian Art: The Nez Perce Connection," *American Indian Art Magazine* 6(1): 54–63.

1984 "Classic Crow Beadwork: Upper Missouri River Roots." In *Crow Indian Art: Papers Presented at the Crow Indian Art Symposium,* pp. 61–68. Mission, SD: Chandler Institute.

1987 "E.O. Who?" *American Indian Art Magazine* 12(2): 52–61.

Lewis, Meriwether, and William Clark

1904 *Original Journals of the Lewis and Clark Expedition 1804–1806.* 8 vols. Edited by R. G. Thwaites. New York: Dodd, Mead and Co.

Linderman, Frank

1972 *Pretty-Shield: Medicine Woman of the Crows.* Lincoln: University of Nebraska Press.

Lottinville, Savoie, ed.

1973 *Paul Wilhelm, Duke of Wuerttemberg: Travels in North America, 1822–1824.* Translated by W. Robert Nitske. Norman University of Oklahoma Press.

Lowie, Robert H.

1909 "The Assiniboine." *Anthropological Papers of the American Museum of Natural History* 1, pt. 4.

1909 "The Northern Shoshoni." *Anthropological Papers of the American Museum of Natural History* 2, pt. 2.

1922 "Crow Indian Art." *Anthropological Papers of the American Museum of Natural History* 21, pt. 4.

1956 *The Crow Indians.* New York: Holt, Rinehart, Winston.

McClintock, Walter

1910 *The Old North Trail.* London. Macmillan and Co. (Reprinted Lincoln: University of Nebraska Press, 1968).

1936 *Painted Tipis and Picture-Writing of the Blackfoot Indians.* Leaflet Number 6. Los Angeles: Southwest Museum.

Mails, Thomas E.

1974 *The People Called Apache.* Englewood Cliffs, NJ: Prentice-Hall, Inc.

Mallery, Garrick

1886 "Pictographs of the North American Indians." *Fourth Annual Report of the Bureau of American Ethnology for 1882–1883.* Washington, D.C.: Smithsonian Institution.

1893 "Picture Writing of the American Indians." *Tenth Annual Report of the Bureau of American Ethnology for 1888–89.* Washington, D.C.: Smithsonian Institution.

Markoe, Glenn E., ed., and Raymond J. DeMallie and Royal B. Hassrick

1986 *Vestiges of a Proud Nation: The Ogden B. Read Northern Plains Indian Collection.* Burlington: Robert Hull Fleming Museum, University of Vermont.

Marriott, Alice

1956 "Trade Guild of the Southern Cheyenne Women." *Bulletin of the Oklahoma Anthropological Society* 4: 19–27.

Maurer, Evan M.
1977 *The Native American Heritage: A Survey of North American Indian Art.* Chicago: Art Institute of Chicago.
1992 *Visions of the People: A Pictorial History of Plains Indian Life.* Minneapolis: Minneapolis Institute of Arts.
Maximilian, Prince of Wied-Neuwied
1843 *Travels in the Interior of North America.* Translated by Hannibal Evans. Vols. 22–24 of *Early Western Travels,* ed. R. G. Thwaites. Cleveland: Arthur H. Clark Co., 1906.
Minneapolis Institute of Arts
1976 *I Wear the Morning Star: An Exhibition of American Indian Ghost Dance Objects.* Minneapolis: Minneapolis Institute of Arts.
Morrow, Mabel
1975 *Indian Rawhide: An American Folk Art.* Norman: University of Oklahoma Press.
Myers, Thomas P.
1984 "American Indian Collections of the University of Nebraska State Museum," *American Indian Art Magazine* 9(4): 50–57.
Opler, Morris Edward
1965 *An Apache Life-Way.* New York: Cooper Square Publishers, Inc.
Painter, John W.
1992 *American Indian Artifacts: The John Painter Collection.* Cincinnati: George Tassian Organization, Inc.
Penney, David W.
1992 *Art of the American Indian Frontier: The Chandler-Pohrt Collection.* Detroit: Detroit Institute of Arts; Seattle: University of Washington Press.
Phillips, Ruth B.
1987 "Like a Star I Shine." In *The Spirit Sings: Artistic Traditions of Canada's First Peoples,* pp. 51–92. Calgary, Alberta: Glenbow Museum and McClelland and Stewart.
Porsche, Audrey
1987 *Yuto'keca: Transitions: The Burdick Collection.* Bismarck: State Historical Society of North Dakota.
Powell, Father Peter J.
1969 *Sweet Medicine.* 2 vols. Norman: University of Oklahoma Press.
1973 "The Enduring Beauty of Cheyenne Art," *The American West* 10(4): 4–11.
1976 "They Drew from Power: An Introduction to Northern Cheyenne Ledger Book Art." In *Montana Past and Present,* pp. 1–54. Los Angeles: William Andrews Clark Memorial Library, University of California.
1977 "Beauty for New Life." In *The Native American Heritage: A Survey of North American Indian Art,* ed. Evan M. Maurer, pp. 33–56. Chicago: Art Institute of Chicago.
1988 *To Honor the Crow People: Crow Art from the Goelet and Edith Gallatin Collection of American Indian Art.* Chicago: Foundation for the Preservation of American Indian Art and Culture.
Ruby, Robert H., and John A. Brown
1981 *Indians of the Pacific Northwest.* Norman: University of Oklahoma Press.
1986 *A Guide to the Indian Tribes of the Pacific Northwest.* Norman: University of Oklahoma Press.
Schulze-Thulin, Axel
1976 *Indianer der Prärien und Plains.* Stuttgart, Germany: Linden-Museum Stuttgart, Staatliches Museum für Völkerkunde.

Scriver, Bob

1990 *The Blackfeet: Artists of the Northern Plains.* Kansas City, MO: Lowell Press, Inc.

Skinner, Alanson

1923–25 "Observations on the Ethnology of the Sauk Indians." *Bulletin of the Milwaukee Public Museum* 5(1–3): 1–180.

1926 "Ethnology of the Ioway Indians." *Bulletin of the Milwaukee Public Museum* 5(4): 181–354.

Spier, Leslie

1925 "An Analysis of Plains Indian Parfleche Decoration." Seattle: University of Washington Publications in Anthropology 1(3): 89–112.

1931 "Plains Indian Parfleche Designs." Seattle: University of Washington Publications in Anthropology 4(3): 293–322.

Taylor, Colin

1984 "Crow Rendezvous: The Place of the River and Mountain Crow in the Material Culture Patterns of the Plateau and Central Plains. Circa 1800–1870." In *Crow Indian Art: Papers Presented at the Crow Indian Art Symposium,* pp. 33–48. Mission, SD: Chandler Institute.

Teit, James A.

1930 "The Salishan of the Western Plateaus." *Forty-Fifth Annual Report of the Bureau of American Ethnology for 1927–28.* Washington, D.C.: Smithsonian Institution.

Thayer, B. W.

1947 "A Santee Dakota Buffalo Hide Parfleche Bag," *Minnesota Archaeologist* 13(2).

1947 "A Cheyenne Parfleche with Some Woodland Decorations," *Minnesota Archaeologist* 13(2): 38–41.

Thompson, Judy

1977 *The North American Indian Collection: A Catalogue.* Berne, Switzerland: Berne Historical Museum.

Torrence, Gaylord

1984 *Native American Parfleche: A Tradition of Abstract Painting.* Kansas City: Kansas City Art Institute.

Torrence, Gaylord, and Robert Hobbs

1989 *Art of the Red Earth People: The Mesquakie of Iowa.* Iowa City: University of Iowa Museum of Art.

Wade, Edwin L.

1986 *The Arts of the North American Indian: Native Tradition in Evolution.* New York: Hudson Hills Press.

Walker Art Center and Minneapolis Institute of Arts

1972 *American Indian Art: Form and Tradition.* Minneapolis: Walker Art Center; Indian Art Association, Minneapolis Institute of Arts.

Walton, Ann T., John C. Ewers, and Royal B. Hassrick

1985 *After the Buffalo Were Gone: The Louis Warren Hill, Sr., Collection of Indian Art.* St. Paul, MN: Northwest Area Foundation.

Weltfish, Gene

1965 *The Lost Universe.* New York: Basic Books, Inc.

Wildschut, William

1975 *Crow Indian Medicine Bundles.* Edited by John C. Ewers. Contributions from the Museum of the American Indian, Heye Foundation., vol. 17. 2d ed. New York.

Wildschut, William, and John C. Ewers

1959 *Crow Indian Beadwork: A Descriptive and Historical Study.* Contributions from the Museum of the American Indian, Heye Foundation, vol. 16. New York.

Wissler, Clark
1904 "Decorative Art of the Sioux Indians." *Bulletin of the American Museum of Natural History* 18, pt. 3.
1907 "Some Protective Designs of the Dakota." *Anthropological Papers of the American Museum of Natural History* 1, pt. 2.
1910 "The Material Culture of the Blackfoot Indians." *Anthropological Papers of the American Museum of Natural History* 5, pt. 1.
1912a "Ceremonial Bundles of the Blackfoot Indians." *Anthropological Papers of the American Museum of Natural History* 7, pt. 2.
1912b "Societies and Ceremonial Associations in the Oglala Division of the Teton-Dakota." *Anthropological Papers of the North American Museum of Natural History* 11, pt. 1.

Wright, Robin K., ed.
1991 *A Time of Gathering: Native Heritage in Washington State.* Seattle: University of Washington Press; Thomas Burke Memorial Washington State Museum.

Lenders to the Exhibition

American Museum of Natural History, New York
Kenneth and Barbara Canfield
The Carnegie Museum of Natural History, Pittsburgh
Continental Insurance, Courtesy Douglas Drake Gallery, New York
Denver Museum of Natural History
Field Museum of Natural History, Chicago
The Thomas Gilcrease Institute of American History and Art, Tulsa
Glenbow Museum, Calgary, Alberta
Benson Lanford
Masco Corporation
Michael and Sherry Maxwell
Maxwell Museum of Anthropology, University of New Mexico, Albquerque
William A. Miller
Milwaukee Public Museum
Minnesota Historical Society, St. Paul
National Museum of the American Indian, Smithsonian Institution, New York
National Museum of Natural History, Department of Anthropology, Smithsonian Institution, Washington, D.C.
Oklahoma Museum of Natural History, Norman
Peabody Museum of Archaeology and Ethnology, Harvard University, Cambridge, Massachusetts
Peabody and Essex Museum, Salem, Massachusetts
Richard A. and Marion D. Pohrt
Staatliche Museen, Museum für Völkerkunde, Berlin
State Historical Society of Iowa, Des Moines
Trustees of the British Museum, London
The University of Iowa Museum of Art, Iowa City
The University Museum, University of Pennsylvania, Philadelphia
Anonymous Lenders

Photographic Credits

With the exception of those listed below, all plate photographs in this publication are by Mark Tade.

Plate	
1	Linden-Museum Stuttgart, Staatliches Museum für Völkerkunde. *Photo by Ursula Didoni.*
3	Peabody Museum of Archaeology and Ethnology, Harvard University. *Photo by Hillel Burger.*
4, 22	Staatliche Museen, Museum für Völkerkunde, Berlin. *Photos by Dietrich Graf.*
23, 68	The National Museum of Ethnography. Stockholm. *Photo by Bo Gabrielsson.*
38	Masco Corporation. *Photo by Tim Thayer.*
45	Peabody and Essex Museum, Salem. *Photo by Mark Sexton.*
52	*Photo courtesy of the British Museum.*
77, 79, 93	These loan materials are reproduced with the permission of The University Museum, University of Pennsylvania, Philadelphia by which all rights are reserved.

Index